THE TENACITY OF ETHNICITY

THE TENACITY OF ETHNICITY

A SIBERIAN SAGA IN GLOBAL PERSPECTIVE

Marjorie Mandelstam Balzer

PRINCETON UNIVERSITY PRESS   PRINCETON, NEW JERSEY

Published by Princeton University Press, 41 William Street,
Princeton, New Jersey 08540
In the United Kingdom: Princeton University Press,
Chichester, West Sussex

Library of Congress Cataloging-in-Publication Data

Balzer, Marjorie Mandelstam.
The tenacity of ethnicity : a Siberian saga in global perspective
Marjorie Mandelstam Balzer.
p. cm.
Includes bibliographical references and index.
ISBN 0-691-00674-1 (cl : alk. paper). — ISBN 0-691-00673-3 (pb : alk. paper)
1. Khanty. 2. Ethnology—Russia (Federation)—Siberia.
3. Indigenous peoples—Russia (Federation)—Siberia. 4. Siberia (Russia)—Ethnic relations. I. Title.
DK759.K53B35 1999
957′.004945—dc21 99-22818

This book has been composed in Sabon

The paper used in this publication meets the minimum requirements of ANSI/NISO Z39.48-1992 (R1997) (*Permanence of Paper*)

http://pup.princeton.edu

Printed in the United States of America

1 3 5 7 9 10 8 6 4 2

1 3 5 7 9 10 8 6 4 2
(Pbk.)

TO MY MOTHER

Eve Natalie Mandelstam

WHO FIRST ENCOURAGED ME TO ASK QUESTIONS

TO MY HUSBAND

Harley David Balzer

AND

TO ALL THOSE WHO HAVE THE INTERESTS OF INDIGENOUS PEOPLES IN THEIR HEARTS

Contents

Illustrations and Figures

MAPS

PHOTOGRAPHS

FIGURES

Acknowledgment of Biases and Debts

ALTHOUGH the United Nations has declared the 1990s to be the "decade of indigenous peoples," more awareness of Native peoples' plights and the politics of their potential recovery within diverse state systems is needed. One relatively neglected area, Siberia, both fits and defies standard conceptions. Whether termed tribe, ethnic group, or nation, peoples pushed to the brink of their land and their spirit, whose communal existence in a homeland predates the arrival of hegemonic, land-grabbing state representatives, have much in common. Throughout the North and beyond, suffering and survival have led to indigenous peoples' mobilization at many levels, up to and recently including levels that cross state boundaries. In this sense, I use the word "global," to indicate awareness of processes that come from many mutually influencing intra- and interstate political and economic trends, rather than to imply commonality or convergence of world culture.

In the 1970s, I became interested in the history of indigenous peoples of Siberia because I was hoping to find, somewhere in the world, some sort of Native success story. I wanted to believe Soviet propaganda that "their" Northern peoples had been treated well by settlers and were prospering under Soviet rule. It was not to be, because it could not be: once in archives, and then in "the field" on several cultural exchanges (as one of the first Americans in Siberian villages in the Soviet period), I was not that blind. However, I did find glimmers of light in the literacy campaigns of the Soviet period, in some impressive bicultural individuals, and in the "districts" named for some indigenous peoples.

In the 1990s, I have been privileged to participate in a series of transnational meetings of indigenous peoples, exchanges between Native Siberian and Native American leaders. During one 1998 workshop, hosted by the generous Seminole of Florida, the Siberian (Far Eastern) Chukchi politician Vladimir Etylin turned to themes that had initially intrigued me. Struggling with the propaganda of his youth, he explained that indeed the Siberian colonial experiences had been "relatively softer" than the initial "genocides" of North America. Workshop participants then discussed Native resistance to colonialism in its various guises on both sides of the Bering Sea, in terms of its relevance to today's political and economic turmoil. The interchange reminded me that complex, multilayered understandings of local histories and comparative theory must be guided by indigenous experience.

A word is appropriate about the power of words in an anthropological text. Born in Washington, D.C., I am not Native, nor do I speak for any indigenous group, including the Khanty featured in this study, no matter how much I care about them as individuals and as a group. I acknowledge we are living in a postmodern world rife with cynicism, with gaps between rhetoric and belief, belief and ritual, meaning and content, truth and fiction, perception and reality, psychology and representation, self and other. This world has provided the context for a key concept of anthropology, "culture," to be with good reason deconstructed and re-construed. But healthy reflexivity does not mean we should become paralyzed by our inability to write "objective" texts—only that we should admit preconceptions and strive to create narratives as accurate and detailed as possible. Our texts should be filled with the voices of our interviews and friendships, across continents and through time. By the end of the twentieth century, we should be reflective enough to create a synergy of relevant theories and methodologies, even when the theories may be perceived by some to be mutually contradictory.

My theories and practice are indebted to many people, whom I should acknowledge. My first thanks are to those who have helped me in the Northern Khanty villages of Kazym and Tegy and the Association for the Salvation of the Ugra. In the late 1990s, weighing issues of privacy, credit, and accuracy, I have chosen not to disguise Tegy and Kazym or many of my interlocutors, especially those from 1990s friendships. When material was personal, or when people have requested anonymity, I of course have omitted names.

Khanty to whom I am especially grateful are Tatiana Gogoleva, Tatiana and Timofei Moldanov, Olga Kravchenko, Nadezhda Taligina, Antonina Siazi, Agrafina Sopochina (Pesikova), Joseph Sopochin, Vladimir Kogonchin, Nadezhda Lirshikova, Pëtr Moldanov, Nina Nicharchova, Galina Obatina, Ronalda Olzhina, and Yakov Vandymov. Insider insights into Siberian indigenous life have also come from Larisa Abriutina, Vladimir Etylin, Evdokiya Gayer, Yakov Iadne, Vladimir Ivanov, Zinaida Ivanova, El'vida Mal'tseva, Vasily Robbek, Sergei Karyutchi, Gavril Kurilov, Leonid Lar, Yuri Samar, Vasily Robbek, Yuri Vella, and Uliana Vinokurova. Russian and Siberiak friends and colleagues deserving thanks include Sergei Arutiunov, Olga Balalaeva, Leokadia Drobizheva, Andrei Golovnev, Liuda Iodkovskaia, Valery Kozmin, Nadezhda Moldanova, Elena Novik, Natalia Novikova, Valery Tishkov, Nikolai Vakhtin, Natalia Zhukovskaia, and the late Il'ya Gurvich, Rudolf Its, Alexander Pika, and Galina Starovoitova.

For fieldwork and research support, I am indebted to the International Research and Exchanges Board (IREX), which gave me preparatory fellowships, cultural exchange participation (1975–76, 1985–86), and travel grants, beginning in 1973 and extending periodically to 1997. I am also grateful for support from the Social Science Research Council (SSRC), the Harvard University Russian Research Center, the Averill Harriman Institute of Columbia University, the Kennan Institute of the Smithsonian's Wilson Center, and the John D. and Catherine T. MacArthur Foundation.

Institutions that have assisted me in the Russian Federation include the Academy of Sciences Institute for the Problems of Northern Minorities (Yakutsk), the Academy of Sciences Institute of Ethnography (Saint Petersburg, then Leningrad), (the former) Leningrad State University, the Academy of Sciences Institute of Ethnology and Anthropology (Moscow), and the State Committee of the North (Goskomsevera, Moscow).

Invaluable access to archives and museum collections was given by the Peter the Great Museum (Kunstkamera) of Saint Petersburg, especially Alexander Teriukov; the Central State Historical Archive (Tsentral'nyi Gosudarstvennyi Istoricheskii Arkhiv: TsGIA) of Saint Petersburg, especially Svetlana Sergeevna; and the National Museum of Finland (Helsinki), especially Finno-Ugrian scholar Ildigo Lehtinen.

My participation in relevant seminars is recalled with great thanks: the 1991 ethnographic film workshop at Kazym, organized by Asen Balikci and Mark Badger (U.S. National Science Foundation); the 1993 Moscow conference "Traditional Cultures and their Environments," organized by Olga Balalaeva and Alexander Vashenko (Gorky Institute of World Literature); the University of Alaska 1996 seminar "Development and Self-Determination among the Indigenous Peoples of the North," organized by Gordon Pullar; and the annual seminar "Problems of the Peoples of the North," which has met regularly since 1995 and is coordinated by Olga Balalaeva, Andrew Wiget, and Anatoly Volgin (with support from Goskomsevera, the MacArthur Foundation, IREX, and George Soros's Humanities Foundation). Special thanks are due to Gail Fondahl, for organizing the 1996 meeting of this serial seminar at the University of Northern British Columbia, and to Franklin Keel of the Bureau of Indian Affairs, for organizing it in 1998.

Native American friends and colleagues to whom I am grateful include Smithsonian American Indian Program Director Joallyn Archambault, Chief James Billie (host of our 1998 seminar on indigenous problems), writer Nora Marks Dauenhauer, psychologist C. W. Duncan, BIA executive Franklin Keel, anthropologist Bea Medicine, and Professor Gordon Pullar. For insider insights I thank activists Mary Black (Canadian ambassador-at-large), Bill Day (Director, Cultural and Historical Preservation, Tunica-Biloxi), Honorable Keller George (President, United South and Eastern Tribes), LaDonna Harris (Director, Americans for Indian Opportunity), Mary John (of Stoney Creek, Northern British Columbia), Harry Nyce (Chief, Nisga'a Tribal Council), and Rosita Worl (Board of Directors, SeaAlaska Corporation).

Professors who have guided my thought without being responsible for my words include Jane Goodale, Ward Goodenough, Igor Kopytoff, Alfred Rieber, Thomas Greaves, and especially Frederica de Laguna, who sensitized me to many issues crucial to my fieldwork, including the concept of reincarnation. Anthropologists to whom I am grateful include Michael M. J. Fischer, Roberte Hamayon, Mihály Hoppál, Caroline Humphrey, Laurel Kendall, David Maybury-Lewis, Gail Osherenko, Juha Pentikäinen, Nancy Ries, Eva Schmidt, Katherine Verdery, Evon Z. Vogt, and the late Ernest Gellner and Dmitri Shimkin. For stimulating team teaching (in two Social Science Research Council graduate seminars), I thank colleagues Michael Herzfeld and Nazif Shahrani. I am also grateful to colleagues Murray Feshbach, Paul Goble, and Blair Ruble, and to research assistants Matthew Curtis, Sharon Kay, and Rachel Ong.

Particularly deep and special thanks are due my husband and colleague Harley David Balzer and my colleague Bruce Grant (founder, with Nancy Ries, of Soyuz) for careful, insightful readings of this text. Warm thanks also to Beth Gianfagna, Mary Murrell, Elizabeth E. Pohland, and, especially, Victoria Wilson-Schwartz and Lauren Lepow of Princeton University Press, and to other readers.

Finally, a word is appropriate about the terms and spellings I use, for here too, political decisions are latently or blatantly made. The most significant policy decision I have made is to favor the post-Soviet, official designation the "Russian Federation," or "Rossiia," over "Russia." This does not mean I see "Rossiia" as always functioning as a federation, but rather that I hope to stress its multiethnic potential for federation. "Rossiia" is not accurately translated into English as "Russia," since non-Russians view "Rossiia" as a multiethnic composite state and see themselves as "Rossiiany" (peoples of Rossiia) not "Russkie" (Russians). I use Russian terms for various levels within the administrative hierarchy of "Rossiia." Other terms in Russian or in Khanty dialects are noted as such, unless context alone is explanatory.

Geographical and personal names are spelled using the U.S. Library of Congress transliteration system, unless convention has rendered other spellings more familiar. For some indigenous leaders and published scholars, I honor the foreign passport or European spellings of their names.

Abbreviations

GATOT	Gosudarstvennyi Arkhiv Tobol'skogo Otdelenii (Government archive of Tobolsk).
GOM	Gosudarstvennoe Okhotnicheskoe Ministerstvo (Government hunting ministry).
OGPU	Ob"edinennoe Gosudarstvennoe Politicheskoe Upravlenie (Unified state political administration).
RAIPON	Russian Association of Indigenous Peoples of the North (also, Association of the Minority Peoples of the North, Siberia, and the Far East)
RIK	Regionnyi Ispol'nitel'nyi Komitet (Regional administrative committee).
TsGIA	Tsentral'naia Gosudarstvennaia Istoricheskaia Arkhiv (Central state historical archive; post-Soviet: Rossiia state historical archive). Cited by *fond* (collection), *opis* (section), *delo* (file), and *list* (page).
RAIPON	Russian Association of Indigenous Peoples of the North (also, Association of the Minority Peoples of the North, Siberia and the Far East).

THE TENACITY OF ETHNICITY

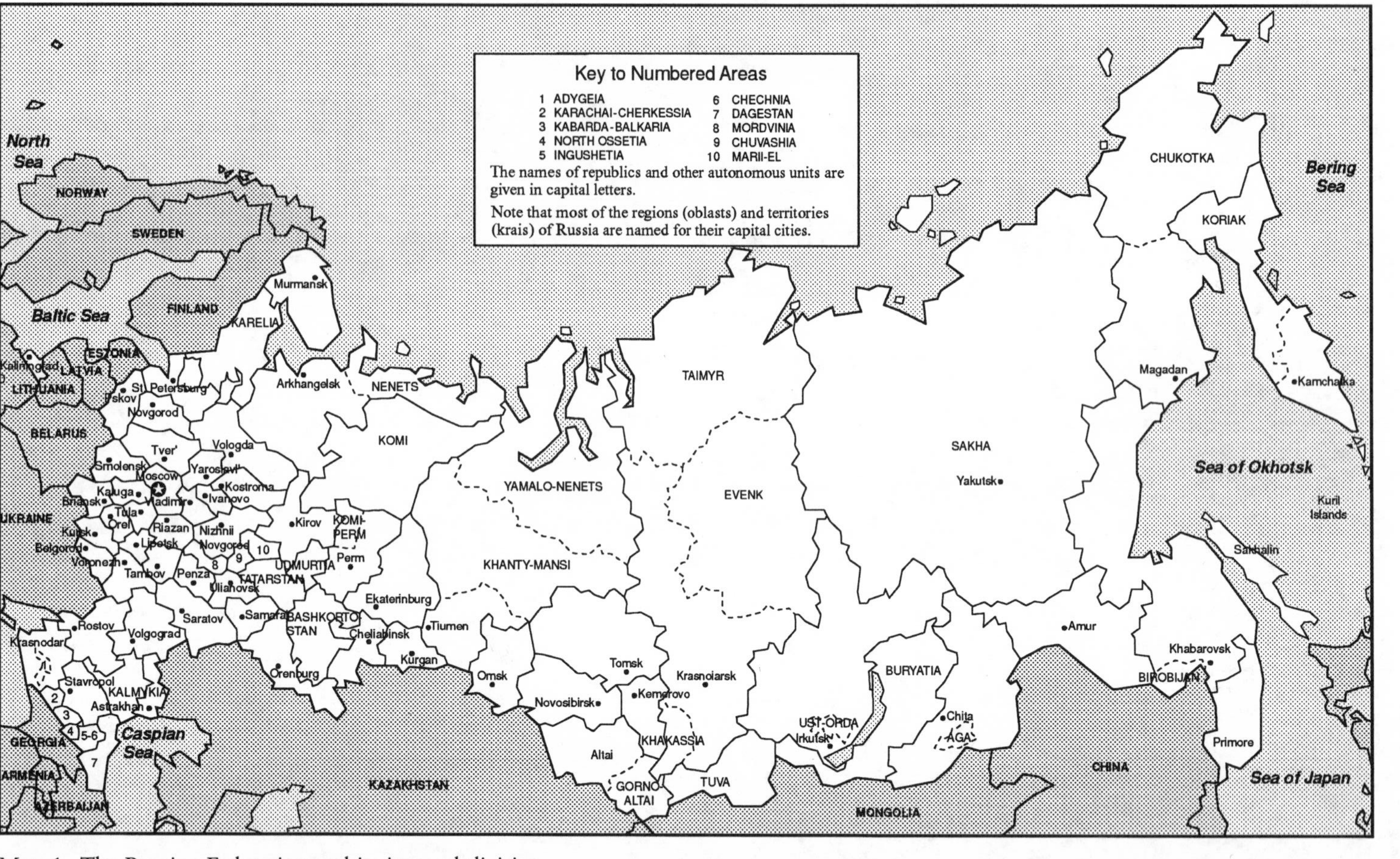

Map 1. The Russian Federation and its internal divisions.

INTRODUCTION

From Romanticism to Realism

> The main questions that concern the Yugan Khanty are self-rule, preservation of our territory, and how to survive under conditions of economic reform. Without adequately addressing these questions, nothing else matters.
>
> (*Vladimir Kogonchin, head of the Yugan Khanty* Obshchina *[Community] "Yaoun-Yakh," May 1996*)

"GLOBAL" and "traditional" mean something different to each generation of a people. Late- twentieth-century international energy corporations, collapsing collectives, and interpenetrated mafia-government alliances represent contemporary versions of much earlier multileveled relationships based on multiethnic trade, war, and shifting nomad-settler interaction. The shaping of group politics is an ancient art. To acknowledge this is not an invitation to project a specific group's identity backward in time, using some analytical shopping list of frozen ethnic characteristics, such as language, lifestyle, religion, worldview, or "tradition." The time for indulging in an imagined primordialism has long passed in anthropology. Rather, I invite readers to empathize with a people through their changing self-definitions.

This book is a contemporary version of what anthropologists do best: it is my telling of a dramatic nonfiction story of how a small group in West Siberia, the Khanty, has formed, survived, and remade itself over multiple generations of strife generated by the interaction of external and internal pressures (map 1). It is about the politics of power and powerlessness over time: from a period before the contact of Khanty ancestors (Ob-Ugrian Ostiak) with Slavonic peoples (not yet called Russians and Ukrainians) to the current post-Soviet jostling for land, wealth, and dignity. It is a micro-study of macro-issues. It is at once remote and immediate, for I hope to take the exotic out of Siberian images and individuals without making them "just like us."

Cultural revival movements that stimulate or exacerbate a politics of difference are occurring under tense conditions in many areas of the world. For some Native American activists, the term "revival" is itself offensive, since ongoing vitality rather than mere cultural reconstruction or re-creation is viewed as the key to understanding rituals and ways of life perpetuated privately or in remote communities of "traditionals." In

Siberia, although romantic images of isolated communities persist among some Russians and Westerners, "cultural revival" may be an all-too-appropriate term for processes occurring within indigenous groups buffeted by globalizing patterns of colonization and Christianization, compounded by more region-specific and far more harsh Sovietization. The post-Soviet age, chaotically combining "wild east" marketization with paternalism, and regionalization with Moscow administrative control, leaves indigenous Siberian groups in ever more precarious positions. In such conditions of uncertainty, political movements of cultural survival are emerging with varied intensity and resonance.

Khanty outrage at the forced relocation of numerous villages and the destruction of much of their environment by the energy industry has been expressed throughout the 1990s, beyond their tentative cries of anguish in 1986–89. In an atypically extreme incident in 1992, a group of armed Khanty hunters encircled a camp of Russian geologist-prospectors and demanded that they leave within twenty-four hours. The hunters, fearing that their tiny settlements would be moved once again, were trying to curtail yet another influx of outsiders into their territories. Frightened and surprised, the tough Russian geologists packed up, but vowed to return.

A more organized, multiethnic protest occurred around the same time, when Khanty, Mansi, Nentsy, and Nganasan activists used a large conical tent to block the planned route of a railroad spur into the Yamal peninsula. They also occupied the main supply road north into the Yamal, attracting the attention of local authorities, who had been giving indigenous rights only lip service. In 1995, the poet Yuri Vella protested threats against his family territories by placing a tent at the parliament of the Khanty-Mansi *Okrug* (District) in its capital, Khanty-Mansiisk.[1]

Public, organized protests have been rare, however. Far more common is a seething anger voiced within local communities and to a few outside supporters. A Khanty museum activist, for example, returned from a trip near Kazym, where the roadside is littered with debris for kilometers, exclaiming, "How can people hate themselves so much as to spoil their own environment like this? They must not think of it as theirs, even though they have taken it from us."

In the late 1980s, such feelings combined with shifting political conditions, enabling a few members of the Siberian intelligentsia to form an "Association of the Minority Peoples of the North." One of the first planning meetings took place in early August 1989, in Khanty-Mansiisk. Regional meetings led to a full Congress of the Minority Peoples of the North in Moscow's Kremlin in March 1990, with the explicit goal of empowering indigenous Siberians to have a greater voice in the distribution of resources, power, and authority in their own territories, and to monitor government programs ostensibly designed to improve their lives (see appendix A).[2] Within the Association, smaller regional activist groups were formed, among them the Association for the Salvation of the Ugra, headed by Tatiana Gogoleva, to formulate and defend Khanty and Mansi cultural, political, and economic rights.

The Association of the Minority Peoples of the North was a response to increased opportunities for local peoples throughout the Soviet Union to participate in the political and cultural processes changing the country and fostering newly revitalized identities. These opportunities were illustrated by the famed catch-words of the Gorbachev era, *glasnost'* (frankness) and *perestroika* (restructuring). But the cultural and political ferment did not begin in a vacuum. Rather, people's participation in new political forms had roots in their historical experiences and in the nurturing of ethnic identities they defined on the basis of cultural differences.

The history of ethnic interaction in Siberia's northern Ob River area reveals examples of ethnic group formation, survival, and persistence against considerable ecological, demographic, and political odds. The process has been painful, uneven, and unstable. For the Khanty, it was volatile enough to include a harshly repressed "rebellion" in the 1930s and sporadic local conflicts in the nineteenth century and earlier. In the twentieth century, expressions of ethnic consciousness have persisted in varying degrees, with varying influence on surrounding Russians.

In a café in Paris in 1997, I noticed some "New Russians" (slang for newly rich Russian businessmen) enjoying themselves. As the evening progressed with internationally customary libations and table-hopping, I landed next to their leader, an energy executive from West Siberia—Khanty territory. The executive was adamant: "All Khanty are alcoholics and die by age thirty, far too young to absorb any wisdom from any elders, who do not exist anyway. . . . No land exploration deal can be negotiated without a bottle, for the Khanty want and expect it that way. Khanty like to shoot at energy prospectors, and it has gotten quite dangerous to venture into the woods of the Eastern Khanty Surgut region." He concluded, "Let the few pitiful Khanty who are left on this earth live in town. Russian villages are dying too. The world needs gas. You need all we can pump."

The executive's logic and prejudice were sobering. He refused to believe that any Siberians were leaders, members of an intelligentsia, or were capable of writing books and producing films. Sadly, his views cannot be dismissed, for they are characteristic of many in his industry. And his chilling words "Whose homeland is it, anyway?" pointed to the crux of the tension, as Khanty writers, hunters, and reindeer breeders compete with newcomers for a home they thought was theirs.

GOALS

My first task is to tell a story of West Siberian development, strife, and accommodation that brings indigenous views of their history and current life into focus. Like most tales of human interaction, it has moments of transcending hope for interethnic communication as well as moments of despair. Having lived through the break-up of the Soviet Union, and seen its initial ramifications for indigenous peoples of the North, I hope to make the Khanty better known to a wide range of Western and Russian readers. Three stages of my field data are integrated with historical, sociological, and census materials, for perspectives on changes in Khanty society and differences within it. No Western ethnography of the Khanty based on post-1917 fieldwork and research has been published, and few works on Siberians have appeared since the former Soviet Union and then Russia (Rossiia) opened itself haphazardly to anthropologists.[3]

The Khanty (Ostiak in historical accounts) are an Ob-Ugrian people with hunting, fishing, and reindeer-breeding adaptations to the harsh Siberian north, a complex kinship organization, and a rich ritual life influenced, but not eclipsed, by Russian settlers. They are significant as a posttribal people with a difficult historical legacy struggling to remake themselves into a mobilized political and cultural group. Nomadic camp and lineage identities continue to be important, as other levels of identity (regional, national, international) are added.

Study of Russian and Khanty interaction can contribute to a more general understanding of ethnicity, nationalism, and change. My approach to ethnicity stresses self-identity, encompassing group and individual awareness of social-cultural differences. I see ethnicity as a mildly politicized construction of cultural difference and nationalism as a striving for some level of self-determination. In practice, the distinction dissolves, making the word "ethnonationalism" appropriate. Study of specific cultural values and behavior can reveal how social groups are maintained and why conflicts emerge. Analysis of responsive ethnic interactions can help illustrate the futility of theoretically pigeonholing the material and the ideological, the real and the perceived, the practical and the ideal, or the cultural and the political. An underlying assumption of my work is that, just as ethnonational groups are interactive, so these theoretical realms are interpenetrating and mutually influencing.

Narratives out of Siberia should transcend notorious stereotypes of cold and cruelty, as well as reverse stereotypes of selfless hospitality. The experiences that have compelling correlations for me are those of Native American (First Nations, Indian) groups, whose own painful histories of colonization and community power are (or should be) important factors shaping American consciousness and conscience. Native American comparisons are relevant for Native Siberians in the 1990s, as they emerge from one version of colonialism (under the Soviets) only to encounter new varieties of exploitation. I hope that readers familiar with North American history will find similarities and contrasts in my Siberian accounts; I call attention to some of the most salient correlations. The comparison is especially significant because newly politicized Siberians and long-mobilized Native American Indians are themselves interested in meeting and understanding each other. My participation in projects helping Native Siberian and Native American leaders communicate has permitted insights into adaptable models of hard-won Native American political and economic success, as well as development and reservation ghetto plights that Native Siberians are trying to avoid.[4]

A further goal is to describe Siberian ethnic interaction in sufficient detail to permit comparisons with the experiences of other Soviet and post-Soviet ethnonational groups. While many comparisons must remain implicit, my account of ethnonationalism, especially in the chapters on the 1990s, addresses concerns of political and economic specialists fascinated by the Russian Federation transition. Chaotic post-Soviet conditions invite a range of new scholarship and the generation of new theories.

My account of West Siberia also sheds retrospective light on "nationalities issues" raised by Soviet officials and ethnographers, engaged in what they perceived as one of history's grandest experiments in national relations and (re)construction. Before *glasnost'*, some Soviet ethnographers contributed to the study of ethnic relations. Their varying views of "ethnos," nationalism, bilingualism, and ethnic intermarriage can be compared with a range of Western analysis. By the end of the Soviet period, Western and Soviet analyses of ethnonational problems converged to an extent previously inconceivable, as ethnic conflicts erupted in former Soviet republics.[5]

FIELDWORK

A Khanty fisherman in Tegy village proudly told me in 1976: "My children study in different places, in Tiumen', in Omsk, in Berezovo, and in Salekhard. They will be able to read what you write about the Khanty." I take his words seriously, though the context of his statement has changed dramatically in the 1990s. Multiple kinds of interaction, dialogue, and observation have contributed to my comprehension of ethnic relations and social life in the former Soviet Union and the post-Soviet

Russian Federation. Periodic fieldwork since 1976 has been in many of the republics of the former Soviet Union and its successor Russian Federation. Most of my field time, especially in the 1990s, has been spent with Siberian colleagues and friends in and out of Siberia.

Since 1987, visits of Siberians to my home and to conferences in the U.S., Canada, and Europe have provided opportunities for updating and supplementing my Siberian work. As with many "post-modern" anthropologists, the "near" and "far" of standard fieldwork have been wonderfully confounded. Consultations with Khanty in 1993 (Moscow), in 1995 (at home outside Washington, D.C.), 1996 (Northern British Columbia), in 1997 (Moscow), and in 1998 (Florida) have been especially relevant. While these have been mostly with leaders and members of the intelligentsia, they have also provided more insights than I once thought possible into continuities of nomadic camp life in the post-Soviet period. In many ways, this makes the shock of recent oil industry excesses all the more tragic. One Khanty leader, Joseph Sopochin, explained to Bureau of Indian Affairs executive Franklin Keel in 1995, "We experienced colonialism by oil development, beginning in the Soviet period and continuing even more intensively today." Many Khanty add that they would like more control over local development, plus negotiated percentages of energy profits, but understand that they cannot realistically expect a total halt to energy projects in West Siberia.

I have lived nearly forty months in villages and cities of Rossiia, on nine trips, two lasting over a year. The first thirteen months of my exchange experience were in 1975–76, when I did research for my doctorate in cultural anthropology in Leningrad (now Saint Petersburg) and traveled widely. My first addictive taste of Siberia was a 1975 Novosibirsk conference on Siberian-Alaskan cultural connections. In 1976, I was able to join a Leningrad University summer ethnographic "expedition" to Khanty territory, thus becoming the first American permitted, in the Soviet period, in Khanty villages of the Northern Ob River near the Arctic Circle. In 1986, I lived in Yakutia (now the Sakha Republic) on the official cultural exchange, an experience that strongly influenced my views of the entire Siberian North and what Russians call the Far East. In 1991, I returned to the Khanty area and the Sakha Republic, beginning a series of yearly visits.[6]

The circumstances of my July-August 1991 fieldwork at the old Soviet "culture base" of Kazym, where I had first lived in 1976, were remarkable for what they symbolized about changing life in the last months of the Soviet era. I arrived alone, by plane, at the newly developed oil boomtown of Beloiarsk and phoned local representatives of the Association for the Salvation of the Ugra. Two Russians with a car were found to take me the forty-five-minute drive to Kazym, where I was brought to the warm and welcoming home of Khanty activist Tania Moldanova's widowed mother, Nadezhda Karpovna. Several days later, members of the ethnographic film seminar that I had come to take part in moved to the local boarding school (*kasum kutup*, in Khanty), empty for the summer. My lively and talkative roommates were a Mansi leader of the Association for the Salvation of the Ugra, a Nenets director of a folklore museum in Salekhard, and a talented young assistant to the Association, of mixed Khanty and Mansi background. Neighbors included Tania and Timofei Moldanov, the Khanty folklorist-intellectuals most responsible for bringing our film seminar to fruition.[7] In addition to film seminar activities, I had time for diverse home interviews, berrying in the woods with friends, jam making, mushroom picking and processing, breadline waiting, Russian-style bathhouse female solidarity, occasional group-heckle TV news viewing, participant-observation at the Saturday night disco, and socializing of a more low-key variety (photo 1).

My 1991 field interests had three main overlapping aspects: (1) the nature and development of the Association for the Salvation of the Ugra and its ethno-political context; (2) a general ethnographic study of cultural change and spiritual revival, using comparisons especially to my

Photo 1. The Kazym community during the 1991 ethnographic film seminar. Note Tatiana Moldanova kneeling.

observations in 1976; and (3) the multiethnic and multivoiced dynamics of the film seminar.

First contacts with the Association for the Salvation of the Ugra occurred in Moscow, where I had discussions with their capable and impressive president, Tatiana Gogoleva. Even before meeting Tatiana Gogoleva, I had heard from Sakha friends that she was one of the most effective of the emerging leaders involved in founding the umbrella group "Association of the Minority Peoples of the North." When we met, she outlined Salvation of the Ugra activities that combined hard-nosed political-economic activism against indiscriminate energy development with sponsorship of Native rituals such as weddings and bear festivals.

I was pleased that the Association for the Salvation of the Ugra, by focusing on both internal and external Ob-Ugrian relations, was becoming a fulcrum for precisely the issues that I considered most crucial and most fascinating about the new efforts at Khanty political-cultural revival. Yet I also understood, especially later in Kazym, that I would have to temper my own enthusiasm for their activities with a more broad-based sense of how extensively their influence was spreading. I interviewed more than twenty people of various ages, sometimes through personal connections and sometimes in casual talks on the village street. Over half of the street interviews developed into home visits. Some Kazym Khanty, from young to elderly, were excited about the Association, but some had barely heard of it. One sad and cynical young woman, who had health and housing problems, was very sarcastic when I suggested she might want to contact the Association for possible support and advocacy. "What possible good could they do? The real power to do anything around here is still in the hands of the [former communist] Zyrian [Komi] local village [council] president, and he helps his own people." I also had two interviews with this friendly yet nervous local president, who proclaimed himself a Yeltsin-style reformer, criticized the ecological devastation of his region, and was defensive about his relations with the Association.[8]

It was impossible to measure Khanty cultural changes in any standardized way, yet it was easier in 1991 than 1976 to discern that many Khanty appreciated not only their "traditional" (non-Christian, non-Soviet) rituals but also the spiritual beliefs that underlie them. This was brought home when I accompanied three sisters to the graveyard to pay respects to their ancestors. It emerged in my discussions with several (young) believers about their yearning for a revival of effective shamanic practice, "before it is too late." But most striking was the acknowledgement of a continuity of ritual life (including reindeer sacrifices for ancestral spirits, bear festivals, and some wedding rituals) that had persisted under the surface of Soviet rule. Crucial to this was a key tenet of Khanty personhood: belief in reincarnation and the need to divine proper Khanty names for babies. In 1991, elderly, middle-aged, and two younger Khanty women were regularly divining to determine soul transfers for newborns. Thus the spirit of Khanty specialness and continuity, expressed through soul beliefs, persisted amidst a morass of interethnic marriage, atheist propaganda, and sheer alcoholic apathy.

My 1991 role in Kazym was not just outsider ethnographer, collector and sifter of bits and shreds of information, but also teacher-facilitator, part of a team of Western, Russian, Bulgarian, and Hungarian specialists leading seminars on ethnographic film (see Appendix B). Our goal was to give Siberian seminar members skills with which to film their own cultures, however they cared to define that challenge.[9] During intensive classroom sessions, we traded information on methodology and diverse philosophies of cultural anthropology, as well as on video film techniques. Conflicts arose between some participants, who defined "culture" as only traditional and folkloric and others who wanted to include "modern," Russified Native youth. We ate meals together in the school cafeteria, shared adventures during filming, and helped organize a Khanty "traditional sports" festival for the community on a cold damp day that was saved for me by a bonfire that generated gossip as well as warmth.

During frenetic evenings in the school, we had Western ethnographic films running in one room; videos of a four-day Khanty bear festival (filmed in the winter of 1991) in another; and tea, conversation, and singing in a third. In all three rooms, members of the Kazym community mingled with seminar participants, who included not only Khanty and Mansi but also Nentsy and Sakha. Informal discussions lasted past midnight in all three rooms. The room with the bear festival was the most popular with elderly Khanty women and drew a few elderly men as well. They came to watch themselves and their friends, reliving their joy at being able to dance and sing openly in a rite honoring the sacred bear. Eager to talk and explain, they made that room sacred for me. Later, when a Khanty widow proudly showed me a bear skin, complete with head, that she kept above her dresser, kissing and talking and making offerings to it, I better understood her feelings. I was pleased when she let me help her put the bear away.

Participation in the film seminar provided insights into aspects of Kazym life that I might not have been able to see so quickly in another field situation. The presence of outsiders-with-cameras catalyzed, and in some cases polarized, community opinions about the opening of their village to foreigners, to reform, and to overt issues of ethnicity. Such mixed community feelings were aired in two village meetings, and more informally around many kitchen tables. Slavic-Native tensions exploded in my face one day when I was scolded by a Ukrainian woman for my friendship with "Khanty nationalists." Native rights and ecology advocacy, seemingly congruent, also turned out to be fraught with tension when a Russian ecological activist appeared, asking us to make a film on local ecology problems.

Debates were continual about where lines should be drawn in exposing sacred rituals to outsiders. During filming of the winter bear festival a related sacrifice of seven reindeer in a sacred grove was not permitted to be filmed. One of our Khanty colleagues had tears of sorrow and anger in his eyes when he saw a film of a shamanic ritual that included an animal sacrifice (see appendix B.) He did not think it should have been filmed, because he felt aspects of "insider" sacred life should be kept hidden from "outsider" viewers, whose atheist, Christian, or other perspectives might interfere with their understanding or good will.

The problem of mystical secrecy is familiar in anthropology: I try to explain insights Khanty have given me about named souls and reincarnation without revealing confidences about personal spirituality. The task became far easier later in the 1990s, when some Khanty have urged greater openness and themselves are writing eloquently about spiritual concerns (e.g., Kravchenko 1996).[10]

The focus of the seminar was on using ethnography and film morally, creatively, and productively, to help serve community purposes. Thus, we courted diverse community input. We debated the meaning of Soviet rule, patriotism, what constitutes "anti-Soviet propaganda," and what it means to lose one's "national soul." Similar pulse-taking opportunities emerged, with higher stakes but less overt intensity, during the August 1991 coup.[11]

Discussions of ethnography and ethics brought out stories of how a few Khanty purposely deceived certain Russian ethnographers, including one case of systematic misinforming on the subject of lineage identities. Ethnographers perceived to be potentially exploitive, or too closely allied with local Russian authority figures, were given misinformation throughout the Soviet period, raising alarming questions about the nature of some seemingly apolitical ethnographic and historical data.

When I was first given permission to participate in a university "ethnographic expedition" to the Khanty in 1976, I was concerned about my ability to learn very much during summer fieldwork. However, the trip enabled insights into Soviet anthropology and Native-Russian interaction. Most important, I became intrigued by Khanty culture: fieldwork provided focus for further archive and library research, and for future contacts.

In 1976, members of our "expedition" lived in two villages, one a

Photo 2. The Kazym main square, women cooking, 1976.

fishing collective (Tegy) and the other a reindeer breeding center and "culture base" (Kazym). In both, I was impressed by the importance of rituals stressing life passages. It is crucial to emphasize that I did not initially set out to study this topic. Rituals were not immediately apparent upon arrival at Tegy via modern hydrofoil. But their significance soon became clear, modulating first impressions of impoverished, Sovietized, dispirited lives (photo 2).[12]

Many opportunities arose to confirm my growing impressions of active yet discreet ritual life, beginning with ceremonies and beliefs focused on the graveyard. In Tegy, I observed the Khanty librarian at a traditional memorial feast; in Kazym, I watched preparations for another remembrance ceremony. Although I had been told religion was dead, I heard recently made tapes of sacred bear festival songs and listened to a Russian and a Khanty consultant accuse two other Khanty of shamanic misdeeds. Just before a thunderstorm, I watched a woman, buffeted by a life of many misfortunes, run out of her cabin and beg the Sky God, Numi-Torum, not to harm her family. I learned of recent weddings that featured adapted older rituals. I was shown, from a boat, the site of a sacred grove still considered off-limits to women, and I experienced firsthand the fear that a Khanty man evinced when I attempted to climb to his attic. I was by his definition "impure," as a woman, and would contaminate the house below.[13]

In Tegy, our group stayed in the grade school, empty for the summer and located conveniently in the center of the village near the Malaia Ob River. In Kazym, the collective director placed us in a small building that also housed the local library and Communist Party headquarters, on the main square. Such arrangements enabled easy but not ideal access to consultants, whom we sought ourselves. While some villagers felt free to visit me, most of my serious discussions took place in Khanty homes, where Khanty casually encouraged visitors to enter after calling "uusia" (hello).[14]

Several consultants lived in the same households, which became places I frequented at all hours of the long summer days. Others entertained me (and sometimes other expedition members) at length with songs and legends. I taped such expressive data, which then (with permission) became currency for breaking the ice with other consultants. Only one woman, a reputed shaman, completely refused to talk. A few of my most significant interviews took place by chance, sitting on the bank of the Amnia River waiting for a boat to take me between Kazym and the more "traditional" village of Amnia on the opposite shore.

I collected life histories to the extent that it was polite and politic to do so.[15] Expedition members pooled historical and kinship information (especially from male elders) that I was then able to check with my most trusted middle-aged or elderly female consultants. In everyday visits with Khanty women, I helped clean fish, make tea, and carry wood, although I was all too often treated as a guest without work obligations.

Twice I was able to leave the villages and learn something of the active and strenuous camp life that many Khanty lead. One occasion was a day-long scything trip made with a Khanty elder, his son, and our expedition leader, Valery A. Kozmin. On this trip, I cut grass for cattle feed, and helped prepare a Khanty-style meal of boiled fish. I watched our host check fishnets in what he described as his traditional lineage territory and listened to his stories of World War II.

On a second trip, our group traveled in two motor boats to a fish camp near Kazym to see a six-person fishing crew in action. We watched the solitary Khanty woman of the camp rapidly splay fish to dry on lines for the long winter ahead. A young Khanty fisherman described sacred groves and local history.

Descriptions of rituals and ethnic relations often varied in detail and emphasis. Some differences could be resolved by correlating them with Tegy and Kazym accounts; others were undoubtedly based on memory lapses and changing practices. Only rarely did anyone attempt to misinform, and their information could usually be checked against other sources. When questioning the extent of contemporary belief in gender-linked prohibitions, for instance, I discovered that a whole group of

Khanty women of various ages, sitting in the same room, could not agree. The incident confirmed that, for certain issues, a valuable technique is to encourage friendly debate. Anthropologists clearly cannot attempt to find one right answer to complex questions about culture change, conservatism, and ethnicity.

From 1975 to 1998, I have had fascinating conversations with Russians, in and out of Siberia, about their attitudes toward the Khanty and other Native Siberians. The Russians varied from staunchly idealistic Soviets, such as the collective directors of Tegy and Kazym, to snobbish townspeople of Berezovo who disdained learning a Native language, to mixed Russian-Native "Siberiak" women in nineteenth-century Russian peasant dress who bragged about knowing the local Khanty dialect, to energy executives, to post-Soviet officials of the Moscow Government Committee of the North (Goskomsevera), most of whom are Russians, not Natives.[16] In West Siberia, evidence of Russian-Soviet culture was everywhere: in village stores, in the first two-story apartment building in Tegy, in post offices, in log-cabin hospitals, and especially in the energy boomtowns like Beloiarsk. In 1976, I observed that the Russians had relatively better housing, jobs, and possessions than the Khanty, but the life-style gap had become much greater by 1991. It has increased through the 1990s, as the dachas of energy executives rim lakes where Khanty sacred groves were once the sites of rituals.

ARCHIVAL, MUSEUM, AND LITERATURE RESOURCES

"It is important for the outside world to learn something about us, and to realize that not everything about our culture is dead," Tania Moldanova reassured me in 1991, when I expressed concern about writing Khanty history as an outsider. In this spirit, my work combines diverse historical and contemporary data, forgoing generalized descriptions in the "ethnographic present," and featuring, now that they can finally be heard, diverse Khanty voices. Historical sources are uneven. Particularly rich are the Soviet household demographic and economic records of Tegy and Kazym, since they were kept by officials who did not intend to use them for anything other than their own information. Prerevolutionary archival data on legal conflicts, taxes, leadership, government reform policy, and intermarriage are also quite reliable, provided each is weighed in terms of the background (class, occupation, opinions) of its author.

My most significant historical sources relate to indigenous protests, called "rebellions" by authorities, and collectivization. These include accounts in Russian in obscure journals, by participants, witnesses, judges, and other officials. I have tried to augment Russian and Soviet descriptions justifying the taxing, jailing, killing, and relocating of Natives with indigenous or foreign accounts. Native versions of a little-known, searing hostage crisis at Kazym in 1931–32, resulting in the killing of high-level Soviet officials, are recounted here for the first time in English.

A panoply of impressionistic local resident and traveler descriptions of Northwestern Siberian life since the eighteenth century has been sifted for nuggets concerning the Khanty. These are revealing even when the authors were clearly racist. Ethnographies by usually well-meaning Russians, writing more or less professionally since the nineteenth century, have been combed for data related to the themes stressed here.[17] Finally, museum records in Saint Petersburg (Leningrad) and Helsinki, accompanying collections of religious materials, have provided insights into Khanty spiritual life. These insights were subsequently reinforced when I saw precious, secret items in the field for the first time in 1991.

SYNCRETIC THEORY THROUGH MULTIPLE PERSPECTIVES

Arjun Appadurai urges us to "re-think concepts of family, civil society, political society and the nation . . . avoid[ing] the trap of de-historicizing 'tradition.'"[18] His discussion of fresh perspectives in "transnational" contexts is aimed at better understanding complex societies where people often do not expect to live and work where they were born, and where "collective imaginings" take place through electronic media. His plea to go beyond concepts of the "nation-state" or accusations of "tribalism" when ethnic conflicts break out is as relevant to studies of Siberia as to India, Europe, or America. It is appropriate even for people without computers who are trying to stay in their own homelands.

Accounts of ethnic interaction ideally should be multisided and multileveled ethnographies, so that ethnohistory is more than a study of European political-economic impact and "Natives" are more than passive, acculturated recipients of outsiders' cultures (Wolf 1982:385–91; Ortner 1984:143; Ortner 1995). The reverse stereotype of Native overaction implicit in the expression "the natives are restless," must also be avoided. This stereotype may be implicated in the wave of reflexive soul searching in anthropology that rejects the word "native" entirely.[19] Relations of Europeans, including Slavic peoples, with Native peoples, including Siberians, have been too unpredictable and diverse to define as corrupt or benevolent or to permit the clear demarcation of "friends" and "foes." Sherry Ortner's now classic statement (1984:143) that history should not be "something that arrives, like a ship, from outside the society in question" still serves as an appropriate warning.

The task of selecting the most significant interactions is made difficult by insufficient material illuminating Native perspectives on events described by majorities holding formal or informal power (Slezkine 1994; Brown 1980). Western anthropologists thus often attempt radical revisions, presenting and interpreting Native views and Native resistance. My approach is similarly Khanty-centric, although I have tried to understand the situations of nearby Siberians and of Russians in diverse positions of power. I integrate various individual "ethnoscapes" into my text without overgeneralizing about ethnic groups as "collectivized individuals" (Appadurai 1996:48–65; Handler 1988).

My interpretation of Siberian data seems least distorted using models of "longue durée" ethnohistory that represent standards of comprehensive description.[20] While acknowledging the hidden strings of phenomenology in any analysis and the reflexivity of any field situation, I see in various aspects of Khanty narratives diverse theories and theoretical applications. I have gradually evolved a precarious balance between my worldviews and an openness to others that enables a "situational ethics" approach to theory, data, and writing.[21]

Like a fur animal eluding capture, ethnicity has come to mean so much to so many that the most humanitarian way to view it begins with individuals' self-labels of cultural identity, ethnonyms (Proschan 1997). Ethnic consciousness can be mobilized or simply fostered in social group behavior and ethnic interaction. Ethnicity is constrained from leading to chauvinist brands of nation-dreaming separatism when a given ethnic group is a tiny minority in its own homeland. Yet chauvinist nationalism can supersede defensive nationalism when desperation leads to ethnic polarization.

Within the Russian Federation, many ethnic group members aspire to increased degrees of self-determination for the ethnic group to which they belong but stop short of radical or chauvinist nationalism. Thus the American theorist Walker Connor (1994) argues for the encompassing term "ethnonationalism." For Connor, the rational and the irrational are part of the dynamics of ethnonationalism, spurred by diverse and interactive conditions prevailing between ethnonational groups, especially in an evolving federal context.

Many social theories distinguish between a culturally, especially linguistically, "homogeneous" ethnic group (*ethnos*, or *ethnie*) that has developed through time (identified as coherent by ethnohistorians) and a group that is in the process of defining for itself a more politicized ethnicity.[22] Indeed, anthropologists' current critique of culture hinges on awareness that our disciplinary ancestors often saw "culture" as an unrealistically fixed and integrated system (Fox 1995:1–5). My focus is on the rooted-in-history politics of ethnicity, not on ethnicity or culture as homogeneous.

In the Norwegian anthropologist Fredrik Barth's view (1969), people cannot become aware of their own ethnicity until they chafe against ethnic others, and thus need to define ethnic boundaries. Ethnicity becomes inherently political, using the language (idiom, discourse) of cultural differences to make us/them distinctions. While for Barth, this could theoretically happen in premodern times, for Ernest Gellner (1983), the self-conscious definition of an ethnic group as a sociopolitical unit becomes possible only in an industrialized, modern world of intense, often colonial or unequal, interethnic relations.

Similarly, Benedict Anderson (1991) calls national groups "imagined communities," and finds their roots in the development of printing, literacy, and the break-up of colonial empires. His "imagined communities" are limited and self-conceived as sovereign, yet European patterns are imprinted in the brains of their members, whether they like it or not. Taken too far, this argument misses the power of non-European worldviews to shape outsider messages, or coexist with them. John and Jean Comaroff (1992:49–67) address this problem by arguing that people acting in the name of ethnicity (consciousness of difference, shaped by specific historical processes) become complicit in its dynamics, and yet can change the rules of its deadly serious games of categorizing.

Creative and multifaceted approaches to nationalism are illustrated by some of its early European theorists (e.g., Mazzini (1907)), who wedded traditions of liberalism and nationalism, and by more recent theorists struggling to make sense of the diversity of ethnic and nationalist movements from non-European perspectives. Especially useful for stressing the constructedness and responsiveness of ethnonationalism are the ideas of non-Western political anthropologists Yael Tamir (1993), who uses Middle East politics to illustrate her points, and Partha Chatterjee (1993) writing on India. Tamir's *Liberal Nationalism* argues that loyalty and patriotism to a state or federal republic need not preclude other identities and loyalties or take priority over them. Just as there is a linguistic distinction between the words "selfishness" (egoism) and "individualism" (taking care of oneself without hurting others), so too nationalism need not imply an automatic or blind mass chauvinism. People have "human rights" as both individuals and group members in this conception. "The morality of community" means protection of group rights first for ethnically related members, but also for all minorities within a given multiethnic state, on the basis of citizenship (Przeworski 1995:31; Hann and Dunn 1996).

Formation of Khanty ethnicity in the pre-Soviet period involved shifting levels of cultural awareness, and occasional political use of that awareness on a group level. In the early Soviet period, ethnicity was state-sponsored, through the creation of the Khanty-Mansi Okrug (District). With education, Khanty gradually became more aware of their group identity, based on cultural differences in relation to other peoples, but rarely overtly politicized. More recently, Khanty (and Mansi) ethnicity has become politically strengthened, viable, and credible, at the same time that Khanty are joining with other Siberian peoples to reinstate and protect their interests. Some Khanty leaders advocate self-determination through "preserves" (not reservations) and *obshchiny* (land-based communities).[23]

The significance of self-identity has been emphasized by psychological anthropologists Lola Romanucci-Ross and George De Vos (1995), among many others. Soviet census takers were instructed to use self-identity as the basis for recording national statistics, although debate has raged over how much self-defining the census permitted, given preconceived nationality categories and the existence of a "nationality" designation in Soviet passports. Russian ethnographers usually define *ethnos* in more complex terms, beginning with self-identification but assuming an evolving and hierarchic set of historic and ethnolinguistic categories.[24]

While ethnonationalist identities are often crucial keys to understanding behavior in the former Soviet Union and the Russian Federation, they are hardly the only keys. The concept of "social identity" discussed by Ward Goodenough (1963:3) and Michael Herzfeld's "levels of identity" (1989:155) stress the plural and situational nature of self-identity, placing ethnicity and gender in broader perspective. In different contexts diverse actions and identities may be appropriate, particularly in situations of ethnic or international interaction. New rights and duties are constantly learned or adapted but do not preclude old relationships.[25]

Examples of multiple, situational identities in the Soviet context include urban Russian Communist Party members who secretly attended family funerals or baptisms. Among the Khanty, I met many who were balancing multiple identities. They included a collective worker who played a major role in a traditional graveside memorial feast and a party leader who participated in a bear ceremony. Precisely because multiple levels of social-cultural participation became widespread in the Soviet period, the post-Soviet transition has been somewhat more flexible, diverse, and democratic than often predicted or claimed (Balzer 1990, 1992, 1994, 1995).

The term "biculturalism" does not begin to describe all the options for individuals, nor should we assume hypocrisy as we analyze changes of heart in Native leaders who were Communist Party members. For any given individual, the distinction between conservative and progressive often depends on social context and opportunity. An established, educated young Siberian man living outside of Siberia conspiratorially said to me in 1976, "I may be wearing a business suit, but inside is my traditional culture." During *glasnost'*, the Evenk poet Alitet Nemtushkin (1988), speaking for many Siberians, proclaimed in public: "Thanks to all the Soviet peoples for their fraternal help. . . . However, we have outgrown the children's trousers and no longer need to be under guardianship. Give us the right to take charge of our destiny."

Concern with individual identities and strategies of ethnonational survival should not mask the serious social and political constraints impinging on those strategies (Royce 1982; Gellner 1983, 1993, 1994; Verdery 1996). Prejudice, ethnic conflict, and ethnic stereotyping all lead to attributions that are unwelcome and hard to shake. Such negative aspects of ethnicity can push people into boundary crossings, "passing," or the opposite, exacerbated ethnic consciousness and embittered chauvinist nationalism. But bloodshed, escalating and tragic in many places, is not the norm, either for the world community or the post-Soviet peoples.[26]

Ethnic conflict and accommodation should be seen in the context of the politics of demographics. For most Khanty, the Soviet-Russian influx into the North has been all too rapid and extensive, reducing indigenous groups to only about 3 percent of the Khanty-Mansi Okrug by the 1990s. Yet many villages and settlements remain predominantly Native. In 1976 in Tegy, a young Khanty man remarked to me, "I think there are more Russians than Khanty living in this village." Startled, I checked the collective records and asked local officials. I discovered the youth's impression was inaccurate, as there were almost a third more Khanty than Russians in Tegy in 1976. However, the incident revealed a different kind of truth: many Khanty perceived themselves as besieged, knowing themselves to be a minority in the region as a whole. This perception has only grown.

In their turn, some anthropologists stress processes of acculturation and assimilation in complex societies with dominant and minority groups. Such trends need to be tested rather than assumed.[27] Assimilation is used here in the sense of social assimilation, especially that involving ethnic intermarriage. "Russification" may result. Yet intermarriage in Rossiia is as often between members of non-Russian groups as between Russians and non-Russians. In the past, when children of mixed Russian and Native Siberian marriages chose their "official" ethnic identity at age sixteen (for internal passports until 1997), the choice of Russian was not assured.[28] This was especially true while Soviet-style affirmative action programs were in place. In the 1990s, however, such programs and the attitudes that produced them have been curtailed, as Siberian regional leaders, often Russian nationalists, take control of local areas.

Acculturation describes a process of incorporating values. While acculturation usually results from the influence of one dominant culture on another, the concept allows for influences to flow in multiple directions, involving multiple groups. Peoples of the North were not passive recipients of outsiders' sacred (Orthodox, Soviet) words, but active integrators and interpreters of those words. Soviet propaganda was often ignored and values compartmentalized, so that bi- or multicultural behavior did not seem insincere to its practitioners (Abrahamian 1994).

To assess the Soviet legacy, it is necessary to confront the degree to which certain aspects of Marxist-Leninist thought took hold among Native Siberians and Russians. Ideology and social behavior were filtered through different levels of awareness of Marx and different experiences of local history. Yet for many, pragmatic faith in progress, objectivity, and civilization became part of an unevenly shared worldview even when people were cynical about local conditions (Grant 1995).

In folk Marxism-Leninism, separation of political trends (cadre building, purges, and labor organization) from economic programs (collectivization and industrialization) is superfluous. The two were also enmeshed in Soviet planning. And some Soviets believed that they were building, against horrendous obstacles, the strong economic-technological base necessary for effective, enduring social and spiritual change. In this crude materialist view, endorsed by some Siberian officials, changes in the means and modes of production set the pace and determine the nature of social-cultural advance, yielding a domino theory of culture change. Such a functionalist utopian framework, still embraced by many graduates of the Soviet education system, posits meaningful change as occurring first at the economic, then at the social, and finally at the religious level, conquering superstitious false consciousness only with great difficulty.[29]

Sensing from experience, if not from theory, that changing material conditions were not by themselves enough to move a population quickly toward Communist goals, Soviet leaders gave sociologists, ethnographers, and Marxist philosophers the task of seeking functional alternatives to religion (Kryvelev 1977). Faced with the persistence of religion, party cadres waged elaborate propaganda and secularization campaigns, creating secular rituals based on Russian cultural forms (cf. Stites 1989; Lane 1981). Rather than replacing the religious opiate of the people with communist rituals, authorities in effect substituted methadone. This was less successful than hoped, particularly when the "masses" were devout national minorities, and when individuals responded to religion as forbidden fruit, not opium.[30]

To analyze Siberian ethnic relations, I view religion as neither an opiate nor a handicap but rather as a bulwark of potentially tenacious personal and social-cultural significance. Religious belief in itself did not necessarily lead to political dissent in the Soviet period, since many loyal Soviet citizens practiced their religions quietly. However, in the Soviet milieu, religious belief often became a symbol or marker of ethnicity (Petro 1990; Ramet 1992). Religious practice changed, without its significance being diminished. In the whole Soviet (dis)Union and in Khanty territory, many aspects of traditional religious life declined, while others grew stronger in new ways. These patterns have become especially clear in the post-Soviet 1990s, as some Siberians are attempting what they and others call "neo-traditionalism" (Pika and Prokhorov 1994).

THE KHANTY IN CULTURAL, DEMOGRAPHIC, AND ECOLOGICAL CONTEXT

The Khanty are closely related in language and culture to their neighbors the Mansi (Vogul). This "Ob-Ugrian" cultural commonality was reflected in Soviet political geography, with a large portion of northwestern Siberia designated the Khanty-Mansi Autonomous Okrug. The region was established in December 1930 and until 1937 was called the Ostiak-Vogul National Okrug. The name discrepancy was symptomatic of Soviet politics, for 1930s ethnographers claimed that "Khanty" and "Mansi" were more authentic ethnonyms than the terms "Ostiak" and "Vogul," which were loaded with tsarist legacies (see Appendix C).

The Khanty in 1926, when the first Soviet census was taken, numbered 17,800 and the Mansi 5,754 (fig. 1). In the late 1990s, they number approximately 25,000 and 10,000, respectively. While not all Khanty live within the bounds of their *Okrug* (District), most live within the Tiumen' *Oblast* (Region). In the Soviet political framework, the Khanty and Mansi were midway between Siberian groups without a formal administrative unit based on nationality (the Yukagir and some Amur River groups) and the two largest Siberian groups, the Buryat and the Sakha (Yakut), each numbering over 375,000 in 1989, with its own "autonomous republic" within the Russian Soviet Federative Socialist Republic. Since 1991, the nesting "matrioshka doll" has endured declarations of greater republic and regional status, but hierarchy is maintained through the Federal Treaty signed in March 1992, the 1993 con-

	1897	*1926*	*1939*	*1959*	*1970*	*1979*	*1989*
Khanty (Ostiak)	17,211	17,800	18,500	19,410	21,138	20,934	22,521
Mansi (Vogul)	7,473	5,754	?	6,449	7,710	7,563	8,474
Nenets (Samoyed)	?	15,462	?	23,007	28,705	29,894	34,665

Figure 1. West Siberian demography (by census year).

Sources: Chislennost' i Sostav Naseleniia; *Natsional'nyi sostav naseleniia* (Moscow: Finansy i Statistiki); and Murray Feshbach archives, Georgetown University. Question marks indicate data are unreliable.

stitution, and bilateral treaties. Despite some debate, Khanty and Mansi boundaries have not changed (maps 1 and 2).

The Khanty, Mansi, and Hungarian languages comprise the Ugrian branch of the Finno-Ugric language family (fig. 2). The Khanty language is divided into three major dialect groups: Northern (including Kazym, Obdorsk, Berezovo, and Sherkaly Khanty), Southern (Irtysh-Konda, Altym, and Leusha Khanty), and Eastern (Surgut, Salym, and Vakh-Vasyugan Khanty). These divisions also reflect subtle cultural distinctions that Khanty sometimes make. Variable interactions with Russians, Tatars, and Samodeic [formerly Samoyedic] groups, especially the numerically dominant Nentsy, have led to further indigenous distinctions.

On the basis of language, environment and ethnic interaction, the most significant distinction is between Northern and Southern Khanty. In the more southerly portions of the Ob region, the Khanty historically had greater association with Russians than in the north. I have worked with Northern and Eastern Khanty and have found that these groups have preserved a relatively strong sense of ethnic and local identities, despite Samodeic, Tatar, and Slavic influences. Today, in the 1990s, about 60 percent of the Khanty speak their Native language (Vakhtin 1993:48).

The Khanty have long been patrilineal in social organization, tracing descent and significant inheritance through the male line. Awareness of widely ramifying levels of kin group identity is common, although kin groups became less relevant in the Soviet period. Many Khanty are patriarchal, highly valuing male authority, and patrilocal, preferring a woman to live with or near her husband's family.[31]

In a given area, the relative importance of fishing, hunting, and rein-

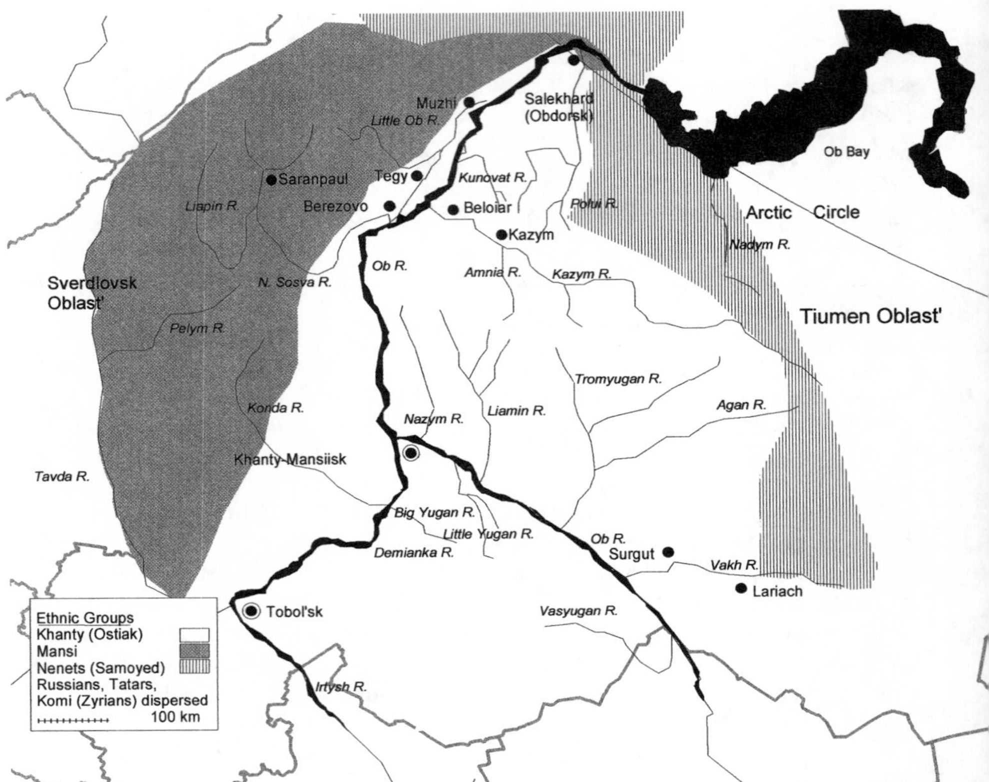

Map 2. The Northern Ob river region. Khanty-Mansi Okrug of the Tiumen Oblast.

deer breeding varies with natural resources, and, since the 1930s, with government planning. In the 1960s, some Khanty reindeer breeders living along the Ob moved to the Kazym region, since the Kazym collective was one of the last to actively support reindeer breeding. Khanty fishermen catch a wealth of fish, including pink and white salmon, pike, sturgeon, trout, and carp. Khanty hunters shoot or trap squirrel, polar fox, elk, otter, marten, sable, wolverine, ermine, and, occasionally, wild reindeer and bear (cf. Ponomarev 1973). In addition, grouse, partridge, geese, and ducks abound in regions not affected by the energy industry and are easily trapped or shot. Waterfowl are especially easy prey during summer molting season, when the defenseless birds can be clubbed.

The environment that supports such rich animal life is diverse, including taiga, tundra, and forests of cedar, beech, pine, and larch. Traveling

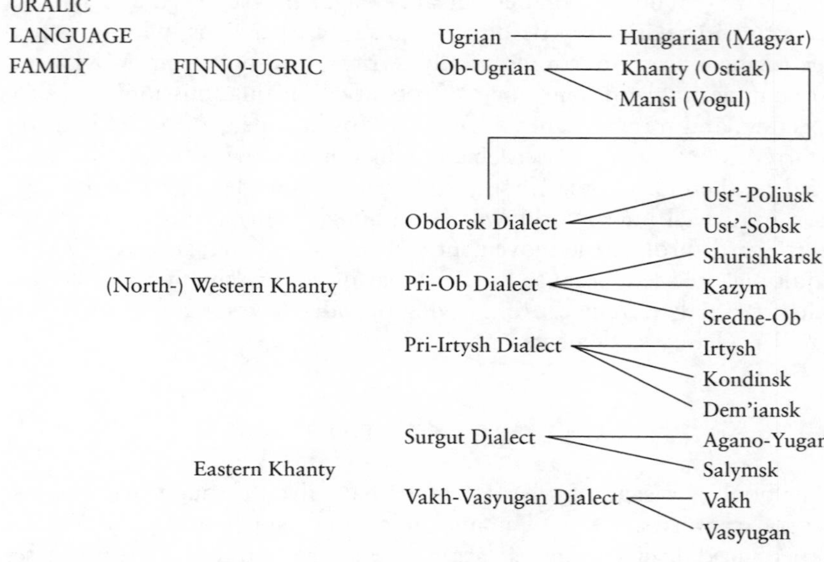

Figure 2. The Khanty (Ostiak) language as seen by Khanty linguists.

Source: Adapted from Sengepov, Nemysova, and Moldanova 1988:3–7.

north, or away from riverbank forests, one reaches taiga, with its stunted vegetation and grasses, and then tundra, with its huge expanse of permafrost. Aerial views of Khanty territory in summer show rivers overflowing their banks and glimpses of large moss-covered swamps, peat, and marsh pine.

Large segments of the Surgut (Eastern Khanty) region as well as parts of other Khanty territories have been devastated by wasteful and destructive oil and gas excavation. Networks of Ob River tributaries support Khanty fishing settlements, while expanses of taiga and tundra enable nomadic reindeer breeding. The Ob, as well as some of its tributaries, have been polluted to varying degrees, with a diminution of fish resources notable since the 1960s. Yet fish spawning grounds relatively free from pollution still exist in this vast region larger than France.

Khanty often asked how long the winter is in America. It was clearly a matter of great concern, for they would solemnly trump my answer of "four or five months" with the figures "seven or eight months." Their climate is severe and continental, intensely cold in the "dark days" of winter (minus twenty-five to minus fifty degrees centigrade) and hot in the "white nights" summers (fifteen to twenty degrees centigrade).

The sub-Arctic environment meant that many Northern and Eastern Khanty had relatively little direct exposure to Russians, who long perceived the extreme north (especially territories distant from waterways) to be undesirable, despite some efforts at colonizing, missionizing, prospecting, and trading. Only since the 1960s has the gas and oil industry spurred more extensive settlement.[32] In this ecological and behavioral climate, therefore, some Khanty survived without demographic inundation until well after World War II, although many changes percolated northward through the movement of Khanty and Mansi themselves. In addition, precisely because of the threat of cultural inundation, certain Khanty rituals were kept from prying outsiders' eyes, particularly in the smaller Khanty settlements.

ORGANIZATION

This book is a saga of what Siberians have lived through over the last several centuries. As with many indigenous Northerners, the Khanty experienced displacement, isolation, and interpenetration. The processes of ethnic interaction in the Ob River region may be characterized by sweeping trends that overarched and strongly affected Khanty lives: colonization, Christianization, revitalization, Sovietization, and regionalization. These processes incorporate suprastate and state politics, as well as more local social dynamics and movements. Recent devastation stemming from the energy industry's land thefts has led to upheaval and nuanced resistance in many styles. Such changes might seem to presage the complete demise of Khanty ethnicity. Yet the final chapters demonstrate ways some Khanty have found, in the midst of crisis, to preserve cultural values and dignity and strive for cultural empowerment. Khanty ethnicity has varied with the politics of individuals, groups, and generations. It has been shaped by recent grass-roots mobilization, ecological activism, and religious revival, as well as older historical memory, language-based solidarity, and loyalty to a homeland. At each historical turn, Siberian experiences help shed new light on old debates concerning the concepts of colonization, conversion, revitalization, and ethnicity.

The term colonization is used here with awareness of fluctuation in Russian/Soviet historiography on the issue, and relief that recent Russian assessments have refuted Soviet ideological emphasis on a history of ethnic friendship between early Slavs (mostly Cossacks) and Siberians. Colonization describes a combination of conflict and accommodation that occurred as soldiers and settlers arrived in Ob Ugrian territories. Colonies (networks of fortified outposts) were where officials demanding fur taxes often treated Siberians in less than respectful ways. Colonists (settlers) forged into Native lands hoping for personal survival and private gain. Some became Siberiaki, combining Slavic and Siberian values.

Christianization was equally inconsistent, with missionary zeal for large numbers of converts at first taking precedence over more thorough and patient approaches. The term Christianization is used to stress the process rather than the result. Focus on conversion to Russian Orthodoxy inappropriately implies finality. Missionaries were, in effect, fomenting a de-ethnicization process. Most, in the name of civilization, hoped to change individual consciousness on such a scale that whole cultures, from funerals to choice of chiefs, would be transformed.

Complete Khanty transformation proved elusive. Two small revitalization movements arose in the nineteenth century, and others may be undocumented. One movement, of a Nenets shamanic leader named Vavlyo Nenyang (Vauli Piettomin), united some Khanty with Nentsy neighbors against Russians and a few Natives seen as tsarist middlemen. Its Robin-Hood–like demands included redistribution of resources to the poor, alleviation of taxes, and appointment of new leaders. A second movement, in response to a smallpox scare, was more religious, involving massive animal sacrifices and a return to traditional values. Neither movement resulted in a new religion, but they contained the seeds of syncretic ethnic regeneration for several West Siberian groups.

Khanty ethnicity was most influenced by Sovietization (chapters 4 and 5). Soviet life began violently, and only slowly came to be part of many citizens' conscious and unconscious values. This does not mean that every Khanty individual was delighted with every decision made at collective meetings. Rather, many learned to think in Soviet terms of collective work and ethnicity. Federal "nationalities" definitions shaped the politics of ethnicity, yet not always in the ways officials planned. In the Soviet period, Siberian Russians too came to be "ethnic" and gradually responded to the growth of non-Russian ethnonational movements with their own.

In chapter 6, analyses of trends toward regionalization in Siberia focus especially on the development of Khanty politics through the Association for the Salvation of the Ugra, local claims against energy companies, and agitation for community (obshchina) self-rule. Interaction of the indigenous intelligentsia with Russian leaders has reached new levels of complexity, conflict, and potentially productive negotiation. And Russians who have become "Siberiaki," committed to staying in Siberia and developing it for themselves, pose a new version of an old threat to Khanty and other Native Siberian groups.

"The tenacity of ethnicity" becomes most clear in chapter 7, where tenacious values and symbols of Khanty spiritual life are explored. The importance of reincarnation for continuity of the Khanty and the significance of rituals marking life passages reveal the main channels of Khanty ethnicity before political activism became possible. These cultural expressions of ethnic consciousness were striking in the antireligious Soviet milieu.

Crucial questions about ethnicity in a global context center on behavior as well as cognition. Theories of ethnicity should take into consideration its multiple potential roots in social-group boundary maintenance, linguistic differentiation, resource competition, political struggle, descent principles, religious values, and underlying psychological needs. Combining, yet not homogenizing, the work of many theorists in my conclusion, I review and analyze further those concepts of ethnicity that have aided interpretation throughout the text.

Each major change in Ob River ethnic relations represents some degree of manipulation of Khanty life by outsiders. Yet multiple levels of ethnic interaction can trigger radicalized reactions of self-preservation, as well as adaptation and partial cultural destruction. Khanty individuals have long been nurturers of a valued yet changing culture and reshapers of outside messages, as their nineteenth-century revitalization movements testify and their current responses to educational, political, and economic developments reveal. The West Siberian energy executive may discover more than the debilitated Khanty he bargained for.

CHAPTER ONE

Colonization: Forming Groups in Interaction

My grandfather lived one hundred years, in time to tell me tales of the old days, when the words "Ostiak," "Vogul," and "Wild Man" had the same meaning.
(*Mansi writer Yuvan Shestalov, 1985*)

Russians sometimes speak in the Ostiak [Khanty] language to each other; it is possible even to meet some who nearly have forgotten their native language.
(*Russian doctor B. Bartenev, 1896*)

WHAT'S IN A NAME?

ANALYSTS of colonial histories, whether debunking the "Wild West" or the "Orientalized East," have called for perspectives that reveal diverse sides and mutual influences of colonial encounters. Local histories have turned upside-down generalizations about majorities and minorities in various settings. The coherence of old-style colonial apologists gave way to a reverse focus on "minority" and "ethnic" discourse. Each style created some imbalances and obscured power relations. As the historian of the American West, Patricia Nelson Limerick (1997:34) points out, "the formula 'active agents, not passive victims' has unintentionally proven to be a good way to draw attention away from the agency, name, and responsibility of those who accumulated coercive power and used it to injure culturally enriched but economically ripped-off groups."

Similarly, the Seminole chief James Billie told me (personal communication, July 1998), "what I have against most anthropologists is that they constantly generalized about our culture without highlighting individuals."[1] To the extent possible, I highlight individuals, agencies, power imbalances, and local contexts. Together, these are what helped shape identities at multiple levels and enable diverse claims of cultural authenticity (cf. Limerick 1987; Handler 1988). Khanty identities changed as Slavonic peoples (Russians and Ukrainians) and Native Siberians (Khanty, called Ostiak; Mansi, called Vogul) influenced each other.

The history of Khanty ancestors (pre-Ob-Ugrian, Ob-Ugrian) began before colonial contacts. The term "prehistory" is misleading: the unwritten history of Khanty roots existed in epics, rituals, and memories. Khanty ancestors did not necessarily call themselves "Khanty," although *khantē* came to mean "person"and *kantakh*, "people" (Kulemzin and Lukina 1992:6).

Archeological and linguistic evidence demonstrates the importance of multiple contacts for the Ugrians. Before "Ugra," as early sources called them, came north, they intermixed with Turkic and Iranian peoples (Kosarev 1984; Novikova 1991). By the ninth century, at the verge of the Iron Age, Ugra probably spread into the Ob region, where they encountered Samodeic Ural groups (Nentsy ancestors, formerly called Samoyedic). Perhaps in this time of interethnic mixing, the Ob-Ugrian social organization evolved into a dual phratry, or moiety, system. The system defined rules for marriage and influenced group dynamics, including the gradual separation of the Khanty and Mansi.[2]

Archeological evidence from the Bronze to Iron Age transition in the Surgut area points to rapid population growth, fortification, and the development of a military elite: sixty fort settlements of over two thousand households have been excavated (Kosarev 1984:146; Solov'ev 1987). Discoveries concur with narratives valorizing pointy-helmeted "warrior-princes" (*urjurt*) of such fort villages as Emder and Tapar-Vosh. Evidence accumulates for early Ugrians having a "war democracy," with an elaborate social-political organization comparable to that found in other groups reliant on abundant animal and (dryable) fish resources, such as certain Amur River peoples and Northwest Coast Indians.[3]

Early Khanty history was marked by conflicts with Mansi and Samodeic neighbors. War councils gathered as many as eight hundred fighters. Captives, taken from groups defined as nonhuman, became servants, slaves (male, *tey*; female, *tey-nen*), or sacrificial victims (Patkanov 1891:49). Bride wealth (called "bride price": *kalym* in Turkic, *netym* in Ugrian) and dowries included such captives. Humans for sacrifice were also bought, especially on the eve of war campaigns.[4]

Gradually, fighting declined, interethnic marriages increased, and human sacrifices nearly ceased. One oral history about the founding ancestress of the Kazym Khanty tells of her initial marriage to a Nenets warrior near present-day Salekhard. Eventually she felt the need to flee with her kin, so she cut off her husband's legs as he was sleeping. She could not bring herself to kill him, for he was the father of her children.[5]

Early Slavic and Tatar contacts influenced Ugrian movements, as indicated in chronicles (*letopis*) from the eleventh to sixteenth centuries.[6] Many group names, including those of Ob-Ugrians, derived from descriptive terms invented by Slavs and other neighbors. Ostiak, originally As-iak, people of the Ob River, came to be a generic name for Ugrians encountered by Novgorodian or Muscovite traders. To the Ugrians, more narrowly defined local names distinguished kin and friends from enemies. For instance, *Khondy-kho* meant person of the Konda River.

Conflicts with Tatar and Slavic colonizers kept Ugrian groups in cycles of war and peace until the seventeenth century, when Russian imperial hegemony led to relative peace. A wide indigenous knowledge of ecology was crucial, since seminomadic reindeer breeders, hunters, and fishers fled into the northern tundra when they felt settlers were encroaching. Political savvy was equally significant, although Cossack conquerors and "Ostiak princes" often misperceived each other.

CONQUESTS AND COLLABORATION

The first Slavic people to arrive in Ugrian territory probably were Novgorodian traders, eager for sable and marten. An episode in the Kievan Primary Chronicle, written by Kiev monks and dating from 1096, tells of a Novgorod explorer-trader named Guriata Rogovich who encountered "Ugra," neighbors of "Samoyed," bartering iron in the Ural Mountains. The Novgorodian Primary Chronicle contains an entry for the year 1193 about the bloody defeat of Novgorod *Voevoda* (Commander) Yadreik and his men, who were "cut to pieces" in a Ugrian campaign east of the Urals. Trade contacts between Slavic groups and Ostiak, as the traders came to call the Ugra, were sporadic for the next century. Even this early, the Slavs considered furs they received from Native Siberians—termed as a category *inorodsty*, literally, "not our kin"—as tribute. But the Slavic strangers liberally distributed iron objects as gifts, encouraging Native views that they were engaging in trade.[7]

In the thirteenth century, Khanty ancestors were more intensely involved with Tatars than Novgorodians. A Siberian Tatar dynasty ruled them, as well as many other Siberian peoples, under the Siberian Khanate. Simultaneously, Ugra competed with Samodeic groups (Nentsy ancestors) for reindeer-breeding tundra, sparking a series of confrontations still remembered by Khanty. I was shown an ancient hill fort site said to date from the period of "Nentsy wars." The wars were fueled by dispersion of Ugrian and Samodeic groups, driven north and east.[8]

Slavic military campaigns against Ob River peoples continued in the fourteenth century (1346), when Cossacks Aleksander Avakunovich and Stepan Lyapa fought skirmishes against Tatar Khans Ediger and Bekbulat, who were neglecting what the Cossacks considered to be their rightful tribute. The campaigns were mostly ineffective against migrating Ugrian nomads, but incursions intensified along the Ob after Novgorod fell to Moscow in the mid-fifteenth century. Cossacks met Native resistance but also found occasional cooperation from some Khanty elders, who gained personal advantages as middlemen. These elders wished to defeat the Tatars and lessen tribute obligations.[9]

The leader most responsible for defeating the Tatars in West Siberia was the Cossack *Ataman* (Headman) Ermak Timofeevich. Ermak's successful lightning tactics against the Tatar Khan Kuchum and Kuchum's violent death by drowning are celebrated in Russian *byliny* (poetic song narratives).[10] Ermak was supported by a Russian noble family, the Stroganovs, who sought not only the glory of a multinational Russian state but also a direct source of furs for their private sable treasury. Ermak's campaign began around 1578–81, after Ivan IV (the Terrible) granted the Stroganovs a *gramot* (deed) in 1547 increasing their territory east of the Urals.[11]

Pacification proved easier than expected, since Khanty and Mansi elders and warriors who had previously supported the Tatar Kuchum joined a Cossack and Muscovite triumph in 1582. People calling themselves Khanty came in large numbers to Ermak at the river Demianka, bearing furs and pledging allegiance to Moscow (Miller 1787:110). The delighted Cossacks called the Khanty leaders "princes [*kniazy*]," though the leadership of Khanty elders and warriors was based as much on war exploits, ritual power, and community support as on heredity.

The Cossacks maintained good relations with some Khanty. In the mid-1580s, Cossacks spent a terrible winter on the verge of starvation in their Kashlik stronghold, near what was to become Tobolsk. In a manner reminiscent of the origins of the American Thanksgiving holiday story, some Ob-Ugrians saved the Cossacks with supplies of meat, fowl, and fish. Cooperation developed especially between the Koda Khanty and the Cossacks in the 1590s, when Koda elders of the Alachev family were given the right to collect fur tribute from two conquered Khanty administrative areas. The Koda Khanty helped build forts (such as Makov) and population centers (such as Tomsk) and participated in military campaigns extending north and east. With the aid of Khanty "Prince Bardak," Cossacks also established the pivotal fortress of Surgut.[12]

Although some Khanty, like Bardak, were ready allies of the Cossacks, others were either aligned with Tatars or attempting to stay neutral. As these Khanty were conquered, the Cossacks demanded hostages, or *amananty*, from them, particularly in the Berezovo area. Amananty were usually elders held by Cossacks until their communities paid fur tribute (*yasak*), but they could also be children, as I discovered in dramatic archive accounts.[13] Cossacks conquered Siberia for glory, gain, Christendom, the Stroganovs, and the Moscow tsar.

Fur tribute (yasak) was a major motivation. By the seventeenth century, the average demand was eleven sable per person. In some areas tribute was ten sable per married man and five per single man. Khanty formally protested tribute demands to Russian authorities in 1586, 1603, and 1610.[14] In the seventeenth century, tribute was lowered to two sable per family elder, but this limit was not always honored by local collectors. Centers for sable collection were set up, with Khanty elders assigned the tasks of census taking and delivering tribute.

Many elders became dissatisfied with Cossack rule, sparking violence in Berezovo, Surgut, and Obdorsk.[15] Even the Koda Khanty were disillusioned after their special fur tribute collection privileges were revoked. Obdorsk and Berezovo Khanty besieged Berezovo in 1607, with the aid of Koda Khanty, but they were defeated. The Koda "Princess Anna," with "Princes Chumey, Keul of Surgut, and Tair Samorov," unsuccessfully "rebelled" (as tsarist authorities termed it) in 1608. Some Khanty then turned to their former Tatar enemies, but their "plot" was discovered and its leaders executed. Russians came to fear all large gatherings of Khanty, even when their purpose was ceremonial.

After Cossacks established forts along major rivers, families of Slavic peasants and traders deemed the area safe for settlement. In the seventeenth century, the government encouraged peasants to settle in areas where they could grow food to support themselves without dependence on long-distance supply transports. Tomsk, Tobolsk, and Surgut grew into important trade centers. On the Lower Ob, Irtysh, and Vakh Rivers (especially near Surgut), land was simply taken, as state peasants, sharecroppers, serfs, craftspeople, and traders traveled into Siberia from northern Russia. Many were volunteers, hoping for land and freedom; others came by government order, to help establish monasteries and settlements.

COLONIAL CONTEXTS

By the eighteenth century, Slavic peoples of varied cultural traditions, classes, and occupations came to the Siberian North. Slavic groups were colonists in the narrow sense, as settlers in new lands, and in the broader sense, as newcomers with a dominant centralizing power behind them.[16]

Three major interaction areas and patterns prevailed: (1) *Russian dominance* in the southern Siberian townships, such as Tobolsk, a relatively desirable agricultural area occupied increasingly by Russians and impoverished, marginalized, or assimilated Khanty; (2) *uneasy interdependence* in northern Siberian villages, such as Berezovo on the Ob, founded by Slavic groups reliant on government supplies, fishing, and Native trade; and (3) *Khanty dominance* in the northern and eastern backwoods and tundra-edge settlements, such as those along the Kazym and Vasyugan rivers, where a few Slavic families maintained fishing, hunting, trading, and marital ties with reindeer-breeding Khanty.

Each of these communities represented contrasting life-styles and approaches to each other. The three main kinds of interaction vary in demographic context, socioeconomic relations, interethnic perceptions, and degree of assimilation. My description is therefore a fluid model that moves across time and space. By the nineteenth century, colonial policy encouraged further settlement away from major centers. Colonists were urged, with offers of horses, cattle, money, and supplies, to found new settlements, the very word for which, *slobody*, also had a connotation of tax exemption.[17] Ethnic boundaries were created, maintained, and crossed from the beginning of Ob-Ugrian and Slavic interaction.

RUSSIAN DOMINANCE: IRTYSH AND OB RIVER TOWNSHIPS

Southern Siberian towns developed in the seventeenth century on the basis of Cossack military establishments, buttressed by missionaries, settlers, and adventurers. Ambitious Tatar, Zyrian (Komi), and Slavic traders became additional spokes of a wheel of influence extending into Khanty territory. This area of steppes and forest had some grain-growing potential and much seemingly empty space, given the low population densities of seminomadic indigenous hunters, fishers, and reindeer breeders. The distant tsarist government encouraged settlers to stake land claims. Townships grew in wealth, administrative complexity, trade ties, and population, as newcomers from Russia continued to arrive.

Towns like Tobolsk and Surgut were built after rapid, albeit incomplete, conquest of Natives. Mutual influences through intermarriage, cohabitation, and trade proceeded awkwardly. Slavic and Native Siberian integration was due in part to a shortage of settler women well into the eighteenth century. Conditions for mutual respect and intermarriage diminished with greater influx of Russian merchants, industrialists, miners, and government personnel in the nineteenth century. Provincial towns like Tomsk, Tobolsk, Tiumen, and Surgut mirrored Russian society, with a nobility and several levels of trade guild status. Townspeople also included increasingly prosperous Cossack, service, and peasant families.[18] Native-Slavic interaction grew complex, as Khanty of the region became entwined in domestic service and labor obligations.

By the mid-nineteenth century, newcomers greatly outnumbered impoverished Khanty in the major towns. A few Khanty families lived on town fringes, and some lived in surrounding villages. In Surgut in 1869, Russians, with a population of 1,644, were overwhelmingly dominant, although in the surrounding region (okrug) they were outnumbered by the Khanty by about 40 percent.[19]

In 1882, only one Khanty man, listed as Ostiak, lived within the city limits of Tobolsk (Dmitriev-Mamonov 1884: appendices 7,8). He was unusual, for he was both literate and Russian Orthodox (cf. Aipin 1990:259). Natives, who appeared as "inorodtsy" on official lists, made up only 14.49 percent of the population in and around Tobolsk. This included Tatars, Burkhatsi, and Bashkir, as well as Khanty, Mansi, and Nentsy.[20]

Scattered and ethnically divided villages surrounded main urban centers by the mid-nineteenth century (Abramov 1857). Slavic groups (Russian peasants and some Cossacks) had their own villages. Natives settled nearby. Alternately, Slavic villages were established near existing Khanty winter villages, chosen as prime locations for fishing, hunting, and cedar nut gathering. While some Khanty villages were identified in government tax records as merged with Russian villages, Khanty usually had separate *yurt* settlements, listed under Russified versions of their traditional names.

Russian laws and policy encouraged ethnic divisions, to protect Natives from Russian interference and to preserve government tax revenues from depletion through illegal trade. But the norm of living in separate villages was altered on the lower Irtysh River, where land was available to settlers for grain and vegetable growing.[21] The geographer Poliakov reported that in villages like Bazian, Karimka, and Kashilev, the Natives "even have houses near those of Russians . . . and it is hard to recognize them as Ostiak" (1877:54). Poliakov praised the local "Ostiak" for their comparative stability, cleanliness, and "orderliness in family life."

Interethnic contacts in southern Khanty territory were shaped through the politics of labor and land. Russians rented choice Khanty fishing beaches and inlets for minimal sums; they then hired Khanty as laborers, sometimes on their own traditional patrilineal fishing grounds. While rentals were often as low as 150 rubles a year, fishing yields amounted to thousands of rubles. Rental arrangements extended beyond the short terms allowed by the government, with some Russian families passing on rented lands to their children. Cedar nut groves were rented by Russians, with similar Khanty losses, especially near Surgut.[22]

Exploitation evolved because the Khanty, like Native Americans and other indigenous peoples, considered themselves not owners but caretakers of lands for their lineages. Russian payment for temporary use of land did not at first seem to disturb the basis of traditional usufruct and social organization.

Khanty laborers near the towns of Tiumen, Tobolsk, and Surgut had options besides fishing and nut gathering for Russian employers. Commissioned work for merchants and traders meant intensive sable, fox, and squirrel hunting. Payment for hunting was usually in iron goods, flour, sugar, tea, and tobacco, but Khanty hunters were often in debt (Patkanov 1911:177; Shvetsov 1888:59–61). Individual Khanty tried to extricate themselves from credit accounts and increased dependence on Russian goods, but Russian employers sometimes forced Khanty to become servants, woodcutters, and builders.

By the late nineteenth century, Russians hired Khanty workers for logging, road building, and mining. The interrelated economy and ecology of the Ob-Irtysh area changed. The geographer Iadrinstev, after several trips through Siberia, described the hard and impoverished life of Khanty men reduced to living in barracks on work projects, separated from their families. "The impoverishment of the Ostiak has gradually taken such hold that they have had to look for work as stable hands, on boats and ships, and even in mines, where they are dying, both materially and spiritually" (Iadrinstev 1891:75).

Khanty were rarely hired in the distilleries, mills, or candle, glass, brick and leather-working factories that were prospering in Siberian towns (Pamiatnaia Kniga 1881:339). This was due both to Native preference and to employer prejudices that included images of lazy, deceitful aboriginals. To an extent, Khanty competed for jobs with Russian exiles and workers. They received lower pay for the same work and were charged higher prices for the same goods.[23]

The exploited, impoverished, and demoralized state of Khanty workers was periodically bemoaned. Count S. Shvetsov (1888: 59–61, 80–82, 85), a long-term resident of Surgut, castigated local Russians for lack of morality in their relations with the Khanty. He made the valuable distinction between those Russians living in or near towns, who viewed Khanty and Nentsy as "dogs," and those Russians living in the "wilderness," who were more dependent on Khanty friendships and trade. The Russians of Surgut would not sit with a Khanty man at their table nor stop on the street to save a freezing Siberian, Shvetsov confessed. He watched Russians picking the corpse of a frozen Khanty man, and, in another incident, beating a drunken Khanty who appeared on the streets of Surgut. Children in Surgut could taunt a Khanty visitor with impunity. Their parents had warned them of the "abhorrent" and "polluted" nature of Natives (especially loiterers near local taverns).

Shvetsov concluded, "Even the death of an Ostiak does not stop a Surgutian; he continues to think of that Ostiak as merchandise [*tvar*]—only now that merchandise is becoming scarcer" (1888:81, 84–87). The Russian doctor Bartenev (1896:27) confirmed that the Khanty of Surgut had particularly "unfortunate life-styles [*obraz zhizni*]."[24]

Just as forest fires were sparked by imprudent logging (for example in 1827, 1847, and 1867), so the flames of sickness and starvation were stoked through increasing Khanty reliance on Russians (Iakobii 1893: 46, 51). Although he knew of Khanty ill-health, Iadrintsev (1891:75) was still shocked to find, near a tavern at the confluence of the Ob and Irtysh, "a huddle of sick people (men, women, children, especially children), in the most exceptional straits, covered with sores, ragged, with pale, unexpressive, and blank faces." Administrator Dmitriev-Mamonov (1884:12–13, 135, 236–41) reported that the once healthy and prosperous Khanty were being "completely destroyed" by alcoholism, syphilis, typhus, smallpox, anthrax, and other serious, sometimes epidemic, diseases. Few Russian doctors were willing to treat them.

Ethnic relations bred through a cycle of labor exploitation, land theft, prejudice, and alcoholism were hardly conducive to warm interethnic friendships or intermarriage. Yet closer analysis of the social fabric of Siberian townships reveals a mix of relationships and backgrounds. Russians in southern Khanty territories could be divided into those who staunchly maintained Russian ethnic purity and those whose blood, to use their own terms, was clearly mixed with that of the Khanty. These groups roughly coincided with locally perceived social divisions: recently arrived nobility and administrators maintained ethnic purity, while Cossacks, bourgeois (*meshchanstvo*), and settler-peasants with long local family histories might not. Exiles varied in their approaches, with political liberals or revolutionaries often befriending Siberians. Some Cossacks and Russian settlers intermarried or cohabited with Khanty women. But as Cossacks and merchants became established in Siberian towns, intermarriage was considered inappropriate for the upwardly mobile. Class, historical, and regional perspectives are all needed to understand intermarriage and cohabitation patterns.[25]

Russification through intermarriage and "mestization"(mixed ancestry) occurred intensively through the eighteenth century, and sporadically in the nineteenth. Iadrinstev (1891:169) claimed that in the early contact period Russian peasants and Native Siberians were at "quite a close level of culture and growth." Patkanov (1911:178) similarly argued that Cossacks, Russian hunters, escaped serfs, and legal settlers were conditioned to "primitive" and depraved life-styles. They therefore did not flaunt their physical and spiritual differences from indigenous Siberians. Russian men were ready and willing to mate with Siberian women, particularly when women from home were scarce. Many children of these unions were officially considered Russian.

Iadrinstev and Patkanov couched their arguments in elitist terms, concerned that single Russian adventurers had a too easy tolerance of Native women.[26] Russians were also open to communication with Natives when help was needed in initial Siberian adaptation. But not all unions were voluntary or based on mutual tolerance. In the early contact period, Siberian Cossacks were notorious for raiding villages and carrying away women and children.[27] In lean years, Natives themselves sometimes approached Russian towns and forts, offering women and girls for sale. Only in 1825 did Russian laws make it "forbidden to buy Kirghiz, Kalmyk, and other Asians," although "due to the insufficient numbers of women in West Siberia, it [was still] allowable to trade with nomads for female children" (Pamiatnaia Kniga 1881:98). Later authorities found Native women working as unpaid labor in wealthy households. A decree of 1831 singled out Russian merchant offenders.

Seizing or buying women was a blatant assertion of cultural and physical dominance. For some raided peoples, such as the Central Asian Kirghiz and Kalmyks, retaliatory raids were possible (Iadrintsev 1891:170). But the more impoverished and less numerous Khanty, among the earliest "Asians" incorporated into the Russian empire, could not easily fight back. Cossacks on tax and administrative business "not rarely" took for themselves "the most beautiful Ostiak women and girls" (Abramov 1857:348). Native peoples were thus cast into similar and demeaning ethnic categories by colonizing Russians, despite indigenous differences in cultures, nomadic patterns, and responses to tsarist administration. Russification of children born to Native female servants and Russian men proceeded rapidly.

Fear of precisely this kind of Russification caused Russian Orthodox church authorities, as early as the seventeenth century, to issue warnings against interethnic mixing. By the nineteenth century, housing laws segregated Natives and Russians, except for administrators.[28] Authors of the often violated laws sought to discourage mixed marriages ("miscegenation") and to control taxes and trade. Reformers also hoped to shield Natives from economic exploitation.

Russian-Native intermating and resulting mutual influences increased by the twentieth century. The majority of Russian unions with Khanty were unofficial. The few registered weddings were usually of Khanty women to Russian peasant men, as only Russians of low status made their liaisons with Khanty women official. Liaisons often took the form of Khanty women working as housekeepers for Russian men, sometimes even priests.[29]

Russian women were stigmatized for having relations with Khanty men, and they had less opportunity for contact with Natives. Russian women might meet Native men at village churches or trade fairs, but they usually stayed behind when their men went off to hunt, fish, and trade with the Khanty. Russian (including Cossack) women were independent, responsible, and powerful, but only within their own domain.[30]

Along the lower Irtysh, in relatively mixed communities, a few Christianized Khanty men tried to take Russian wives because they had to pay "little or no bride price for them" (Poliakov 1877:54). When Khanty men acquired Russian brides, an ethnic boundary crossing occurred between individuals with marginal identities in their communities: poor and outcast Russian women with somewhat Russified and economically dependent Khanty men. Material markers and solidifiers of "proper" marriage were often dispensed with in these atypical unions. Russification of resulting offspring was by no means assured. This was lamented by Poliakov (1877:54): "When an Ostiak man manages to find a Russian wife, it is not he who is most under her influence, but rather she who is forced to adapt to customs and beliefs of his ancient ancestors." Male dominance in these marriages seems to have outweighed Russian cultural dominance. Such examples illustrate the relative and incomplete nature of Khanty assimilation, even in southern Siberian townships.

UNEASY INTERDEPENDENCE: NORTHERN TOWNS AND VILLAGES

If Russification was limited in southern Khanty territory, it was even less pronounced further north, where the Khanty were in greater control of their land, wealthier, more nomadic, and on relatively equal footing with local Cossacks and Russian peasants. This contrast was apparent in ethnic interrelations around Berezovo and was striking in northern villages near Obdorsk (now Salekhard) at the Arctic Circle.

Berezovo marked a rough natural line beyond which extensive agriculture was practically impossible. As such, it was a symbolic entryway to an area where Slavic families were dependent on the Native population.[31] Well into the nineteenth century, Berezovo was also the northern limit for steady postal service and legal alcohol distribution (Bartenev 1896:31). This changed with the development of Obdorsk late in the century, but even growth of the Russian population did not radically alter Khanty and Russian interdependence. Crucial protectionist restrictions meant that Russian land appropriation (ownership or rental) north of Berezovo was illegal without Native permission (Patkanov 1911:177).

In the nineteenth century, the farther north along the Ob River and its tributaries one traveled, the greater were the distances between villages and the smaller the ratio of Russians to Natives. In 1875, the Khanty of the Berezovo region outnumbered Russians seven to one.[32] Northern Khanty numbers fluctuated, as some families moved from the south. Migration and nomadism made accurate counts nearly impossible. Censuses were based on winter village (yurt settlement) residency, but some Khanty intentionally escaped into the tundra to avoid the census and taxation.[33]

The northern Slavic residents were predominantly Russian Cossacks whose ancestors had conquered the area by founding fort-villages at strategic sites like Berezovo. Berezovo had been a Khanty winter village and a sacred site in the seventeenth century. Government-sponsored peasants, clergy, traders, and exiles made up the rest of the populace, settling by the late nineteenth century in fishing villages and small towns along the Ob, Sosva, Kunovat, Kazym, Polui, and Yugan Rivers.

Russians controlled three *volost'* (subdistricts) of Berezovo Region, while Siberians were legally dominant in five *upravlenie* (districts), where rights to land were maintained by Natives.[34] By 1900, when Natives refused to rent land, local Russians became resentful. Colonists griped that Natives kept land after their families dwindled, leading to low population density and good fish yields for the Khanty but crowding for the Russians.[35]

On the Little Ob near Old Tegy, some Khanty refused to participate in sale or rental of their lineage lands. When members of the important and prosperous Nettkin clan allowed a sale at the turn of the century, the local Khanty considered it scandalous. Their descendants remembered the sale in 1976. A Russian trader wanted desperately to buy waterfront land on the Northern Ob and had difficulty finding Khanty who would even allow fishing rights. Nettkin elders sold him a small portion of their extensive lands for nine hundred rubles, then a huge sum. Proceeds were divided among all the male family heads named Nettkin, although some had moved far away and had to be located. They had stopped using the land, but their right to a share was honored.

Khanty land use was based on the need for riverbank fishing and for hunting territories that extended from riverbanks. Reindeer breeders, who hunted and fished part-time, needed large tundra areas where their animals could graze for lichen in transhumant patterns. Because lineage members usually included reindeer breeders and fishers, Khanty had multiple economic and ecological options. In a few areas where fishers predominated, they bartered with reindeer breeders. Families fishing with nets were expected to take from the river what they needed but no more.

Fishing restrictions were built into the organization of Khanty lineage territories along a given river. The best territories were those at the mouths of rivers or where two streams joined, for the occupants had the first opportunity to catch fish swimming to spawn. Early arrivals in the area claimed the best positions; offshoot families had to find another river or to move upstream, where fishing was less productive. Only those who had no relatives upstream could freely set nets or create blockages across the width of a river. With population increases, partial blockage became the norm, so that fish would be left for other settlements. The Russians ignored this delicate socioecological system, and therefore the Khanty were loath to sell them waterfront land (cf. Voronov 1900:29).

Economic and commercial relations were intertwined with social and political power. Khanty control over most northern territory was reinforced by Count Speransky's 1822 reforms. But the laws did not prevent illegal use of especially desirable lands by Russians. The laws alone cannot explain the different quality of relations between Russians and northern Khanty.

The interdependence of northern Khanty and Russian socioeconomic relations was probably the main factor saving Khanty from the extremes of exploitation typical in the south. Interdependency was reflected in binding trade ties and cautious social contacts. Northern Khanty and Russians based their mutual tolerance (if not respect) on complex and relatively stable exchange relationships. The crux of their bond was a trade partnership that individual Russian men constructed with individual Khanty men. Relationships often endured through generations of willing participants. Some Khanty customers were satisfied to emphasize the credit, rather than debit, side of the partnership. Both parties regarded the deals as profitable, although many were monetarily to Russian advantage. Many traders behaved as capitalists, enjoying high profit with low investment. Yet the northern Khanty did not see themselves as helpless victims (cf. Limerick 1997:34). They required little and, if dissatisfied, could change trade partners or withhold furs.

Key trade commodities were food (flour, tobacco, tea, and sugar), tools (knives, axes, iron nails, and needles), household goods (brass plates, copper kettles, incense, and samovars), and adornments (beads, jewelry, scarves, calicos, and tapestries).[36] In return for Russian goods, Khanty hunters supplied fox, squirrel, and sable pelts, plus reindeer hides, as well as fish in huge quantity. Cedar nuts, sheaves of birch bark and pieces of birch fungus (for mixing with snuff), game birds, and water fowl, including geese, ducks, and swans, also were traded.

Khanty contributions included processed products. They made and sold *aihop* (hollowed canoes of single tree trunks), sleds, skis, snowshoes, *gimga* (fish traps), walrus thongs, birch baskets, and boxes.

Khanty men crafted mammoth ivory into intricately carved pipes; women worked reindeer hides and fox and sable furs into appliquéd *gusi* and *malitsi* (gowns and parkas). Their fur clothes, boots, mittens, and hats were valued by local Russians as the clothing best adapted to Siberia.[37]

Each Khanty family head dealt predominantly with one "merchant" family, with credits calculated in skins. The Khanty were trusted, since "as long as any member of the family survives and can take part in hunting and fishing, the creditor may be certain that at some time or other his debt will be faithfully discharged" (Felinska 1853(1):199). Profits in furs could be greater than 300 percent for a Berezovo trader.[38] Only when the pressure for furs had become so great, by the start of the twentieth century, that fox and sable became scarce, did Khanty hunters have difficulty maintaining preferred levels of consumption. They were reduced to trading in squirrels (Voronov 1900).

Traders had to learn enough about surrounding nomadic groups (the Khanty and Nentsy) for at least minimal rapport in indigenous languages. "Acquaintance with the usages and manners of the different tribes, with their periodic changes of residence, and, if possible, a personal acquaintance with the principal heads of their widely dispersed families . . . [were] indispensable" (Felinska 1853(1):199). By the nineteenth century, Berezovo, Obdorsk, and even Surgut Cossacks were known not only for their knowledge of Native languages but also for their poor Russian or Ukrainian. Their admixture of Russian and Native languages in everyday speech was notorious, and their proficiency in Native languages was high.[39]

When Khanty visitors came to Berezovo, they sometimes stayed with their trade partners, or, more often, camped on the edge of town. Twice, for a wedding and a baptism, Khanty stayed in the Cossack home where the Polish exile Felinska lived. Khanty with reputations for wealth had little trouble finding Russian hosts. But destitute Khanty also came to Berezovo "when pressed by hunger," making the rounds of Russian houses, where they sometimes received moldy bread, flour, and animal entrails in dishwater (Felinska 1853(1):220). Less frequently, Russians fled to the Khanty in times of personal or financial trouble. A few genuine friendships were generated.[40]

A focal point of northern trade was the annual Obdorsk fair, held in January and attended by members of ethnic groups from as far away as Arkhangelsk and Tobolsk. Timing was dictated by the ease of sled travel in midwinter. Local Khanty considered the fair an occasion for celebration and inebriation as well as trade. While members of a few fast-growing Russian families, such as the Kaigorodovs, Novitskiis, and Protopopovs, controlled much of the personalized Ob River partnership trade, the Obdorsk fair provided an opportunity for more diverse transactions.[41]

Before trading at Obdorsk could begin, tsarist officials set up a station where Natives, through appointed elders, paid taxes (yasak) in furs or money. This practice, common through Siberia, ensured that the government would get its share of furs. Officials feared trader competition. Russian peasants gained the right to trade legally for Native furs only in the 1820s. Earlier, trade guild membership was required.[42]

The Obdorsk fair, begun around 1820, provided a lively riot of goods. Northern residents came for their year's supply of cloth, salt, flour, grain, meat, and fowl (Potanin 187?:201; Bartenev 1896:8). As the market grew, so did the town, and each January its population swelled severalfold.

A current, if not currency, lubricating many transactions was vodka. Northern Natives, with famously little experience with alcohol, succumbed to its properties, leading to serious and uncharacteristic acts of aggression against each other, as well as to vulnerability in trade negotiations. "The passion of Ostiaks [Khanty] and Samoyieds [Nentsy] for drink is so strong that they will travel one hundred versts [66.3 miles] for no other purpose than to muddle their heads with whiskey," wrote Felinska (1853(2):280). Although reformists periodically attempted to restrict the time and place of sales, vodka was sold widely, making "every house a tavern" in Obdorsk (Bartenev 1896:31). In 1889, a legal bar opened; prices were regularized, exploitive illegal sales declined, and alcohol tax revenues helped support a local school and hospital. Some Khanty may have derived advantages from the new system, but most shunned the school and hospital.[43]

A few northern Khanty were forced to have more complex labor relations with Russians. In the nineteenth century, this meant working in the fish processing factory of the merchant Diakonov, outside of Obdorsk (Kornilov 1828:75). Khanty also hauled wood for Russians and herded reindeer for settlers who had bought them from impoverished Native families.[44]

Regional Native rule cushioned the blows of Khanty labor exploitation. Obdorsk was designated to have indigenous, not Russian, rule. In practice, this meant that Obdorsk was run by Russian officials and Native elders. The elders were from lineages designated by the Russians as princely. They acted as middlemen in tax collection and Native courts. Regional court records afford a rare glimpse of Russian-Native disputes and Native customary law in action. Cases involving Russian employment of Natives did not begin until 1893. Punishments were no stricter for Native crimes against Russians than for intra-Native disputes, and sentences were harsh for all repeat offenders.[45]

Most Russian complaints against Khanty defendants involved vandalism during drunken binges, nonfulfillment of work obligations, attempts at working for two employers at once, and the sale of food, clothing, or equipment issued to the worker. Complaints were brought more frequently against Nentsy than Khanty. Most involved intra-Native disputes: in nineteen years, only 8 out of 144 cases involved Russians. Very few cases could be construed as outbursts of Native anger against Russians. In one rare and scandalous 1894 case, a Native snatched a bottle of vodka from a Russian peasant, on an Obdorsk street in daylight.[46]

The degree of power wielded by Native Khanty leaders has been disputed. Whether Khanty elders were princes or pawns, their ability to guide Russian-Native relations was limited. Despite their middleman, culture-broker status, their power was constrained by their own people and by tsarist law. Their legal mandate, set forth in "Jurisdictions on Natives," ruled that only the less serious crimes were to be judged according to Native tradition. Murder and government sabotage were handled by Russian administrators.[47]

Within Native traditions, restrictions on power and influence were more subtle. To be successful, Khanty elders could not rely on illustrious lineage alone. Leaders had to prove that they were wise and generous providers. Despite epic traditions of heroic princely deeds, there was no Native royalty by the nineteenth century. This was recognized by the Russian governor Kornilov (1828:78), who explained that many leaders "in no way differ from ordinary people." Some were called princes only because their ancestors had received symbols of Russian favor: insignia, robes, and a *gramot* (document).

Two cases of nineteenth-century leaders, Taishin and Artanzeev, reveal contrasts in Native attitudes toward Russians, as well as the unstable nature of Native prestige and wealth. Taishin and Artanzeev each had Russian documents proclaiming their rule over local Khanty (Abramov 1857b:217–19). Taishin enjoyed wealth and respect, at his peak owning about eight thousand reindeer. He lived extravagantly; his large, well-made tents and access to women, furs, tobacco, and vodka were renowned in the Berezovo and Obdorsk areas. Artanzeev, in contrast, had only two hundred reindeer and was considered poor. He had little wealth to distribute and less influence, despite his rank.

The Taishin and Artanzeev families used dominant, brokerlike positions with Russians as levers to gain trade goods, usurp taxes, control court cases, and arrange land rentals. But Artanzeev and his descendants lost power and were little respected. Taishin was a well-known power broker who continually bragged about a trip to Saint Petersburg in 1854, during which he received a royal medal. He was respected and feared, but by age seventy, even he had lost his fabulous wealth and was living in a cabin "no different from that of other Ostiak."[48] Taishin lost his wealth to unstable natural conditions and generous giveaways. His prestige was augmented by "the power of the Russian circle" (Popov 1890: 458). But power derived from the Russians was also unstable. A midcentury story about the "impotence of the Prince of Obdorsk," probably a kinsman of Taishin's, recounts his humiliation at an Obdorsk inquest.[49]

Even those, like Taishin, with the most to gain by learning Russian ways did not necessarily speak Russian or convert to Orthodoxy. Conditions for acculturation were limited, and ethnic boundaries were evident in marriage patterns. At the end of the nineteenth century, Obdorsk resident Bartenev (1896:24) found "little intermarriage" between Natives and Russians, although many Obdorsk residents had come from the Tobolsk region rather than directly from Russia. As in many colonial contexts, more intermating than intermarriage occurred.[50]

The extent of Khanty influence within a mixed ethnic household varied with its location. Few Khanty women formally married Russian men, since Khanty girls or widows had little opportunity to move from their communities. Khanty considered leaving be a serious defection: "to leave the [Native] community means to become Russified" (Bartenev 1896:25). More common were living arrangements in which a Russian man surreptitiously set up housekeeping in a yurt with a Khanty woman. In such cases, local Russians and Khanty considered the children to be Khanty.

The class consciousness that affected ethnic intermarriages further south was to some extent also present in northern Russian communities. Only poorer Russian peasants made official their liaisons with Khanty women. Russian merchants and Cossacks preferred to maintain the illusion of keeping their blood pure. Russian attitudes toward Natives were frequently prejudiced, despite trade partnerships, Native courts, and wealthy Khanty with thousands of reindeer. Russians feared that intermarriage would entail participation in "pagan" and "drunken" Khanty festivities, and they regaled each other with rumors of such festivities (Poliakov 1877:54–56). They reasoned that "bride price" meant slavery (Kostrov 1873; Poliakov 1877:54). They disdained nomadism and the "stench" of Khanty camps (Felinska 1853(1):219). Prejudice was so strong in Berezovo that many were averse to eating reindeer flesh "merely because it is the favorite food of the Ostiak . . . Contempt for the subjugated race and anything belonging to them is general among the Russians; insomuch that any admixture of Ostiak blood in children is considered a degradation" (Felinska 1853(2):192).

In Berezovo, the women of the Russian elite may have felt threatened by the complex trade arrangements and sexual liaisons their husbands maintained with the Khanty. Married women were the least likely of the Russians to develop friendships with Natives and were therefore especially prone to high levels of ethnic stereotyping. Given these prejudices, most Khanty who were in an economic position to maintain their independence from northern Russian villages and towns did so. They kept pragmatic trading and working relations with Russians to a minimum to avoid unpleasant incidents.

Khanty men were as loath as Russian women to see their kin crossing sexual boundaries, since Russian women did not know the proper gender-linked behavior maintained within Khanty communities, the elaborate rules that kept Khanty households pure. Fears of interethnic mixing were enacted in satirical plays during sacred Khanty ceremonies honoring the bear.[51]

KHANTY DOMINANCE: BACKWOODS SETTLEMENTS AND CAMPS

Ethnic interaction was more conducive to friendships in the backwoods of Khanty territory, where the Khanty predominated numerically and culturally. Khanty influence was strongest on Russian pioneers who homesteaded along rivers like the Vasyugan and Kazym. For their very survival, these pioneers relied on Khanty trade and knowledge of the subarctic. Newcomers were often exiles, peasants, Old Believers, or adventurers, trying to escape Russian authorities. This in itself made them acceptable to some Khanty.

Out of backwoods interaction developed a new culture, a mixture of Slavic and Native Siberian traditions that Siberians themselves, as well as outsiders, termed Siberiak. While scattered through the Siberian North, its members exemplified a significant ethnic trend. Through ethnic interaction, newcomers merged aspects of their previous worldviews and behavior with indigenous practice. On the Northern Ob River, individuals and families created a local Siberiak culture, without consciously using their new identity for political ends. Though some assimilated into Khanty families, most who learned the Khanty language, attended Khanty shamanic seances, and mated with Khanty neighbors considered themselves neither Russian nor Khanty but "Siberiak." The term was also used derogatorily by urban Russians who wished to disassociate themselves from Siberian life and Native life-styles.[52]

Prerevolutionary demographic statistics for the northwest Siberian backwoods are unreliable. While Khanty everywhere dodged detection to avoid taxes, the practice was particularly rampant in remote areas.[53]

And Slavic hunters, settlers, and fugitives also had reasons to evade government notice. Small communities of exiles and Old Believers lived along remote Ob tributaries. Although rumors of such communities were probably exaggerated, the existence of internal refugees was widely confirmed.[54]

Khanty who were pushed northward to the fringes of their earlier territories had a large expanse of forest, river, and tundra nearly to themselves. One elder recalled that his family and nine others had fled Cossacks of Surgut to found villages on the Vasyugan River in the nineteenth century (Grigorovskii 1884:36–37). They encountered no opposition from local Khanty or Russians.[55] The area around the Kazym River, 236 square versts of successful Khanty seminomadic adaptation and little Russian influence, was typical of the backwoods. The 1828 census recorded 525 Kazym Khanty and 218 Nentsy (Iadrintsev 1893: 282).[56]

Backwoods Khanty were victimized by smallpox, alcohol, and increasing dependence on trade goods, but they were far from Russified. Nentsy neighbors and Tatar trade contacts probably influenced them more than the Slavic settlers.[57] Ethnic boundaries were relatively fluid, and cultural ties among ethnic groups stemmed from barter, adaptation to newcomers, and need for mutual support in the rugged northern climate. Contact resulted in intermarriage, linguistic changes, and mutual religious influences.

The Khanty seminomadic subsistence schedule shaped yearly socioeconomic relations. In the nineteenth and twentieth centuries, the adaptive strategies of northern and eastern Khanty were based on multiple resource exploitation. So-called "reindeer Khanty" (living North of Berezovo or near the rivers Pima, Tromyugan, Vasyugan, Agan, Nazym, Kazym, Vakh, and Yugan) combined fur animal hunting, fishing, and reindeer breeding with varying degrees of success (Dunin-Gorkavich 1904:41).[58] Horses were only beginning to appear on the Vasyugan in the 1870s (Grigorovskii 1884:53) and in Obdorsk at the turn of the century (Bartenev 1896).

Khanty living far from Russian trade centers were more likely to have Tatar and Nentsy trade partners than Russian (Cossack) ones. However, the long trading arm of a few leading Russian families extended to the Kazym and Vasyugan Rivers (Poliakov 1877:78). Some, with family names like Kishtov, Mefodeev, and Alekseev, intermarried with Natives. Such Siberiak traders and trappers had mixed attitudes toward the Khanty, profiting from the trade and justifying profits by keeping Khanty well supplied with credit. On the Vasyugan, one Old Believer peasant from Tarsk controlled trade by traveling the river in fall and spring with goods brought from the central Siberian town of Tiumen.

His fluency in the Khanty language, his literacy in Russian, and his quantities of sugar, tea, flour, and grain made him more popular than five competitors throughout an area of two thousand square versts.[59]

A few newcomers maintained social and cultural distance. Rumors about secret Old Believer villages included tales of Natives disappearing, killed by settlers who did not want their location known. Old Believers also had conflicts with Khanty over rights to fish in specific lakes, for example, one near Aipalov. But in other cases, Natives and Siberiak hunters were "received, fed, and given bread for the road" in Old Believer villages (Grigorovskii 1884:1, 32–33).

Young Siberiak boys often chose hunting and trapping over fishing to attain a more solitary and free-wheeling life. They scorned agriculture, which, save for a few vegetable plots, was impossible anyway. Even group fishing with nets required more work than they wished. Many hoped to avoid conflicts with Khanty over fishing sites. But only under duress did Siberiaki respect the Khanty norm of paying for hunting usufruct with part of the catch (Dmitriev-Mamonov 1884:37; Grigorovskii 1879:14).

Slavic settlers in Khanty territory maintained more reindeer than horses or cattle, according to official census records of 1869 and 1875. By 1875, 1,396 peasants were listed in northwestern Native Siberian jurisdictions, living in 83 homes and owning 45 horses, 43 cattle, 2 bulls, and 3,200 reindeer. Many reindeer were herded by Natives, but some were tended by their Slavic owners. Such Siberiaki were living seminomadic life-styles, although their summer hay gathering was decidedly in the Slavic peasant tradition (Iadrinstev 1891:190, 283–85).

Siberiaki often combined Slavic and Native technologies for survival.[60] Settlers learned they could not rely on potatoes, carrots, barley, or wheat in the subarctic. By the twentieth century, Siberiaki had come to depend upon reindeer meat and blood soup. Hardworking Siberiak wives learned to process reindeer hides, sew Native-style parkas, and make birch baskets, even copying Khanty geometric designs. Siberiaki used Native canoes and fish traps on Ob tributaries, ate fish raw (especially when ill), and processed fish in indigenous ways. They also adopted local techniques for handling dogs, constructing sleds, and occasionally for installing stoves in semisubterranean huts.

The adoption of Native technology was a practical necessity and helped to mitigate ideas of Native inferiority. Although literate observers viewed adoption of Khanty technology as a decline in cultural level, the settlers themselves acted in their own best interests. If peasants forgot how to build roads, sow barley, or make carts in the subarctic, it was because these skills were irrelevant.[61]

Technological adaptations required Native-Siberiak contact, and interethnic relations were in general richer in the backwoods. Visitors saw Native influence in Siberiak linguistic patterns, socializing, mating, and spiritual values, including Siberiak belief in local shamans and spirits. Contemporaries like Iadrinstev (1891:190) mourned such "trends away from national character."

Khantization was particularly evident in language changes. Not only did Slavic traders use the Khanty language for business, but other Siberiaki used Khanty words so naturally that they did not realize they were not speaking "pure" Russian. Pronunciation was also affected, so that some Siberiaki spoke Russian with a Khanty accent. In the Obdorsk area, most Siberiaki spoke the Khanty and Nentsy languages, and some spoke to each other in the local Khanty dialect.

Northern Khanty rarely learned to speak Russian, since this represented a deliberate effort to step outside cultural norms. Given their trusting approach to trade, many felt that learning Russian was not worth the effort, when Russians could speak the Khanty language. Others learned enough to avoid being cheated. A Russian Orthodox priest's efforts to teach Russian to Khanty in the Vasyugan River area in the 1880s met with little success. Most Khanty avoided conflict, adjusting hunting and herding to prevent encounters with outsiders. Some protected illegal settlers, refusing to divulge their names to authorities, while others occasionally succumbed to temptation and reported them (Grigorovskii 1884:33, 44, 56–57).

Backwoods Khanty were as strongly attracted to alcohol as those in other areas but were less victimized in exploitive trade schemes. Siberiak women were known for their home-brewed "wines," local staples of relaxation. No holiday, whether for the Siberiaki or the Khanty, could be celebrated without alcohol. Siberiak youths met Khanty in home-based "taverns" and caroused with them, "tavern hopping." While binges could end with Siberiaki stealing or winning fur clothing from Natives, some provided the basis for friendships, fish site rental agreements, hunting rights, and even dowry and "bride price" arrangements.

Over generations, interethnic mating could result in full Khantization, where Slavic roots were forgotten or deemphasized. But more often assimilation was less than complete. Siberiak families with government service backgrounds tended to remain wedded to the idea of superiority over the Khanty. Such families were less likely to be completely assimilated, even when intermarriage occurred.

The Ob North population was mixed, combining Ugrian, Samodeic, and Tatar elements, as well as Slavic. Diversity stemmed from intermarriage and from the widespread Siberian practice of temporarily sharing daughters and wives (usually with their consent) with travelers.[62] Slavic hunters and traders occasionally participated in wife sharing, and thus "new Russian blood [grew up] in traditional Ostiak [Khanty] . . . households" (Grigorovskii 1884:58).

The degree to which populations mixed varied greatly. Greater Khanty aloofness during travel in seminomadic reindeer-breeding cycles logically led to fewer social contacts. However, a shortage of Khanty women worked against full endogamy for Khanty reindeer breeders. Statistics recorded by river and settlement consistently reveal fewer Khanty women than men.[63] The imbalance resulted from traditions of female infanticide and maltreatment of ill-favored Khanty girls (Voronov 1900:24). Gender disproportion caused tensions in Khanty communities. By the twentieth century, the average age for a Khanty bride had fallen to ten, in contrast to the traditional Khanty ideal of fourteen. Khanty marriages were increasingly made through abduction rather than negotiated arrangement. Khanty bachelors without means had trouble finding brides. Wealthier men offering "bride price" turned to Siberiak women, whose families gratefully accepted the financial aid, without calling it "kalym."[64]

Khantization was a relative process. Even among those who saw themselves as Siberiak, differences in approach to the Khanty were considerable. In a world where Khanty were sometimes called "primitive pagans" and sacred groves and graves were occasionally raided for their wealth, mutual respect had to be earned. Some settlers called their unbaptized children "Tatars" or "Ostiak." Yet the atmosphere of the Siberian backwoods was by far the most conducive to complex interaction. Low population density and little competition for land fostered Khantization, which was enhanced when newcomers had to rely on local technology for northern survival, and when cohabitation was socially permissible. When a basis for common linguistic and spiritual communication was established, Khantization thrived.

CONCLUSION: PRIDE, PREJUDICE, AND PASSION

The preceding portraits of ethnic interaction show ethnic groups-in-the-making in three different situations. Russian dominance led to Khanty impoverishment and Russification in the townships of the south, while Khanty dominance led to Khantization of Russians in the east and north backwoods. Between these poles, Native and Slavic peoples of the Northern Ob River villages maintained group social and political boundaries in a context of uneasy interdependence. Social stratification and ethnic stereotyping emerged to some extent in all three contexts, but varied in their saliency. Variables in demography, power and labor relations, cohabitation, and spiritual life reinforced each other, enhancing or discouraging opportunities for interethnic rapport.[65] Historical periods also reveal variation: southern Siberian towns of the eighteenth century may be compared to northern towns like Obdorsk in the late nineteenth century.

Contrasts developed within Slavic and Ob-Ugrian groups as much as between them. For Slavic groups, the most significant division may be that between the agricultural and the hunting-fishing way of life; for the Ob Ugrians, between the nomadic and the settled. Each is based on a south-north distinction that developed during colonization and was recognized by Natives and newcomers alike. An ethic of freedom from agricultural labor contributed to the formation of Siberiak ethnicity, just as an ethic of nomadism shaped northern Khanty culture.[66]

Ethel Lindgren's (1938) analysis of Cossack-Tungus trade relations in Manchuria as characterized by "contact without conflict" only begins to describe ethnic relations on the Ob River. Absence of conflict does not necessarily mean absence of prejudice. And "exchange by itself says little or nothing about power differences" (Cohen 1978:391; cf. Appadurai 1988:24–25).

Interdependencies fostering a relative balance in ethnic reciprocity and social distance on the Northern Ob River in the nineteenth century should be seen as part of a changing dynamic in a system tilted into inequality. Indeed, the trade partnerships and mutual tolerance that characterized interethnic relations during the early period in southern areas were mostly later destroyed. By the twentieth century, Berezovo and Obdorsk ethnic relations were headed in a similar colonial direction, due to increasing population, resource competition, and Russian political control. Overexploitation of fur animals had tipped an ecological balance in many areas and was affecting interethnic socioeconomic relations. Slavic peasants were also agitating for Khanty fishing territories and the abolition of protectionist rental restrictions. In Berezovo, the Khanty were not considered "merchandise" (as in Surgut), but many were pitied for their poverty and sickness.

Changes from symbiosis and reciprocity to contempt and conflict have occurred in many areas, most notoriously in former Yugoslavia, most poignantly in North America after "first contact."[67] Western fascination with lore about trade partnerships, Thanksgiving, and Pocahontas perhaps stems from a guilt-ridden desire to imagine a time when Natives and newcomers opened arms to each other, rather than firing arms at each other. Proximity of peoples defining each other as different has bred contempt, love, and every emotion in between, but it has not bred stability or escape from the sexual metaphor of Natives being screwed (cf. Taussig 1987:46–47; Trexler 1995:118–72). Pocahontas and John Rolfe stories were mirrored through the Siberian North, but with less romanticism and with a stronger assumption that the children of such a union would become Native.[68] Dominant trends of Native exploitation were mitigated by strong countertrends of colonists becoming Siberiaki. Yet ethnic barriers were maintained. Increased interaction enhanced the salience of ethnicity. It stimulated ethnic awareness in areas remote from industrialization or modernization, although certainly feeling their ripple effects (cf. Perry 1996; Gellner 1983; Wolf 1982).

The theoretical midpoint of Khanty-Russian interaction, exemplified by the northern nineteenth-century village, can be identified. This point is central in several senses: on a continuum of cultural change, on the ground, and in time. Salient characteristics are: (1) little cohabitation, less intermarriage, and limited socializing; (2) bilingualism (though often asymmetrical) and tolerance without warmth; (3) ecological niching (particularly of nomadic Khanty and settled Cossacks) in areas of low population density; (4) interdependency through trade reciprocity; (5) culture brokers as middlemen on both sides of ethnic relations.

The interactive, personally responsive nature of ethnic relations, setting these factors off-balance, led to increased Russification or Khantization. Analysis of this complexity, beyond generalizations about "creolization," must encompass the issue of personal choices and the multiple ways groups are formed through social and political processes. Personal decisions, affecting ethnicity patterns, are both constrained and stimulated by cultural preconceptions, gender, and political contexts (Stoler 1996:290–91; Ortner 1995:178).

As Russians became dominant demographically, materially, and politically in southern Siberia, Khanty personal survival options narrowed to fleeing north and east, hunting and fishing in poverty, or settling as partially Russified agriculturalists or laborers. In the Far North, Slavic survival was affected by the demographically, materially, and spiritually successful Natives. Native reindeer breeders could rival Russian traders in their wealth. Tsarist reforms of 1822 also gave the Khanty and Nentsy some political clout in courts and land rentals.

For some Siberians, ethnic boundary crossings were literally forced, when Native women were taken by Cossacks in early raids or later rapes. But for many families, social change meant difficult decisions about settlement, livelihood, and cultural values. This is not to imply that all were in complete maximizing control of their lives (cf. Barth 1969). As individual Khanty decided to enter into labor relations with Russians, unforeseen and often unpleasant consequences ensued (sickness, alcoholism, debt relations), setting off increasingly negative responses by local Russians. In Surgut, this led to ethnic relations reaching such a low point that Russians could leave a drunken Khanty man to freeze in the street. Reportedly, Surgut area Khanty felt a reciprocal stereotyped contempt for Russians (Shvetsov 1888:80–82).

In sum, ethnicity becomes socially salient in numerous political contexts, with colonization often providing a significant trigger, but no set prescription, for polarization or accommodation. Acculturation, too often conceptualized as a uniform, stifling process of blanket change, has a range of manifestations and consequences (Hallowell 1971). For Siberians, as for many Native Americans, partial and, to a degree, reversible acculturation was more common than total cultural absorption or the squeezing of individuals into fixed categories, such as "creoles," "traditionals," or "moderns." The superficial character of much acculturation became particularly clear as Russian Orthodox missionaries intent on converting the Khanty consistently experienced frustration.

CHAPTER TWO

Christianization: Processes of Incomplete Conversion

> Torum-Asti, the Sky God-Father, is the second of our main Gods. We have Mir-Susne-Kum, or Asti-Ikki [God Old Man], and Kaltash-imi, the Goddess who sends children, and others. Most of the gods are near to us, not high up and removed. They are our ancestors."
>
> (*Timofei Moldanov, Kazym, 1991*)

> People also had male icons and female icons, and men and women could pray to both. . . . In Berezovo, nearly everyone has icons."
>
> (*A Tegy woman, 1976*)

WHAT IS CONVERSION?

KHANTY oral history tells of ancestors who originally fled north to the Ob River from the steppes of Permia, precisely when Bishop Stephen tried to convert them to Russian Orthodoxy. These ancestors, called "Ugra," reportedly carried with them a gilded "idol" called "Christ" that they carefully protected, along with carved images of patrilineal ancestors. Their mixture of Christian symbolism with Khanty religion exemplifies a syncretic pattern that many Khanty mastered over the centuries.[1]

The Khanty received Christianity in their own terms. While the immaculate purity of the Virgin Mary was questioned, icons of the "Mother of God" were related to a family of deities surrounding one of the Khanty Sky Gods, Torum or Numi-Torum. The Khanty merged Ugrian and Turkic-Iranian ideas of a pantheon of deities with the Christian concept of a supreme God. Icons were placed in the same spots as ancestor images, and sometimes treated in the same ways, with offerings of cloths, coins, and food.

The nature and success of Christianity in northwest Siberia paralleled the process of Russification. A continuum roughly representing degrees of Christian influence developed from south to north in the Ob River region. By the twentieth century, some settled Khanty families had adopted Russian Orthodoxy with fervor in southern Khanty territories. But superficial or syncretic Christianity predominated in the northern and backwoods areas. Northern and eastern Khanty preserved many pre-Christian rituals and beliefs, despite centuries of Orthodox missionary activity.

An exploration into the ways Khanty adapted and sometimes rejected Christian influence provides insights into the correlation of religious and ethnic identity. As in many areas of Christian missionizing, far more than tax concessions, baptism, and boarding schools were needed to change the cognition of indigenous peoples (Taussig 1987; Kan 1987, 1998; Harkin and Kan 1996; Hugh-Jones 1994). Conversion to any religion, despite the finality implied in the term, is rarely absolute.

PRE-CHRISTIAN BACKGROUND

Ob-Ugrian socioreligious concepts and rituals resonated in a wide range of interrelated pragmatic and spiritual activities. As reflective Khanty explain today, major premises guiding Khanty thought included reincarnation (transmigration of souls), complex beliefs in multiple named souls, and shamanic mediation between the human and spirit worlds, all imbued with natural cycles. Key rituals focused on naming, male initiation, provisioning ancestors, and placating animal spirits. Spirits of bears, foxes, geese, and hares were associated with major kin groups. Through dance, mime, and satirical plays, social tensions and realignments were sometimes expressed during festivals honoring dead bears. The social settings of Ob Ugrian religion varied from personal and family worship to elaborately planned patrilineage and phratry ceremonies. The pantheon of deities, with their own extended family relationships, partially mirrored local social organization.[2]

The Khanty marked life passages and seasonal transformations by performing animal sacrifices before patrilineage or phratry figures, called "idols" in missionary and ethnographic accounts (Novitskii 1884: 50–52; Karjalainen 1927:148–51). Northern Khanty term them *itérma*, a receptacle of spirit power; or, more euphemistically, *agan*, figure. These human or animal images, usually carved wooden statues ranging from five inches to several feet, are covered with layers of clothing, metal ornaments, and face plates. Representing links with the Khanty past and the spirit world, the images are sometimes distinguishable by gender and are associated with specific accounts of ancestral travels or heroism.

By the time missionaries arrived, certain ancestor spirits had become widely known deities. These spirits, through their figures, were honored by Khanty men in sacred groves where horses, reindeer, and occasionally human captives were sacrificed with drama and ritual feasting. Communicants smeared the noses and mouths of the figures with sacrificial blood and grease, while chanting under the leadership of shamans and patrilineal elders. Feeding the spirits with tokens of respect helped ensure that poetic prayer-chants would be well received.

In 1715 the Russian Orthodox missionary Grigory Novitskii (1884:47–52) gave a detailed, albeit biased, account:

> Some of them deceivingly worship various gods, in the form of birds, reptiles, or fowl; others bow to [human-shaped] idols associated with animals, especially the bear. . . . They serve without shame multiple gods. . . . [Valuables] are blindly brought to these idols. . . . "Shamans," cohorts with the devil, perform magical predictions and consider themselves leaders. . . . Those living near Tatars prefer to sacrifice horses, while others sacrifice wild animals and reindeer. . . . Over the animals, the priest [shaman] sings mythical songs and prayers, to insure successful hunting and fishing. . . . When the priest has finished singing, he taps the animal on the head. . . . [After the animal is killed] they take it by the tail and drag it three times around the idol. . . . They draw blood out of the beast into a consecrated vessel, to drink and to anoint their houses. . . . They dress and eat the flesh with great rejoicing and singing. . . . They imagine that the unclean spirit housed in the idol dances with them in the surrounding air.

A few special "idols" were revered by interlineage groups, bringing Ob Ugrian tribes together as a people conscious of common roots associated with certain named multilineage phratries, especially Por and Mos. One of these unifying male images, called the Old Man Ob, was believed to guide fish yields. Novitskii (1884:56) was particularly struck by his imposing height, gold breastplate, and "devilish horns." Symbolizing his broad appeal, the Old Man Ob spent a term of three years in each of two sacred groves, one at the Irtysh-Ob confluence and another further north along the Ob River. He was to become a special target of missionary fire.

CHRISTIAN CAMPAIGNS

The trappings, if not the spirit, of Russian Orthodoxy penetrated deep into West Siberia with the first Cossack soldiers of Ermak Timofeevich in the 1580s. A small tent chapel, glittering with precious silver and gold icons, accompanied Ermak's bellicose entourage. Monks carried the icons forward whenever Ermak changed camp, symbolically challenging the "land of idolatry."[3] Khanty in turn used their own symbols to meet the challenge. In 1585, Khanty attacking the winter fort of Ivan Mansurov "brought with them their famed shaitan [idol] . . . placed it on a tree near the fort and brought sacrifices to it, asking for help in defeating the Russians" (Miller [1763] 1937:267; cf. Golovnev 1995: 147).

The challenge grew heated as Russian settlers arrived and helped organize chapels, churches, and monasteries in Tiumen and Tobolsk.[4] Khanty leaders who became Russian allies were encouraged to travel to Moscow for audiences with the tsar, and to be christened. In 1600, one Khanty "princeling," Vasili of Obdorsk, returned from Moscow with enough fervor, whether political or religious, to sponsor the building of a wooden church named for Saint Vasili. Members of the Native Alachev family also built a church in 1602 and married into a Russian noble family (Abramov 1854:17, 337).

These early alliances reveal an official attitude toward Native leaders as educable and ripe for enlightenment. Khanty cooperation, however, was minimal. Few actively participated in church building or Christian worship. Khanty leaders, seeking political and economic advantage, did not acknowledge that Orthodoxy demanded religious exclusivity. When Vasili and the Alachevs became disillusioned with Russian rule, they led "rebellions" and became the first of a long line of Native Christian "backsliders" (Miller [1763] 1941:212).

Provincial authorities were eager to bring Natives into steady tax (yasak) obligations by baptizing them and recording their new Christian names. Though Christian converts were initially exempt from taxation, the names gave officials the ability, at least in theory, to track Natives when exemptions expired. Officials also proclaimed concern for saving souls, since they felt that the Ob River Natives represented extremes of idolatry. In 1618, Russians received a Mansi (Vogul) request for permission to sacrifice a tax-paying Native (probably a Khanty captive) in a local sacred grove. Permission was denied, but the sacrifice was held in secret, a strategy that persisted through the centuries.[5]

The first archbishop of Siberia, Kiprian, arrived in Tobolsk in 1621, with the moral authority and resources of the Russian Orthodox church behind him.[6] His mandate from Patriarch Filaret was to cleanse Russian Orthodox settlers of their already infamous immorality and to teach conquered peoples the love of Christ. Kiprian expressed his views particularly strongly when honoring the wild and unruly Ermak and his men as "martyrs" who had triumphed over "impure and vile" peoples (Miller [1763] 1941:67–68). But by the end of the seventeenth century, official focus shifted to battling Old Believer schismatics and consolidating monastery lands in Siberia.[7]

Russian civil and religious authorities often went beyond diplomatic persuasion to encourage Native conversions. In the seventeenth and eighteenth centuries, decrees were issued deploring baptism by force (and exposing its prevalence). One such decree in 1625 declared: "If any of the natives should desire to be baptized into the Orthodox Christian faith, then you are ordered to accept and baptize them. But you are prohibited from converting any native against his will."[8]

In the eighteenth century, Christian missions and monasteries were hampered by Siberian settlement conditions, the elusiveness of the reindeer breeders, and the lack of consistent administrative support. Novitskii lamented, "Without the riches of the East Indies and China, missionaries were not eager to go to such a poor and savage nation as the Ostiak" (1884:69).

Novitskii, who learned at least one Khanty (Ostiak) dialect, took part in a major proselytizing campaign led by Filofei Leshinskii (Metropolitan Fedor) during the reign of Peter the Great. Although missionaries were encouraged for the first time to learn Native languages, emphasis remained on quantitative, not qualitative, conversions. In the summers of 1712 to 1714, Filofei and Novitskii traveled as far north as Berezovo, destroying idols and baptizing Ob-Ugrians in mass ceremonies. Their approach was to baptize first and convince later.

The campaign, described in military terms by its organizers, provoked widespread anger and confusion. In some Native villages, missionaries were greeted with arrows and abuse. In others, tearful men begged Filofei to spare their wives and children from baptism. They pleaded that "idols" be taxed instead of burned. A prominent human image with a silver face was burned at Shorkovsk, as "an appearance of Satan" (Novitskii 1884:72). But some Khanty managed to hide their ancestor images deep in the Siberian wilderness. Novitskii (1884:58) lamented that "during this time of scourging of idol worship," precious "idols" from Belogar were spirited farther from Russian control.

The Khanty were told that human sacrifice was "savage," that their shamans were evil, that thirty-year-old men should not marry seven-year-old girls, that polygamy was blasphemy, and that unconfessed "sins" resulted in horrible judgment after death (Novitskii 1884:94–95). The difficulty of translating these concepts into the Khanty language, much less into Khanty practice, casts doubt on contemporary claims of conversions by the thousands (Businskii 1893:21).

Although Novitskii (1884:80) believed that God supported the Orthodox side with good weather, the situation was more complex. One intractable shaman, whom Novitskii (1884:75) described as an enemy with an "evil, black, and small face," stirred "about one hundred" Khanty to successfully expel all Christians from his area in 1713. However, conversions did occur, especially in the area already Russified, near the Kondinsk monastery. There, an Alachev prince made a great display of his change of heart, "having been told the story of the ancient Prince Vladimir of Kiev's conversion from idolatry" (Novitskii 1884:73). He and his followers celebrated lavishly with the missionaries, in an "auspicious" mass baptism and feast "not seen since the days of Vladimir" (Novitskii 1884:73). A shaman of the Karinkarsk settlement converted after a spiritual struggle between his helper spirit, who threatened to afflict him with anthrax, and God, who offered him blessings and a cross (Novitskii 1884:95–96).

In 1726, an aging Filofei was turned back on the Ob River near Obdorsk (today Salekhard) by arrows shot from surrounding cliffs (Abramov 1857a:350). Novitskii was killed by Khanty he had been trying to convert. Ten years after Filofei's campaign, despite the huge numbers of "idols" he burned, nearly fifteen hundred "idols" were found in the Berezovo area alone by frustrated missionaries. Some had escaped destruction, while others were recreated. The Old Man Ob was rumored to have "risen out of flames as a swan."[9]

In 1762, Khanty from the Narikharsk yurts near Berezovo "killed a horse and presented it to the devil as a sacrifice," although they were officially baptized. Their leader, Afanasi Loshmanov, probably a shaman, led them in prayers "for ample fish in the water, animals in the forest." After feasting, remains of the carcass and head were put into the Ob and scattered in different directions. As punishment, Loshmanov was forced to spend three years in the Kondinsk monastery, and the others were made to bow and pray fifty times.[10]

Material incentives supplemented punishments. Grain gifts were made through monasteries and churches, some newly built at Malo-Atlym, Shorkarsk, Kazym, Sukhorukov, and Berezovo. The monks Gideon and Zinoviev were especially active at the Voskresensk monastery of Berezovo (Abramov 1857a:346–47). Twenty-three churches were established in the northern Ob River area in the eighteenth century. Fur tax exemptions for newly Christian Natives were granted in 1720 and 1731.[11] While the amount and length of exemptions varied, this policy continued into the 1800s.

The church had great potential impact in protecting Natives from abuses by local government officials and Slavic settlers. Filofei, concerned about the "gullibility" of the newly Christian Khanty, began what was to become a fluctuating Native-rights advocacy role for the clergy. This led to a decree (Ukaz Pravlenie Senata, July 29, 1726) stipulating that taxes were to be collected peacefully, that Natives in service or marriage against their will were to be freed, and that it was a serious crime to "forcibly harry" either "Christian or non-Christian natives." After the decree, in the village of Berezovo alone, fifty Khanty men and women were freed from "involuntary service" to Russians (Abramov 1857a:349).

Similar reforms were reintroduced in the 1760s under Catherine the Great and in the 1820s by the liberal Siberian Committee, under the leadership of Count Speranskii. The need to repeatedly promulgate similar reforms indicates that concerns nurtured by high church and government officials far from Siberia did little to alleviate local tax corruption, excessive trade in alcohol, and un-Christian social abuses. The clergy themselves violated Native rights when they collected choice furs, forced baptism, or jailed Khanty for shamanizing and polygamy.[12]

Russian Orthodoxy was more successful when conversions grew out of long-term relationships with churches and missions. In a few southern areas, Khanty leaders were designated as official church affiliates. Their tasks included convincing parents to volunteer children to learn Russian grammar and the Orthodox catechism. "The best pupils were sent to the Tobolsk Slavic-Latin school" (Abramov 1857a:347). This extended a tradition, dating from the first period of Slavic contact, of teaching Christianity to Native child hostages, amananti.[13]

In the 1800s, church building intensified, with some churches consciously placed on sacred spots formerly occupied by "idols." The Kondinsk monastery in southwest Khanty territory became a center for several surrounding Khanty villages. Natives grew dependent on mission trade, charity, and services (Kornilov 1828:67). By the 1850s the monastery school enrolled twenty boys, half of whom were Khanty. This was, however, only a token few, and the impoverished mission was unpopular with monks.[14]

As late as 1885, the influential newspaper *Sibirskii Vestnik* (3:9–10) editorialized that missionaries still focused on accruing large numbers of superficially converted Natives rather than thoroughly teaching them Orthodox principles. The Tobolsk Guberniia record book listed only 205 "rural" schools, "all exclusively in Russian areas" (Dmitriev-Mamonov and Golodnikov 1884:251).

In this climate of failure, an idealistic monk and scholar, Arkady Ivanovich Iakobii, sought a site for renewed missionary activity. Traveling in a caravan of fifty-four reindeer, he found an ideal spot at Nadym, near northern Khanty and Nentsy. It was close to a sacred grove and had fertile soil and marvelous fishing potential, conducive to a diversified mission economy.

During Iakobii's search, he discussed the proposed mission with Natives. Khanty elders agreed that, combined with the mission, a local tax and trade center could be convenient. They accepted the church on the condition that Zyriany (Komi), whom they considered deceitful traders, would be excluded from the congregation (Iakobii 1895:6). Iakobii learned that for most northern Khanty, church holidays and Christian rituals were superfluous. He hoped, rather, to protect Natives "against the dark side of our civilization" (Iakobii 1895:13). He encouraged church donations to the hungry, regardless of their religion, and believed that sermons, social services, and schools were the best "weapons" of Christianity (Iakobii 1895:35).

The hoped-for networks of parish schools remained elusive. Qualified teachers were rare even in rural European Russia (Eklof 1986). In Siberia, it was difficult to find literate Christians willing or able to teach the Khanty. Local Russian helpers who claimed fluency in the Khanty language turned out to have vocabularies geared to practical, not spiritual, matters (Iakobii 1895:27).

Most missionaries were reluctant to become reindeer-owning nomads for the sake of their faith. They found an ample mission field in Russian villages and the few surrounding Native settlements farther south. They hesitated to fight the medical and alcohol problems of northern Khanty. In the subarctic, missionaries could ride hundreds of kilometers in fifty-below-zero weather and then be ill received in a Native village. On the Kazym River, missionaries rarely risked such disappointment (Shukhov 1916:30). They simply avoided the area.

In sum, the success of a missionary varied greatly with his character, with the locale of the Khanty he was trying to reach, and with the extent to which the Khanty perceived Christianity as a means to power, tax relief, and trade goods.

KHANTY RESPONSES TO CHRISTIANITY

While Khanty in retrospect confirm that the act of baptism itself rarely meant sincere conversion, aspects of Russian Orthodoxy did become meaningful. Most significant was the *Pax Slavica* that Christianity, along with Muscovite and Petersburg rule, represented. Khanty elders welcomed relative peace, after a series of resource-depleting and demeaning wars with their Nentsy, Mansi, Komi, and Tatar neighbors. Perhaps this is one reason why representatives of the Russian empire were able to make such a remarkably rapid advance across Siberia.[15]

A second major Christian influence was curtailment of human sacrifice. On moral and pragmatic grounds, empire officials were loath to waste a taxpayer. Ugrians quickly learned not to ask official permission for sacrifices held during periodic lineage ceremonies. Eventually human sacrifice, part of the complex Ugrian war-related rituals that included scalping, waned after Slavic conquest. Perhaps Khanty leaders who adopted Russian Orthodoxy were aware of the special terror this practice produced in their Slavic allies. Even so, the skeptical explorers Finsch and Brem (1882:487) found informants who remembered that human sacrifices had been made at a sacred center near the site that Iakobii later chose for a mission.

A third aspect of receptivity to Christianity involved more subtle issues of syncretic belief. Despite variations with time, place, and individual, a few patterns emerge. Some Khanty came to see one of their deities, Numi-Torum, as the single Sky God Christians revered. Some priests encouraged such correlations, leading to the identification of the Khanty afterlife with heaven. Khanty then adapted their gospels, called "myths" by outsiders, to fit Christian ones.[16]

In the unfriendly competition between priests and shamans for the respect of Khanty followers, shamans often won. Russian Orthodox allegations of shamanic collaboration with the devil, excessive greed, and quack doctoring did little to dispel Khanty, and sometimes local Slavic (Siberiak), fascination with shamanic curing seances (Startsev 1928:92).

By the twentieth century, the majority of northern Khanty were officially baptized Christians but retained much of their pre-Christian outlook and behavior. Many had fled northward from the Irtysh area to avoid Slavic Christians. They were incensed over Russian and Zyrian thefts of valuable cloth, furs, and money from their sacred groves and graves. But they were also attracted to the trade goods and grain that were bartered or given away at mission centers. This ambivalence, combined with limitation of contacts due to seminomadism, produced a view of Russian Orthodoxy as powerful but negotiable.[17]

A young Khanty couple exemplify this flexible approach. They arrived in Berezovo to be married at the church, having already spent about a year living together (Felinska (1853(2):19–21). They stayed at their Cossack trade partner's home to prepare for the wedding. The pregnant bride elaborately arrayed herself in a green caftan with beads and jingling bells. But when the couple reached the church, the priest refused to marry them since they had forgotten their Christian names. Unperturbed, they returned to their tundra home. Having attempted to meet the social and political demands of Slavic contact, they felt no further obligation.

A second case of incomplete conversion involved a Khanty man from the Obdorsk region who became a deacon's assistant (Poliakov 1877:55). This enterprising young man was considered so upstanding by the local Russian community that he was allowed to marry a Russian woman, in a rare mixed-ethnic ceremony. His bride was then chagrined to discover that he attended "pagan" sacrifices before ancestral "idols," broke Christian fasts, and generally behaved in an "unclean" and "debauched" manner. He had been using his perceived spiritual power and authority as a deacon's assistant to enhance his standing in the local Khanty and Russian communities.

The doctor Bartenev (1896:94–95) claimed that among Khanty converts were "more thieves, drunkards, and laggards than among shamanists," leading to local Obdorsk speculation that converts were Natives who, living near Russians, had seen "the worst side of civilization" and had been corrupted by it. Bartenev noted sadly that the "Christian" Natives he met were quite cynical, converting "for practical reasons," to get white shirts as offerings to ancestral images and to acquire "bits of civilization." Iakobii complained (1895:20) that Khanty men accepted mission jobs out of necessity, not religious fervor.

Northern Khanty "did not attach great meaning to baptism" (Bartenev 1896:92). One Obdorsk missionary was visited by a Khanty hunter who wanted to have his small son baptized. The delighted missionary asked if the parents were themselves baptized and was told they were not. The hunter explained: "I went hunting, and walked and walked, but I could not manage to meet any animals; such was my luck. Then I prayed to Nicholas: 'Nicholas, said I, if you bring me luck I will have my son baptized.' Well, Nicholas helped" (Bartenev 1896:92). The missionary countered that a baptized son should have parents in the faith, to raise him properly. But the hunter instead resolved that he would give Nicholas an offering of rubles and forget having his son baptized.

From the 1600s to the 1900s, the Khanty were influenced by Russian Orthodoxy, but not nearly to the extent that might be expected, given the length of time involved. Explanations include the strength yet adaptability of Khanty religion; and the haphazard, undermanned, and at times brutal nature of missionary actions. Multiple views of the interactive history are crucial for understanding mutual influences. The relative scarcity of effective Russian Orthodox models among Slavic settlers of peasant backgrounds played a significant role in justifying Khanty religious perceptions. The homestead-oriented faith of Slavic colonizers was often a blend of pre-Christian belief, lapsed Orthodoxy, and awe of Native shamans.

SLAVIC ADOPTION OF NATIVE RELIGION

Northern Slavic peoples, particularly Siberiaki, adopted Native religion and syncretized it with their own beliefs. Khantization worked on technological and spiritual levels, with the two processes reinforcing one another. Siberiaki appealed to Native shamans, attended shamanic curing seances, and participed in sacrifices to Native spirits far more commonly than missionaries cared to admit. The ethnographer Nosilov (1904:16–19) observed, "I know many Russians who are not ashamed to take part in sacrifices, who eagerly consult the magicians of these people [Ob-Ugrians], and who even carry out their rules, according to which, starting out on a journey, they lay out fish or offer some sort of valuable article to spirits."

On the Liapin River, Russians, chanting the proper words, "as indigenous believers do," shared part of their hunting and fishing gains with the spirits they felt had helped them (Nosilov 1904:17). On the Vasyugan, a Khanty shaman taught a Cossack who was ill with fever how to place sacrifices at a local sacred site (Grigorovskii 1884:29).

While the Khanty rarely invited settlers, even Siberiaki, to sacred groves, many settlers felt free to ask for shamanic advice in curing and divining, and such appeals lessened Khanty suspicion of backwoods newcomers. Local Khanty shamans had varying reputations for success with Khanty and Siberiak clients. The traveler P-rovskii (1866) reported widespread adoption of "shamanstvo" by settlers, and Shvetsov (1888:77) lamented its popularity.[18]

Settlers were predisposed to shamans by their own background, despite their professed Russian Orthodoxy. "It is not surprising that shamanism was taken up by the Russians in Siberia," a Russian Orthodox priest explained to me. "Their own priests behaved like shamans with their 'boxes of miracles.'" Peasant settlers brought to Siberia pre-Christian practices and beliefs: they propitiated domestic and forest spirits, revered bears, purified with fire, cured with incantations, and believed in sorcerer-magicians who could change shape. The similarities to Khanty religion are striking.[19]

In the Surgut, Berezovo, and Obdorsk areas, syncretism flourished on the basis of perceived parallels. For instance, Siberiaki believed that a woman could at will become a forest spirit (in Russian, *susedko*) by changing into a bird, in order to commune with spirits, eavesdrop on humans, and cause sickness (Shvetsov 1888:76–78). This had roots in Russian concepts of witchcraft or "spoiling" (*porcha*), shape-changing magicians (*volkhi*), and fear of unclean power (*nechistaia sila*).

Russian beliefs about spirit communication and shape changing into animals and birds resembled Khanty shamanic ideas. As evident in their incantations, the Russians probably once had shamanic folk doctors (*znakhar*) who performed healing-trance journeys and activated amulets, but many of these talents had been lost in Christian times (Maikov 1869; Zguta 1977). Many analysts have described Russian folk religion as "double faith [*dvoeverie*]," though a more nuanced term, with less pejorative load, might be "multifaceted faith."[20]

Settlers openly maintained pre-Christian spirituality long after it was purged in Russia and Ukraine (Bartenev 1896; Rusakova and Minenko 1985). They turned to Native shamans for specific help with illness in an environment they perceived to be ruled by alien spirits. When home remedies failed, they lacked access to scientific medical practitioners. In contrast, the Khanty appeared to have a steady feedback system of symbolic communication with their spirits, and they confidently demonstrated control over them in dramatic, audience-impressing seances.[21] Shamans provided a direct link to the spirits and the spiritual.

Shamanic seances, with their passionate thunder of drumming, drama, and catharsis, drew Russians to the Khanty in an environment that both groups perceived as spirit ridden. For Siberiaki, the Christian God remained supreme, but lesser Khanty spirits (or devils) were nonetheless forces to be feared, tamed. Visitors were sometimes astounded to find local Russians "still moving within the precincts of the invisible world . . . the most poetical element of their existence" (Felinska 1853(2): 163). The congruence of Slavic peasant and Siberian shamanic beliefs provided fertile ground for syncretism.

KHANTY SYNCRETISM

The mingling of Christian ideas with Khanty shamanic cosmology presents a familiar challenge for anthropological analysis. Part of the cognitive process of coping with Christian conversion pressure, and indeed of adjusting to colonization, involved melding aspects of new ideology with older worldviews. Far from representing a route to complete conversion or acculturation, with attendant loss of ethnic consciousness, syncretism became a process of cultural creativity, providing sometimes spiritually weakened cultural bodies with infusions of new meaning. As a merging of beliefs and actions from different cultural traditions, syncretism is mentioned frequently in religious studies, though without enough detailed description or interpretation of its dynamics.[22]

To grasp the complexity of missionary dialogics in the Latin American context, Michael Taussig (1987:196) describes "an interacting doubleness of epistemology, two universes apart, each requiring the other, each demolishing the other." The resistance of certain religions to change may vary with the extent of their hierarchical organization and their elaborated, especially written, body of gospel. Nonetheless, organized religions like Russian Orthodoxy, as well as shamanic philosophies, reveal deeply syncretic thinking. Even at the height of their clash there is mutual recognition, for their universes turn out to be less different from each other than first appears.

In Clifford Geertz's (1968:1, 56) famous passage, the religious sphere is one "where old wine goes as easily into new bottles as old bottles contain new wine." In syncretic dialogics, a better metaphor might be permeable skin bags that can accommodate new wines with particular frequency. Several wines can flow into the same malleable containers. Culture becomes not a rigid form but a filter through which innovations are perceived and adapted even when competing cultural "histories," "myths," and "traditions" do not meet on equal terms. Mavericks can function outside cultural practices and values or become driving forces for change.[23]

Syncretic situations often involve the collision of two cultural traditions, only one of which has a well-developed hierarchy of official practitioners and a written gospel of exclusivity and truth. This has been a typical pattern of contact as European Christians penetrated tribal areas throughout the world. Perhaps because of their own acknowledged history of "paganism," Christians often assumed an attitude of "noblesse oblige" toward the spread of their faith, rationalizing conversion as the equivalent of Progress and the index of Civilization. But Christian missionizing varied widely, sometimes within the same region. The effectiveness of kind, well-meaning missionaries like Iakobii was undermined in Siberia by more debauched and exploitive missionary-traders.

After initial heavy-handed efforts, Russian Orthodox tolerance of folk syncretism became the norm. This relative tolerance, coupled with a tenacious retention of ancient beliefs and actions among Uralic and Altaic peoples of Siberia, suggests that Siberia is a particularly apt place to study syncretism and missionary dialogics. Appropriate comparisons include Russian Orthodox communities of Alaska and indigenous communities of Canada, where each generation continues to negotiate meanings of spirituality.[24]

Khanty religious history is complicated and enriched by influences that preceded Russian Orthodoxy. Such influences, integrated by Ob-Ugrians into their beliefs about deities and sacrifice, came from Iranian and Turkic peoples and possibly early Nestorians.[25] Recently, however, Russian Orthodoxy provided the most sustained stimulus for religious syncretism. Syncretic gospels, sacred objects, and rituals illustrate some of the cognitive processes involved in creative Khanty responses to Orthodoxy.

SYNCRETIC GOSPELS: BEARS AND HARES

Christian influences are particularly clear in several Khanty versions of the origin of the bear, reported in the early twentieth century (Dunin-

Gorkavich 1904:43, 1911:37; Karjalainen 1927:193–234). As a rebellious son or brother of the Sky God Numi-Torum, the bear, who had a remarkably human form, was kicked from the sky for the sin of pride. He fell between two sacred trees (birch or cedar) and lay there for a long time. Finally, he supplicated Torum, begging him to remember their kinship and exalted origins. Torum responded: "I will give you the life of a bear. Then people will fear you and worship you. But all the same, they will hunt you." Moss on the spot where the divinity had fallen became his fur, and his humanlike figure was transformed to that of a bear. But he did not lose all of his God-like characteristics. He remained all-knowing and all-seeing. For this reason, the Khanty used his paw or head for oaths and performed respectful rituals when hunting him. When humans encountered a bear in the taiga, the bear would stand on its hind legs. People believed that this was the bear's way of asking Torum if the human should be spared.

A slightly earlier version was collected by the ethnographer Gondatti (1887:78) in an area of mixed Khanty and Mansi settlement. One day the bored bear, who was the son of God, broke the locked doors of his golden sky house and went outside, discovering the earth below. The bear wrecked his home when he realized he could not travel. For this, Numi-Torum punished his bear-son by having him dangle for three days in a cradle held by chains over the edge of the sky. Torum then relented, put the bear on earth, and extracted a promise that his son would not eat the humans' stores of supplies. Torum told the bear to live in his lair peacefully, hurting only those who were sinful or disrespectful of the bear. But the bear quickly yielded to temptation and ate the entire contents of a storehouse. Torum had said that if this occurred, people would have the right to hunt the bear, and so they did.

In all the Ob-Ugrian versions of bear origins, the bear has the ability to judge sinfulness in humans.[26] For this reason, Khanty considered false oaths taken on a bear paw or head to be extremely dangerous. In the tsarist period, officials demanded loyalty oaths to be sworn on bearskins, because this ensured that the Khanty would keep their word (Businskii 1893:21). Khanty, at least through the 1920s, invoked the bear to ascertain criminal guilt or innocence, since no one would utter "may the bear eat me if I am guilty" without meaning it (Startsev 1928:103). As the words were said, the oath taker was usually required to tap a bear skull with an axe. Bear oaths were also used to make pacts, usually between hunters on joint outings, to share the spoils.

Khanty narratives about the sacred bear reveal struggles with new concepts, such as Christian sin. The bear became equated with Jesus Christ, the Son of God, and also with Lucifer, the rebellious angel. In some Khanty versions, the bear was Numi-Torum's brother, reflecting

Khanty fraternal kin priorities.[27] Khanty combined Christian explanations of Jesus Christ's martyrdom with Satan's expulsion from heaven, revealing concern over the frequent Russian Orthodox identification of what was sacred to them (bears and ancestral spirits) with the devil. Ambiguity was resolved when the bear became Jesus Christ.

Other Christian themes included the significance of prayer and the existence of the Supreme Heavenly God. New prayers became acceptable in place of and together with shamanic animal sacrifice. Numi-Torum acquired multiple meanings and powers, derived from pre-Christian as well as Christian thought. Numi-Torum, also honored by neighboring Samodeic peoples, was associated with thunder and with the highest level of seven golden heavens. He became the Christian Sky God, the most elevated, but not the sole, heavenly deity.[28]

The literal suspension, in limbo and liminality, of an unruly god in a child's cradle, and his transition to bearness through acquisition of moss-fur, demonstrate critical symbolic changes in Khanty mythic thinking: from sacred to mundane, from heaven(ly) to earth(ly), from hunter to hunted, from human(oid) to animal(-like), from child to adult, and from innocent to rule abiding. These transitions could cycle back, in a process that permeated Khanty life. They both reflected Khanty social expectations and inverted them. Probing them helps us understand Robin Ridington's (1988:71) plea: "unless we can find some way to understand the reality of mythic thinking, we remain prisoners of our own language, our own thoughtworld."[29]

Symbolic transitions illustrated relations among humans, animal spirits, and deities that guided Khanty views of kinship, ancestry, and place. Kinship was built partially on Khanty identification of certain lineages and one phratry (the Por people) as coming from an ancient bear mother. Bear ancestry reveals seemingly totemic ideas, yet the bear is sacred for all Khanty. The bear, both sacred and profane while on earth, defies neat structural categorization. Concepts of bear ancestry link reincarnation and personal identity to cultural identity in a cycle that touches, according to contemporary Khanty, the deepest levels of their shamanic ideology. Humans can stem from animals, and animals may once have been human. The bear ambiguously remains "part-God, part-human, and part-animal." This Khanty trinity may well predate the Christian formula "God the Father, God the Son, and God the Holy Ghost."[30]

The second major Ob-Ugrian phratry (moiety) is Mos, whose people are said to have come from the hare, or sometimes the water-bird goose. This phratry is associated with narratives about another major Sky God, the highly shamanic Mir-Susne-Kum, or World Surveyor Man, rider on a winged horse, controller of seasonal changes, mediator between humans and the spirit world. Protector of humans, Mir-Susne-Kum can be correlated to the Iranian Sun God, Mithra, and is a key player in Ugrian bear ceremonies. His mother is Kaltash, in some versions a goddess cast from the sky by her former husband Numi-Torum for the sin of mating with the underworld god-spirit Kul'-Ortyr (Novikova 1991:29).

A bear ceremony song depicts Mir-Susne-Kum and the bear, two half-brothers, as locked in a struggle that ends with Mir-Susne-Kum killing the bear, in his beast form, to protect humans. The linkage of the half-brothers is confirmed when Ob-Ugrian participants in bear ceremonies bring offerings of silver plates, depicting a flying horse with a rider, to altars made of the bear's head and fur. For them, such images depict Mir-Susne-Kum, although the plates, originally bought from Russians, depict Saint George to Orthodox Christians.[31]

SACRED OBJECTS: COOPTING SAINTS AND ANGELS

Sacred objects such as Saint George plates provide further clues, confirmed by some Khanty consultants, to Khanty syncretic conceptions. Saint George, superhunter of mythological serpents, was transformed to a shamanic ancestor-hunter of the sacred bear, whose mission was to protect humans. The archangel Michael, sometimes depicted in icons on a horse dispelling evil spirits with the holy book, was similarly coopted. Moreover, by the early twentieth century, at least one Khanty shaman had painted the image of Saint Nicholas on his drum, amidst iron rings and other representations of spiritual power. This shaman invoked Saint Nicholas as a spirit helper during curing seances (Shukhov 1916a:31).

Saint Nicholas easily appealed to Khanty believers, given the saint's renown among Russian Orthodox priests and peasants as a curer and miracle worker. I asked a Russian Orthodox priest what makes Saint Nicholas so popular, and he explained three aspects: his pure love of God and efforts against heresy; his good works; and his understanding of truth. Truth for Saint Nicholas meant morality, but without the extreme denunciation of theater and dancing that other ecclesiastic figures of his day espoused. The most appealing side of the saint was his active and brave charity, which took the form of wandering from village to village as a curer. He healed people, helped criminals, and saved those accused unjustly. In Siberia, Saint Nicholas the Miracle Worker came to be an all-purpose saint whose icons adorned the "beautiful corner" of many peasant huts. Passionate Russian and Siberiak belief in Saint Nicholas's power was communicated to Khanty neighbors, who bought icons of Saint Nicholas and placed them with ancestral images, praying to them for good hunting and health.

The occurrence of a few Saint Nicholas images even in remote areas like Kazym demonstrates the rapid spread of a powerful "new" symbol of curing, charity, and shamanic mediation. Khanty call this saint Mikkola-Torum and consider that he travels the sky on skis, through the Milky Way, monitoring world order, breaches of social conduct, and the distribution of animals.[32]

Crosses, bells with Slavonic inscriptions, breastplates with images of saints, plus coins, buttons, and keys, became part of many shamans' sacred paraphernalia. These metal symbols were attached to cloaks to enhance jingling calls to spirits during seances (Businskii 1893:35). Iron, brass, silver, and gold were associated with Khanty ideas of strength, longevity, and spirit power. Such ideas were embodied symbolically in the use of metal on ancestral figures' faces and chests, in rituals involving iron knives to protect Khanty souls, and in the placement of iron rings on shamanic drums and cloaks.[33] Metal, particularly iron, can thus be seen for Ugrians as a dominant multivocal symbol, welding old and new meanings about power (cf. Turner 1982:16, 29).

In some Ob-Ugrian areas, images of the god Mir-Susne-Kum, World Surveyor Man, were dressed in hats that adapted the style of Russian policemen of the nineteenth century. This too was an attempt at coopting power, transforming secular (Russian) authority into the sacred (Khanty) realm while bending contemporary times and values back onto the time of the ancestors.[34]

When objects were themselves valuable as Russian Orthodox symbols, Khanty interpreters of the sacred saw extra benefit in adapting perceived symbols of Christian power and wealth. Thus shamans put crosses on cloaks because the crosses gave them access to Christian angels, treated like Native spirits, not because they accepted Christian interpretations of Christ's martyrdom.[35] Throughout the North, Khanty gradually added wooden Russian Orthodox crosses on graves for supplemental spiritual insurance, even when ritual emphasis was on older symbols and forms (Balzer 1980). Some families have continued this practice into the 1990s.

SYNCRETIC RITUALS: MARY HAD A LITTLE RAM

Syncretism in Khanty gospels, objects, and rituals stems from similar cognitive processes and contexts. Their underlying shamanic ideology is not dogmatic, and is sometimes publicly explained or debated.[36] The borrowing or coopting of perceived Christian power was a major trend, building on the complex relations among humans and between humans and spirits. In 1746, Russian Orthodox officials complained that Satyginsk Khanty had practiced their animal sacrifice rituals in honor of male ancestors injudiciously close to a newly built Christian church.[37] Sacrifice of a reindeer stag had proceeded according to sacred custom, with a shaman directing chants. But a major change occurred: the whole ritual was oriented not toward the sacred northern island where ancestors were believed to dwell but toward the Russian Orthodox church. Khanty were appealing to and appeasing new powers. Prayers accompanying the sacrifices could as easily have dealt with improving relations with Russians as driving them out.

In the 1860s, Malo-Atlym Khanty sacrificed a ram inside the local church, reportedly to the chagrin of church authorities. Local Khanty were acting on the instructions of a supposedly Christian Khanty church assistant, who had a dream about Mary, Mother of God. In this vision, Mary, acting much as a helping spirit would when visiting a shaman, had requested "that the following day a ram should be taken to the church and sacrificed" (Poliakov 1877:59). Pious "Russified" Khanty, among whom were leaders, elders, and "peasant-policemen," executed her request, with appropriate incantations. What provoked the Mother-of-God dream and what an animal sacrifice in church was intended to accomplish went undocumented. Church officials found it ominous that the incident occurred in a southern area where the Khanty were supposed to "know better." The incident stretched the limits of the officials' famed tolerance, and they quickly suppressed the perpetrators for breaches of Russian Orthodox law.[38]

Aspects of Malo-Atlym Khanty reasoning can be explained by Khanty beliefs concerning Mary, Mother of God. The Khanty fertility goddess Anki-Pugos (or Kaltash-imi for Northern Khanty) came to be associated with the Mother of God (Kulemzin and Lukina 1992:101). Her motherly and intercessory roles were extended to include beliefs in her highly shamanic powers of clairvoyance. Eastern Khanty also correlated Mary with the powerful women they called *ulom-verta-ni* (dreams doing woman), who could read dreams and foresee the future (Kulemzin 1976:52; Balzer 1987:1086).

In the 1990s, some Khanty families perform animal sacrifices in sacred groves, and many honor bears in special ceremonies featuring bears hunted according to prescribed rituals. At the end of Khanty patrilineage ceremonies honoring bears, plays are performed to entertain the bear spirit. They range from rollicking and bawdy (in the early portion of multiple day rituals) to solemn and sobering (in the ritual climax). One drama reenacts the killing of the bear, followed by sacred preparations for the bear to return to Numi-Torum, his father in heaven.[39] This resurrection scene, woven into ceremonies danced with masks, makes the syncretic equation of Jesus Christ and the bear especially apparent. The equation itself, however, might not have been made if the Khanty had not already had an idea of preserving bear bones so that the souls of bears could be returned to the taiga and eventually reincarnated as new animals. Thus a Christian concept, Christ's resurrection, is fit into Khanty ideas of reincarnation, ecology, and kinship.

CONCLUSION: THE LONGEVITY OF SHAMANIC THINKING

The study of Christianization encounters reveals that one group's gospel is often another's mythology. Adoption of cultural traits, objects, messages, or styles is not enough to produce the integrative reworking of meaning that characterizes the (dia)logic of syncretism and adaptability of shamanic thought. This creative process occurs consciously and unconsciously, chaotically and systematically. It is exemplified by the merging of new symbols or ideas, such as Christ's resurrection, into older cultural filters, such as shamanic curing and bear worship.

The symbols and actions most easily integrated from a contacting culture are those most logically and structurally compatible with existing forms. This "fertile ground" approach explains much Khanty syncretism, especially beliefs about Saint Nicholas the curer. But Khanty shamans also confounded Christian concepts (Jesus Christ and Lucifer) and changed the significance of major Christian symbols (crosses and bells) to fit with earlier concepts about the sacred power of animals and metals. They incorporated Christian structures (from churches to Saint George plates to policemen's hats) into existing rituals, hoping to coopt newly perceived political and spiritual power. More data could reveal other patterns. Of these, cooption comes closest to enabling development of new cultural forms, rituals, and, as we shall see, social movements.[40]

As a syncretic dialogic builds on itself, ethnic interaction may gradually change socialized habits of thought. Sometimes a tradition, such as human sacrifice, is strained to its limits and declared obsolete. Or a particularly difficult shamanic curing seance requires the improvisational introduction of a new helper spirit, for example, the kind and gentle intercessor, troubleshooter of human woe, Mary, Mother of God. Cultural filters can be adapted as people explore the aesthetic and semiotic potentials of multivocal meanings and variations of practice. Ritual action within flexible cultural paradigms at once incorporates accumulated folk knowledge and loss of knowledge.[41] Emotional individuals in times of crisis could rip the paradigms apart, reconstruct them, or live partially outside them (cf. Lutz and Lughod 1990). But shamans, without dogma, were able to understand and balance a variety of "real psychological processes affecting the fragmenting and reintegrating self" in relation to the community (Humphrey with Onon 1996:226–27).

Edmonson (1960:192–96, 202), studying Native American syncretism, long ago argued for a "psychology of syncretism." He suggested two levels of cognitive patterning: micro syncretism, characterized by obvious logical correlations, and macrosyncretism, analogic and semantic. Edmonson's simple distinctions are superseded by analytic work on metaphor, tropes, and mimesis (Fernandez 1991; Taussig 1993; cf. Taussig 1997:25). Particularly productive directions are those delving into the interrelation of cognition, cultural creativity, and sociopolitical context.

Just as fusions of Islam and folk practices took different forms in different areas, leading to various syncretic Sufi brotherhoods (Geertz 1968:48), so fusions of Christianity have led to varied symbolic emphases (Rambo 1995; Hefner 1992). Within Russian Orthodoxy, interesting syncretic differences developed, making for some quite unorthodox Orthodoxies.[42]

Interpreters of Russian Orthodox history range from those who see Orthodoxy as a politically hegemonic extension of empire to those who see it as a benevolent program of salvation. Some stress the unforced quality of Russian Orthodox missionizing (Kan 1989; Soldatov 1977), while others critique its methods (the missionary Iakobii (1895); Businskii (1893)) or challenge its very raison d'être (the Soviet scholar Ogryzko (1941)). The early missionary Grigory Novitskii's life and death provide ample evidence for initial miscommunications and conflicts. But once missionaries settled near indigenous communities and learned Native languages, both missionaries and their targets collaborated in analogies that were to become spiraling distortions of official Muscovite Russian Orthodox concepts. This is a variation on what Ann Fienup-Riordan (1990:69–122), discussing Yupik Christianization, more tactfully calls "negotiated meaning."

Russian Orthodox believers often insist on the special, tolerant nature of their church's historical missionizing among Native Siberians. It has become an article of faith, and one that I for many years accepted as a dominant, if not universal, pattern. But I must temper any generalization about Orthodox tolerance by acknowledging an environment of toughness, prejudice, and brutality in Siberia that, while perhaps not equaling the terror described by Taussig in the Putamayo, certainly must be taken into account. That Spanish colonists and Siberiaki appealed to local shamans for healing hardly proves solidarity with or respect for

Natives. Indeed, Taussig (1987:100) bluntly states, "Going to the Indians for their healing power and killing them for their wildness are not so far apart." The perceived power and danger of Indian "otherness" were motivating relations.

In at least some Siberian areas where colonists were partially dependant on Natives, mutual perceptions of spiritual power worth coopting led to better, less stereotyped communication. As in many newly colonized areas, Russian colonists had a gut fear of a wild evil lurking in extreme environments beyond human settlement. They saw in Siberia overwhelming expanses needing to be tamed. Natives, conceded to be better at taming the spirits of nature by their very "primitiveness," were thus both "wild" and "wise." In Siberia, terror, tolerance, and fascination drove interethnic relations, including missionizing.

The agents of Christianization in Siberia were not only missionaries, who were spread thin across the northern lands, but also settlers. For many Slavic peasants of nineteenth-century Siberia, whose ancestors had only partially adopted Russian Orthodoxy to begin with, Orthodoxy was homestead and spirit oriented, with great emphasis on shamanic, demonological, calendrical, and Mother-of-God symbolism. Ugrian Khanty socialization comparably stressed spirits, an afterlife, souls, resurrection, a Sky God, ancestors, and, eventually, selected saints and angels, integrated into a multileveled cosmology.[43]

The Christianity of Slavic peasants and Native Siberians had ample room for the miraculous and the charismatic. Local Orthodox officials initially condemned and then accepted folk syncretism, though periodic complaints from within the Moscow church hierarchy led to occasional purges of "unclean power" from the church's own ranks. While the Russians held ultimate, though contested, political power, Native Siberians were often perceived to have the stronger spiritual power. Mixed Orthodox signals and Khanty creativity ensured that an ideological dialogic continued through the centuries. For those who see Christianity as a set body of strict beliefs and rituals, this meant the failure of Christianization among the Khanty. But for analysts who interpret Christian faith more flexibly, Christianity had partial success.

Both sides of the Christianization encounter were changed in the process. A more productive trope than conversion, double destruction, or Christian hegemony, can be found in the Old Man Ob ancestor image ("idol"), destroyed by the missionary Novitskii in the eighteenth century. Contemporaries saw a swan rising from its ashes, and late twentieth-century Khanty honor the spirit of Old Man Ob through his recreated (resurrected) image. Other examples of Khanty capacity to subvert Russian power, through combined spiritual and political movements, are depicted in the following chapter.

CHAPTER THREE

Revitalization: The Battleground of Religion and Politics

We do not know our own history well enough, especially the history of "rebellions."

(*Tatiana Moldanova, August 1991*)

In 1896, A Vakh Ostiak [Khanty] had a dream, in which she saw that there would be a great sickness among her people.

(*Dunin-Gorkavich*, 1904)

REVITALIZATION OF AN ANTHROPOLOGICAL TERM

IN the nineteenth century, two social movements arose in the Ob River area that represented efforts of Native peoples to cope with colonization and Christianization. In 1825, a charismatic Nenets leader named Vavlyo Neniang (Vauli Piettomin in Russian) began a protracted protest of Khanty and Nentsy against Russian rule. In 1896, Khanty of the Vakh River near Surgut organized numerous animal sacrifices and agitated for a new morality at the dream-inspired urging of a female shaman. These budding cultural revitalization movements, occurring in socially disrupted areas, involved syncretism of new and old religious and political ideas. By their dramatic scale and emotional intensity, they became socially significant processes.

I view revitalization as a group-level attempt to recapture an idealized past in order to reintegrate it with an uncertain future. Conditions conducive to revitalization are neither easily determined nor generalized. Yet revitalization movements have been studied and squeezed into typologies by anthropologists since they first became aware that tensions produced by ethnic interaction are often symbolized on the battleground of religion.[1]

Revitalization movements, whether "cargo cults," "holy water cults," "ghost dances," "prophet dances," or incipient revolutions, must be analyzed in temporal contexts. They are responses to compelling ideas of internal social reform as well as to pressure from external social oppression. Many political, social, and religious movements have revitalization potential, despite their differing manifestations and end results. Whether called revolutionary, messianic, nativistic, vitalizing, or revitalizing, the psychological-functional vocabulary used to describe such movements often implies mass-level spiritual crisis-easing related to cultural rebirth. Single theories stressing "objective" material causes, charismatic leadership, widespread psychological depression, or relative deprivation rarely do such movements justice.[2]

It is worth rethinking the anthropology of socioreligious movements in terms of accumulated theories, recent comparative studies (Tromf 1990; Trott 1997), and Siberian data. Classic interpretations of socioreligious movements, such as Anthony Wallace's (1956, 1970, 1974) on Native American movements, emphasize personality alterations in leaders and followers, stimulated by rapid culture change, status deprivation, demeaning loss of Native identity, and the overwhelming pressure of new experiences. Resulting cognitive confusion, as well as physiological symptoms, can be alleviated only after a new dissonance-reducing synthesis of ideology, values, and life-style is accomplished. This is often enabled by the vision, dream, or epiphany experience of a stress-ridden leader, who manages to introduce a new religion.[3]

Theodore Schwartz (1976:206), in his cultural and historical analysis of Melanesian "cargo cults," challenges Anthony Wallace's (and Leon Festinger's) assumptions that "cults" are based on efforts to resolve cognitive inconsistency and stress. Rather, he focuses on "cognitive ambiguity, tension and heightened excitement" as productive conditions often sustained or recaptured, rather than resolved, through animated cult behavior. Cults are culturally intoxicating "fixes," with "metastable" (liminal) qualities that enable status inversions, role reversals, the expression of extreme emotions, and full use of conflicting or dissonant values. They are states to be returned to, with revisions and variations, regardless of their failure to produce desired goods ("cargo"). They can occur in remote areas barely contacted by Christian missionaries, as well as areas of intense missionizing.[4]

I view the Siberian social-religious movements featured here as having revitalization potential, but they are intoxicating without fulfillment. While the movements in which Khanty were involved never crystallized into revolutionary or religious institutions, they shed light on the frequently religious idiom of such movements, the roles of charismatic leaders, and the variable consequences of revitalization efforts.

THE MOVEMENT OF VAVLYO NENIANG (VAULI PIETTOMIN)

Beginning in 1825, one notable movement in the Northern Obdorsk region became too widespread and incendiary for officials to ignore. Led by the Nenets shaman Vavlyo Neniang, it united Nentsy and Khanty activists. While Vavlyo's movement is known in the Soviet historical literature as a Native rebellion with strictly political and economic ramifications, aspects of his leadership both evoked and represented syncretic Native religious orientations.[5]

Through the 1830s, Vavlyo, a talented, powerful, and dynamic shaman of the Neniang (literally, mosquito) clan organized Nentsy followers to make Robin Hood–like raids on huge herds of reindeer owned by the wealthier reindeer breeders in the Obdorsk region. It was a time of hardship, when famine and forest fires left many families poor and some facing starvation. At first Vavlyo and his fiery brother Togompada attracted followers from related Nentsy clans. They gained Khanty adherents, including some who threatened to kill Russians in Obdorsk for pressuring them to become Russian Orthodox (Tokarev 1936:110). While Vavlyo's "partisans" were "increased by those who suffered from want or sought his protection," some "joined him from fear of persecution" (Felinska 1853(2):300). A tsarist court later characterized his followers as "those without daily sustenance," implying they were desperate.[6]

As Vavlyo's raids became increasingly successful, with deer and valuable furs being redistributed to followers, incensed Nentsy and Khanty mobilized in opposition. Political alignments cut across ethnic and class divisions. Even defining "rich" was a problem, since epidemics and clan pressure to redistribute wealth to poorer relatives made rich reindeer breeders easy prey to changes of fortune, with or without Vavlyo. Some Northern Khanty were, in turn, readily attracted to Vavlyo's growing wealth and power. Opposition to Vavlyo centered around the Obdorsk Khanty "prince" Taishin and members of the Khudi clan of Nentsy. In 1839, a plot to lure Vavlyo into arrest succeeded, when Vavlyo and a few followers were surrounded in the tundra as they attempted to "liberate" a hundred reindeer from Khozobyko Khudi.

Vavlyo and his friend Magari Vaitin (Khodiakym) were taken to the Obdorsk prison, then handed over to Russian authorities by Taishin. A special Berezovo tribunal sentenced Vavlyo and Margari each to twenty lashes with a knout and a year's hard labor, with subsequent exile in the Surgut region. A higher Tobolsk court intervened, requesting that the governor himself sentence Vavlyo and Magari.[7] The two were finally sent to Surgut, where they began working for a local trader, Nikifor Silin. Not long after, they escaped, taking with them a small boat laden with trade goods.

"Shrewd, courageous and adroit," Vavlyo returned to the Obdorsk tundra, where he gathered more followers than ever before. "He declared that during his long absence he had a personal interview with the White Tsar . . . and though he had been admonished . . . [the tsar] afterward restored him his freedom and entrusted him at parting with many confidential orders" (Felinska 1853(2):301). Followers began to look on him "as some superior being," particularly because of his "[s]hamanic character and rank, which made him a repository of all the secrets and mysteries appertaining to the priestly order" (Felinska 1853(2):301).

A sung epic fragment about Vavlyo comes from the Nenets poet Yuri Vella, who recorded it from his neighbor. "In the song, his name is not mentioned, but it must be about Vauli [Vavlyo]. It tells of how he sat in a Russian house [prison] for seven years and then returned."[8] After confirming that Vavlyo had to be a shaman to have withstood Russian prison, Vella continued:

> He came back to a scattered family and dispersed reindeer. His sacred sled [with ancestor images] had a tree growing up its middle. When he approached, a bear loomed out from under it. And he was startled and reached for his weapon. But the great bear spoke in human tongue, "Why are you trying to kill me? It is I who have gathered your herd back together for you, and kept them from others. It is I who have saved your land."

Vavlyo was adept at both shamanic spirit contact, and the pragmatic politics of changing local Obdorsk leadership. He was intent on revenge against three established figures of authority: the Khanty leader Taishin, the allegedly corrupt Russian judge at Obdorsk, Sokolov, and the police chief Skorniakov. Vavlyo ordered all loyal Natives to withhold their fur tax until the Russian judge of Obdorsk was removed. Vavlyo also gathered large numbers of families into a single camp. He continued to encourage poorer followers to appropriate reindeer from wealthy breeders, although traditional patterns of clan resource sharing gave use rights to many of the impoverished.

In 1840, at the height of his power, Vavlyo had an impressive circle of four hundred tents in his camp (Budarin 1952:98). His popularity was enormous, with rumors of his physical and charismatic prowess spreading from the "Urals to the Yenisei and from Surgut to the mouth of the Pur and Taz rivers" (Budarin 1952:98; see map 2). His chief aides, however, were still members of his own family and clan: his partner-in-exile,

Magari Vaitin; his brother Togompada; and his uncle Motti Task. When Vavlyo's forces were strong enough, they approached Obdorsk during the January market of 1841. Vavlyo told his followers, armed with flintlock guns, rifles, spears, arrows, and knives, that their pressure could lower the prices of Russian trade goods, increase the value of Native furs, and force Taishin to abdicate or to distribute government supplies of grain.[9]

When news of Vavlyo's advance reached Obdorsk and Berezovo, many merchants fled, while frightened Russian inhabitants surrounded their houses "with every available defense" (Felinska 1853(2):303; Budarin 1952:98). Panicky rumors spread that Vavlyo's camp had as many campfires "as the stars in the sky" and as many lances "as trees in the forest" (Budarin 1952:100). Obdorsk itself was poorly fortified, with only a small garrison of Cossacks, many of whom had become traders unaccustomed to police or military duties. Reinforcements were called from Berezovo, and an emergency council of merchants, Russian officials, and a few Native elders, including Taishin, developed a plan to lure Vavlyo into Obdorsk without his full retinue. Key actors in the plan were the Nentsy-speaking merchant Nikolai Nachaevskii (a trading partner of Vavlyo) and Taishin himself.

Vavlyo and a band of four hundred to six hundred men (depending on the account) were camped near Obdorsk. The group included the extended family and followers of a Khanty reindeer breeder named Yaptika Murzin, who Vavlyo wanted to place in Taishin's position as primary elder and middleman for Native relations with the Russians.

On the encouragement of trader Nachaevskii, Vavlyo sent for Taishin, who arrived at Vavlyo's camp on the thirteenth of January, with about ten elders (Budarin 1952:100, 1968:84). The visitors knelt before Vavlyo and kissed his hand, but he harangued them "as in Nenets tales an angry master behaves with a servant" (Golovnev 1995:160; cf. Budarin 1952:100). Taishin agreed to give up his "princely" inherited position to the Khanty reindeer breeder Yaptika Murzin, if Vavlyo would halt his advance on Obdorsk. He was to enter the town with only a few followers, in order to clinch the transfer of power.

Vavlyo, suspecting danger, sent a small advance guard with at least one Russian-speaking Nenets into Obdorsk to learn of plots against him. Hearing nothing, he decided to risk a visit to Taishin. Taking only forty men, with sleds laden with guns hidden under furs, Vavlyo arrived at the government grain store, where he met Taishin. They proceeded to Taishin's house, where a prominent group of Nentsy and Khanty elders agreed to redistribute hundreds of reindeer and three hundred pounds of grain. Meanwhile, the house was surrounded by Cossacks and Obdorsk merchants, some of whom were disguised as Khanty (Budarin

1952:101; Felinska 1853(l2):305). The police chief, Skorniakov, burst in and managed, during a scuffle, to secure a few of Vavlyo's men. Vavlyo escaped to the street but was caught and beaten up soon after. The rest of the retinue mingled with Obdorsk Khanty who were willing to shelter them. By daybreak, many escaped.

Berezovo Cossack reinforcements, arriving after Vavlyo's arrest, staged a jubilant parade through Obdorsk. Skorniakov, concerned about rescue attempts, then had the Cossacks escort Vavlyo and his four arrested followers to prison in Berezovo. A local Russian blacksmith was commissioned to forge special irons to fetter Vavlyo. The blacksmith, as well as many Berezovo residents, feared that "the strongest chains would be inadequate to resist the spell of Waul's [Vavlyo's] shamanic incantations" (Felinska 1853(2):306). But the smith then claimed to devise "chains of an antimagic character, which all Waul's [Vavlyo's] witchcraft would fail to break" (Felinska 1853(2):306).[10]

A special governor's commission, headed by the governor's adjutant Count Tolstoi, was sent to Obdorsk to investigate the uprising. Vavlyo was eventually sentenced to prison and hard labor in East Siberia. In Saint Petersburg, War Minister Chernyshev and Tsar Nicholas I were apprised of Obdorsk's danger before Vavlyo's arrest and of his successful imprisonment. Chernyshev wrote to the Siberian governor-general, Prince Gorchakov: "The emperor, through a report of my own and your February 1 communication, has been informed of the increase of discontent in the Berezovo region among Ostiak [Khanty] and Samoyed [Nentsy] and of the measures taken for their resolution. The utmost approval is extended to you on this subject."[11] Primary figures in Vavlyo's demise, including Skorniakov and Nechaevskii, received medals from Saint Petersburg. Taishin was summoned to Saint Petersburg, where he met the tsar, received lavish gifts, and was awarded a gold medal "for bravery" (Budarin 1952:102–3).

Soon after Vavlyo's arrest, the Tobolsk governor wrote the following summary to the governor-general of West Siberia[12]:

> [T]he Samoyed Vauli Piettomin ran from exile to his tribe and, taking up armed rebellion, led a group of four hundred in thievery among the nomads. His onslaught brought on such fear among the primitives [*dikary*] that no one dared contradict his profit-seeking demands, but each meekly satisfied them. Vauli, finally, having reached the point where he named himself tsar of the nomadic tribes, debased the meaning [of tsar] and took over the power of natural princes, changed the authority of several established [Russian-appointed] elders, forbade the people to pay taxes [*yasak*] to the government treasury, and planned an attack on the Obdorsk government. . . . According to the police superintendent [*ispravnik*], Vauli Piet-

> tomin has been sent to Berezovo for imprisonment, but his uprising is still not fully suppressed and, in the *ispravnik's* opinion, is still dangerous. But I think . . . that the opponents of Piettomin now have seized back their rightful clan power and will prevail over sympathizers of Vauli and not harbor his adherents.

Native reaction to Vavlyo's defeat was mixed, just as support for him had been. According to a report by an Obdorsk policeman, some Khanty "princelings" and "elders" who had stakes in curtailing Vavlyo's Nenets-based power play gave thankful offerings in furs and valuables, totaling around three hundred rubles, to images of Saint Nicholas (Budarin 1952:103).

While most of the feverish support for Vavlyo's causes died down with loss of his charismatic leadership, about thirty men led by a Vavlyo aide named Pani Khodin (also called Pani Tokho) continued to withhold tax payments, take reindeer from the richer breeders, and travel in small bands through the Ob north. Pani and eleven followers were apprehended in the Yenisei area in 1856, having successfully avoided Russian authorities for fifteen years. Most Natives returned to a state of detached cooperation with Russian authorities, as an 1841 report from the Tobolsk governor to the governor-general in Omsk reveals: "In the Berezovo region there is a return to complete peace, with natives promptly paying taxes [*yasak*]."[13]

VAVLYO'S MOVEMENT AS REVITALIZATION

Since most local observers and subsequent analysts emphasized the military and political, rather than religious, nature of the movement, the extent and precise character of religious and ritual participation in Vavlyo's shamanic movement will never be known. No curious ethnographer made a scientific foray into Vavlyo's camp to chronicle what ritual preparations were made before the advance toward Obdorsk. But a clue comes from traveler I. Zavalishin (1862:286), who observed Nentsy and Khanty together dancing "voluptuous dances," and making nighttime sacrifices to communicate with and placate local Obdorsk water spirits. Led by a chanting shaman, offerings included metal money, pieces of metal, and a drowned reindeer.[14]

Vavlyo's political-military-spiritual movement bears only partial resemblance to the inwardly directed, passionate, and desperate Native American Ghost Dance, as practiced by the Arapaho. It is closer, however, to the rebellious Sioux version of ghost dancing that took place in 1890 at Wounded Knee (Mooney 1896:816–914). It is a revitalizing effort with a mixed-ethnic Native base. Vavlyo's vision of himself reportedly was first as a Neniang clan shaman, second as a reformist Nenets (Samodeic) political leader, and third as a protector of the Native poor (both Nentsy and Khanty) against Russian authorities. His movement broadened when he called on Natives to abandon ethnic differences, a preoccupation of Russian authorities, for a new level of indigenous solidarity.

As Vavlyo gained more understanding of Russian power, he increased his syncretic use of Russian political and spiritual symbols for his own shamanic purposes. Vavlyo's assertion that he had a mandate from the White Tsar when he returned from exile in Surgut in 1839 enabled him to gain the respect of Native followers. The White Tsar represented not only the highest Russian political authority but also a higher religious authority, who could be called upon for salvation in the same way that helper spirits were invoked by northern shamans. Vavlyo's exile itself became a shamanic journey.

The nature of follower response, the resonance of a (re)vitalizing message, and the framework of a leader's appeals are situational and culturally guided.[15] For Nentsy and Khanty living in the Obdorsk area in the 1830s, revitalization was desperately appealing, in the face of famine, devastation of local resources, and threats to the relatively free nomadic life-style that they had enjoyed until then, despite Russian rule. The Nentsy especially, as independent reindeer breeders with an egalitarian leadership tradition, found themselves unusually dependent on government grain stores, the Obdorsk market, and local Khanty leadership under Taishin. Their previous system of internal clan mutual aid was breaking down as poverty increased. Vavlyo represented a path toward individual and group self-respect, with appeals couched in terms of Obdorsk politics, anti-Russian emotions, and an adapted shamanic idiom.

While missionary activity had been meager among tundra nomads in the Obdorsk area, influential Russian Orthodox ideas of Saint Nicholas, the major God-in-Heaven, and concepts of sin had begun to affect local Nentsy and Khanty thinking (Veniamin 1855:114; Khomich 1976:40, 1979:12–28). Acknowledgment of Russian spiritual power, even if grudging, meant that certain aspects of Russianness needed to be coopted in order to be understood and defused. Vavlyo was adept at precisely this kind of cooption, placing new Russian ideas in the context of shamanic practice. The resonance of his message transcended the risks.

Although Vavlyo proclaimed himself a "tsar," he was aware of the limits of his power when he requested that the Khanty reindeer breeder Yaptika Murzin take Taishin's place, rather than doing so himself. This support for a Khanty leader may have reflected some knowledge of the Russian legal structure created by Count Speranskii's reforms of 1822, which placed the Nentsy, but not the Khanty, in the "wandering" or "migratory" (*brodiachii*) category and made the Khanty, as "nomadic" (*kochevoi*), relatively more subject to Russian control.[16]

Long-standing use of Khanty middlemen as culture brokers in dealings with Russians, together with the demographic context (Khanty were a majority in the immediate Obdorsk area, according to government tax records), also meant that a Nentsy leader might be less accepted and effective. The 1822 reforms gave Khanty, not Nentsy, control over local Native courts.

Vavlyo's hold over people stemmed from a combination of personal skill, political savvy, and ability to instill fear. In one incident, he first sweet-talked, and then bashed, a reluctant potential follower, a Nenets named Soi (Golovnev 1995:158). Khanty like Murzin had to overcome some traditional Khanty-Nentsy enmity to form an alliance with Vavlyo. However, precisely in the Obdorsk area in the 1800s, marriages between Khanty and Nentsy increased. Though Russian authorities tried to make neat ethnic distinctions for their records, Natives were less focused on ethnic group differences when pragmatic considerations overrode group loyalty. A few Khanty families consistently intermarried and traded with Nentsy, and many of Vavlyo's Khanty followers came from these lineages.[17]

Gifts of reindeer and the promise of a new political order were important factors in Khanty loyalty to Vavlyo. Further, his status as a renowned and respected shaman reinforced the material benefits, since it was advisable to be on good terms with strong shamans. Appeals to shamans often transcended ethnic boundaries in Siberia. The presence of Khanty in Vavlyo's camp involved political alliances that served as prelude to later ethnic boundary crossings and mergings. Even without full success, the movement may have accelerated processes that were leading to a mixed Nentsy-Khanty group or to comfortableness with multiple ethnic identities.[18]

Questions remain about Taishin's concern for his people's welfare in 1840, his alliance with Vavlyo in food redistribution plans, and the genuineness of his regret over his role in Vavlyo's arrest. Contemporary sources indicate that Taishin was an enemy of Vavlyo and a competitor for power that Taishin saw as best gained through the favor of Russian officials. The culture-broker "prince" Taishin had no formal control over his people in traditional Khanty terms. When Vavlyo offered Khanty something more rewarding materially and spiritually, some may have seen Vavlyo as their best chance to remain nomadic, to escape succumbing to a more settled life as hired laborers and fishers in Obdorsk.

Most significant, revitalization of one group can stimulate another's realignment of ethnic identities. Decisions about maintaining one's ethnicity can be flexible, especially given conditions of poverty, danger, and uncertainty on one side and tempting group acceptance, wealth, and prestige on the other. Whether viewed as a thief or a hero, Vavlyo clearly needed, and welcomed, all the followers he could get.

THE VAKH KHANTY MOVEMENT

Followers of a local Khanty dream-seer (*ulom-verta-ni*, dreams doing woman) convened at various sites along the Vakh River in 1896. Their activities constituted an intensification of traditional religious patterns during a perceived crisis. As such, their agitation was taken as a potential threat by local Russians and thus had political implications beyond what the original organizers intended. The Vakh Khanty movement was witnessed first by a local Russian forestry surveyor. He reported it to an intrigued government official and ethnographer A. A. Dunin-Gorkavich, who launched an investigation.

Dunin-Gorkavich (1904:44) recounted: "In 1896, a Vakh Ostiak [Khanty] had a dream, in which she saw that there would be a great sickness among her people. To prevent this, it was necessary to give up smoking tobacco, to build up stores of goods [Native and Russian], and to bring horses for sacrifice." These instructions became the core of a new movement, which Dunin-Gorkavich saw as growing specifically out of the "mixed" and unique combination of Christianity and traditional belief that local Khanty had developed. He concluded, "Christianity, not penetrated very deeply into the consciousness of the Ostiak, is mixed with their pagan approaches, with the result that new religious views combining Christianity and paganism have appeared, with predominance of paganism."

Following the first dream, and after the spring ice break-up, fervor and conviction were so great that word traveled in the region as far as the Ob River. Representatives of the ulom-verta-ni spread her message concerning massive blood sacrifices of horses, a renewed moral code, and altered relations with the Russians. The original dreamer and her growing number of followers held consultations with local elders in every community from the yurt settlements of Vartovsk (near the Ob) to Pokursk (near Lariach village). People arrived in the dream-seer's Vakh settlement, in panic and pilgrimage. The movement's influence extended over one hundred kilometers.[19]

The scale of the Vakh movement and its syncretic character make it striking. It combined traditions of shamanic predictive dreaming, kin-network mobilization, and sacred grove ritual with anti-Russian feeling, diverse offerings of Russian goods, and sacrifices of scarce and prestigious horses.

"It was decided . . . at various points to gather seven horses for sacrifice" (Dunin-Gorkavich 1904:44). The animals were brought to appointed groves and draped in white and black sacrificial cloths, made specially by women for this purpose (cf. Dunin-Gorkavich 1911:50). Seven horses were considered an ideal sacrifice, at a time when people, out of necessity, had become less rigorous in following traditional norms. As local resident Turskii (1898:30) explained, "The usual sacrifice is reindeer, but the most pleasing for the gods is considered the horse, because horses are rare and expensive." Sacrifice sites were mostly already sacred ancestral places, but some were dictated by the vision.

Sacrifices, as was customary, were pledged to ancestors through their images. They also may have been made to the Sky God Numi-Torum, with whom only certain shamans were said to communicate directly, to relevant members of Numi-Torum's family, and, especially, to the female smallpox goddess and the god Kul'-iki (or Kyl'-lunkh), associated with disease, the devil, and the underworld. The sacrifices both placated evil spirits and appealed to those gods or spirits considered best able to intervene in crises. While Dunin-Gorkavich focused on the "placation of enemy [spirit] power," other observers of Eastern Khanty sacrifices have stressed community appeals to ancestral gods.[20]

Substantial offerings of luxurious goods were made: "In the end of June 1896, goods valued at about seventy rubles were prepared near the yurt settlement of Nizhne-Vartovsk, and in the Pokursk area, the value in rubles came to about forty to fifty. Ur'evsk, Ivashkinsk, Komarovsk, and Pokursk Ostiak [Khanty] participated" (Dunin-Gorkavich 1904:44).

In early July, the Russian forestry surveyor stumbled upon a sacrifice and offering site in the Nizhne-Vartovsk area. It was situated on an island between the channels of the Chakhlonei and Ob Rivers, about four versts (2.6 miles) from the Vartovsk yurt settlement. High on branches of a sacred birch tree hung a reindeer skull, placed there after earlier sacrifices. On various tree boughs, goods worth more than was usual for Vakh groves were strewn. "There were designed and simple shawls, lengths of wool material, scarves, chintz, and calico cloth" (Dunin-Gorkavich 1904:44).

At yet another sacred site used for the horse sacrifices of 1896, near the Urevsk Khanty settlement, a forest grove sheltered a special stilt storage hut (*lobaz*), in which images of ancestors were kept, along with offerings of brass, pewter, and iron ornaments, cloths, and embroidered material. This Urevsk community grove was particularly rich, containing the offerings not only of Urevsk but also of Agansk and Tromyugan Khanty (Dunin-Gorkavich 1904:44). Their patrilineage affiliations made them natural associates during the stepped-up and enthusiastic pace of 1896 summer sacrifices. Lineage groups of the Vakh Khanty included the Tym-iakh, or Tym people, Vat-iakh, or town people, and Lar-iakh, "impure-quarreling" (mixed?) people.[21]

The health of the Vakh Eastern Khanty had been relatively better than that of Khanty in other areas up to this time, although they were well aware of devastating epidemics further south. Vakh Khanty were, by reputation, poor but proud, relying on squirrel skins for trade and subsistence hunting and fishing. They lived on the fuzzy border between the reindeer-keeping and horse-keeping Khanty, with many families needing to buy reindeer skins for clothing (Dunin-Gorkavich 1904:37, 41). Potanin had observed (187?:211) that Khanty of the Vakh-Vasyugan area were more influenced by Tatar traders and middlemen than by Russian traders and priests, and that some had "run into the woods from the Ob" to escape Russian influence. Alcoholism, though known, had not yet become a full-scale scourge in the Vakh region. And when Russians had tried to pressure some Northern and Eastern Khanty to move south and live a more settled existence, they had answered, "No, the soul does not want to; it is not good for the heart" (Iadrintsev 1891:197).

THE VAKH MOVEMENT AS REVITALIZATION

The Vakh movement was an outgrowth of Khanty lineage-oriented shamanic practices, made particularly dramatic and extensive by genuine and justifiable concern about Russian-associated sickness, probably the smallpox epidemics that had been sweeping Khanty and Mansi regions (cf. Nosilov 1904:14; Karjalainen 1922:362–64). As with many Native Siberians, Khanty sometimes personified smallpox as a female Russian spirit with unruly red hair. Only powerful shamans were deemed capable of taming her, through appeal to spirit helpers and gods, and success was by no means guaranteed. Called Ves-lunkh, the smallpox spirit was associated with the buckthorn bush, since its leaves were spotted like the skin lesions of smallpox. Sacrificial animal remains were sometimes draped on buckthorn bushes for her. The Vakh movement sacrifices thus were directed primarily against a horrendous and uncontrolled sickness, and secondarily toward acquiring general prosperity.[22]

The founder of the Vakh movement was a shamanic seer (ulom-vertani) with the ability to give warning of disaster, suggest prophylactic prohibitions and rites, and sense the presence of spirits (cf. Kulemzin

1976:52–53). But as a woman dreamer, she was not expected, or indeed permitted, to make the blood sacrifices her spirits had requested. These were carried out by esteemed elders and, especially, by two categories of shamans, the *ëlta-ku*, who had the power to do battle with Kul'-iki and other spirits of illness in séance, and the *isylta-ku*, who could extract (by sucking) evil sickness spirits from human bodies, often in the form of a worm or lizard. One who functioned as a prayer and sacrifice leader, or "spirit gatherer," was called *multé-ku* (Kulemzin 1976:61). The story of how the Vakh people became alarmed about sickness indicates how various kinds of spirit communicators could work together, and how one woman could influence a whole extended lineage system.

The mobilization of followers during the Vakh crisis of 1896 was a variation on ancestral themes. The ulom-verta-ni sounded a warning that was acted upon by male elders and powerful shamans, those best able to travel effectively across Khanty family and phratry lines. People also converged on her, making her village a center of sacred activity and her prestige unusual for a woman.[23]

Vakh Khanty considered dreams of both men and women shamans to be especially significant as direct and action-stimulating messages from ancestor spirits, as well as from various gods within Numi-Torum's pantheon, including Sankë, the Goddess of Light. Torum was variously referred to as Nagi-iki, White-Light-Old-Man; Allé-iki, Great Old Man; Torum-Vokh, God of Iron.[24] By the late 1800s, Kul'-iki (Kul'-Old-Man) was identified with the Christian devil. Also called Kyn'-lunkh, he was believed to eat the heart and control other sickness spirits (Dunin-Gorkavich 1911:36; Kulemzin 1976:107).

Among the Eastern Khanty, the ulom-verta woman (*-ni*) or man (*-ku*) was known to see a variety of messenger spirits in dreams, though it was usually a man termed *chirta-ku* who could dream about animal sacrifices and conduct them. Certain spirits directed the dreamers to create new sacrifice sites, enabling "that territory to become sacred, a place where a figure of the owner-spirit could be placed, where gifts would be brought" (Kulemzin and Lukina 1992:98; Kulemzin 1984: 114).

The Vakh movement was shamanic in its emphasis on animal sacrifice. Shamans were the dominant organizers of reindeer and horse sacrifices in times of sickness or poor hunting yields and at periodic lineage ceremonies (Shatilov 1931:120–28; Karjalainen 1927:245–331). The repeated sacrifice of seven horses during the Vakh crisis indicates a realignment of values, a return to standards of horse rather than reindeer sacrifice and to sacrifices of several animals rather than one. During séances in sacred groves, shamans were believed to be escorting the souls of sacrificed animals to appropriate spirits.[25]

The syncretic, changing nature of Khanty sacrifice symbolism is apparent through comparison of rare eyewitness accounts. One of the most revealing is Karjalainen's (1927:145–55) blow-by-blow description of a day-long cow sacrifice near Demianka, just south of the Vakh River, in September 1898, on Saint Simon's Day. While somewhat idiosyncratic, this sacrifice provides perspective on the rituals adapted to the crisis of sickness in 1896.

The sacrifice honored the Sky Goddess Sankë and a forest spirit ("Waldgeist") called Unt-tonx. It was led by an elder, who probably was a shaman. Active participants were males of the Demjanka area, who prepared themselves by washing their hands and putting on clean shirts. Early in the day, they carried household ancestral images from their homes to a sacred clearing near pine trees, just north of their village. The images were witnesses and focal points for the ritual.

Women related to the lineage by blood and marriage at first waited at the fringes of the sacred clearing. Dressed in homemade and imported finery, they came bearing berry cakes, fish in bread dough, and cooked fowl. Men prohibited them from going near the special white-clothed sacrifice table, the images, the sacred pine tree, or the hearth where men presided during sacrifice. Only after the ritual did they join the men in the grove, and even this concession may have been a relatively recent development.[26]

The sacrificial animal was supposed to be white and male, to assure that it was sufficiently pure to intercede with the Sky Goddess, but circumstances had prevented procuring such an exemplary beast. Instead, a nearly white cow, on which a copper bell had been hung and a white cloth draped, was tied by its horns to the holy spruce tree. The sacrifice leader waved branches of smoking spruce under and over the cow and over the offerings on the table. Standing on the west side of the clearing with the images, all the men then turned toward the rising sun, keening and praying. Women imitated at a distance. The leader spoke his prayer to the Sky Goddess (Karjalainen 1927:148):

> You are the light of the seven lights, O Sankë. You are the light of the six lights, O Sankë. I am bringing you a foaming, horned, good sacrifice. It is a good, foaming-mouthed sacrifice, bound to the holy tree. I pray for a long life. I pray for a long life span. I pray for a long life span for my little daughter . . . for my little son. For my arrow points, I pray for sevenfold good fortune. For my bow, I pray for sevenfold good fortune.

After praying, everyone turned and bowed in the four directions. Attention focused on the cow, whose white covering was hung on a nearby pine. The animal, with its head facing north, was stunned with an axe on the forehead. As the men cried out, the elder quickly knifed the cow's neck, so that blood spurted upward, toward the rising sun. Fresh blood was drunk by communicants and shared with Sankë. While the men fell to their knees, the elder again intoned to her: "The sacrifice you have demanded, I have brought. Do not be angry with me, for I present you with a drop of blood on the palm of a spoon, and in the curve of a ladle. Grant me a long life. Grant me the days of my life" (Karjalainen 1927:150). Bowing in the four directions resumed. Finally, the men poured some berry wine onto a pine bough and shared some amongst themselves.

After the sacrifice, a small offering area with a table was set up near the forest beyond the Sankë center, for a modest, separate, all-male ceremony honoring the forest spirit, Unt-tonx, with brandy and a prayer intoned at a fire. Although meat was not offered to Unt-tonx, the pattern of ritual appeal for lineage protection was similar to that for Sankë.

The men soon returned to the cow, turning its body three times so that the head described an arc like the sun. Participants simultaneously shouted at full strength. Each man dipped his index finger in throat blood and anointed his forehead. Wives and children then were summoned for blood spots to be placed on their foreheads. "In this way, good fortune was assured" (Karjalainen 1927:150–51).

The cow was skinned and apportioned; part of the meat (including the head, tongue, brains, and kidneys) was stewed in a huge kettle in the grove, and part was taken to individual homes. The lungs and liver were hung on a sacred pine bough, for the blood to run out. The cowhide, turned inside out with hooves attached, was draped on a special balance pole and hung between two trees, to ease the travel of the cow's soul eastward to the sky. When the stew was ready, topped with balls of grease, the sacrifice leader threw three chunks of meat and three pieces of fish cake into the fire, as offerings to the female fire spirit. After participants bowed eastward again, the leader and his wife served the stew to the participants and divided the sacrificial baked goods.

By sunset, the solemnity of the day and the strict division of gender roles dissolved into feasting and gaiety. When the company returned home, a sacred white kerchief with a black border and with silver and copper coins tied into its corners was left as an offering. In Demianka, where Khanty were particularly poor, it was permissible to recover the money the following day, and even to rescue the hide, for its trade value, after seven days. Some Khanty, according to Turskii (1898:26), were using the wealth of sacred grove offerings as an insurance system, removing some objects in times of need but promising to replace them in better times.

Late nineteenth-century sacrifices to sky and taiga gods reveal an ancient structural differentiation between sky and taiga, dramatized by the need for communication with each in a different area during the same major ceremony. In Khanty terms, however, the basic unity of these powerful cosmological providers contrasted with the impoverished world of supplicating humanity. With Russian contacts, the rituals changed timing (Saint Simon's day), incorporated wine and beer, came to include women, and deemphasized spears and saber rattling.[27]

Certain key symbols appear in Khanty ritual: blood for anointing, controlled fire, smoked (purified) offerings, the fortune-bringing number seven, ancestral images of metal and wood, and sacred trees (birch and pine). These are integrated with repeated ritual movements, such as bowing in sacred directions, keening, dancing, chanting in unison, and dexterous animal sacrifice. Animal skins hung on bushes and trees or made into altars become mediators between the earth and the sky. Such familiar cultural patterns were at the disposal of innovative leaders searching for new combinations of meaningful symbols that could coalesce to help confront, if not solve, immediate spiritual and all-too-material problems. This coalescence constitutes the genius of what the Vakh Khanty ulom-verta-ni did with her call to sacrifice seven horses at multiple sacred sites.

The sites chosen for the 1896 ceremonies reveal both traditional and contact-related association. The Nizhne-Vartovsk grove was an ancient lineage site, characteristically situated on an island, where the usual blood sacrifice offered to ancestor images had been reindeer.[28] Other sites had explicit connections with Slavic conquest and Christianity. Three Vakh River groves established during the contact period were directly related to Khanty religious ideas about Russian power. The first was near the mouth of the river Sabuna, at three tall cliffs where the first local Russian house (*Rut-kat'*) was built by traders in the eighteenth century. Shatilov (1931:106) speculated that Russians were perceived to have "great natural strength" and that therefore the place of the first Russian house "came to be considered the dwelling of a special spirit 'Pelia-Rut-kat-lunk' [cliff-Russian-house-spirit]." This Russian spirit place evoked fear and respect from Khanty pilgrims. It was a logical location for sacrifices in 1896.

Sacrifices were also performed in the sacred grove at the mouth of the Kolok River, already established as the site of worship of a Vakh Khanty ancestor-hero called Sarniang-avtav-Kantakh-kan (golden-haired Khanty-khan). This hero-prince of Khanty epics was renowned for fighting the original Russian conquerors who came to Ugrian territory.[29]

Other 1896 sacrifices took place on cliffs near Lariach village, where the first Russian missionaries had built their church on traditionally sacred land used by Khanty as a burial ground and a special place of honor for a helper spirit of Torum's called Vont-Iki (Shatilov 1931:105–

6). The Russian Orthodox chapel and subsequent full-scale wooden church established on this site ("to squelch the imagination of the Ostiak [Khanty]") came to be called Torum-kat, or house of God (Shatilov 1931:105–106). The Khanty did not distinguish this "Torum-kat" as different in principle from the storehouses they built in sacred groves to house their ancestral images. Into the twentieth century, they continued to make offerings to the clan spirits associated with the site.

The Khanty practice of moving sacred images and establishing new groves was in part a response to the early Christian missions and later, in the nineteenth century, to the fear that Russians would pilfer valuables left as offerings. Since these valuables increasingly included Russian money, scarves, cloth, and trinkets, Russians and Zyrians (Komi) were attracted to the goods. In the late 1800s, bitter complaints about thefts from groves or graves were recorded. Khanty voiced similar fears of sacred grove and grave robbery to me in 1976 and in the 1990s. Many consider this to be a key historical grievance against the Russians and Zyrians.[30]

Since pilfering was exacerbated with increased colonization on the Vakh River, organization of sacrifices in 1896 included the establishment of new groves in more remote locations. This enabled protection for the unusually valuable objects donated, an important consideration at a time when Vakh Khanty were becoming poor and reluctant to give up precious goods. Sacred grove wealth was in general on the decline (Poliakov 1877:59; Karjalainen 1927:66–166). The 1896 movement was a nativist and revitalizing reaction against the trend of stinting on sacrifices.

Khanty bitterness over thefts from sacred groves reveals a strong source of the anti-Russian feeling that permeated events in 1896. The very idea of massive sacrificing was a direct affront to Russian Orthodox missionary efforts in the area. Association of smallpox with Russian evil spirits further added to tensions that were especially strong in areas of partial colonization. Thus, the 1896 Vakh message, encouraging a return to previous morality and renunciation of Russian trade tobacco and alcohol, symbolized a Khanty yearning for an envisioned "pure" traditional life, unspoiled by the Russians.[31] This did not mean, however, that Khanty reformers wanted an absolute return to precontact conditions. They wanted Russian power and goods without the attendant corruption and disruption. One notable case reveals the degree to which Khanty had become dependent on Russian goods. A shaman was asked to divine when some gunpowder, late in delivery, would arrive at a local trade center. He reassured Khanty hunters that it would come soon, and it did (Dunin-Gorkavich 1911:48–49).

Ambivalence about the Russians was expressed symbolically in insistence on *seven* sacrificial animals, representing pre-Christian, possibly Turkic, concepts, coupled with the stipulation that the blood sacrifices should be horses rather than more accessible cows or reindeer. The sacrifice of seven horses simultaneously in multiple sites must have been a hardship for the Vakh River Khanty, despite immediate benefits derived in sustenance and community feeling from feasting in the groves.[32]

The moral message that spread like a torrent along the Vakh River included renunciation of trade alcohol as well as tobacco. Khanty men and women had become accustomed to smoking, and alcohol trade had begun on the Vakh near the Ob, at Alexandrovsk village, where even young Khanty girls were seen drunk (Sadovnikov 1911:5). Offerings to spirits of smoking and chewing tobacco were common among Ob-Ugrians of the time. Ancestral spirits were also "fed" alcoholic spirits (Poliakov 1877:59; Karjalainen 1927:69–166). Like the sacrificial meat itself, most of the spirit "donations" were consumed by participants in the grove ceremonies, so that some of the sacrifices climaxed in indulgences that the Vakh movement leaders were trying to curtail. In the 1898 sacrifice at Demianka, berry wine may have symbolized sacrificial blood. This homemade wine was preferable to that acquired from Russians. Dependence on Russian traders for vodka, brandy, or grain to make beer was discouraged in the 1896 movement to return to more traditional symbolism and values.

Another reform message, by implication, involved discouraging sexual relations between Russians and Khanty. The sacred grove sacrifices reinforced traditional kin relations, including the importance of observing Por and Mos marriage rules. This fit with a strong Khanty value of correlating morality, including sexual relations, with health (Balzer 1983). Some sicknesses were perceived to be the result of culturally defined "sins" involving human relations with each other and with spirits. Many Khanty saw sexual relations with Russians as a threat to traditional patrilineage social patterns and to interlocked physiological and psychological well-being. Khanty felt newly endangered at the turn of the century, when Vakh population growth was slowed, and syphilis had just begun to appear in the area (Sadovnikov 1911:5). The 1896 message may also have included a return to traditional rights of polygamy, as opposed to explicit and resented Christian emphasis on long-term monogamous relationships.[33]

REVITALIZATION THROUGH COMPARISON

The contrast between the Vakh movement of 1896 and Vavlyo's 1825–41 protest is striking. One was female inspired, secretive, revivalistic, and ritualistic, while the other was male, pragmatic, defiant, and militaristic. Yet each had roots in shamanic leadership, and both were anti-Russian. Although one was solidly Khanty in its membership and the other composed primarily of Nentsy, attributing the differences between the two movements solely to cultural differences would be inaccurate. Under other conditions, during early missionary campaigns and later Sovietization efforts, Khanty were more bellicose. Nentsy, in turn, quietly resisted some missionaries and kept certain sacrifice-oriented rituals secret from the Russians.

The Vakh and Obdorsk movements should be seen as revitalization attempts, as opposed to steady, ongoing processes of vitalization, because they represent creative indigenous reactions to perceived Russian-inspired crises. Siberian data invite focus on revitalization movements as sociocultural phenomena that need not develop into new institutions to be significant.

Settings for religious movements range so widely that general preconditions are unpredictable, but some proximate causes are discernable in hindsight. In Siberia, revitalization efforts became critical and visible only after extensive European contact and heightened colonial frustrations. The form the movements took was shamanic, although the degree to which an active charismatic shaman dominated them varied.

Some areas of ecological and social stress may appear to be fertile ground for revitalization movements but are devoid of them. While "insufficient charisma" or the lack of a prophet may be the "missing ingredient," leadership is not the only factor (Schwartz 1976:168). The cumulative nature of community-based religious fervor and the interethnic politics behind religious activism are also significant. A shifting political dynamic was visible in some of the alliances and battle-ready enmities formed in response to Vavlyo. A huge range of contexts for revitalization movements should be considered: "acculturation, colonialism, oppression, discrimination, class conflict, social disorganization, war and natural disasters" (Kopytoff 1964:88; cf. Trompf 1990).

In Siberia, ecological disasters, not necessarily "natural" in colonial contexts, were especially relevant. Both the Vakh 1896 movement and Vavlyo's initial campaign in the 1820s started with serious disruptions in the delicate Northern ecology, in the broadest sense of the term. The Vakh movement began with fear of an epidemic, while the Obdorsk movement was sparked by forest fires and a devastated tundra. Each situation led rapidly to famine and loss of hands desperately needed for subsistence. Such crises, including epidemics among reindeer as well as humans, had earlier been coped with by shamans who were believed capable of traveling to sky gods or to ancestral spirits to negotiate for prosperity. With increased colonist settlement, however, "natural" crises were often exacerbated by growing Native dependence on Russian grain that did not always arrive in emergencies. Shamans had to negotiate with new and increasingly unfamiliar forces. Although Russian trade and aid should have cushioned some of the blows, instead new populations in the North directly or indirectly caused some of the disasters.

Examination of local history can uncover serial movements that represent accumulated protest energy in a given area. Prior movements may be correlated to impinging state policy, external missionizing religions, internal cyclical patterning, or intensifying crisis fervor.[34] In Siberia, movements were more likely to grow out of existing shamanic practices than out of other movements, although they were triggered in relation to state policy and missionizing. From discussions with diverse Siberians, I am convinced that more such movements existed than have been documented.

Leaders of Siberian movements rarely envisioned the development of new institutions (religious or political organizations) to cope with new problems. The 1896 Vakh dreamer targeted her sacrifices to deal with a predicted epidemic, and the movement lasted less than a year. Local Khanty resumed using tobacco and alcohol. However, they had established new sacred groves farther from Russian depredations.

Other leaders, such as Vavlyo, showed remarkable staying power, accumulating followers for over fifteen years. He left a legacy of legends and one immediate successor. Just after Vavlyo came a smaller movement that developed around the shaman Pani Khodin (Togoi), Vavlyo's friend and heir to his authority. In 1856, Pani, with Nentsy followers Khydy, Ome, and Khorume, plotted a "rebellion" that was uncovered with the aid of Taishin and the Nenets elder Tepki Vankhoze (Tokarev 1936:110). His band, including at least one Khant, was violently apprehended and tortured. In one version, while in the Berezovo prison, he converted to Orthodoxy and was baptized as "Ivan." He later died in the "native hospital." Pani, according to Nentsy narratives, died or was killed in prison. But his spirit, in the form of a white-haired giant, returned to his home tundra, in the Gydan peninsula, where he haunted kin who had betrayed him.[35]

The most dramatically successful Siberian revitalization movement was Burkhanism.[36] It developed in the Altai Mountains in 1904, under colonial conditions similar to the nearly contemporary Vakh movement. Beginning with the visions of a charismatic leader named Chot and his daughter, it evolved into an established religion that buttressed the waning prestige and self-confidence of the Altai-Kizhi people by playing on their nostalgia for non-Russian rulers. Its elaboration was comparable to the Seneca Code of Handsome Lake, surviving after original leaders died or became martyrs.

MOVEMENT MEANS, GOALS, AND MESSAGES

Multiple means and goals may characterize a given movement, negating the value of simple classifications such as Linton's (1943) "magical or rational, revivalistic or perpetuative."[37] Vavlyo's campaign was at once aggressive, resistive, perpetuative, and rational. It also had some magical and reform aspects. Vavlyo mobilized massive protest, validated it in terms of syncretized shamanic tradition, and managed to bring together Khanty and Nentsy in a new version of Northern Native solidarity. The very process of doing this was perhaps as significant as the revolutionary goals Vavlyo did not accomplish.[38]

The 1896 Vakh movement was magical, revivalistic, and nonaggressive. One of the most significant aspects of the Vakh movement was its secrecy, which has made research on it particularly difficult. Secrecy had become a strategy for Khanty cultural survival, whether or not movements on the scale of the Vakh organization were involved.[39]

Questions like "Do the ends justify the means?" become significant for movement participants and their historians, although intense recruitment of followers can blur the line between movement "means" and "ends." In the Vakh case, impoverished participants may well have questioned the need to sacrifice so many animals at once, as happened nearly one hundred years later in arguments over reindeer sacrifices at Kazym. In Vavlyo's case, many Khanty and some Nentsy were repelled by his violence. Yet later, Native pride in his protest superseded critique of his methods.

The ideology proclaimed by a given movement provides clues to leadership appeal, changing cultural values, and interethnic relations, although discrepancies may arise between public and private messages. Initial messages are often couched in negative terms, revealing issues that have sparked community concern. The language of movement fervor thus tends to be oppositional: anti-Russian, anti-Anglo, anti-Christian, antipoverty, antisickness. Transition into more positive goals can be harder to make.[40]

The Vakh 1896 movement remained a limited ideological campaign against selected aspects of Russian culture and Russian-derived disease. Salvation was to be found through a stepped-up pace of worship of ancestral and celestial gods. By rejecting trade tobacco and alcohol, Khanty could at once reject Russian influence and promote self-reliance and community purification, as Mary Douglas uses this concept in *Purity and Danger* (1966:140–79).

Vavlyo's ideology extended beyond this to a dream of equitable reindeer and grain distribution and a balance of ethnic power in the Obdorsk region, if not eventual Nentsy hegemony. However, the discrepancy between Vavlyo's ideals of a new, more equitable social order and his own practice of gathering wealth and power as a tundra tsar was significant.

Vakh movement ideology began with a spirit-derived vision that resonated with Khanty respect for shamanic dreams and trance experience. It focused responsibility for the movement in a spiritual world and can be seen as originating in the culturally influenced "unconscious" of the dreamer (LaBarre 1971:20). But articulation of goals in Vakh settlements required deliberate elaboration on the original vision. Vavlyo's ideology came from conscious and careful politics, although he also drew strength from spirit helpers such as the bear.

Both leaders utilized a combination of traditional, syncretic, and innovative ideas in their appeals to followers. Innovation is often a matter of degree, defying standard anthropological categories and inspiring hope, no matter how "(un-)realistic." Although Vavlyo's movement inspired some short-term tax resistance among a few Nentsy and Khanty, it was less "realistic" in its generation of a new "cultural blueprint" than Altai Burkhanism or the Native American Ghost Dance movement.[41] It was an aborted revitalization effort. The Vakh movement was aborted less by politics than by sickness and despair.

To survive, movement ideologues usually try to create some balance between confrontational opposition and avoidance of violence. Leaders such as Vavlyo gauge risks of arrest. Repressing leaders can sometimes fuel a movement's fire. But advocacy of violence often represents an unrealistic assessment of the readiness of societies for "cultural revolution."[42]

FOLLOWERS AND ORGANIZATION

Siberian movements had ethnic, interethnic, and class appeal. Vavlyo's self-proclamation as a tundra tsar was an effort to impose hierarchy, autocracy, and coercion on a traditional kin-based network loosely built upon mutual aid, consensus leadership, and clan or tribal pride. The movement was proselytizing, and thus exclusive only in that it was anti-Russian and anti-official. Membership turnover was not great, and the movement grew steadily till 1841, when over four hundred families, representing several thousand people, had joined. Vavlyo's Robin Hood raids also provided some economic motivation for his followers.[43]

The 1896 Vakh movement was unstratified, local, and seemingly democratic, with its origins in the vision of one female dreamer and its loose traditional structure of lineage elder guidance. Its consistent membership was a highly homogeneous single-dialect group of Vakh Khanty, who united through the "communitas" of ritual for as long as the crisis of an epidemic held them together.[44] Spurred by the adrenalin of fear, proselytizing was rapid within already viable social and spiritual networks.

Given the dynamics of the Vakh movement, perhaps if one leader-dreamer had not arisen, another might have. Multiple terms for dream-seers and shamans reveal rich potential for spiritual leadership. The cultural and emotional content of the movement was as crucial as the personalities that led it. But follower fervor fell far short of what was needed to carry the movement toward institutionalization or Weberian "routinization."[45] Vakh Khanty returned to tobacco and alcohol consumption, as well as familiar relations with Russians, soon after the crisis had passed.

In contrast, Vavlyo was a larger-than-life figure, whose exploits spawned legends still told today. Several sacred places named after him remain. Some Northern Natives date events as "before Vavlyo" or "after Vavlyo" and believe that his spirit is still aiming accurate arrows at fur animals somewhere in East Siberia. One contemporary Nenets spoke admiringly of Vavlyo as "a big shaman, holding everyone in terror," while another saw him as "a brigand, thief"(Golovnev 1995:156). The success of heroes like Vavlyo is often ephemeral, and martyr "myths" about them do not necessarily translate into long-term cultural changes. Such heroes, however, can become symbols of ethnic and Native pride, as Vavlyo has for some Khanty and Nentsy, including the poet-activist Yuri Vella.

CONCLUSION: REVITALIZATION REDUX

Anthony Wallace (1956:265) defines a revitalization movement as "a deliberate, organized, conscious effort by members of a society to construct a more satisfying culture." He stresses the psychology and ideology behind culture change, rather than the material conditions that foster movements. His theory implies a striving toward unity of values and a coherent system of culture, as movements generate successful religions or revolutions and reach a "new steady state." Yet more recent anthropological analysis suggests that culture acts less like a system than a malleable and uneven filter, as does its interpretation.[46]

By stressing the importance of psychological resynthesis and cognitive consistency, Wallace may overstate the degree of change that revitalization entails. Even bulldozer-style revolutions must appeal to followers in a language they can understand (Gadamer 1976:64–68). The radical changes of the Russian and Iranian revolutions were accompanied by deep-rooted values and sometimes explicitly invoked sociocultural continuities, as their aftermaths have shown.[47] Further, once a movement has gotten under way, the very process, risky, ambiguous and exhilarating, can become its own stimulus, leading to repetitive, addictive patterns.

Analysts of revitalization need a balance between understanding radical transformation of values and nostalgia for variously defined "traditions" and concepts of "authenticity." Revitalization may lead to diverse, sometimes splintered versions of Benedict Anderson's "imagined communities" (1991:187–206). Revitalization movements can both build and break a community. Calling such movements "cults" diverts attention from their importance, or may radicalize them, particularly in colonial and neocolonial situations (cf. Trompf 1990).

In Siberia, different kinds of movements arose that addressed various ecological, social, and political crises. Nostalgia shaped the way these crises were addressed, without paralyzing participants in precise recapitulation of ritual. My focus here is on groups with varying degrees of politicization and heightened religiosity trying to recapture an idealized past in uncertain times. Socioreligious movements that focus on critical rejection of the past, such as that of the Indian (Native American) Shakers, do not fit this framework as well as some others do (cf. Smith 1959). Some recent Native American examples of intensified ritual vitality, including the spread of powwows and Sioux sweat lodges and certain renewals of the Sun Dance, fit better—although they do not attain the fervor of the Ghost and Prophet Dances (cf. Nagel 1997). Precisely those movements that quietly build religiosity through widening community identity and pride are those that last.

Revitalization studies can help clarify knotty theoretical issues of social process commonalities (colonization, missionizing, rebellion, revolution) without cutting down the forest of cultural diversity. The importance of cultural content in a given movement comes not from pan–Native American or pan–Native Siberian psychological generalizations, but from the nuances that emerge as self-identifying cultural representatives make an ideology their own. Examination of such processes for contemporary meanings enables a flexible approach to the politics of ethnic group formation. In Siberia, aborted revitalization attempts reveal Native frustrations and accommodations with representatives of Slavic culture. Few Siberian movements managed to move beyond Wallace's stages of "goal culture" formulation into viable long-term religions or revolutions. But the 1917 Communist Revolution, itself a kind of aborted revitalization for its participants, was to have a profound effect on Siberia, far beyond Christianization or indigenous-inspired agitation for change.

CHAPTER FOUR

Sovietization: Hot and Cold Wars

> My grandfather was taken. He never came back. What did they have to kill people for? We didn't have any reindeer. It wasn't our family who led the trouble. . . . But it is true, too, that our own people killed. They say some Khanty strangled people who came to investigate.
>
> (*Anastasiia Vagatova, 1991, on the 1930s "Kazym Rebellion"*)

LURCHING REVOLUTION, WRENCHING HOSTAGE CRISIS

SOVIET officials aggressively tried to instill in Siberian Natives creeds of Communism and friendship among peoples. As with their responses to Christianization, the degree to which Khanty shared the revolutionary spirit varied. Diverse, and sometimes contradictory, Soviet messages and means to accomplish change influenced Khanty receptivity. The unrealized ideal of a homogenized New Soviet Person, with little or no ethnic identity, permeated schoolrooms and Soviet propaganda. But in the Leninist creed, ethnicity could coexist with Sovietization, as long as ethnic consciousness did not descend to nationalism.

On the eve of the revolution, most Siberian Natives had little education, few livelihood options, and minimal involvement in the world beyond their local communities. That world came to increasingly impinge on them. After a confusing and sometimes violent start, some eventually experienced improvements in their literacy, career possibilities, and levels of political participation. By the late 1930s, some Khanty became genuinely patriotic, convinced that these gains were possible only under Soviet rule (cf. Grant 1995).

Soviet life in the Ob North began late and was marked in the early 1930s by one of the most violent and tragic protests in Soviet history. Like most such explosive dramas, including that of the derogatorily named Central Asian anti-Soviet fighters of the 1920s, "basmachi," it was suppressed literally and symbolically (cf. Paksoy 1992). Nearly unknown, the "Kazym rebellion," complete with a hostage crisis, disappeared into Soviet lore as one last gasp of anti-Soviet, antirevolutionary reaction. Without condoning the violence, I term it a "protest" here, since "rebellion" is the idiom of authority.

Collectivization eventually succeeded, if success is defined in Soviet terms of collective ownership and labor, rather than in terms of the human costs involved. Despite the typically haphazard cruelty of collectivization, local conditions modified standard Soviet chronologies and behavior. Close study of the dynamics of Sovietization reveals mutual influences between the center and periphery. Action and reaction can be discerned, rather than a steady line of "progress" dictated from Moscow. Ethnicity is shaped through struggle (cf. Ortner 1995).

REACTIONS TO REVOLUTION

In the North, the Soviet era began as a rumor. Gradually stories reached the Khanty of a Russian war, of the death of the tsar, and of "Lenin's New Road." Uncertainty plagued them. Most Northern Khanty were not directly involved in the wave of destruction that swept Siberia during the civil war, as Reds fought the White forces of Kolchak. However, Natives were aware of villages being torched in the Urals and on the Irtysh and of supply shortages that forced reliance on traditional subsistence patterns. Some were victims of gun requisitions that caused great hardship. Many were alarmed by the disruption of the Obdorsk market and the demise of earlier trade partnerships.

Farther south, Natives were more politically involved, occasionally using new conflicts to settle old scores. A few, including Zyrian, Khanty, and Mansi, were active as scouts and suppliers for either the Red or White army. Natives of the Narimsk area, including Khanty, reputedly sympathized with Whites. But at Demianka, some Khanty men attended a 1918 Bolshevik meeting. The Khanty revolutionaries Lukha Ernov and Afanasii Druzhinin exposed traditional Zyrian enemies as Whites and eventually helped organize Soviet collectives. A few Natives were caught up against their will on both sides of the conflict, at Demianka, Karymar, and Oshvorakh, and some were among the casualties.[1]

Local Russians first organized their soviets in 1921, but Khanty political organization began much later. In the Surgut region, "counterrevolutionary bands" raided Russians and Natives alike up to 1922, making organization difficult (Onushchuk 1973:43). On the Vakh River in 1921, Khanty took part in a so-called "counterrevolutionary rebellion" that left two Communists and at least one "Ostiak" dead (Kopylov 1994:199). As late as 1925, a few Russian traders collected debts incurred by Khanty hunters before the revolution (Startsev 1928:11).

Many Khanty did not realize until 1926–27 that Soviet power had been established (Shatilov 1929:83–84). They were uninformed about national-level politics, as indicated by one Kazym elder in 1976, who asked me with regret "why Trotsky ran away."

Backed by Lenin himself, research expeditions to Siberia, such as that of academic A. E. Fersman, concluded that "natives of the North are one of the great productive strengths of the country."[2] Idealistic representatives of the Tiumen Society for Scientific Study of the Local Region, such as its president L. R. Shulz (1924:1–9), supported ethnographic work among the Khanty and advocated economic reforms to put hunting, fishing, and reindeer breeding on a better organized, more scientific footing. Fishing was "nationalized" in the early twenties, as was fur hunting by the end of the decade. Some allegedly corrupt Russian traders were arrested and their supplies requisitioned.

To explain and implement economic and political reform, traveling Communist Party members held local meetings throughout the North. A 1922 "People's Commissariat" conference was held in the Tobolsk region at Samarovsk, to which Natives were invited. Although these meetings were supposed to establish "native soviets" (councils), giving new local leaders a degree of "autonomy" (with big-brotherly guidance), few Khanty, Mansi, or Nentsy appeared at Samarovsk. Native reticence and lingering "Great Russian chauvinism" led to official self-recrimination. Bureaucrats chastised each other for "completely ignoring the rights of national minorities."[3] Internal debates about Native governance led to adjustments of Tomsk and Tobolsk power, to a temporary form of "native soviets [*tuzsovety*]" and, most important, to the formation of a Committee for Assistance to the Peoples of the Northern Regions (the "Committee of the North"), on national and local levels (see appendix C).

THE COMMITTEE OF THE NORTH AND NATIVE GOVERNANCE

The Committee of the North, established in 1924 by the highest USSR governing body, the All-Union Central Executive Committee, had the formidable task of organizing the so-called "small peoples [*narodnosty*] of the North."[4] They were to be brought to the level of civilization that Soviet leaders considered appropriate for building Socialism. The Committee's mandate was to protect administrative, economic, cultural, and political interests of northern Natives, "considering the great economic and political significance of northern regions, on the one side, and the catastrophic condition of the tribes, its population, on the other."[5]

The Committee's founding members included Communist activists, president Petr G. Smidovich and the future minister of culture Anatolii V. Lunacharsky, as well as dedicated ethnographer-revolutionaries Vladimir G. Bogaraz (Waldemar Bogaras-Tan) and Lev Ia. Shternberg. Positions on initial policies were divided, with the northernists Bogaraz and D. E. Lappo advocating an "American-style" reservation system for Siberian Natives, to protect them from ravages of rapid change. Party activists pushed for a relatively more integrative political and economic approach, and won.[6]

Committee members worked through regular Communist organs and government ministries. The head of the Tobolsk Committee of the North, a Russian, was also a leader of the governing Tobolsk Revolutionary Committee. The committee sponsored journals (*Sovetskii Sever* [Soviet North] and *Severnaia Aziia* [North Asia]), scientific expeditions, conferences, and key legislation.

Legislation of immediate relief to Siberian Natives abolished taxes and provided supplies, especially bread, guns, and fishnets for those joining early cooperatives. Suspension of alcohol sales was greeted soberly, as were the confusing efforts of Russian outsiders to establish "native people's courts [*tuzsudy*]" and governing "soviets." Advocating the philosophy that Natives should have not only government "for the people" but "by the people," the committee established guidelines for Sovietization in its 1926 "Temporary decree on the administration of the native peoples and tribes of RSFSR northern areas." This crucial decree was oriented toward local conditions, taking into consideration scattered populations, kin-based labor networks, and seminomadism. The means for communicating government policy to Natives and receiving feedback was the "traditional clan" or other established social-kin grouping. Local meetings, local councils, regional Native congresses, and Native executive committees were established on the basis of "traditional" social organization.[7]

Existing clan or phratry elders became moving forces behind the new indigenous governing bodies, so that many Khanty did not at first view Soviet rule as a radical break with previous governance. For most Khanty, patrilineal kin groups already held specific usufruct territories communally; thus the aim of their elders was to protect traditional phratry access rights. Settled populations were administered territorially, while nomadic ones were given more leeway in defining their own "clan" or "tundra" soviets. Elections at first were poorly attended, since the Khanty perceived their elders as validly (albeit flexibly) established by age, kin status, charisma, and wealth.[8]

Russian "secretaries" usually ran local councils and regional congresses. Russians sometimes dominated these ostensible "tuzsovety," since most Native leaders were illiterate (Leonov 1929:231). Despite pressure from Communist Party members, women and youths were rarely involved in council meetings. When Russians tried to deny particularly rich Native elders voting and leadership rights, complaints arose. The Khanty considered these elders successful and therefore wise.

Traditional leaders sometimes approached their new roles in councils and committees as if they personified the institutions. Thus the head of a Native regional executive committee (*tuzrik*) could say, "I am the tuzrik" (Sergeev 1955:235). At this local level, a few Native leaders became active Soviet middlemen. They began, with varying effectiveness, to carry out centrally required tasks of census taking, registering movable property, aiding the poor with credit to buy reindeer, and monitoring illegal alcohol sales. They also coped with local disasters, including forest fires and epidemics. Considerable but uneven resources were available, derived in part from official requisitioning of fur-trader wealth and from government aid in goods (flour, grain, sugar, salt, guns, and nets), credit, and money. Resources were concentrated on settled Native groups, rarely reaching nomadic reindeer breeders.

A new hierarchy of courts was overlaid onto the indigenous political structure, with most cases handled by elders in their council meetings according to customary law, unless national law explicitly contradicted local.[9] Inspectors bridged the gap between government and local leadership. For the Khanty, this meant that practices of "bride price" (*netyn*, Khanty), polygamy, and animal sacrifice in sacred groves were technically illegal. But it was many years before indigenous courts (tuzsudy) consistently enforced these changes. Native, especially nomadic, courts operated in Khanty dialects and focused on resolving movable property and land use arguments by consensus among elders. Punishments included fines, community censure, public labor, and confiscation of property.

EARLY COLLECTIVIZATION, NATIVE RESISTANCE

Any Native illusion of status quo politics was shattered by the first five-year plan in 1928, with mounting pressure on Siberians to organize into cooperatives. Northern Natives slowly joined seasonal "integral" hunting and fishing cooperatives, organized around government trade and credit centers. Poor Southern Khanty joined more quickly, since they had few economic outlets for their fish and furs after private trade arrangements became illegal and many Russian trade partners were arrested. Russian Communist activists eventually organized reindeer-breeding cooperatives, such as the multiethnic "Kharp" near Obdorsk, with special distributions of reindeer, traps, nets, and guns to members. In 1927–28, the northern Tobolsk region had seven "native integral cooperatives" and sixteen trade points. By 1931, fifteen such cooperatives had been established, with fifty-four trade centers. About one-quarter of the Khanty were involved with cooperatives at this early stage.[10]

For the Khanty, advantages of early cooperatives included continuity with earlier norms of seasonal flexibility, local convenience, easy credit, prudent trapping, and other ecological practices. Laws passed by the late 1920s limited fur hunting and trapping to Native peoples, giving them an edge in the newly centralizing market. Trade centers affiliated with cooperatives bought or gave credit for meat, fowl, nuts, berries, and crafts of fur and birch made by Khanty women. This enlarged the range of products transferred into the Soviet economy. Trade centers sold grain, cloth, cooking utensils, guns, and ammunition at fixed, subsidized prices lower than those of private traders. Nonetheless, a few local Russians who had been fur merchants managed to run some of the new trade centers.[11] Some Natives considered the centers serious encroachments on their territories and their freedom.

Natives who joined the first cooperatives, also called "primary production units," had few formal obligations, other than to deliver fruits of their labor to government centers. Indeed, these cooperatives were nicknamed "wild" or "customary" artels. They took advantage of traditional labor groups (both kin and non-kin) who fished or nomadized together, although increased Native contact with Russian newcomers was also common. Their members became an important symbol of the poorer "classes" that Communists and idealistic action-oriented ethnographers wanted to save and elevate. If cooperatives had remained at this level of relatively voluntary and pragmatic association, many more Khanty might have become members in the 1930s. But Stalin's intensive collectivization campaign, devastating in the rest of the country, reached the Siberian north by 1930, and Siberian Natives were not immune.

For the Khanty, intensified collectivization meant attempts to channel the main economic activities of a region, for example, fishing or reindeer breeding, into one collective year-round "commune." Organization by locality rather than by ethnic or kin group meant that some collectives had a more mixed ethnic composition than previous artels. Most significant, some of the new communes tried to collectivize everything, from reindeer breeders' tents to fishnets and samovars. The process was involuntary, with Khanty roughly and hastily herded into collectives like wild reindeer. Local Russian party members and government officials, following ominously sketchy decrees from Moscow, frantically attempted to "complete the five year plan in four years," to introduce grain agriculture in hopelessly unsuitable northern areas, to "eliminate *kulaki* [rich exploiters] as a class," and to "collectivize all means of production."[12]

While some hunting, fishing, or reindeer-breeding artels remained seasonal and voluntary, others were turned practically overnight into *kolkhozy*, profit-sharing, locally run collectives.[13] In the Berezovo region, officials reportedly collectivized 85 percent of the population in one week, dispossessing both rich and middle-level households (Skachko 1934:37). According to those in 1976 who remembered this painful period, requisitions from Russians and Natives alike ranged from guns, traps, and nets to reindeer, cattle, horses, and dogs.

Officials who carried out collectivization orders were a mix of quickly promoted peasant sons from Russia, local Siberiaki of Cossack background, and veterans of Red civil war units, accustomed to treating noncooperative peasants harshly. With orders from Stalin's bureaucracy, such veterans were willing and able to nearly recreate civil war conditions. Some, with little respect for Ob River Natives, revealed chauvinist attitudes that were shocking to senior Committee of the North administrators like A. E. Skachko (1931:106). Abuses were especially rampant in the Berezovo area. Without bothering to learn Native languages or explain Soviet policy, officials misappropriated possessions not only for the government and new collectives but also for themselves.

Some of the new collectives were strikingly poor. An early reindeer kolkhoz called Khandy (Khanty), was established in 1930 near Berezovo with only five households, nineteen individuals, and ten "yearly workers" (Pervukhin 1930:79–80). All property was shared, as well as board and housing (five winter yurty and five tents). New communal housing was planned. Meager collective resources included sleds, boats, and thirty-eight nets. Members had only one horse, five dogs, and twenty-seven reindeer, but were allowed bank credit for 295 more reindeer. Although ten other families were expected to join, many Khanty reacted angrily to such impoverished collectives and to requisitioning animals.

The overzealous campaign created a backlash of complaints from its victims and Committee of the North officials. By spring 1930, Smidovich and Skachko sent an emergency telegram to local officials excoriating the mistakes of forced collectivization and "dekulakization." Communes had been pushed "without enough preparation" and "without active participation" of the poor (*bedniaki*), the laborers (*batraki*), and the middle layer (*sredniaki*). Smidovich and Skachko "sternly reminded" local activists that collectivization was to be voluntary and to begin with simple "integral cooperative production units" until a greater "class consciousness" had been developed.[14]

Soon after, the dramatic 85 percent collectivization statistics tumbled. Some new communes collapsed, with nomadic Khanty and Nentsy once again disappearing into the northern tundra.[15] Ethnic tensions accumulated. In one newly formed Khanty-Zyrian kolkhoz near Sartyn, Khanty requested separation from local Zyrians, who were called "overbearing" (Skachko 1931:106). After the request was denied, ethnic and economic tensions resulted in Zyrians (Komi) murdering Khanty.

Tegy and Kazym Khanty in 1976 recalled with bitterness Soviet efforts to round up livestock and to designate which areas would become fishing collectives and which would feature reindeer breeding. They did not view giving up family territories to collectives as voluntary, and they resented pressure to move from scattered, temporary winter and summer villages into established Soviet centers. Some Khanty, loaded with supplies, fled deep into the tundra to escape collectivization.

REGIONAL ORGANIZATION AND CULTURE BASES

The attempt to channel Native populations into collectives was paralleled by a new stage in the political restructuring of Native-government relations. Clan, band and yurt soviets had been mandated in 1926 only as a temporary measure, to give Natives time to understand Soviet policy. Soviet scientific researchers then had a chance to determine logical national-territorial boundaries for Natives whose group activities rarely extended beyond the phratry or local level, but who were aware of local ethnic differences. By 1931, the Ostiak-Vogul National Okrug was officially inaugurated as a basis for territorial jurisdiction of the Khanty and Mansi within the Russian Soviet Federated Republic. (It became the Khanty-Mansi National Okrug in the 1940s.) Whereas earlier the Khanty and Mansi had been spread amongst six regional districts, with their local councils subordinated to Russian-dominated regional centers, the new organization was intended by its Committee of the North planners to enhance Native participation in Soviet government and Native "self-awareness" of various levels of ethnic and national affiliation (Terletskii 1930:5–28). The new organization was also supposed to help streamline the economy, the transport system, the bureaucracy, and the settlement of nomads. As usual, local conditions produced a wide gap between ideals and reality.

Within the new Okrug were the following initial subdistricts: Berezovo, Mikoianovsk, Kondinsk, Samarovsk, Surgut, and Lariach, roughly corresponding to existing cultural and economic orientations. These local areas served as the bases for party elections to newly monitored councils and regional executive committees. Trusted Russian party cadres, often not from the immediate region, monitored elections and spotted "class enemies." Their major task was to encourage new and younger Native cadres, whose members could attend party congresses and then help enlighten local communities with accurate renditions of the party line. Only thirty Khanty were party members in 1930. By 1934, the number had increased to 121.[16]

The first Okrug Congress was held in 1932, with 118 delegates, 69 of whom were Native Khanty or Mansi, 52 of whom were already members of collectives, and 32 of whom were women.[17] The congress focused on the need for radical economic reconstruction and industrialization, through stimulation of indigenous cadres, literacy, and more stable local soviets. At the very moment when frightened northern Natives were absconding into the tundra, party planners were hoping to phase out "nomadic soviets," regularize the court system, and settle the population into collective centers and "culture bases."

Culture bases were planned predominantly by Soviet and Committee of the North leaders to impress Natives with the benefits of settled life near stores, schools, hospitals, and communication systems.[18] Developed in the late 1920s and 1930s, the bases were model villages in remote areas of Native resistance to Soviet rule. They were social experiments in culture change on an almost unprecedented scale, and in some areas, depending on their personnel, they worked well at providing initial services for skeptical Natives. Bases also were supposed to be research stations for gaining knowledge of local populations and resources. Only two culture bases were focused on the Khanty, at Lariach (on the Vakh River) and at Kazym. A third northern base served Khanty and Nentsy at Yamal, and bases were situated on the Konda and Taz Rivers for the Mansi. They served as centers for supplies, for adult education, and, crucial to Soviet planners, for political agitation. From these bases and from regional centers, Red tents and Red boats traveled with political activists and medical personnel who explained Soviet policies, from collectivization to sanitation.

When news that a culture base was to be built at Kazym reached the Khanty, some reacted with enthusiasm and helped to cut the lumber for its split-log buildings (Skachko 1930c:7). Propaganda emphasizing increased trade opportunity, rather than settlement or collectivization, may account for this initial reception. Some Kazym Khanty ominously expressed suspicion of the Soviet nickname for such bases, *kul't baz*, since their word *Kul'* refers to a specific evil spirit (Panov 1937:98).

The imposition of Soviet life on the Khanty was a fragmented process with mixed early results, depending greatly on the attitudes and personalities of Soviet representatives. Humanist-ethnographers like Grigori Startsev or M. B. Shatilov made more friends for Soviet rule than Russian officials of Berezovo who forced the Khanty into unproductive collectives. Most damaging to Soviet interests were zealots who imposed "class warfare" upon the North without understanding Khanty traditions or patterns of interethnic relations.

CLASS AND ETHNIC CONFLICT

After initially tolerating Native elder-based leadership, Soviet officials began "class warfare" in the North. By the late 1920s, targets were rich reindeer breeders, elders from well-known families (former "princes"), and shamans. They were lumped into a "class enemy" category of "kulak-shamans," who were to be denied voting rights in elections to councils.[19] Those with over seven hundred reindeer were heavily taxed and their reindeer confiscated by "people's courts." In the 1930s, however, many Khanty continued to admire and obey these traditional leaders.

In the more inaccessible villages along the Kazym and the Sosva, leaders urged mass sacrifices of horses and reindeer before sacred ancestral images, to sabotage collectivization and beg assistance from ancestors. Hundreds of animals were killed. A shaman named Iarkin was particularly active at Narikarsk as an "agent against collectivization" (Kartsov 1937:120). He was accused of organizing a plot to kill Soviet party workers, but the "conspiracy" was discovered and squelched, its leaders jailed. Party records reveal the arrests and trials of 70 "kulaks" in 1932, 91 in 1933, and 181 in 1934 (Kartsov 1937:120).[20] The fever pitch of purge-oriented condemnation of Soviet "enemies" that rocked the rest of the country had reached the Ob River area.

Party workers defined "kulaks" by an elastic range of activities, including bigamy, economic exploitation of orphans and female relatives, trade speculation, and ownership of large reindeer herds.[21] Since the Khanty did not necessarily view their elders as exploiting poorer family members when they offered them shelter and herding tasks, the concept of "kulak" was often difficult to communicate. Natives argued, "It is not right to divide one people into rich and poor . . . rich and poor live together in one life" (Sergeev 1947:136).

A few reindeer breeders did control large herds. In 1928, in the Pur tundra (north of Kazym), six "master-reindeer breeders" owned 10,500 of the existing 13,080 head of reindeer (Koshelev 1930:112–13). Around Kazym in 1930, the "kulak" Zakharov had about 3,000 deer, nearly half the amount of all other local herders combined (Medvedev 1931:47). For Russian activists like Sergeev, Koshelev, and Medvedev, these discrepancies represented class differences and injustice. But large-scale reindeer breeders usually functioned as patrons for Khanty extended families. Subject to enormous losses of reindeer during bouts of epizootic diseases, they could not easily build the aristocracy of generation-to-generation control that Russian ideologists presumed. A few well-known families had enjoyed prestige and power for generations, but this was mostly due to support from tsarist officials.

Many Khanty understood why some Russian and Zyrian traders were accused of exploitation. They had long resented certain traders, as evidenced in Khanty satirical plays and official complaints. But assumptions of criminality directed at rich breeders and shamans polarized northern communities in unprecedented ways, introducing new class distinctions between those who could benefit from Soviet power politics and those who could not.

"Kulak-shamans" reacted with bewilderment, defensiveness, and fascinating creativity. Some, like Zakharov, offered to pay new government representatives a "self-assessment" tax of five hundred rubles (Medvedev 1931:47). Others, who had been active in the "clan" or "band" councils near Obdorsk, insisted that they were identified with the revolution and that party workers should protect them against true "anti-Soviet elements."[22] Some temporarily gave reindeer to poorer relatives to make themselves appear less wealthy. Others hid their deer in collective herds. A few tried to take over the collectives, donating reindeer and designating themselves as best qualified to enhance the Soviet economy. They became collective presidents and labor brigade leaders (Kopylov and Retunskii 1965:167). Still others moved to areas where they were less well known to Soviet officials. Sometimes they too managed to be elected to new councils through kin networks (Sergeev 1955:356).

In official leadership positions, "kulaks" and their assistants could mistranslate the statements of party visitors or warn their followers about requisitions of reindeer. A red banner at the Kazym culture base proclaiming "Integral cooperatives—the path of natives from darkness and from kulak-shaman hegemony" was allegedly mistranslated as a warning for Khanty to run away (Sergeev 1937:112). Surgut Khanty leaders consistently translated "Soviet power" as "burty khon," the power of the Red Khan (Gudkov and Senkevich 1940:79). When the party worker Butinov traveled through the Obdorsk tundra, the president of a Native soviet called a meeting and announced: "A Russian has arrived. He is going to take away our reindeer."[23] Natives quickly disappeared from the meeting and the area.

At the "Khandy" kolkhoz, shamans were in charge of reindeer herds, while at the "Berezovo" kolkhoz, Native bosses, reputedly allied with shamans, paid their followers not to work. In other areas, shamans were accused of infiltrating collectives as herders to steal reindeer and even to spread epizootic diseases. In the Surgut area, two Khanty named Kuznetsov and Kondakov set up a rival artel to that of the local poor and garnered enough credit and trade so that the original artel failed. Having coopted local authorities and "middle-level households," they then disbanded their own association. Only later were they punished by an outside public prosecutor for economic disruptions.[24]

In 1932, two Native leaders named Khozianov and Shubin attempted to take over the Labovozhsk council of the Berezovo region. They organized a four-day "shamanic festival," during which they allegedly plotted to undermine the council by demanding new elections. The "party cell" of the region had "great difficulty" diverting "the masses" from these "kulak influences."[25] Similar trouble occurred at Shuryshkar (near Berezovo), where "kulaks" packed the local council with shamans. Throughout the Ob North, Native leaders bought votes with reindeer or trade goods and held "illegal" meetings parallel to those of party agitators. As a direct result, Native councils voted resolutions condemning new trade arrangements, schools, and female participation in meetings (Pervukhin 1930:82).

Besides attempting to subvert the system from within, Native leaders sponsored direct economic and political opposition. Such opposition was pronounced following the harsh collectivization campaign, when party workers laid themselves open to legitimate accusations of abuse. In Polnovat, a delegation of Khanty threatened to kill all cattle, horses, and reindeer if supplies were distributed solely according to the state's economic plan (Kopylov and Retunskii 1965:167). In the tundra, wealthy breeders bought as many reindeer as possible to prevent them from going to collectives and also required debts owed to them to be settled with valuable polar foxes, in order to prevent those furs from reaching government trade stations (Orlovskii 1930:51).

Far from easily giving up family territories and prized herds, some Natives directly fought government representatives. Such "rebellion" usually led either to jail or escape into the tundra. Near Lariach in the early 1930s, a Khant named Prysin killed the president of an integral cooperative and set fire to the cooperative's trade center. He was arrested, tried by a Soviet court as a "kulak" and "terrorist," and undoubtedly shot (Kopylov and Retunskii 1965:69).

THE KAZYM PROTEST

The most dramatic and extensive opposition to Soviet rule in Siberia occurred in the early 1930s in an area encompassing Kazym and the sacred lake Num-to, 150 kilometers east.[26] Many Khanty and Nentsy refused to send their children to the culture base boarding school or to participate in local cooperatives and elections. Some, defined as "kulaks," had lost their right to vote in local meetings. A respected Khanty elder, Ivan Andreevich Ernykhov, who earlier had been chosen as head of the Polnovat village council, decided to gather Khanty in meetings. He sent a wooden staff, "shum-ty-iukh," carved with his family symbol (*tamga*), around to various Khanty families of the whole Kazym river system. The first meeting was held at the camp of Maksim Petrovich Kaksin and a second, more numerous one at the mouth of the "Vozh-egan" (Vosh-yugan) at the base of the multigenerational Moldanov family, whose forbears had been princes under Tatar and Russian rule. Sources differ on the numbers involved, but from twenty-nine to forty Khanty men (rich, poor, and in-between) came to these meetings. They decided to "collect all of the Kazym people, advance on the culture base, and make demands of the Russians."

Decisions and demands included:

- "countermand the taxes on kulaks and return their voting rights and rights to participate fully in meetings and local judiciary councils";
- "take all children from the school, refuse to give any more children up, and thus effectively close it";
- "refuse to give any [further] aid to the culture base, whether in reindeer, wood, or labor";
- "fish, furs and reindeer should be sold freely and not by government demand";
- "remove from the Kazym culture base and the Num-to lake their Ural-fur processing points";
- "reelect the local council, since the current one had not supported the interests of the natives, particularly by allowing children to be taken to the school."[27]

The meeting climaxed with a séance and a blood sacrifice ritual (*pory*), led by two Moldanov shamans, of fifteen reindeer. Using the sacrifice to communicate with the spirits (*lunkh*), the shamans announced that the spirits approved the demands, concluding, "It is not necessary to bow to the Russians, and those who do will be punished" (Golovnev 1995:168).

By December 1931, a fresh gathering at the Khulor yurts attracted 150 people, armed with hunting weapons and resolve. Danil Ernykhov with a few others was sent to the brothers Petr and Andrei Nemysov of Polnovat village, so they could widen the movement to all Ob River Khanty. Fifty more were sent to Kazym to collect the children. Those remaining in Khulor hoped to have officials come to them, but men returning from Polnovat ran into four worried Berezovo officials, who convinced them to hold a general meeting in Kazym. The Ob Khanty based at Polnovat, allegedly numbering as many as 300 to 320, decided not to wait and scattered.

The Kazym meeting of January 8, 1932 went poorly for the Russians. When officials tried to oust leaders Ivan Ernykhov and Vasily Zakharov (known as Vas'ku-Sorum) as kulaks, Native participants replied, "We do not have kulaks. All are equal, and all must participate in the meetings and in decision making." In this mood, participants changed part of the Native council (tuzsovet) leadership, naming the elder Prokopii Spiridonov as head and approving some of the Native demands. This included not allowing Russians to fish at "native rivers and lakes" (Golovnev 1995:170).

Russian officials decided on a new tactic, arresting "kulaks" one by one. One of the first victims was Sergei K. Moldanov in spring 1932. Pavel Tarlin, Maksim Kaksin, and Ivan and Timofei Moldanov later were arrested and were given three- to five-year sentences for anti-Soviet, especially antischool, activities. Frightened and ill-provisioned Khanty, including members of the Moldanov, Kaksin, and Ernykhov families, disappeared into the Kazym tundra to nomadize until the crisis passed. This was later interpreted as spreading anti-Soviet agitation. Despite dispersion, they vowed to continue seasonal and emergency rituals.

A relatively small midsummer sacrifice took place on the Liamin River at the yurts of Ivan Tarlin.[28] Local Khanty family heads, led by at least one shaman, sacrificed several reindeer. Rumors spread that shamans at an accompanying séance in Tarlin's tent had seen a vision "from on high" of "Whites [tsarists] returning on ships and routing the Reds [Bolsheviks]."

At a fall sacrifice in 1932, about thirty Khanty of the Kazym region gathered, voting to elect Kirill Ivanovich Senchenov as an *eesaul*, or spokesman. In a sacred grove described as "Lunkh-khot" (Spirit-place), two shamans, Andrei (Khrom) and Nikolai Moldanov, confirmed that the *lunkh* predicted the return of tsarist power and the demise of the Soviets. Khrom suggested reinforcing contacts with the Nentsy. Many also agreed to "live in the tundra two to three months until the Whites come."[29]

The Whites did not come, and by the summer of 1933, further trouble was brewing at Num-to (Spirit Lake), sacred to both Nentsy and Khanty, and also called Torum-lor by Khanty. The secretary for the Ostiak-Vogul Communist Party, A. Ia. Sirson, reported:

> Nentsy are harassing a fishing brigade at Lake Num-to, threatening to burn the [Kazym] culture base, and demanding the freedom of the four im-

> prisoned Ostiak kulaks, arrested by the OGPU [secret police] in connection with the Kazym events of winter 1931–32. . . . In spring 1933 the Kazym culture base sent a fishing brigade of Ostiak and Russians as part of their "integral cooperative." They did not consider that the lake has an island sacred for Nentsy.[30]

Inconclusive negotiations ensued, and, consonant with the harsh times, some of the more conciliatory Russians were removed from their jobs. Natives came to view each Soviet action as "Russians preparing for war" (Golovnev 1995:172). A larger sacrifice of twenty-one reindeer was organized in November at the sacred grove Tor-Khop-Iukh-Pai. At least forty-one Nentsy and Khanty men attended, and the large number of deer sacrificed attests to sacred symbolism (three times seven) and to the growing crisis. Participants, electing Efim Vandymov (Yän kow-iki) as leader, decided not to allow Russians to fish at Num-to and to fight with them if necessary. They also discussed the possibility of taking hostages to get the four arrested men returned to the community. Through the shamans Khrom and Grigori Moldanov, the lunkh confirmed that Russians should be "captured and tied up" (Golovnev 1995:173).

At this point, the elected tuzsovet leader Prokopii Spiridonov appeared and over tea mentioned that arrest warrants were out for eighteen more kulaks. His main message was that the Russian authorities wished to speak only with Nentsy living at Num-to about the issue of fishing there. But he was sent back with the answer that it was a matter that concerned more than a few Nentsy families.

Eager to avoid violence, Prokopii Spiridonov was active in providing assurances on all sides.[31] Spiridonov, an elder who had dramatically cut his long traditional-style braids, had been a delegate to party meetings in Samarovo (later called Khanty-Mansiisk), and had collected Khanty children for the Kazym school. His adult sons, however, sided with the protesters, and his own sympathies were wavering during his middleman role.

Tension escalated with the arrival at Num-to of a group of Soviet officials sent to investigate the Native complaints. Led by the Russian (Yenisei-born) president of the Berezovo District Executive Committee, Petr V. Astrakhantsev, who had directed the construction of the Kazym culture base, the distinguished group included a woman named Polina Schneider, head of the Ural Communist Party Regional Committee, and Zakhar N. Posokhov, the first Khanty Chekist (member of the secret police). "Comrades" Smirnov and Nestorov, Russians in charge at Kazym, and two Native guide-translators (E. Kaksin and P. Voldin) completed the group. As they slept, a séance was held during which the lunkh confirmed that the Russians should be killed. Participants agreed that the signal to take them should be the cry "ta-ta," Nentsy for "hold, hold," so that the Khanty translators could not understand.

In the early morning, to Efim Moldanov's cry of "ta-ta," the seven-member brigade was taken, beaten, and tied. An unlucky eighth, G. Nikitin, was taken as he arrived with a message for Astrakhantsev. Khanty and Nentsy delivered an ultimatum:

- "Return the four arrested Ostiak immediately. If not, consider the hostages killed";
- "Close the boarding school and return the children to their parents";
- "Abolish the levies on kulaks, and submit no more cases to the courts . . . return voting rights to kulaks";
- "Take no more reindeer for the culture base, and require no further Native labor there";
- "Change the norms on furs and fish collection, and let us buy products for money";
- "Close and remove all trade points in the Kazym tundra, and forbid Russians to fish at Num-to";
- "Have all Russians leave Kazym; otherwise we'll wage war and oust them with force."[32]

Spiridonov and Nikitin, who had written the demands, were sent back to Kazym, leaving guides Kaksin and Voldin as hostages. Spiridonov, caught in the middle, said that if his elected leadership was not acceptable, the tuzsovet should be reelected. At Num-to, shamans again began a séance and divined with an axe. The axe was heavy, "sticking to the table," which meant that "the Russians are destined to be killed."[33]

All the hostages except Kaksin and Voldin were bound to sleds and led to ritualized (sacrificial) deaths. Later Mikhail Ia. Moldanov testified: "We left the camp of six Samoyed [Nentsy] tents, going the distance of a dog's bark, and reached a tall hill. Circling this, we stopped; then we led the sleds on which lay the tied Russians to the hilltop, and there took them from the sleds and undressed them."[34] Then they were strangled with nooses and placed on the ice of the lake. The strangulation occurred in sync, with all participants pulling on the rope ends together. "This way responsibility for the crime lay on all the Khanty and not on separate people." In a chilling postscript, Astrakhantsev's wife claimed the bodies were scalped, raising questions of hearsay or specters of ancient soul beliefs.[35]

Some accounts described the contingent of Khanty and Nentsy who sacrificed the brigade to be three hundred strong, though it was more likely well under one hundred. Armed only with hunting weapons, the "rebels," including the Moldanovs and the Spiridonov sons, allegedly threatened again to burn down the Kazym culture base and even to destroy the Soviet establishment at Berezovo. While waiting for the return of the jailed Khanty, they instead received further Soviet messages and calls for meetings. An indication of how desperately far apart the two sides were can be seen in a letter of December 25, 1933 from the president of the Ural Regional (Oblast) Court, Chudnovskii, to the Num-to leaders:

> These [brigade] members have conducted themselves as Soviet people and in no way deserve your displeasure . . . the personal weapons which they had, they not only did not use against you, they did not even reveal them. The people who are being held by you have committed no crimes against you and intended no evil. Even Zakhar Posokhov, who has arrested various Ostiak kulaks, is personally not guilty before you, since, working in government service, [he] was fulfilling written orders. . . . If he had not followed these, he would have had rough punishment. Especially grave is your breaking of the law in detaining . . . Astrakhantsev, chosen by the people of the Berezovo region. In taking the brigade with the intention of an exchange for four of your convicted people, you have broken Soviet law in an unprecedented way. Indeed, your people in their turn were arrested for counterrevolutionary activities against the worker-peasant government and were judged in an open court. . . . You, under the instruction of evil people, have treated the brigade treacherously.[36]

The rebels began to split among themselves and worry about provisions. Rumors of Ob Khanty support reached them, but so did the information that a special operative group of the OGPU had arrived at Kazym. A posse using some of the first planes seen in Siberia chased the rebels through northern tundra and forests for eight months. Few resisted arrest, although the Khant Grigori Sengepov and his wife were killed as they tried to fend off OGPU operatives. Eighty-eight were apprehended, with thirty-four eventually released for lack of evidence or time served for "petty crimes." Three died before sentencing, among them the elder Ivan A. Ernykhov, who died (suspiciously) of "heart failure and lobar pneumonia." In June 1934, the Ob-Irtysh regional court found fifty-one Natives guilty of rebellion and deserving severe punishment, including fourteen sentenced to death for treason. In the social categories of the day, twenty-four were kulaks, thirteen were shamans, nineteen were middle level (sredniaki), and eight were poor (bedniaki).[37] All property of the guilty was confiscated, including from 979 to 2,000 reindeer (depending on the account), furs valued over 2,000 rubles, and all shamanic accoutrements (most going to the Berezovo regional collection). Spiridonov, his sons, Efim Vandymov, and many Moldanovs were among those arrested. Some, however, remained hidden in the Yamal tundra, where they were accepted by the local nomadic groups. Others sheltered in the regions around the Nadym, Pur, Taz, and Yugan rivers.

The Kazym protest was a foiled, last-ditch effort to assert some Native control over a frightening new Soviet order, seen by many Khanty as waging a lopsided war on themselves and their way of life. As Khanty consultants looked back on the "rebellion," whispering hints to me in 1976 that grew louder in 1991, they remembered the out-of-control protest as sparked especially by unrest over the new Kazym boarding school (*internat*), built literally on the graves of some Khanty families. The four Khanty fathers, arrested (among other reasons) for refusing to give their children to the new school, became heroes. Khanty recall that local outrage was compounded when schoolchildren were taken by force from their homes and housed in the boarding school during a rumored smallpox epidemic.[38] Khanty strongly associated sickness and unpalatable food with the Russians. The children reputedly were not allowed to return to their homes, for health reasons. Their families converged on Kazym and prayed for the deliverance of their children and themselves from incomprehensible Soviet policies. Led by shamans, they addressed, through reindeer sacrifices, the important female ancestress whose image was housed in a famed sacred grove near Yuilsk. A Soviet "brigade" of seven elite Communists, sent to quell the disturbance, violated sacred space at Num-to and was taken hostage to bargain for the return of jailed Khanty, but was killed when Khanty releases were rejected.

The Khanty writer Eremei Aipin (1990a) has described how Khanty secretly passed on stories of this "so-called Kazym war," which lasted by some accounts into 1935. Attributing the main cause to the "devastations of collectivization," he explained that Khanty leaders "wanted to reestablish full electoral rights, change the punishments against kulaks, recreate the Native Council, change the basis on which furs were given to the government, close the boarding school." Most of all, "Khanty wanted themselves to orient and control their own lives," according to their own spiritual beliefs (Aipin 1990a:24).

The Khanty activist Tatiana Moldanova has described the suffering and embitterment of her people during and after the rebellion, and how difficult it was for the remaining women and children to survive the winter. When men of her family were arrested, "two came into the yurt: one armed Russian and one well-dressed, nonlocal Khant in furs. Already, on their many sleds, sat Khanty, tied up two by two."[39] Her grandmother had premonitions of trouble when their clan spirits refused an offering. Anastasiia Vagatova, whose voice opened this chapter, moaned that members of her family had been swept along in "the trouble" and arrested without justification.[40]

The magnitude of this joint Khanty and Nentsy attempt to retaliate against perceived injustice reveals how politics in northern Siberia had become acrimonious, dividing people along Soviet/anti-Soviet, religious/antireligious, and Russian conciliator/Russian hater lines. Ethnic differences played an important role, with old anti-Russian or anti-Native prejudices emerging during collectivization, party meetings, and purges. In addition, radical social change made everyone victims, caused by the unhealthy cycle of forced reform by order and counterorder from above. In Kazym, neither industrialization nor the need of urban populations for grain could excuse the brutality, accusations, involuntary settlement, and misunderstanding of Native values that characterized Soviet rule. In response, the Khanty and Nentsy "rebels," panicked and desperate, resorted to hostage-taking tactics that had not been used since the first century of Russian rule. The resulting shamanic sacrifice, allegedly endorsed by the spirits, was as frightening and confusing for some of the Natives themselves as it was for the Russians. It left a legacy of sorrow, cynicism, and, for a few, enough desperation to attempt suicide.

CONCLUSION: DOMINANCE, PATERNALISM, AND ETHNICITY

At the start of the revolution, ethnic identity was often fluid and situational. Some Khanty used the revolution as cover to compete with their "traditional" enemies, the Zyrian (Komi). Others joined with Nentsy against Russians. While the Soviet period may have sharpened ethnic distinctions by formalizing categories and boundaries, in documents and on the ground, Soviet officials hardly invented politically useable concepts of ethnic difference (cf. Bremmer 1997:3–4).

Idealistic reforms by some Russian culture-base organizers attracted a few elders like Spiridonov, who shared their goals of literacy, economic equality, and social dignity for Native Siberians. Like younger progressive Natives at party congresses in the newborn Okrug, Spiridonov judged Soviet Russians as individuals, not stereotypes. This made repressive Soviet policies and resource failures especially disillusioning, since they violated a fledgling trust.[41]

By 1935, when Native Siberians critically needed protectors and leverage in Moscow, the Committee of the North was disbanded, officially because it had fulfilled its mission but probably because its sensitivity to local conditions had become a dangerous luxury. Some of its functions were assumed by the development-oriented Main Sea Route Administration (Glavsemorput), including operation of culture bases. But an official editorial concluded:

> The culture bases of the Glavsemorput, which are supposed to be centers for all kinds of cultural organizations in the Far North (schools, hospitals, public baths, veterinary stations) do not justify themselves and are in de-

> plorable condition. In spite of large appropriations, the construction of culture bases is far from completed, . . . Attendants are using hospitals, veterinary stations, etc. for living accommodations. . . . All the culture bases are suffering greatly from a shortage of teachers, doctors, agronomists, and other specialists.[42]

By the late 1930s, political activism was reduced to cover-ups and mutual recrimination, leading one Obdorsk official to see "disorientation of the whole party organization" (Serkin 1937:10). Many cadres, according to Serkin, obeyed the old Russian proverb "Do not throw the dirt from the hut." Thus, they hid resource shortages at culture bases and at new fish- and fur-processing plants. They failed to explain local Soviet elections and Stalin's new constitution to the Natives, yet blamed "class enemies" for the low level of Native participation in the new plants and logging camps and for fur trading that resembled the old exploitive merchant style.

The Khanty learned to approach Soviet authorities cautiously through limited economic contacts, sometimes working as temporary wage laborers at processing plants and logging centers. Some treated Soviet life as an extension of the tsarist period. Miasnikov, a prize-winning ("Stakhanovite") worker pinned his various Soviet awards next to an old tsarist medal (Serkin 1937:9–15). Many tried to retreat further into back-river areas.

Double standards and paternalism were evident in the slow integration of Native leaders into Soviet life. Soviet political culture under Stalin was plagued by numerous, often contradictory decrees. Leninist ideals affirmed the rights of national minorities, but Stalinist violence was condoned against individuals who embodied those ideals. This was more than a simple discrepancy between ideals and practice, since ugly purges came to have their own set of justifying standards. In the Siberian multiethnic environment this translated into the emergence of simmering Russian chauvinism in some officials, who at best considered Natives "naive," "childlike," and ruled by "kulak-shamans." Lip service to the need for Native cadres was accompanied by Russian domination of most councils, conferences, and collectives.

At Kazym and Num-to, the Native reaction to Sovietization was bitter and extreme. The Soviet counterreaction was massive by any measure of human injustice. On December 29, 1993, after a Native petition, the public prosecutor of Tiumen Oblast looked over the records of the Kazym protest and refused to rehabilitate forty-nine participants.[43] This did not stop the cycle of pain. In addition, certain streets of Berezovo are still named for the hostages and the OGPU officers Kibardin, Durkin, and Solov'ev who died trying to arrest Grigori Sengepov. Natives in the 1990s whose kin participated in the Kazym protest feel a special solidarity with each other. Many have become leaders of ethnic revival efforts.

The Kazym "rebellion," stimulated by a clash of values and executed with a lack of international or even national publicity or awareness, represents one of the major hostage crises of Soviet history. It is a shame that the Khanty involved knew nothing of what later was to be termed the "Stockholm syndrome," when hostages become sympathetic, even empathetic, to the cause of their captors. Indigenous leaders could have used the empathy of a high-level Soviet brigade. Instead, one of the Khanty leaders, the shaman Iakov P. Moldanov, clinched the argument that the Russians should be killed by observing, "no matter how long one holds a fox, one still cannot feed it enough."[44]

CHAPTER FIVE

Sovietization: Hearts, Minds, and Collective Bodies

After boarding schools, and after the army, who is going to want to herd all year, to live in a tent?
(Kazym reindeer breeder, quoted by the Khanty journalist Klepikov, 1967)

PROPAGANDA AND PRIORITIES

ONCE overt rebellion was quelled, Sovietization became a bumpy process of political indoctrination and economic change, influenced by fluctuating Moscow-directed policy, pragmatic behavior of local officials, and complex Native responses. Development for some meant hardship for others, especially in the Stalin period, but also with the discovery of oil in the 1960s. An amalgamated version of the principles of MELS (Marx, Engels, Lenin, and Stalin) may have guided change, but they were interpreted extremely loosely (cf. Humphrey 1983).

In the Soviet literature, massive Northern economic and development programs were described as catapulting Siberian Natives "from patriarchalism to Socialism," while bypassing the Marx-ordained stage of capitalism (Sergeev 1953, 1964; Uvachan 1971; Kiselev 1974). A parade of leaders, from Lenin to Gorbachev, provided theoretical and political justifications for this unconventional leap, supported by scholars (Kartsov 1937; Sokolova 1971a; Gurvich 1985) and local officials (Loshak 1970:11–56). The propaganda picture of ethnic interaction, social progress, and economic development was often unquestioningly positive, although perceptive exceptions occurred even before "glasnost" (Sokolova 1971; Pika 1982) and increased with policies of openness (Arutiunian and Bromlei 1986; Simchenko 1992; Pika and Prokhorov 1994).[1]

In two major areas, officials were determined to make radical changes that could lay the groundwork for more thorough Sovietization of subsequent generations: gender relations and the settlement of nomads. Only when these perceived problems were managed (never really solved) could "consolidation" of collectivization and education ensue. This consolidation was followed by extensive economic and political "development" in the postwar Soviet period.

GENDER AND THE SURROGATE PROLETARIAT CONCEPT

Committee of the North conferences stressed that Native women were an "oppressed" and "backward" class, prone to "cultural survivals" and in critical need of literacy.[2] This became the crux of an ideological argument that placed women in the forefront of the early Soviet cultural and political revolution. If poor workers were hard to find in nonindustrial societies, then surely, the objectifying argument went, the closest thing to a true proletariat in such societies must be the oppressed women, sighing in place of the masses.

This ideology-driven policy was famously foregrounded by Western historian Gregory Massell (1974), who focused on propaganda to bring Central Asian Islamic women into an unveiled Soviet fold. Interestingly, the parallel between Central Asia and Siberia goes further than a simple redefinition of the proletariat. The Khanty female practice of modestly covering the face with a scarf before certain categories of male in-laws made Soviet officials see red. To them, this custom symbolized all that was retrograde in Khanty culture and became an early target of concern.

Unveiling ceremonies were held, in which women in groups, on makeshift stages, dramatically (blushingly) uncovered their faces before their in-laws, other kin, and friends. The embarrassing ceremonies, clumsily imposed attempts at social control, did not "take," at least at first. They were rituals divorced from full understanding of the beliefs behind the "veiling" tradition. Even in 1976, I saw some, though by no means all, Khanty women modestly covering their faces with scarves in appropriate contexts. I also heard Khanty women debate the relative merits of the practice, based on concepts derived from the impurities of menstrual blood and the need for women to be cognizant of their special roles as fertile mothers, guardians of tradition, and socializers of the young (Balzer 1981) (photo 3).

As elsewhere, local Soviet officials recruited women workers and political activists to expand the pool of cadres in a mobilizing, reforming society (cf. Shalin 1996:6, 72). They condemned the conservatism of Khanty men that kept women in the home. Official propaganda ignored the traditional divisions of labor that had given Khanty women considerable clout in running households while their husbands were away hunting. The Russian activist I. Pervukhin (1930:82) reported frustra-

Photo 3. Khanty mother and child, in Amnia with a view of Kazym, 1976. Note the mother's scarf is loose, ready to be pulled over her face in respect before a male in-law.

tion when Shuryshkar Khanty balked at females attending local meetings. Well into the 1930s, women stayed away from village councils. As seen from the fallout of the Kazym protest, some Native women paid a tragic price in the clash of cultural values, losing their men to jail or death. As widows, they gained the dubious legal honor of becoming heads of their households, in both the 1930s and during World War II.

Another "front" on which the battle for women's hearts and minds was waged was the issue of "bride price" (*kalym*, or, locally, *netyn*). The self-confident Soviet definition of social "progress" ignored traditions of kin reciprocity that were at the heart of the payments. *Kalym*, a Turkic word, came to mean in Russian simple payment for a bride—the buying of a human being in a transaction little better than the buying of a slave. Indeed, in some cases, the argument was legitimately made that women were "sold" against their will by male relatives oriented to money and prestige, not the best interests of their female kin. But this was not always the pattern in 1920s Khanty practice, when women had pragmatic and love matches and were under varying degrees of familial pressure.

Marriage practices that Soviet workers called "survivals" (*perezhitki*) continued well into the Soviet period. As late as 1937, a Khanty groom from Polnovat paid eighteen hundred rubles in bride price (Gudkov and Senkevich 1940:95). But usually, after they were made aware of new Soviet laws, families found it safer to donate reindeer toward lavish wedding parties than to pay bride price (Pervukhin 1930:82). They broke no laws but could still demonstrate their wealth and participate in kinship exchanges (cf. Leonov 1929:253–54; Sergeev 1955:243).

In extreme cases of "bride theft," or abduction of brides without ceremony or payment, some brides' families were able to complain successfully to Native or Russian courts. But families hoping to recover unpaid "bride price" in Soviet courts of appeal were sorely disappointed; most resolved such questions informally and locally. By 1930 in the Shuryshkar area, a few cases of known bride price payments were successfully prosecuted through Native courts (Pervukhin 1930:82).

The creation of Native female political cadres occurred particularly slowly in Khanty areas, given local Russian and Native male skepticism concerning women's capacity for public and political life. Some of the early elder-dominated Native councils (tuszovety) officially resolved to deny women the right to vote (Sergeev 1955:236). In the 1930s, Khanty women gradually became aware of new Soviet laws encouraging their participation in craft brigades, clubs, women's conferences, and regional meetings.

Courses in sanitary health care were focused on Khanty women, as householders and primary socializers of children. A Ukrainian party activist named Denisenko (1957:54), who worked in Kazym in the early 1930s, described initial efforts: "When the doctor Veronika Martynovna led the women to the clinic, they burst into discussion. The doctor emphasized to them the great importance of sanitation . . . [designating] sanitary activists to teach others about cleanliness in yurts and tents."

Despite this optimistic start, many Khanty women still considered themselves "impure" because of menstruation.[3] They obeyed rules restricting their activities and continued to give birth on furs in remote forest huts, relying on midwives, shamans, and elaborate purification rituals featuring sacred birch bark doll offerings and smoked beaver. They remained in seclusion for several weeks, fearing to bring contamination into their homes. Although birth and menstrual huts became illegal in the 1930s, infant mortality remained high. It was a shocking 60.8 percent in the early 1930s. Female mortality was higher than male, but the gap was gradually closing (Iag'ia 1980:57). Maternity clinics only gradually became available.

Traveling "red tent" propaganda programs encouraged changes in gender relations to facilitate expanded roles for women as nurses, teachers, and craft workers. Khanty women were also taught to plant potatoes, in experiments that pushed agriculture to its northernmost limits. An Obdorsk Khanty woman named Makarova was among the first to organize an artel for sewing furs, but the artel had difficulty obtaining raw materials (Pervukhin 1930:81). The few young Khanty women who ventured away from home to conferences and schools were censured in their home communities, where powerful elders, older women, and female shamans remained staunch conservatives, enforcing time-honored beliefs about female purity and pollution (cf. Douglas 1966).

In sum, gender divisions of labor and status were difficult to alter, because many Khanty women were suspicious of reforms perceived as driven by Russian males. A. P. Mikhailov (1936:34–39), the Native head of the Obdorsk "political section," publicized with pride a few exceptional Khanty female models of Soviet-style productivity, cleanliness, and political participation. In northern areas such as Obdorsk and Kazym, where Khanty and Nentsy reindeer breeders remained nomadic, change in gender relations and women's labor was predicated on yet another massive campaign: settling the Natives.

HERDING NOMADS INTO SETTLEMENT

Early Soviet planners believed the healthiest and most productive way to bring Siberian women and men into active participation in building Soviet society was to settle the nomads. Skachko (1931:94–98) documented that fertility was lower and mortality especially high for nomadic Khanty. Soviet officials viewed nomadism as unclean, uncontrolled, and un-Marxist. Nomadic reindeer breeding was a primitive form of "wretched labor" that the inevitable march of Progress could only obliterate (Sergeev 1964:489).

Soviet policy was geared to both enticing and forcing Siberian Natives to settle, so that they could be taught the principles of brigade organization, Soviet law, sanitation, and Communism.[4] Russian newcomers expressed scorn for the ethic of nomadic freedom that reindeer breeders had cultivated through the centuries, as they escaped what they called the "Russian noise" of civilization. In effect, each side saw the other as a "primitive other," and each viewed the other with fear.

Through the Soviet period, the nomadic ethic weakened, so that many young people came to prefer the films, food, education, and social life of central villages or towns to the tundra. Teenage Khanty in Tegy explained in 1976: "Reindeer breeding is not desirable to young people, who want films, volleyball, and to leave from here. Many try to live in Tiumen. Some return."

Attraction to cities was previously rare. In the 1920s, many Khanty were frightened by the influx of Russians into their previously isolated areas and moved further north or east. A Khanty leader, who became the secretary of a new Native sel'sovet (village council), advocated less Russian settlement: "Natives are worried. Since 1920, Russians have begun to settle in native regions. Before the revolution, this was forbidden, and for that reason natives are saying 'we lived better earlier.' Now the newcomer Russians burn the taiga and kill the red squirrel."[5]

Before collectivization, many tiny villages were arrayed along the banks of northern tributaries of the Ob. They included Khanty winter camps and a few Russian communities. Settlements, consisting of only several families each, were often ten to one hundred versts apart. Along the Vasyugan, for example, were eighteen Russian villages, ten Khanty camps, and thirteen with a mixed Native and Slavic population (Orlova 1926:66–70). Even Russians (Siberiaki) seasonally moved their housing for better hunting and fishing access.

When her guides on a boat trip along the Sosva river thought she was sleeping, the ethnomusicologist Senkevich (1934:100) overheard a debate about moving to escape Russians.. The guides, a Khanty couple from Voitikhovsk, bitterly quarreled over whether to leave for Kazym. This couple considered the Kazym region the epitome of traditional, remote Khanty life, despite the new culture base. The wife maintained that their local shaman had just moved and that it would be best for them to stay away from Russian centers. She was worried that Russians would take her children to a boarding school. Her husband feared losing his animals, his hunting and fishing territory, and his familiar yurt community. But the wife finished the argument: "Look at Vashka Grigoria, who has gone to school. His mother now bakes Russian bread, and his father's hair is cut. Our children too will soon be taken to school. They will spit in your face and ruin the Khanty life."

Extensive forced population transfers during the Soviet period provide a context for understanding interethnic tensions and accommodations. For example, during the anti-kulak campaign of 1930, allegedly rich Russian and Ukrainian peasants from the southern Urals were forced northward in a chaotic migration. About seventeen thousand were sent to the Berezovo region and sixteen thousand to the area around Surgut (Skachko 1931:109). In their haste to establish the newcomers in fishing and forestry, Russian officials housed some in Khanty winter yurts during the summer. The so-called kulaks were later supposed to move to Khanty summer homes in time to winterize for the Siberian cold. The Moscow activist A. E. Skachko (1931:109–10) admitted, "all this was done without any consideration of native interests, [and] without any agreement from them." The shocked Khanty had little recourse. Only a few Khanty councils had the nerve to protest local "Russian chauvinism" and demand fair division of land and water resources.[6]

Changing ethnic ratios in Western Siberia can be charted since the turn of the century, with the 1926–27 census serving as a rough baseline for the Soviet period. In his prerevolutionary survey, S. Patkanov (1911:36) claimed that the number of Vasyugan Khanty men was decreasing at an alarming rate of 8.45 percent a year, and that the Khanty in general were "dying out." The Khanty population slightly increased only in the Kazym and Surgut tundra, where they encountered fewer Russians, suffered from fewer epidemics, and enjoyed nomadic lifestyles. In the official 1926–27 Soviet census, the Khanty (as Ostiak) were listed at 17,800, a slight increase over a 1903 figure of 17,211 (see fig. 1, introduction).[7]

By 1939, the Khanty population had stabilized (at 18,500), but the Russian population had ballooned to over 50 percent its 1926 size. The Khanty, Mansi, Zyrian, and Nentsy together constituted only one-fifth of the population of the whole Khanty-Mansi National Okrug by 1939.[8] From 1932 to 1939, the region's population nearly doubled, mostly due to massive Slavic population influx, not natural growth.

Khanty reindeer breeding involved varying degrees of nomadism, according to geographical area and size of herd.[9] As with most ecologically attuned nomadic life-styles, conditions of animal breeding and seasonal adaptation dictated patterns of transhumance. Herders did not wander but rather conformed to established yet flexible economic cycles, congruent with kin and other social group patterns.

In the Kazym region, reindeer breeders ranged from those with large or multiple herds (Upper Kazym) to those with fewer than fifty deer for winter transport (Lower Kazym). Those with many deer traveled north and east into the tundra for summer. In fall, the returning reindeer foraged in forest-taiga areas and at the first snow were rounded up for winter, after the rutting season. Breeders with smaller herds stayed in the taiga.

Some families with smaller herds pooled their animals and rotated responsibility for summer pasturing. Those left behind fished in the plentiful Ob tributaries and paid their herders with fish and reindeer products. Those who kept reindeer relatively close in the taiga sometimes built enclosures for their deer, to reduce herding watches. They concocted smudges of slow-burning smoke to help protect deer from insects. Even the poorer Kazym families summered in tents or huts and wintered in yurts well sealed for cold weather. Winter camps were composed of five to fifteen extended families.[10]

Reindeer breeding in the Sosva-Berezovo-Tegy areas was less significant than hunting and fishing. Those who maintained herds of deer (fifty to five hundred) migrated north with their extended families in the summer, into the open, relatively mosquito-free tundra near the Ural mountains where moss, lichen, and grasses could be found. There they also hunted large numbers of geese and ducks. Fall camps, where the reindeer rutted, were set between the open tundra and more southern or riverbank forests. A main winter base was established in the forest-tundra zone, where supplies had been stored from the previous winter. Khanty often moved their skin tents at two-week intervals, depending on lichen conditions in ice and snow. Herders made rounds nearly every day, keeping track of their deer with herd dogs. Families pitched winter camps where they found game (fox, wolf, bear, and beaver), wood for fuel, and shelter from wind.

By spring, supplies were often low. The first appearance of the raven, around April, was marked with great celebration. Spring camps were transitional, along familiar routes, often set on riverbanks and lake shores for maximal fishing opportunity as Khanty traveled back to the open tundra, past stunted larches and firs. In spring, attentive herders watched for newborn reindeer and cut their ears with family marks.[11]

On the Vakh, Vasyugan, and other more southeastern rivers, fewer reindeer were kept, with much less supervision. In this area, horses were more common than reindeer and were preferred for transport and ritual sacrifices. Once a year, in late fall, the reindeer were herded, in a protracted family-level search.

Given the complexity of differing Khanty calendars and nomadic patterns, Soviet officials had difficulty applying general orders for settlement to local ecological and economic situations. To aid them, I. M. Suslov (1930:29–35) systematized five Siberian economies involving reindeer : (1) tundra, with primary dependency on reindeer herding; (2) tundra, with primary focus on hunting polar fox, but with some reindeer; (3) forest-tundra, with focus on small reindeer herds; (4) forest-tundra, with primary attention to fur animal hunting, but with some reindeer; and (5) taiga, with primary dependency on hunting and fishing, but with a few reindeer for transport. Kulaks, politically suspect as too rich, were those with excess reindeer and those who hired herders and helpers, including family members. Local conditions determined how excess was defined.[12]

Impoverished hired herders were the target of the most active settlement campaigns. Hunters who kept small reindeer herds were also encouraged to remain in their settlements as collective workers. Only a few authorized reindeer-breeding brigades were expected to nomadize, and even they were encouraged to leave their families in settlements. Authorities, without considering the nomads' wishes or the nature of reindeer breeding as a family enterprise, declared "all other working strength could go into fishing, fur hunting, agriculture, [settled] animal husbandry, and the transportation system" (Khrapal' 1937:27).

By the late 1930s in the Khanty-Mansi Okrug, only about one-third of the Khanty reindeer breeders were still nomadic. Officially, 625 households had switched to a settled collective life (Khrapal' 1937:30). The government rewarded collectives for each family settled, providing ample motivation.[13] Retired breeders of Tegy and Kazym recalled that they had viewed living in one place as filthy and feared the draftiness of cabins, as opposed to their cozy yurts. They mourned the demise of private herds and resented the pressure put on families to have women and children stay in the villages.

PAINS OF WORLD WAR II (THE GREAT PATRIOTIC WAR)

Consolidation of Soviet ideas could not effectively begin until the perceived war on Native elders and the values they represented subsided. New generations had to come into their own, rebelling against their parents' "backward and primitive traditions," accepting broader definitions of patriotism and education. This process of consolidation was advanced by a new kind of campaign, World War II, as the whole "Soviet people" came together (more or less) against outside enemies.

World War II was and is called the Great Patriotic War, not only by Russians but also by minorities within the former Soviet Union. During the war, Khanty exposure to multiethnic life increased, as did exposure to hardship. War sacrifices came on the heels of renewed pressure for collectivization in the late 1930s. Once again, livestock was confiscated. Some Khanty, particularly literate men, were drafted. Siberian Natives had been exempt from service until the 1936 Constitution. In 1941, many Natives volunteered for Red Army duty, to participate "in the defense of our country, alongside all the other peoples of the Soviet Union" (Sergeev 1964:509).[14]

The talents of Siberians were needed and welcomed in World War II. Khanty men fought well in the front lines and worked as scouts, snipers, and ski patrol messengers. Over four thousand men from the Khanty-Mansi Okrug were active, including in the bloody and protracted defense of Leningrad (Kiselev 1974:197–98). They became immersed in the Russian language, in party politics, and in military technology. The half-Khanty historian Kiselev (1974:201) has stressed that fighting alongside Siberians "was always their older brother—the Russian soldier and officer." This suggests that Khanty recruits rarely became officers and were patronized. However, by the end of the war, party membership among Natives of the Ob North had increased significantly.[15]

Khanty who were not drafted contributed to supply efforts. According to one reindeer breeder, the government set high quotas for reindeer herds. If a breeder could produce as many animals as were demanded, he could be exempt from the draft, because he provided an unusual degree of sustenance for the home front. The breeder who explained this had met the demand; his brother, who had not, was killed in the war. Pragmatic approaches to defense meant that in many areas, pressures to collectivize were eased during the war. In other areas, cooperatives worked frantically to provide furs, fish, and game needed on the northern front.

The home front was a scene of great suffering, where impoverished women, children, and elderly cast fishing nets, collected cedar nuts and berries, and tried to prevent reindeer from escaping into the tundra. Many deer were lost or eaten, despite strict party exhortations. Workers at logging camps and processing plants volunteered labor for the defense fund. Teachers in places as remote as Kazym and Lariach collected thousands of rubles (Kiselev 1974:192–94). Villagers were left with little after requisitions of livestock and contributions of food and valuables.

The entire war experience was so shattering that many Khanty became disillusioned about regaining the psychological security that their cultural values and isolation had provided. War dead had to be mourned from afar. Neither shamans nor burial rites conducted in absentia could console the living. A woman who lost ten brothers and sisters during the war mournfully sighed, "people saw how their praying did not help."

The few Khanty men who survived the war remembered it vividly. In

1976, they wore their war medals proudly, discussed American "lend lease" donations of tanks and guns, and recalled the staggering losses of Khanty placed in the front lines. Survivors became respected Khanty elders, with political savvy and impressive proficiency in Russian. They did not abandon all shamanic belief and ritual, but they were more apt than others to hide it under a patriotic Soviet guise.

The war served as an unplanned stimulus for social change. To a lesser degree, the draft continued to influence Khanty youth. Some drafted after the war considered service a chance to see the Soviet Union. Some were stationed in Vladivostok, while others served outside Siberia. Their multiethnic experiences were mixed, since derogatory epithets for Siberians and ethnic jokes about them became fixtures of Red Army life. Far from ensuring that young men would want to leave their homeland, army service ended with the return of some soldiers to their collectives.[16]

CONSOLIDATING COLLECTIVIZATION

During and after the war, carefully coordinated cycles of reindeer pasturage were affected by new forestry projects and collectivization of land. Lichen, requiring years to replenish naturally, was overgrazed. Wolves found easy targets in overextended, underwatched herds. Thus some reindeer-breeding families found sale of their animals and settlement necessary. Between 1942 and 1945, 231 homes and 19 bathhouses were built in the region.[17]

In the 1950s, officials renewed their efforts at settlement, during the consolidation of the collective economy and the switch to *sovkhoz* (government wage) collectives. The task was easier with younger generations. Nomads' children, educated in boarding schools, rarely wanted to return to hard tundra or taiga life. Culture bases had become attractive, gradually making small winter settlements unpopular. Supply stores, clubs, and medical points were not available in tiny communities of two to ten yurts. Thus Soviet policy created conditions for voluntary movement toward larger population centers.

In 1955, the executive committee of the Tiumen Communist Party offered new livelihoods and homes to some remaining seminomadic families. Natives were given goals to meet in fishing, hunting, fur farming, and forestry. Reindeer breeders assigned to collectives emphasizing fishing had a hard choice: to fight for traditional herding patterns as a minority or to agree to donate their reindeer to other collectives.

In areas like Kazym, where reindeer breeding was supported, official goals of universal settlement were unrealistic. By the 1960s, 20 percent of all reindeer breeding in the Soviet Union was in the Tiumen Oblast (Region), and much of this was in the Kazym area. An elderly reindeer breeder lamented to the Khanty journalist Klepikov (1967:141): "The young people . . . are spoiled. Studying has spoiled them. The army has taken them—and also spoiled them. . . . With old people dying, who will herd? Or perhaps now we do not need reindeer breeding?"

Kazym reindeer breeders have an astute metaphor for this problem. They consider some children of Native herders to be like young reindeer, *avka*, brought up in tents rather than in the wild. A Khanty brigadier explained that such a reindeer "does not live with its own kind, does not eat moss, but is fed leftovers in a soup bowl. He does not sleep in the snow. When he grows up and is let into a herd, he dies. . . . My fellow tribesman is also an *avka*. Long ago he was taken to school. And when he finishes school, he cannot do anything; he has forgotten the reindeer" (Klepikov 1967:142).

The contradiction between maintaining reindeer and settling the breeders worried Soviet planners and scientists. They attempted to establish new life-styles that would allow reindeer breeders to remain longer in collective centers. Their experiments in rendering reindeer breeding a science worked best when Native veterinarians traveled with reindeer herds in transhumant cycles. Attempts to fence large pastures for more efficient and less labor-intensive herding, rotate responsibility for herds, and use residential tractor-wagons were controversial.[18] Reindeer breeders explained that tractor-wagons failed because huge amounts of gas were needed, and reindeer wandered too often into the tractors. Dependence on planes and helicopters was unsafe and expensive. Monthly herd duty rotation only worked with smaller herds and was unpopular with herders used to knowing each animal.[19] A herder concluded: "How can we live without a *chum* [skin tent]? The family in a village and us, [sleeping] wherever we might land? . . . What kind of family life will that be? . . . Reindeer have to be watched day and night, and wolves have to be chased. [The wife] has to sew and cook" (Klepikov 1967:143).

Distances required for effective reindeer breeding around Kazym are formidable and not easily decreased by experiments. Klepikov (1967: 141) traveled by reindeer sled twenty hours from Kazym to reach the first brigade in the tundra. This had not changed by the mid-1970s or indeed by the 1990s, according to Kazym Khanty.

Some extended families were still nomadizing together in the 1970s. Women delivered to the Kazym collective fur and thongs, worked by hand during the winter. They had the customary obligation of putting up and taking down skin tents. Reindeer breeders agreed that "a tent without a woman is not a tent" (Klepikov 1967:143). But by the 1970s, a few younger brigade leaders had houses in Kazym, where their families lived most of the year. Helicopters and planes were increasingly reliable and had become an important source of supplies, emergency transport, and help against wolf predation.

In 1976, reindeer breeding involved a combination of private and collective herding, although most reindeer were under collective (sovkhoz) jurisdiction. Many reindeer breeders had sold, eaten, or given up their deer to the large collectives. Soviet authorities, in their drive to "rationalize" herding, declared small herds unproductive. In Tegy, one former reindeer breeder lamented, "Reindeer breeding is dying out as a trade here, because collectivization came in the form of fishing." But in places like Kazym, Khanty were able to convince authorities that nomadic reindeer breeding could be profitable. Brigades averaging five to seven men tended herds of about fifteen hundred to twenty-seven hundred deer, some of these dangerously large for adequate control.[20]

Economic recovery after the war to some extent dulled the pain of the 1930s and the war years. However, competing demands for postwar reconstruction slowed the healing process. Prices for furs and fish remained nearly at prewar levels, while costs of basic goods like grain and sugar had multiplied. Infusions of government credit became critical, as cooperatives attempted to rebuild the reindeer, fishing, and logging industries. Reindeer, fishnets and motorboats were provided; collectives devised jobs for Khanty needing to relocate for personal reasons.

Collectives were organized in new, more flexible patterns, enabling several industries, such as logging and fishing, to be stressed in one collective. Local initiative to some degree determined economic activities. By 1948, tax concessions (*l'goty*) were offered for Northern workers, and members of collectives were given additional freedom from government levies. By 1950, the government raised fish prices and subsidized other goods, thus bolstering the whole Ob North economy.[21] "Motor fishing stations," affiliated with collectives, began to dot the banks of the Ob river system.

New centers with schools, clubs, party headquarters, medical facilities, nurseries, cattle barns, air fields, food and hardgoods stores were established or refurbished at the organization points for expanding collectives. Bigger came to mean better—not always a valid economic concept in the North. Consolidation continued through the 1950s. For example, forty small cooperatives of the prewar Northern Vartovsk area became twenty-seven collectives by 1952, and eleven by 1956 (Sokolova 1968:27). These combined agriculture, animal husbandry, and fishing.[22] In some cases, such as that of the Lenin's Way kolkhoz near Sherkaly, a Russian agricultural and a Khanty hunting and fishing collective awkwardly merged 106 households.[23]

Collectives sponsored, singly or in combination, not only herding, hunting, and fishing, but also reindeer stud farms, silver fox farms, cattle breeding, vegetable gardens, and logging complexes. Those that included hunters came under a government hunting administration (GOM) guided by new decrees limiting kills and streamlining fur collection and processing. Jurisdiction for the increasingly lucrative fishing industry was divided among profit-sharing kolkhozy, new sovkhozy, and government-run fish-processing plants and canneries. Directed against those who felt the Native populations should become service personnel for incoming settlers, new protectionist laws were supposed to insure food, shelter, clothing, and shoes for Native children.[24]

Major economic trends in the Ob North included gradual transition from profit-sharing kolkhozy and artels that were somewhat independent to government-run, wage-based sovkhozy; an increase in the percentage of the population involved in fishing; increased settlement of nomadic peoples; and increased specialization of collectives according to local ecological conditions.

Khanty workers cooperated in new labor brigades and participated in collective administration. In the Kazym region, rather than bucking the system, members of the famous Moldanov family were winning Soviet labor awards in reindeer breeding, hunting, and fishing. Nonetheless, during repeated field trips, the ethnographer Zoia Sokolova (1968:27) observed, "Not everywhere have these transformations proceeded smoothly . . . consolidation has been mismanaged; sometimes instead of [building] economic centers and productive participation, former kolkhozy established new villages in unfortunately chosen places, isolated from [fishing and trapping] resources, [even creating] unemployment."

Despite failures, by the 1970s many Khanty members of collectives received salaries based on individual productivity, had access to food and hardgoods stores, lived in Russian-style cabins, and owned or had use of motorboats or snowmobiles. Some were employed in the fish canneries of Surgut, Khanty-Mansiisk, and Berezovo, although most were hunters and fishers.[25]

In 1976, Soviet officials bragged of economic security that Siberians had gained under their influence and with their support. They claimed to encourage aspects of "aboriginal Khanty culture," that fit well into their development scheme, for example, men's communal fishing and women's fur working. They pointed to new fish- and berry- processing plants, oil presses, and lumbering centers that enhanced the regional economy.

Soviet-Russian influence was strongest in technology. The Khanty recognized the advantages of modern snares, guns, seines (nets), and propane stoves. Introduction of modern techniques in fishing, reindeer breeding, hunting, and fur farming enabled regional officials to increase Native interdependence with the Soviet economy, shaping a predominantly subsistence orientation into a centralized market one. Reindeer breeders benefited from modern veterinary methods to control epizootic disease, from reindeer stud breeding, and from the spotting of wolves from helicopters. Fishers substituted weirs (traps) of twigs for seines.

In the late Soviet period, the Khanty still dominated the fishing industry in the Ob North, with fishing administered through the government bureaucracy "Goslov." Some profits from fishing in the Tiumen Region went into building new villages, such as Tegy, Kharsaim, and Dorkovo-Gorshkovo. The villages accommodated Natives relocated, not always voluntarily, from remote and poor taiga areas.[26] The chairman of the fishing collective at Tegy bragged: "Even a lazy fisherman can take in nine hundred rubles [in fishing season], and that is lots when there is not much to pay for. What is there to spend money on? Vodka and boats. Some fishermen own seven-thousand-ruble boats which can be comfortably used for sleepovers. What would we want with cars? They would just get stuck in the tundra." But profits from salmon, trout, pike, sturgeon, and caviar declined by the 1980s, because steps were not taken to curtail pollution of the Ob-Irtysh system resulting from increased settlement and energy industry excesses.[27]

The fishing outpost I saw in 1976 was several hours by motorboat down river from Kazym (photo 4). Between a sandy riverbank and a pine forest, the Ishyugan camp had three canvas sleeping tents, two small storage huts on stilts, and a long, low cabin. Inside the cabin, against the length of its back wall, was a platform piled with reindeer furs where several brigade members could sleep in a dormitory row. A crate at the edge of the bed served as a table, while an old wood stove, near the sole window, warmed the cluttered cabin. Fish gear lay about, mingled with pots and crates.

Only one woman lived at Ishyugan when we visited. She sat under a small wooden lean-to near a tent, rapidly and skillfully cleaning fish. Her small children danced around a nearby smudge pail of smoking wood. Wearing a traditional appliqued dress and head scarf, she smiled shyly and gave our group several fresh fish to boil. Throughout the camp, lines of splayed and drying fish hung from poles, testimony to the hard work of one or two women preparing for winter. Near the forest, a canopy-like wooden roof sheltered a long rough-hewn table, which served as a communal work and eating place.

The main Ishyugan fishing site was five minutes from camp. Six brigade fishers went by motorboat to this prime location, then switched to quieter canoes (*kaldonki*), so as not to disturb the early evening fish. In one circling, a canoe spread an enormous seine. Twenty minutes later,

Photo 4. Khanty boy at the Ishyugan fish camp, 1976.

six pairs of hands closed the net, trapping multitudes of pike and trout. While the fish were poured into crates, nets were fed back into the boat, to renew the process throughout the Northern white night. Although the hundreds of fish seemed unbelievably plentiful, a few Khanty explained that "earlier fishing was better." While salmon and sturgeon were available in the Ob, they were dwindling at other prime sites. Nonetheless, sturgeon caviar was consumed by the spoonful in some Khanty homes, and sometimes sold on the "grey market" of semilegal trading in the Soviet Union.[28]

Like fishing and reindeer breeding, fur hunting was modified by Soviet technology and economic planning. Hunters came to catch muskrats, introduced in the 1930s, with modern spring traps that protect the catch from incidental predators. Sable, nearly driven to extinction by overexploitation, made a small comeback, thanks to seasonal hunting limits. While Khanty complained of hunting restrictions in 1976, they benefited from Native priority (at least in principle) for hunting licenses.[29]

In the late Soviet period, most Khanty hunters delivered fur animals to the collectives for fixed prices, unless they found other (illegal) channels of trade. They were not subject to the whims of old-style Russian traders or the demands of fur-tax collectors. But prices were controlled and kept low, with state sponsorship of fur-animal hunting for foreign-currency export continuing a prime source of profit for the Soviet, as for the tsarist, government. Hunting jurisdiction, through Glavokhota, was reformed in 1969, to increase official government profits. But these reforms and the merging of small villages into larger centers coincided with a decline in hunting productivity in many areas, and a decline in the world market for furs.[30] The average age of an Ob North hunter rose to over forty, indicating what was commonly bemoaned: Khanty with boarding school educations did not want the low prestige and hard work of hunting for a livelihood. A Tegy woman was embarrassed as she recalled the poverty of her parents: "Father sold furs to traders, and he did not work at anything else."[31]

In order to generate more luxury furs, "soft gold," for the market, the Soviets introduced a nontraditional form of economy into the North: fur farms. By the 1970s, fur animal husbandry in the Tiumen Region surpassed fur hunting in yields for the state. Farms to raise silver foxes were run by Natives and Russians in the Kondinsk, Samarovsk, Surgut, and Berezovo areas. In 1976, I visited a silver fox farm outside Kazym and learned that the seven hundred restless animals raised there in small cages were all for export. Thirty employees worked in shifts on the sovkhoz, including Khanty, Nentsy, Zyrian, and a few Russians. Many were women who lived in Kazym. They were glad to be employed, for the steady income, but admitted that they did not enjoy constantly tending voracious caged animals and feeding them with stinking fish.[32]

Soviet collectives introduced cattle and horse breeding into the Far Northern economy on an unprecedented scale. In 1976, Tegy and Kazym Khanty benefited from milk products obtained from collective cows. These cattle were tended by wage-earning Khanty, who also herded a few privately owned cattle together with collective animals. Several milkmaids were employed, who were expected to fulfill monthly plans. Cattle or horses peacefully wandering through or near the villages were an index of prosperity. Members of the collectives put in their fair share of summer labor scything hay for winter feed.

Avoiding collective work was considered anti-Communist. Khanty workers were subject to the centralized "gosplan" that required fulfillment of quotas for such diverse activities as milking cows, hunting sable, and catching fish. Even though some initial plans were set by local officials eager to ensure success, many Khanty considered any government goals alien and artificial. Like all Soviet workers, the Khanty were constantly exhorted by billboards to "meet the plan." In the Tegy post office, fish catches, cattle gains, and milk yields were monitored by comparison of reported yields to planned targets. In the town of Khanty-Mansiisk in 1976, I saw a huge roadside billboard with year and month target figures for hunting fur animals. The high numbers (in the hundred thousands) testified to a renewed danger of overexploitation, one that became increasingly problematic in the 1980s and 1990s, as covertly corrupt Soviet officials became even greedier post-Soviet regional authorities.[33]

The ecology of West Siberia was far more threatened by the high-priority oil and gas industry, for example, near Surgut and Berezovo. Oil was discovered in the Ob region in the 1960s, bringing an onslaught of nonindigenous workers to the region and a gush of development money from Moscow. While at first only a few Khanty were directly involved, they came to be increasingly affected by discoveries of oil and gas in their areas. Some were moved, with little notice or choice, to make way for whole new communities; others were forced to cope with the ramifications of a new, destabilizing development boom.[34]

By the early 1980s, the portion of Ob North Natives working on oil and gas projects was only 8.7 percent; less than 4 percent of these were Khanty (Pika 1982:235). Although propaganda photographs featured Khanty men standing in front of gas extraction machinery, most energy workers were of Slavic origin, with many skilled technicians recruited, for double and triple salaries, from other parts of the Soviet Union. For the Khanty, "the traditional northern economic triad—hunting, reindeer breeding, and fishing—has remained firm even in the modern context" (Pika 1982:235). High-rise minicities, growing out of the tundra to service the energy industry, became predominantly Slavic enclaves, sharply contrasting with even the largest of the Khanty collective villages (cf. Mozgalin 1981:132). Regardless of opportunities for technical education, most of the Khanty I interviewed in Northern villages in 1976 and 1991 neither expected nor wanted to become workers in the energy industry. Nor were service-sector jobs in energy centers considered prestigious. Newly arrived Slavic workers and Northern Natives maintained informal ethnic boundaries, and sometimes clashed in more open ethnic conflict, leaving Soviet officials with an increasingly awkward social, political, and labor problem.[35]

NATIVE POLITICS AND ETHNIC INTERACTION, SOVIET STYLE

One of the first Khanty leaders to support oil development in the Ob North was Nifon Vokuev, first secretary of the Nizhnevartovsk Regional Committee of the Communist Party, in the Surgut area. He galloped on horseback to the Magion gusher in 1961, only hours after its discovery. "On seeing the fountain, [he] cried for joy" (Salmanov

1970:69). But most Khanty were removed from the excitement of discovery, development planning, or profit sharing.

The typical regional or village council in the Ob North was headed by a Russian chairman, with sometimes a younger Khanty leader appointed as Secretary. Alternately, the roles were switched, with de facto power still accruing to the Russian. In important towns like Salekhard, Berezovo, Surgut, or Tiumen, Soviet leadership was predominantly Slavic. For Khanty who bought the line that Russians were "big brothers," this felt natural. But others, remembering more egalitarian Leninist goals, by the 1970s preferred to see more Khanty in positions of influence. All were reasonably loyal Soviet citizens, with some becoming educated members of the Communist Party.[36]

In the 1970s, party propaganda stressed the multinational nature of local party organs, rather than the participation of the area's "titular" group. This may be why the word "national" was removed from the official name of the district (okrug), as from all the ethnic-based districts at the time. In the Khanty-Mansi Autonomous Okrug, fifty-six different nationalities were represented in the local party organization (Gryzlov 1982:14). Relative to the rest of the country, West Siberia had a low percent of Communist Party members, and this was all the more true for Siberian Natives.[37]

Political perceptions were nonetheless changing significantly. Khanty were taught from grade school on that they were first Soviet citizens; then members of the Russian Soviet Socialist Republic; thirdly, occupants of the greater Tiumen Oblast; and finally, residents of the Khanty-Mansi Autonomous Okrug or the neighboring Yamal-Nenets Autonomous Okrug. These multiple, state-imposed identities, activated at different times and validated with passports, broadened the Khanty political universe by the late Soviet period.

Many Khanty understood that key decisions in economic and political planning were made in Moscow by the Russian party elite. Only routine administrative decisions and stop-gap strategies for fulfillment of economic plans were left in the hands of regional committees (*raikom*) and village councils (*sel'sovet*), where Native leadership was permitted and concentrated.

The ideal leader, as discussed in 1976, was in effect bicultural, combining old-style and Soviet values. An elder-patriarch who could hunt, fish, and perform rituals properly was respected, particularly if he was a World War II veteran or head of a work brigade. Children were reminded, "Not all are like your grandfather—bringing home much on the hunt, fighting in the war, and knowing legends." Khanty leaders were often members of influential families, with old claims to choice lineage territories and ties to powerful shamans. But they also had to generate respect through consensus, and the nature of that consensus changed in Soviet times.

By the 1970s, Khanty leaders no longer needed to be elders of specific families or even male, although many were. Routes to prestige and political power were multiple, with elders often retaining informal influence, while younger leaders perceived to be more progressive got official Soviet recognition. By 1976, a Khanty leader occasionally could be a young woman, as was the Secretary of the Kazym soviet. She confessed that male in-laws had objected to her marriage, claiming she was headstrong, modern, and unlikely to show them traditional marks of respect, such as covering her face with a scarf when they approached. Her job, one of the most responsible and powerful in the village, required membership in the Communist Party.

Another exemplary young leader was the Secretary of the soviet in Tegy, a lively and confident young man whose early promotion presaged a party career. He was an important role model for younger Khanty, with a meticulous command of collective economic data (kept in kolkhoz records for the party) and a middleman's orientation to helping Tegy residents cope with the outside world. Indeed, by 1985, he had risen to chairman of the district soviet.

A major problem for Khanty and Russian village leaders alike was political apathy and boredom. One well-educated and somewhat frustrated Khanty youth explained: "The problem is boredom. It is hard to organize activities. Try [to organize] even a concert of traditional Khanty music. No one comes to practice." Despite trouble harnessing collective energy for special cultural or propaganda projects, a traveling library of Russian and Khanty literature, run by a Khanty woman, operated in outlying areas. Only a few Khanty hung portraits of Lenin next to family pictures on their cabin walls.

The organization of local collective meetings lay with chairmen beholden to the party. Participation was expected for all members of the community, including part-time workers or relatives of collective members. But turnout for some of the meetings was sparse, and voting a perfunctory endorsement of decisions already made. Elections brought out nearly everyone, since failure to vote was considered one of the most serious breaches of Soviet citizenship. Until the 1989 elections, voting meant supporting a single Communist candidate for each post.

By law, a general meeting of collective members was considered the main governing body of the collective. But the governing committee of the collective was a more manageable forum. The chairman decided when to hold more broad-based meetings and personally agitated to bring out members on the evening of the meeting. Issues were usually those that the party, through the regional center (*obkom*), had suggested and those for which the chairman had already lined up support.[38]

While I was in Tegy in 1976, a local meeting was held at the community center, attended by many, not all, members of the collective. The following is an excerpt from my notes:

> Some of our group heard late that there was going to be a meeting this evening, and so three of us hurried to the community center. The meeting had already started. We tried to slip in unobtrusively, but could not. The Russian chairman [*predsedatel'*], who was talking at the podium, smiled at us and waited as we took seats. The room held a mix of Khanty, a few Nentsy, and Russians, with the men in work clothes or old suit jackets or parkas and some Khanty women in traditional dresses with bright scarves. There did not seem to be any pattern of segregation. Women sat with each other or with men and Khanty sat with Russians. The main issue for the evening was a gun control petition. People were heavily encouraged to sign and pledge money, but the chairman stressed this was "voluntary." The petition [proclaimed] that signers would not bear or own arms [unless their hunting jobs, special licenses, or military service required it]. Considered an important "peace" gesture throughout the Soviet Union, it is also a "gun-control" issue [although crime is not publicly stressed]. . . . People in the meeting focused on the idea "Now is a time of plenty. Young people can not even imagine the horrors of war." One passionate Russian got up and announced that he had suffered at the front in World War II, wanted to have nothing more to do with weaponry, and believed we were on the way to a relaxation of world tensions. He pledged ten rubles. Others stated their names and pledges. When the meeting broke up, both men and women thronged to the front desk to sign. Only men had spoken, and more Russians than Khanty.

This meeting raises questions about the potential behavior-influencing nature of our expedition, as well as the role of the Communist Party in day-to-day collective organization. Timing and content of the meeting were undoubtedly "not accidental," as was often said in the Soviet Union. Before we appeared, Tegy residents had been asked to cooperate with our "scientific expedition" and to be on better behavior than they had evinced the previous week, during rowdy and drunken celebrations for the "Day of the Fishermen." After the holiday, the chairman invoked a "dry law" so that people could fulfill their work obligations and be more presentable to visitors. He could do little, however, about the continued and pervasive use of vodka as a medium of exchange in the informal barter economy.

The petition had political ramifications relating to Tegy's place in the Soviet propaganda system. A "peace campaign" was indeed sweeping the country, as I later confirmed in (then) Leningrad. But its appearance while an American was in Tegy was suggestive. After the meeting, the chairman asked why I did not sign the petition. I replied that I was for peace between our two countries but did not think it was appropriate for me, as an outsider, to be involved with their petition. I was perhaps perceived not only as a catalyst for a propaganda show but also as a potential activist to advance propaganda.

A leap of faith was required to link the issue of individual gun ownership with international conflict. Since questions of war and peace are hardly decided at the grassroots level, especially in countries like the Soviet Union, an underlying concern here was crime control. Ironically, I had assumed guns were already well under control, despite the black market. The meeting was significant as a demonstration of how responsive local party officials were to directives from above. Within this context, it illustrated the personal power and influence of the collective chairman in using those directives for village control.[39]

Several days later, I was approached by a young Khanty man who wanted to know about violence in the United States. Having heard Soviet propaganda concerning ubiquitous crime in America, he was surprised that neither I nor any of my friends owned a gun. With considerable concern, he confided that "propaganda about lack of violence in the Soviet Union is a lie." He showed me knife scars left from an encounter with a Russian gang in Tiumen.[40]

It is hard to judge the extent and nature of crime, gangs, and violence in pre-1991 Siberia, much less their ethnic ramifications. Soviet control of statistics and most crime reporting was effective until the Gorbachev period. With its frontierlike toughness, notorious drinking binges, and high labor turnover, Soviet Siberia was popularly, unofficially perceived to have more crime than many other areas.

I cannot describe the Siberian towns I visited in the Soviet period as consistently "wild and violent," nor can I recognize a description of a fishing village in the Khanty-Mansi Okrug as filled with Khanty "almost permanently drunk."[41] The tone and level of violence in a given community could obviously fluctuate over time and from village to village, but careful distinctions should be made between Khanty and non-Khanty behavior and attitudes, and between local and nonlocal "hooligans."

By the Brezhnev era, Tegy and Kazym villagers had developed a subtle sense of wariness regarding potential problems. Drunks were to be avoided, or treated gently. Young women were to dress carefully and modestly for all social contact. A member of our group in 1976 was scolded for wearing only her robe to receive an early morning gift of fish. "It could have been perceived as a provocation," she was told. Personal theft, quite rare, was to be reported immediately, but "borrowing" of collective property was overlooked. Authorities were told as little as possible about family arguments, the activities of shamans, relations with exiles, and incidents with overtones of interethnic conflict. Such informal mechanisms of self-control and discretion do not convey a sense of chaos in Siberian villages, but rather the reverse.

Perhaps the most recalcitrant concern, just under the surface of village life, was that of interethnic tensions and prejudice. Clues peppered local conversations and behavior. A Russian photographer in Berezovo cursed the local "do-nothing" Khanty, calling them popular derogatory names like "churka" (wood chip; implying something small, insignificant, and mindless, barely able to start a fire). He asked why members of our group would bother to study "*them*." Two young Russian toughs hastily stopped beating up a small Khanty boy when I happened upon them on a beach. During a rainstorm, several Russian teens came charging into a Khanty cabin without knocking, asking if they could "rescue" me from the family whose company I was enjoying. They retreated without apology.

Several Khanty also confided their resentment of Russians and "Zyrians" (Komi) who, in the past and recently, had stolen sacred goods from graves and ancestral shrines. The lack of respect was as upsetting as the loss of valuables. Such incidents and comments stem from a legacy of mistrust that some Russians tried hard to change. The roots of the problem may lie in Russian images of "primitive" yet dependent Khanty, who have indeed suffered for generations in conditions of poverty, sickness, and alcoholism. As in other indigenous peoples' invaded homelands, these conditions have contributed to images of ingrown passivity and weakness. Russians made patronizing comments, such as "Our Khanty are all very kind and very naive. They have never lived elsewhere and so they have not seen much."[42]

CONCLUSION: EDUCATION, AFFIRMATIVE ACTION, AND ETHNICITY

Sovietization of the Khanty was neither uniform nor predictable in its actions and repercussions. In some areas, Soviet rule alleviated some of the worst problems of Native debt and interethnic distrust, but massive influxes of Slavic newcomers also exacerbated interethnic tensions. Some of these new arrivals continued to view Siberian Natives as dependent and ingenuous, "like children," creating a vicious cycle of misperception. Chauvinist misperception was typical of the Russian administrators and many teachers within the Soviet education system (Ventsel and Dudeck 1998: 92).

Many Khanty became bicultural, with a pragmatic respect for Soviet technology and economic improvements but a wariness of official demands. Native participation in local Soviet leadership improved opportunities for conservation of resources, but development decisions made in Moscow nullified many economic gains. The wounds of early requisitions, the war, protracted collectivization, and population displacements left scars on ethnic relations.

Education programs had an equalizing potential only when Natives took advantage of them. Many Khanty dropped out even before finishing secondary school, and few went beyond it. The most successful became veterinarians, teachers, and other members of the Soviet "rural intelligentsia." Native cadres were trained predominantly in the technical schools of the larger Siberian towns like Salekhard, Tiumen, Khanty-Mansiisk, and Tobolsk. A few attended the Herzen Pedagogical Institute in Leningrad and returned to Siberia as teachers with political grounding. Others attended adult political and literacy programs.[43]

Those Khanty wanting education today would hardly recognize the psychology of Kazym parents' protests against sending children to schools. By the Gorbachev period, few Siberians said, as some did as recently as the 1940s, "It is necessary to teach reindeer . . . but why teach a human? [Humans] know how to obtain food and how to live. What possible use could come of . . . school, especially a Russian school?"[44] Yet Khanty and other Native educators have been engaged in a renewed, more refined critique, asking what programs are most productive for their communities, to alleviate the effects of standardization and Russification (Kravchenko 1996).

Soviet schools improved literacy and sought to teach Native Siberians to be loyal Soviet citizens. From the 1960s through the 1980s, increasing emphasis was placed on the Russian language, with Native languages and the history of Siberian minorities taught as supplemental subjects in rare and token "nationality" programs. Many Khanty mourned the loss of their language, as they became reliant on Russian to function in the Soviet world.[45]

Siberian Natives were given special-admissions access to higher education by allowing them to pass entrance exams with lower scores than was normally demanded. Such affirmative action programs, to use a Western term, produced a backlash of Russian resentment and slurs about the quality of indigenous scholarship and Native writers. While the programs could have been more sensitively and consistently administered, they were attempts at producing a multiethnic Soviet community of development-minded citizens.

Propaganda about a harmonious "multinationality" Soviet society, as well as affirmative action programs, heightened ethnic consciousness without giving it much outlet, particularly in a society that was markedly hierarchical, in terms of both class and nationality. Soviet policies raised Native expectations, and the gap between expectation and reality fueled Native ethnonationalist feelings of resentment against Russians (cf. Connor 1994). By the Gorbachev period, resentment coalesced around issues of forced moves during collectivization, unchecked energy development, and ecological despoliation.

Soviet education efforts resulted in a small, tame Native intelligentsia, who used their ethnicity to get ahead in Soviet society and to explore their personal roots in new but restricted ways. Repressive Soviet policies and indigenous demography never allowed them to fit Hroch's (1985) or Gellner's (1983) progressive, intelligentsia-oriented models of nationalist development in contexts of modernization. Nor could they, under conditions of print socialism, easily construct an "imagined community" through the media (cf. Anderson 1991:139–40). The intelligentsia was too tiny, too splintered, and too Sovietized to act on a politicized ethnonationalism until Gorbachev's policies enabled informal groups like the Association for the Salvation of the Ugra to form.

Early examples of the Khanty intelligentsia are the poet G. D. Lazarev; the progress-praising historian L. E. Kiselev, whose father was Khanty; and the linguist Nikolai I. Tereshkin, who was a stenographer during the Kazym "rebellion" trials. Recent, contrasting examples include the museum curators Ronalda Olzina and Antonina Siazi, folklorist-activists Tatiana and Timofei Moldanov, the poet Maria Vagatova, the artist Tatiana Taligina, and the activist Agrafina Sopochina.

Particularly renowned is the Khanty writer Eremei Aipin, who in the post-Soviet period has become a prominent Native leader. Aipin's novel *Khanty*, written in Russian with Khanty phrases amply explained, poignantly expressed Native generational and identity tensions (1990:196):

> [Old Man Demian] felt that his sons were growing farther apart from him and his way of thought. . . . Without ties to the earth of one's birth, in big or small matters, there will be no success . . . the spirit-soul of a person will die. And that spirit-soul dies along with the people's singers, storytellers, and "singing ancients"—musical instruments of bone, wood, skins, reindeer sinew, and horse hair.

Sovietization was the form this process took.

Perhaps the most enduring legacy of the Soviet period was the introduction of not only literacy but an appreciation of its value. One Khanty elder, musing on the success he anticipated for his children, remarked to me in 1976, "I do not remember [as well as I would like to] what my fathers said, because I cannot write."

In sum, the scale and conception of Sovietization of indigenous peoples was unprecedented as a form of highly ideologized colonization. The motives of outsider-activists ranged widely, and local responses were correspondingly diverse. Through the Soviet period, official policy manifested an underlying tension between dragging Natives into a modern economy with settled life-styles and allowing them to keep some aspects of their traditions, values, and senses of self-worth. For many, the biculturalism that developed was uneasy, far more complex psychologically than the Stalinist propaganda ideal "National in form, Socialist in content." In interrelated personal and cultural matters, the reverse more often pertained: "comrades" became superficially Socialist, with deepened national cultural values and loyalty.[46] Natives were not passive victims; their options were both constrained and opened by Soviet policies. Tensions and clashes of values, having subsided but never vanished during the Soviet period, became at once worse and more evident in the post-Soviet period of self-aggrandizing regionalism.

CHAPTER SIX

Regionalization: Lands and Identities in Crisis

We do not want to always have to be the fire brigade.
(Anatoly Volgin, Ministry of Nationalities official, 1993)

We are not disappearing from the face of the earth.
(Yuri Vella, poet, 1996)

DEBATES IN AND ON TRANSITION

IN 1991, leaders of the Association for the Salvation of the Ugra thought they were going to be given a chance to pour out concerns about the political and economic transition in West Siberia to newly elected Russian Federation president Boris Yeltsin in a private meeting. Like much associated with that moment of optimism, the opportunity "to tell it all" never came. Russians and indigenous peoples alike are left struggling to make sense of a transition that seems to stimulate land grabbing and money laundering as often as resource sharing and federation building. The 1990s have represented so much to so many that pinning a label on it is premature. Yet the pushing and pulling of power from the Moscow center to resource-rich periphery regions has been a dominant trend, one that does not bode well for Native Siberians.

From the birth of the Association for the Salvation of the Ugra in 1989 to the wail of pain expressed in a 1997 community letter of protest to the United Nations against an illegal land auction, indigenous leaders have tried to express what they see happening to their peoples. The letter, naming specific parcels of endangered land that include part of an existing ecological preserve, declared, "The National *Obshchina* [Community] Yaoun-Yakh of the Khanty people . . . refuses to accept the putting up for auction . . . the following land parcels for the use of their subsurface resources."[1]

I am still haunted by the outburst of Ronalda S. Olzina, the Khanty-Mansiisk ethnography museum director, after she saw the energy boomtown Beloiar, and the trash-strewn gas-pipeline road from Beloiar to Kazym: "I have a deadening pang of hurt when I see the road and what people have done near it. How much does one have to hate the land to do that to it?"[2]

This chapter explores the ramifications of regionalization and development, initiated before the full collapse of the Soviet Union and continuing within the Russian Federation. I frame the discussion in terms of debates that help define the dimensions of cultural survival for Native Siberians. Perestroika and glasnost' unleashed a cacophony of voices worthy of attention. One set of debates involves the rise of indigenous activist groups in the midst of center-periphery dynamics. A second set concerns land in the political and economic transition. Third are issues of demography, intermarriage, and health; and finally, questions of education are raised in the context of trends toward Native "neotraditionalism" (cf. Pika and Prokhorov 1994).

The debates speak to wider concerns about the nature of post-Socialist society, as global human rights values reach the far corners of Siberia and as the outside world is in turn influenced by post-Soviet transitions (cf. Verdery 1996; Hann and Dunn 1996). Tensions between constructing a locally viable civic society ("sustainable democracy") and retreating into regional oligarchies are playing out especially sharply in West Siberia (cf. Przeworski 1995; Dawisha and Parrott 1997). Nesting levels of politics are reflected in the dynamics of obschina (community) versus okrug (district) versus oblast' (region) versus Moscow interaction that analysts of the transition in the regions need to confront (cf. McAuley 1997; Stoner-Weiss 1997).

NATIVE LEADERSHIP: "WE HAVE OUTGROWN CHILDREN'S TROUSERS"

In 1991, Tatiana Moldanova explained: "Our most important questions, [our] appeals to President Yeltsin, must be about the land. They need oil and we need land. We need to control our own land." Her plea would sound familiar and understandable in the context of 1990s U.S. and Canadian First Nations politics, but in the maelstrom of Russian Federation politics, it was considered radical. Khanty schoolteacher Olga Kravchenko (1996:44) adds a further, soul-searching dimension: "What place should my people occupy among other indigenous minority peoples and among the larger peoples?"

The Evenk writer Alitet Nemtushkin's earlier (1988) cry of the heart, "We have outgrown the children's trousers," was more than rhetoric, for many educated Native intelligentsia came to feel their Russian "big brothers" were more paternal than fraternal. These attitudes were reflected in the old Soviet term for the twenty-six groups lucky enough to come under affirmative-action-type legal protection (*l'goty*) categories: "small peoples." By the glasnost' period, this was clarified to mean "numerically small peoples," but the stigma was there, symbolized by a plethora of ethnic "Chukchi" jokes.[3]

The Khanty writer Eremei Aipin jumped into debates about political self-determination with a now famous article, "Not by Oil Alone," with subsections entitled "Where are my people [*rod*] going?" and "How can my people be saved?" (1989:8–9). The article was part of his campaign for election as a deputy to the 1989 All-Union Congress of People's Deputies. He won. Aipin explained that his "ancient ugrian people" were in danger of "destruction" and outlined how, since the beginning of the energy boom, indigenous people had lost traditional family territories in the Yamal-Nenets and Khanty-Mansi okrugs of the Tiumen Region: eleven million hectares of reindeer-grazing land; twenty-eight productive rivers, and vast hunting and gathering lands. The article began with a blood-chilling story about Aipin's seventy-six-year-old father, who had been waylaid on his reindeer sled by two workers in a truck. One grabbed him from the back by the shoulders while the other snatched his fur-appliquéd boots and made off with them. The old man made his way home in his socks. Luckily it was not far, or his feet would have frozen.

Aipin, who eventually became head of the Moscow-based Association of the Peoples of the North, Siberia, and the Far East, ended his article with a plea for each indigenous group to have a national region, national village councils, and national villages, where "self-determination" would be established by multileveled agreement. His land claims for his people included Khanty-Mansiisk, the capital of the Khanty-Mansi Okrug, though he recognized that an "autonomous region cannot solve all problems."[4]

Aipin's ideal, similar to the goals of the Association for the Salvation of the Ugra, was highjacked by Russian administrators of the Khanty-Mansi Okrug and the Tiumen Oblast to take power from Moscow for themselves. It was also foiled by President Yeltsin's court-ordered dissolution of the village and regional councils in 1993, a move intended to dislodge entrenched Communist leaders but one that also swept out reformist indigenous leaders from influence in local political organizations. In place of village councils some obshchiny have developed. They are modeled on prerevolutionary indigenous, land-based councils, organized by small kin groups. But even such obshchiny as Yaoun Yakh of the Eastern Yugan Khanty have had to prove their validity in local courts.[5]

The Association for the Salvation of the Ugra was founded in 1989, prior to the first congress of the "peoples of the North," held in Moscow in 1990. Based in Khanty-Mansiisk, it developed informally from the friendships of a new-style matriarchate, as Tatiana Moldanova described in 1991: "Women have started and been the backbone of the whole thing. Really seven women. It started at the home of Ella's [Elvida I. Mal'tseva] mother, plus the Ethnography Museum head Ronalda S. Olzina, her sister, and Tatiana Gogoleva [founding president]." Tatiana Moldanova, activist-ethnographer, Timofei Moldanov, reindeer breeder turned folklorist (both originally from Yuilsk), and Zoia Riabchekova (from Tegy) were also founding members (photo 5).

Women recently have become the "backbones" of Khanty and Mansi village and town life, as elsewhere in Siberia, in part because they are often better educated and have tended to be less prone to alcoholism, though that too was changing by the end of the Soviet period.[6] The Association not only named itself "Ugra" because they wanted the broadest incorporation of Khanty and Mansi participants, but they also encouraged Nentsy living in the Khanty-Mansi Okrug to join. Nentsy have a comparable association in the Yamal-Nenets Okrug, called Yamal Potemkom (Yamal for our Progeny). Female leaders of these organizations explicitly hoped to transcend stereotyped divisions among the groups by adopting names with broad ethnic and historical resonance.

Photo 5. Tatiana and Timofei Moldanov, founding members of the Association for the Salvation of the Ugra and organizers of the Kazym ethnographic film seminar. Timofei is reading the local newspaper, *Beloiarskii novosti*. In the background is Nadezhda Lirshikova, math teacher in Khanty-Mansiisk and participant in the film seminar. Kazym, 1991.

Controversy over having a young, attractive woman as a spokesperson, however intelligent and articulate, led eventually to Tatiana Gogoleva's temporary departure as president in 1994.[7] Her place was taken by a Vakh Khanty man, Valentin M. Molotkov, who represented the informal, old-style Khanty male leadership of good hunters and known families. However, his performance (and Communist Party background) was such that Tatiana Gogoleva was again elected president by 1996, when membership had considerably expanded. Tatiana Gogoleva described the goals of the Association in a 1991 interview with me:

> It was the wish of our intelligentsia to join together to reclaim our culture and our rights. . . . We were inspired by the activism of the Inuit Circumpolar Conference, which was begun in Denmark back in 1977. But we in the Soviet Union have had no political experience. . . . We had to begin somewhere. We are trying to develop ties and create an organization. Our main issues are the culture . . . and land, the most important of all. Even now many of our people are living scattered in small communities, as they have traditionally. . . . We have to protect them. . . . Because of the gas and development, people are kicked out of their homes.

The majority politics of snide dismissal that Tatiana Gogoleva and Valentin Molotkov have encountered in the Khanty-Mansi Okrug local Duma (parliament) is clear from a report in *Tiumenskaia Pravda* (Shilnikov 1995):

> The Duma started its sessions with discussion of the Khanty-Mansi Okrug charter. . . . The essence of the disagreement: "We have to understand what the Khanty-Mansi Okrug is. Whose land are we living on? Who is the master here? At least 25 percent of the land use fees should go to the indigenous peoples" (V. Molotkov). [Response:] "Have you read the part of the constitution regarding land and mineral resources, Valentin Mikhailovich?" (P. Volostrigov).

The deputy chair of the okrug Duma, Volostrigov, a Russian aligned with the energy development community, was sarcastically referring to the Russian Federation constitution, passed by the federation Duma and narrowly ratified by voters in December 1993. It allocates subsurface rights to the central government or puts them under the "joint jurisdiction" of the central government and the affected region, thus leaving indigenous peoples in the vulnerable position of hoping for specific instances of goodwill in "joint jurisdiction" discussions. Usually they are left out entirely.[8]

On the street outside the Duma, a small, symbolic protest was organized by the Association, complete with a *chum* (tipi-like tent of animal skins). Indigenous protesters were hoping not only for some legislated percentage of land use fees, but also for their own "miniparliament," with veto power over cases of land encroachment and misuse. On this too, the Duma debated: "'We need to create an assembly made up of six deputies and give them veto power' (V. Molotkov). 'You can have the assembly, no problem. The charter envisages this, Valentin Mikhailovich; regarding veto power, however—this way we will never adopt a single decision'(S. Sobianin)" (Shilnikov 1995).

The creation of a token miniparliament for local Ugra, written into the third draft of the Khanty-Mansi Okrug charter, was conceded in the context of increased pressure on local and central authorities by indigenous peoples since 1990. Three dimensions of this still shaky dynamic have coalesced: local indigenous protests, however weak and poorly advertised; the organizing of indigenous peoples of the North, Siberia, and Far East, beginning with their 1990 Kremlin Congress, however controversial and splintered; and international awareness and solidarity, however limited and haphazard.

Important international solidarity has been established with the Inuit Circumpolar Conference, Saami (Lapp) organizations such as the Saami Nordic Council, the Estonian Society of Ugrians, and some Native American leaders and communities. Indigenous-rights advocacy by United Nations support groups (in New York and Geneva), M. C. Van Walt van Praag's Unrepresented Nations and Peoples Organization, and the human rights division of the World Bank, which has investment interests in West Siberia, has also improved morale. News of diverse indigenous advocacy programs traveled through informal channels and eventually enabled some Khanty participation in international meetings. But the dominant stimuli toward Siberian activism have been local conditions, combined with the basic knowledge that organizing "from below" no longer led to jail.

The 1990 Kremlin Congress was at least a partial "victory" for indigenous peoples, because it foiled some Communist attempts to coopt and orchestrate the gathering "from above." The congress represented the first political steps toward coalition by indigenous peoples sharing similar Soviet experiences—"brethren in misery," as Teleut spokesperson Nikolai Todyshev said.[9] Dislodging the planned leadership of the Nivkh ethnographer Chuner Taksami, the congress (past midnight) elected the Nivkh writer Vladimir Sangi, who served as president until 1993. They dismissed the presentation of Soviet Fuel and Energy Minister Rafikov, whose promises to "establish normal social and economic conditions for native peoples of the North" rang hollow and familiar (cf. Chichlo 1990:112). Subsequent congresses have been less dramatic and have revealed deep splits among the leaders.[10] But an important document of protest, outlining specific grievances and concrete proposals and addressed to President Yeltsin and other government authorities, was signed by the leaders of all constituent activist groups in 1996, in a significant gesture of solidarity (see appendix A).

Local protests, in addition to those outside the Khanty-Mansi Duma, have focused on rail, pipeline, and road projects. The most widely known of these was the fight against further rail and road development into Yamal, deemed crucial by the Yamal energy industry, in 1990. The protest, in the Varegansk area, was organized by the writer Yuri Vella (Vella-Aivaseda) and included such well-known indigenous leaders as Nanai ethnographer and politician Evdokiia Gayer, in addition to local Khanty, Nentsy, Russians, and Ukrainians.[11] A *chum* was put up across a road, and drivers were stopped as Russian Central TV cameras captured the action and anger. According to participants, some of the (Russian and Ukrainian) drivers joined in the protest, although the issue polarized the community, torn between hopes for a better local economy and ecology concerns.

Joseph Sopochin, in 1995, recalled: "When they put up the *chum*, a lot of drivers were angry. But everyone explained to them what was going on, and a lot of people joined the Native side. It [the publicity] worked, though some sat in their cars and trucks and fumed, waiting for the local administration to remove the roadblock." "Was there any later result?" I asked. "Well, there were some specific demands," he replied. "I think they got some improvements in local village building projects. . . . It was not completely wasted."

The complex Yamal energy development program encountered so many technical and political problems that the major Western backer, AMOCO, had pulled out, or at least put the project on hold, by 1996. On the other hand, excavation for a gas pipeline to run from Yamal to Germany was begun in Belarus in February 1997.

Another roadblock protest, on a bridge over the Tromyugan River at Nizhnevartovsk, in Eastern Khanty territory, was staged in 1993. It too featured a *chum* and was focused on local concern for the ecology of the Russkinskie area. Some oil company truck drivers joined the protest, and a later referendum that went against the Surgutneftegaz firm (headed by the extremely wealthy Alexander Bogdanov) showed that Khanty voters were not the only ones worried about damage from oil drilling. Okrug officials funneled compensation money for damaged lands into the mixed-ethnic community of Russkinskie, where new apartments were built as much for non-Native as Native occupants, and where a new school turned out to have been constructed with contaminated materials, rendering it useless.[12]

Demonstrations cannot achieve long-term solutions to Native concerns, as indigenous leaders acknowledge. Demonstrations have drawn dangerous attention to specific local leaders, who are then threatened by non-Native regional administrators and sometimes even beaten by local police.

VIOLENCE, LAND GRABS, AND RESOURCE COMPETITION

Violence erupted in 1993 at Russkinskie, after an unusually public Khanty sacrifice ceremony of seven reindeer that had crowned the Fourth International Finno-Ugric People's Folklore Festival. The Estonian Society of Ugrians reported:

> Violence of the militia toward the native people of the area continues. On June 25, a sacrifice ceremony took place at the IV International Finno-Ugric People's Folklore Festival in the village of Russkinskiye. The following night militia sergeant Aleksandr Ludvigovich Dyagilev, with a car from the Fedorovskoe Militia Department, along with another unknown man, destroyed the sacrifice structure. The same night, Leonid Sopochin and Evgeni Multanov, the shamans who had conducted the ceremony, as well as natives Daniel Devlin and Ivan Vylla, were savagely beaten by the militia. The two others who had assisted with the ceremony were not found, although they were hunted.[13]

In 1998, a Khanty friend recalled the violence that had occurred after the reindeer sacrifice: "they tried to beat people they thought were shamans. . . . The devil knows why they did it." "They" were somehow tied to the local police and administration. "They wrecked the ceremonial structures that had been set up and scattered the fire. But they did not find everyone they were looking for."

Folklorist and activist-fieldworker Olga Balalaeva shared her insight into this event in March 1994: "The sacrifice was more open this time because it was for the festival. The destruction of the sacrifice structure was a threat, a symbolic way to show the locals they must give up land to Surgutneftegaz." Energy and okrug administrators claimed that the leaders of the sacrifice were the same people who had been telling Natives not to sign over their land for energy exploration, and so the administrators decided to teach them a lesson. No one was arrested for the beatings, although it was commonly known who was involved. The attack occurred as the celebrants were preparing an additional ceremony, so witnesses were numerous; but they were intimidated into silence.

Political maneuvers also have involved attempted changes of local administrative boundaries. These attempts point to patterns of using indigenous peoples to gain access to resources and of splitting indigenous territories so that activists will be less able to influence development in mixed-ethnic communities. The plots fit into larger political games designed to wrest power (and tax revenues) from Moscow. Many attempts to alter boundaries have failed, but a few at local levels have succeeded.[14]

One example is a referendum in 1993 on a small territorial adjustment in Eastern Khanty territory, transferring a part of Russkinskie to Liantor. The change went through, although the Khanty uniformly voted against it. Since Khanty are relatively more numerous in Russkinskie than Liantor, where many Russians connected with energy development are based, the redrawn boundary meant that Khanty voices favoring ecological restraint would be drowned in any votes on development taken in Liantor.[15]

A second, more high-profile example was an attempt in the early 1990s to get Mansi leaders to split the Khanty-Mansi Okrug into two, with the Mansi seceding from Tiumen Oblast and joining neighboring Sverdlovsk Oblast. Sverdlovsk administrators (including the famed Edward Rousell, later elected governor) wanted some of the energy wealth of the okrug, but they did not promise enough benefits and were outmaneuvered by Tiumen authorities. Mansi writer Yuvan Shestalov was at first talked into supporting the move. He backed down when other Mansi did not follow and when he was promised only cultural support and political "autonomy," rather than any concrete, land-based self-determination. This was a case of how Russians tried to exploit Khanty and Mansi rivalry in the dynamics of regionalization.[16]

Rivalry among Russian-led administrative levels is revealed by attempts of the Yamal-Nenets and Khanty-Mansi Okrugs to secede from the Tiumen Oblast. Okrug authorities tried to prevent residents from voting in the Tiumen gubernatorial race in 1996, declaring the okrugs to be independent, with "charter" rights allowing direct lines to Moscow, bypassing Tiumen. Surgut authorities in the Eastern Khanty energy-boom region were quite active in pushing the election boycott, but a newly elected okrug Duma eventually voted to participate. At stake, one report claimed, were tax levels and percentages of export rights for 53 percent of the federation's oil and 90 percent of the country's natural gas reserves.[17] Indigenous groups benefited only marginally from energy profits, in that any advantageous deals struck by the okrug might trickle down to them, if they cooperated with local authorities. Officials were ready to use (small) carrots as well as (large) sticks.

Some "carrots" have come in the form of cultural support, most publicly for the Fourth International Finno-Ugric Peoples Festival, the Association for the Salvation of the Ugra, and the Institute for Ob-Ugrian Revival, the last two both based in Khanty-Mansiisk. The Association's acceptance of energy money, even indirectly, has created controversy in the 1990s, with moralists arguing that they cannot effectively fight development if they are in the pay of okrug administrators, who are in turn too cozy with energy company officials. But others argue that it is precisely energy money, in fixed percentages, that should go toward cultural revitalization and toward building and maintaining "infrastructure," such as schools, housing, and clinics.[18]

Some social benefits have ensued, not only in Russkinskie but also in Kazym and elsewhere. In 1991, Kazym residents acknowledged that they were grateful for their new school, paid for with compensation funds from the development of nearby Beloiarsk. But they noticed a contrast between the relatively luxurious health and educational amenities provided for energy workers in Beloiarsk and what was given to Kazym. One matron griped: "The city of Beloiarsk has grown up with an indoor swimming pool and even a music school for the children, plus indoor plumbing for the parents. Why couldn't this have been done in Kazym?" Kazym Khanty were also infuriated at the theft of the sacred lands around a nearby lake at Kislor, where energy workers were building dachas.

In 1990, the composure of villagers on the Tromyugan River was disrupted when an oil company representative (an ethnic Bashkir) arrived to begin explorations in the area. He announced, according to Finnish ethnographer Juha Pentikäinen (1997:106): "We will not take anything from you. We will only investigate what riches may lie under your reindeer pastures. If we find oil, your backward life will change."

They found oil, there and in the whole neighboring region. Joseph Sopochin, one of the leaders of the area, tried to work for the oil company Surgutneftegaz but found he could last only a few months. In a 1995 meeting at the Bureau of Indian Affairs, he explained: "We were always told that the state priority was oil, and that we were lucky to live in an area with such resources." He called it "colonization in the form of oil development," noting it had begun long before the Soviet Union collapsed, but intensified with privatization.[19]

The Tromyugan community of Joseph Sopochin at first refused to negotiate with the Bashkir oil representative, and in a meeting asked Juha Pentikäinen's group (1997:106–7) to publicize the following points: "The immemorial usufruct of the wilderness guarantees its ownership. Geological research in the areas inhabited by the Khanty must be forbidden, because it upsets the ecological balance of nature. The indigenous inhabitants of the area must have the right to local autonomy." They were later caught up in the kind of energy-company politics that people had most feared would come with privatization: playing off one family against another. Vladimir Kogonchin elaborated:

> The Soviets did not recognize Native people's land as communal land. There was never even the recognition of any kind of principle of their sovereignty. But recently privatization has meant that family territories have been defined, and borders drawn more specifically than they had been. This means people have some recognized territories, but also that the oil companies can try to lease them, and they do. There is a real danger of selling them off or leasing for mere snowmobiles. In many cases, people have not even known what they signed. The government still claims subsurface rights to everything. And the obshchiny [communities] are only "voluntary associations."[20]

Leasing land for a mere snowmobile is only a slight exaggeration. Some families were promised snowmobiles, supplies for a winter, money, gas, and, if they were lucky, funds or materials to build a new house. In short, various bribes have been offered for individuals to sign away exploration rights. Some of the "carrots" depend on where the families live, and who (how influential) they are in their communities. This is why it has become crucial for the Khanty to organize their obshchiny as groups, to defend their rights to a set of family territories, so that no one family's personal finances or temptations can ruin an entire community's reindeer breeding and hunting. Development decisions and negotiations in this context can then be made as a group, with extensive consultations, and with less danger of alcohol-induced lapses of judgment.

In communities where signatures have been hard to get, some local authorities have resorted to other means. One local administrator in 1991 had the bright idea that he could simply forge the signatures, and he proceeded to do so by signing local names without bothering to disguise his handwriting. Attempts by indigenous leaders and others to reveal this tale in Moscow backfired. The whole incriminating package landed back in the hands of local court authorities—hardly people inclined to prosecute their own district bosses.[21]

Deadly serious games over signatures have continued through the 1990s. The Institute for Ecology and Action Anthropology reported in 1997 that Khanty on the Pim River, within Surgutneftegaz jurisdiction, were being pressured over exploration rights. For example, an "Anna Petrovna" nearly had her lands negotiated out from under her by her sons-in-law. "They said they had been taken directly to Senur Markianovich Khuseinov [head of the Kamynskoe oil field], where the table had already been laid with bottles of vodka. While they emptied the bottles a lot of promises were made. But what exactly they said, they could not remember when they came back, urging Anna Petrovna to sign . . . that the helicopter could not wait." Anna agreed to a limited one-year winter exploration with three drilling platforms. But if oil is found, further pressure will be on her to agree to derricks, a road through marshes, dams, pipelines—and the destruction of nearby reindeer pastures.[22]

Since 1989, fourteen new exploration or production platforms have been erected on Yaloki Nimperov's lands, with derricks clanking day and night. To calm his fury about his lands and the poaching perpetrated by energy workers, the oil company put him in charge of a checkpoint, with a regular salary. But when the company wanted three new production platforms, and he did not want to sign, they threatened him with loss of his new job. His only victory to date has been that a bus from the oil company now picks up Khanty on its way into town. The bus had refused to stop until Yaloki threatened to blow up a nearby bridge. Yaloki wrote recently to Khuseinov: "If you take one hundred pounds of my gold, then why can't you leave me just two [?]."[23]

An elder, Peres Iki (*iki* means "old man"), has fared even worse, for he has not known how to fight the company. Each year new derricks have appeared on his lands. He was shocked to find that the company had switched the position of one derrick without consulting him, placing it in the center of his summer reindeer pasture. Caring little for proffered videos, he had accepted a promise of building materials for a new home. The company has yet to provide the materials.

Olga Balalaeva returned from 1995 summer fieldwork in the Nizhnevartovsk area with similar stories. "I got to one camp, where people were living very close to one of the new energy boom 'villages of the town type.' The Khanty are frightened even to defend their sacred groves from vandalism. One man tried and was beaten. . . . One group of Khanty were told they had to sign away their family lands. This was ordered by a known local official with ties to Megionneftegaz [energy company]." I asked indelicately: "Russian?" "Yes, Russian. People were told they would receive a Buran [Russian-made snowmobile] if they signed, but that things would go badly for them if they did not."[24]

The wild-West (Siberia) nature of unchecked energy company activities had become clear by the mid-1990s. Cowboys were riding through the gaps in a changing legal system rife with poorly enforced laws. In 1994, an American, actually wearing a cowboy hat, told me at a cocktail party about the investments of his Texas energy company, White Nights (no *k*) in West Siberia: "Sure we are helping the local Eskimo. We are building them a culture center." "Eskimo? Culture center?" I asked. "How about a medical clinic for the Khanty?"[25]

The cleaner technology of Western companies could be a boon to the energy industry in the region, as could their support of human rights—if they were paying more attention. In 1997, I had another social encounter, with a high-level Occidental Petroleum executive so removed from local concerns that he did not realize there were any indigenous peoples or any conflicts over land around Nizhnevartovsk, where Occidental has been reworking fields. He seemed genuinely upset when I described the situation.

In this context, the opening story of this book, about the Eastern Khanty men confronting geologists in their camp after a theft from a local sacred storehouse, becomes clearer in its significance. The geologists were given an ultimatum to leave the area within a day, but they inevitably returned. Olga Balalaeva finished her 1995 Nizhnevartovsk description: "It is open season on the Natives. Not only are people being beaten if they show any spunk, but there has been conscious and systematic hunting of their deer. Local geologists and others associated with the energy industry have purposely mobilized their guys to go and hunt the Khanty's deer."

Into this swamp has come a plan, sponsored by the Moscow-based Goskomsevera (Committee of the North, carved from the Ministry of Nationalities), advocated by deputy minister Anatoly Volgin. To save at least one major Eastern Khanty territory, as yet still ecologically clean, from energy development, Goskomsevera has backed the expansion of an already existing "ecology preserve [*zapovednik*]" in the Yugan region. This is the homeland of Vladimir Kogonchin's obshchina, Yaoun Yakh. His community of eight hundred members is fully behind the plan, as confirmed with signatures in 1996. Given varied statuses of "ecology preserves" in Russian Federation law, it was crucial to push for conditions that would permit local Khanty full access to land that was already, supposedly, theirs, for the continuation of their "traditional means of livelihood." Thus the United Nations (UNESCO) "Biosphere Reserve" concept was used, and local and energy officials were lobbied to accept special status for this territory, as the "Yuganskii Khanty Biosphere Reserve."[26]

Local officials agreed in principle to the concept in 1996, with a significant caveat: that lands currently slated for "license" would be exempt. By 1997, it developed that these officials, including governor of the Khanty-Mansi Okrug Alexander V. Filipenko, had known exactly what they were doing, for they had scheduled extensive land parcels in the region to be auctioned. As Wiget and Balalaeva write (1997:25), "Tracts of the Yugan, which the Khanty use to feed their families, are still being sold out from under them without their knowledge or consent." Three parcels, Achimovsk, Multanovsk, and Tailokhovsk, are coveted by Rosinvestneft. In addition to the illegality of auctioning land without the signed consent of its occupants, the Tailokhovsk parcel cuts into the existing, "protected" Russian Federation *zapovednik*, "preserve."[27]

By late 1997, under increased pressure, Governor Filipenko stopped these auctions and appointed a commission to review the possibility of creating a biosphere for the Yugan Khanty. In a public, business-bolstering appearance in Washington, he seconded the confident gloss of his fellow regional governor Yuri Neelov of the Yamal-Nenets Okrug: "We support the traditional way of life of the small-numbered peoples. We should not disturb their way of life. They are not us. One must be especially careful with them."[28] In 1998, Governor Filipenko found a new "solution." He declared the sacred Lake Num-to area to be an Okrug Prirodnyi (Nature) Park, and also authorized drilling there. At a commission meeting on the Yugan biosphere project, he suggested creating another Okrug Nature Park, over the objections of the only Khant, Vladimir Kogonchin, present during the discussion.

DEMOGRAPHY AND SURVIVAL: GIRLS DO NOT WANT TO LIVE IN A TENT?

The Khanty today comprise only 1.5 percent of the Khanty-Mansi Okrug, and number about twenty-five thousand in the Russian Federation. Together, all indigenous groups constitute only about 3 percent of the okrug. The population of the oil-rich Surgut region alone mushroomed from less than ten thousand in 1965 to over three hundred thousand thirty years later, mostly from the influx of Russian workers (Wiget and Balalaeva 1997:22). Khanty thus fit into broader trends of indigenous demographic and cultural endangerment (Miller 1993; Perry 1996). With increased urgency, Khanty scholars and activists debate their destiny and take steps to brake these trends of despair and assimilation.

In 1976, I made much of the existence of the small "traditional" village of Amnia, across the river from the more built-up and Russified Kazym "culture base." And in 1991, when I returned, I was intrigued to find not only that Amnia still existed but that a few Khanty families were moving back to Amnia from Kazym, that abandoned houses were being repaired, and some new ones being built, on the "Amnia" side.

Amnia was a Khanty winter village of yurts long before Kazym was founded. Amnia residents could not recall when their ancestors began staying there, since it had long been a logical camping spot near the Kazym and Amnia confluence. The oldest family in Amnia was probably the Kaksins, who had their hunting and fishing territories up-river on the Amnia. Convenient to Amnia was a sacred grove. Nearby was the site of an old fort village dating from the pre-Slavic period wars of Nentsy and Khanty ancestors. For hundreds of years, Khanty annually canoed to this fort to pay respects to the dead and to celebrate lineage and phratry rituals, featuring reindeer sacrifices.

After Kazym was established, some Amnia families eventually moved across the river to Kazym for its stores, its convenience, and its school. But some Khanty chose to remain in Amnia, limiting their contact with "Russian civilization." In both 1976 and 1991, I saw the relation between Amnia and Kazym as a metaphor for the interaction of many Khanty with Russians. While Russian goods and services were welcomed, many Khanty held back from crossing over entirely to the Russian side. A river flows between them, easily conquered by motorboat, canoe, or walking on ice, but subtly demarcating a relatively traditional way of life from a more modern one. Since Khanty who lived in Amnia were part of the Kazym collective, I extended the metaphor to the realm of identity, suggesting that Amnia residents had learned to add to their Amnia personas new Kazym social identities. They moved back and forth between old and new identities, just as they traveled to and from Kazym (Balzer 1983a; see photo 3, chapter 5).

This cheerful assessment of bicultural flexibility was not inaccurate, but it was incomplete. It left out the pain of some cultural choices and the forced nature of much Sovietization. As in so many other places in Siberia, Kazym was a conglomerate of people who had been forced from their family territories, especially during processes of "consolidation" in the 1950s. In 1991, an elderly man with his grandson ran after me on the beach on the Kazym side, asking me to take a photograph (polaroid) of them on their pretty motorboat. I obliged, and suddenly, looking across to Amnia, he poured out a story that brought him, to his own surprise, to tears:

> I was forced to move from Amnia to Kazym. I didn't want to. When they created the sovkhoz, they squeezed us like this [*wringing his hands together tightly*]. I've had a rough life, but I have managed to get something out of it. Look at these boots, these motorboats [*gesturing toward several*]. These are our family's. And now we are building another house for one of my sons over in Amnia. But I still live on the Kazym side. And what will my sons have? What have they got to look forward to? This perestroika stuff has lost us our discipline. We need some control. But then I look at the past. I did not want to move from Amnia. . . . Look, I have gotten so upset, tears have come.

The message of Amnia is especially significant in the post-Soviet context. Many Khanty, confused and upset, are trying to control the quality and degree of their contacts with Russians on lands Khanty still perceive to be their own, even if larger towns nearby have become inundated with oil, oil money, and "newcomers." Some leaders have attempted reindeer-breeding experiments with villagers long-unused to rigorous camp life.[29]

Despite being a tiny minority in the region, many Khanty do live separately, whether in camps, villages, or towns. Most marry within their group or with other Natives. Between 1957 and 1966 (before the oil boom), of the 1064 marriages in the Tomsk and Tiumen Oblasts involving Khanty or Mansi, 86 percent were endogamous. Even in the capital, Khanty-Mansiisk and its outskirts, 71 percent of marriages were endogamous (Sokolova 1970:96).

High rates of in-group marriage were consistent with the socioeconomic records for the Tegy and Kazym rural jurisdictions in 1976. The Kazym records included data for two small outlying villages that were solidly Khanty, two that were nearly all Khanty (with a few Mansi or Komi exceptions), and two with mixed Khanty-Nentsy families. Even in central Kazym, few intermarriages were recorded, despite the ethnically mixed population and the ethnically mixed composition of some work brigades. In 1976, 10 percent of the interethnic Khanty marriages were with Russians and the rest were with other Native Siberians. About 80 percent of the Khanty marriages were endogamous. Marriages were frequently between members of the founding families; for example, Tarlins, Ernikhovs, and Kaksins.

By 1991 in Kazym, interethnic marriage had increased, by necessity. Young people had trouble finding mates if they did not look to other ethnic groups. But the ideal of endogamy prevailed, and over 60 percent of Khanty marriages were endogamous. Nadezhda Karpovna Moldanova (Tatiana's mother), a lovely Russian lady who had married a Khanty man and learned the Khanty language, explained the tensions: "Our Khanty girls are sometimes taken away by Russians and Ukrainians. They go to work in Rossiia and marry [there]. But then sometimes our sons find [outside] girls and bring them here. And maybe that is all right. Maybe they do not drink so much because they are in love with these girls. . . . It is more common for Khanty girls to find Russian and Ukrainian husbands. . . . There are a lot of mixed marriages. How else are young people going to find spouses?"[30]

Marriage possibilities have been even more limited for the reindeer breeders, in and after the Soviet period. As elsewhere in Siberia, many in Kazym lamented that the reindeer breeders' sons were having a hard time finding wives. "Girls just don't want to live in a tent," I was told more than once. When I asked if it had been that way since the 1960s, people agreed, but said the problem had intensified. Antonina Siazi, Khanty director of the ethnographic museum at Salekhard, confided in

1991 that she had personally found two young women for her two reindeer-breeding brothers. "Our guys are great, worth marrying, do not drink, and they have stayed married. But it was hard to talk these educated girls [from a pedagogical institute], into going out there. Now they are happy they did." In 1993, Northern Khanty artist Nadezhda Taligina provided another angle:

> When I decided I wanted to have a child, I realized I had a big problem. I was not sure I could find a husband I could live with. I have a higher education as a teacher and an artist. I had become used to living in Salekhard, independently. I could see that most of the available men were drunkards, and I wanted to find a husband of my own people. This was one very big problem. I am very lucky. I did find someone who is well trained, an engineer, one of the only workers in the gas industry who is an educated Khant. He has a high-level job and he is very valued, well respected, where he works. But he had one very big deficiency when we met. . . . He too loved his drink. After we became a family, I made it very clear that he had a choice, me and my child or his drinking.

Nadezhda's marriage is a far cry from the arranged marriages of the past, when Khanty brides were expected to marry in the proper category of phratry and lineage, to perpetuate complex exchange relationships.[31] Well versed in Khanty ethnography, she had written a dissertation on life passage rituals (as did I). And in a very knowing way, this elegant urban Khanty woman had gone back to some of the spirituality of her youth, in part through the culture of women's sacred groves:

> I remember how we laughed together and did predictions. We dressed in our best clothes—it was a holiday. We prayed, to the house spirits and to Num-Torum. When I go back home again, I will go again [to the sacred grove]. If a woman who knows how to do predictions is there, it is especially merry. Only some women know how to do this, especially older women, but not necessarily. Women ask questions: 'Why is my child sick? My husband drunk? Who will join our family?'

Many have not adapted as well as Nadezhda Taligina. Tales of desperation and suicide are common in the North, especially among indigenous peoples. Without full statistical information, it is unwise to assert categorically that suicide has accelerated among the Khanty in the 1990s (Pika and Prokhorov 1988:76–83; cf. Pavlenko 1995:119–40). However, life expectancy for indigenous groups in Siberia is eight to ten years below the already low levels for Russian men (fifty-nine) and women (sixty-six) (Feshbach 1995:8). While many deaths are from heart disease, as in other countries, some evidence points to a rise in accidental deaths, often alcohol related, and in suicides as well.

Even in 1976, when the stories were told sotto voce, I collected heart-rending accounts of suicide, including among young people. Some recent Khanty interpretations of suicide suggest that it may be particularly frequent in certain families. In a variation on Western psychiatric studies indicating that depression may run in families (Romanucci-Ross et al. 1996), a Northern Khanty friend confided:

> We have had too many suicides in our family. Not long ago a woman of only about fifty committed suicide. She was much too young to go, and there really was no good reason. But when we got in touch with her spirit, she said that a voice had come to her and told her to go into the woods and hang herself. This is especially in my father's line, as if it is a legacy passed on. The idea of killing came from the spirits, as if they coaxed and taunted her to go to them. She had a family; people loved her.[32]

In Kazym in 1991, I learned of a woman who took her own life because she had become blind (common in the North) and she did not want non-kin trying to assist her. She was helpless and did not want to live that way. A woman who had been her friend said: "Her son had died: had become an alcoholic and a hooligan, and then was killed in an accident. And she had no hope left. That is how suicides occur with us."

Each family tragedy seems to synergistically create another, as loved ones sink into despair. Some would seem like soap operas from another world, too extreme to be believed, if they did not also have certain kernels of human commonality to them. A Kazym friend's mother had been the victim of an alcohol-related car accident, had her legs cut off, and ended up committing suicide. Olga Balalaeva poured out other tales of family crisis and catastrophe (personal communication, November 1995):

> There was the Khanty mother who took her children out in a boat and cut them all and then shot herself to death. Only one child survived, a little crazy after seeing Mama cut his brothers and sisters. She had just reached the end of her rope, thought she could not feed her children anymore and that life was not worth living. The surviving boy is living with other relatives, but has obviously been enormously affected by seeing the mother he loved kill her family. . . . And then there was the lovely bridal couple. A really very beautiful Khanty girl, intelligent and quick, so bright that she had been handpicked by one of the local elders to learn a lot of the old tales and legends. She was a very quick study and could tell stories for hours from memory. At her wedding to a local Khanty guy, they got very drunk with their friends. Some of them went swimming, drunk, and the couple, both of them, drowned. . . . [There also was] the father who came home

> drunk and killed his sons for showing disrespect. He then burned the house down. He was not usually violent like this, but when drunk, became another person. . . . All his anger at the world and his family came out.

In a 1997 electronic alert to Arctic studies colleagues, titled "Government Deception Threatens Destruction of Eastern Khanty Traditional Culture," Wiget and Balalaeva made the case for calling the sum total of energy boom[erang] effects on the Khanty "ethnocide." They cogently argued that the "patterns of deception" of local authorities, combined with the actions of the energy companies bent on quick profit before legal crackdowns are in place, have made the transition economy literally deadly for those who depend on the land for subsistence. Terms like "ethnocide" may be debated, given the haphazard nature of the horrors that have been inflicted on the Khanty, and given the evidence that authorities often would rather coopt than kill indigenous neighbors (some of whom may be connected to them by marriage).[33] Agrafina Sopochina cautions: "Gas workers and aboriginals must work together at the initial stage of law formation, so that mutual interests are considered. The interests of the aboriginals should be represented by a legal entity, such as the obshchina Khanto" (Yaroshko 1998:9). However, Khanty ability to survive surrounded by a sea of oil is an incendiary question.

EDUCATION LEGACIES: LET THEM BE DROPOUTS?

Two friends, one Buryat, one Khanty, got into a potentially hot argument about education for indigenous peoples in a Georgetown University cafeteria in March 1995. Joseph Sopochin, an Eastern Khanty leader with shamanic ancestry (now head of the obshchina Khanto), said: "The boarding school has been terrible for our people. So some of the families are taking their children back to the woods after the third grade." Zoya Morokhoyeva, an ethnologist who has established a "laboratory of cultural anthropology" in Ulan-Ude, Buryatia, politely asked for clarification, hardly believing her ears. "Yes," Joseph answered, "it is fine with me if they want to do this. This way the boys will be able to come right up to a bear and nab him, the way I can. Otherwise, with too much education, they cannot do this." Zoya, quite upset, told Joseph to notice how Indians in the Southwest (where he was about to travel and where she had visited) were educated, living relatively well by Siberian standards and also maintaining their traditions.

While he made the point provocatively, Joseph's position is advocated by a number of Khanty, who feel children should learn to read and to fend for themselves in a multiethnic environment, but require minimal formal education. In Kazym, the reindeer breeders who could not find wives to herd with them (for the girls were all "overeducated") illustrated a perceived ill fit between mass, homogenizing, Soviet-style education and the way of life of a previously well-adapted specific local group. One matron said (1991): "Guys are pushing thirty and still not married. No one wants this. They made a big mistake the way they forced education on everybody. Let the young people learn to read and write and then let them free." The problem, for her, was the coercion of boarding school education and the need of parents to have their children at home to help with the reindeer breeding. She continued: "The parents want them to herd the family deer. If someone else herds them, they will lose them. The deer are their inheritance, and their heritage too. . . . But the young people do not want to live in a *chum* after ten years of school."

Continuing through the tenth grade seemed especially useless, according to Kazym Khanty, some of whom condoned dropping out at the eighth. Similarly, by 1993, Russian Federation law had dropped its mandatory education requirement from ten grades to eight. Even this is too much for some Kazym residents: "Those who do not want to study should not have to. . . . It is torture for them. The little kids run away from the boarding school and then have to be brought back." This has resulted in some dangerous situations, with children exposed to the capricious Siberian weather, lost and hurt.

One Kazym elder recalled that school protests were one of the reasons the Kazym hostage crisis of the 1930s had begun: "The rebellion started against the school. . . . Those parents were right. Were the Khanty to blame? Of course not." The history taught in the Kazym schools, for example about the "rebellion," was a Soviet legacy still fought over, contributing to Khanty pain and insecurity. A friend nearly committed suicide in eighth grade over the discrepancy between how the crisis was remembered in her home and how it was taught in school. She could not stand to be told that the Khanty were traitors. She was also ashamed and angry when Soviet authorities, including local schoolteachers, dismantled the sacred grove at Yuilsk in the 1960s and carted precious ancestral images off to museums glorifying atheism.

These "glasnost'" revelations paled in comparison with complaints about language use. Problems required far more than revising textbooks to remedy. The Khanty language was first used in schools up to the fourth grade, but in the 1970s, at "autonomous [sic] district" levels, this policy was phased out, so that all classes were in Russian, with only a few token courses taught in Native languages. In the Kazym boarding school (*kasum kutup*, in Khanty), strict Russian or Russian-speaking schoolmarms (for they were indeed mostly women) punished Khanty for speaking their own language during recess and after classes. The official policy may have been "bilingualism," but its effect was to make the Khanty language private, not public.[34]

The multiethnic atmosphere of Kazym was such, however, that some local Russians (Siberiaki) did learn the Khanty language in childhood, or through mixed-ethnic marriages. For a few, therefore, the propagandized ideal of a "balanced bilingualism" was met. More often, especially with the influx of energy workers, bilingualism was unbalanced, with Khanty learning Russian and trying to hold on to their own language too, but Russians making little attempt to learn Khanty. Timofei Moldanov described some Khanty families where the grandchildren spoke only Russian, while one or more grandparents spoke only Khanty. Other families were rumored to speak a composite that had few of the charms of either language. The official census of 1989 recorded that only 60.5 percent of the Khanty spoke their Native language, a drop from 67.8 percent in 1979.[35]

Though I observed that many Khanty spoke the Khanty language at home, by the 1990s Khanty intellectuals of the Association for the Salvation of the Ugra were alarmed enough to start emergency language recovery programs in the schools. One pilot program, begun by Olga Kravchenko in Kazym, was called "cultural anthropology for national school programs," aimed at language and cultural revitalization. Olga has written eloquently about the program, as "an ethnopedagogical system oriented to the preservation of the ethnos and the transferral of cultural values" (Kravchenko 1996:45). The crux of the program is to have children use their Native language at all times and to have elders actively involved in the school. Yet Olga herself frightened her relatives when she admitted in 1991 that the language of the bear festival songs was so archaic and metaphorical that she missed some of its import. "Listen harder for three days and you will get it by the fourth," she was told.[36]

Khanty language texts in the Soviet period were in short supply and were sometimes confusing to pupils and teachers alike, since the differences in various Khanty "dialects"—for example, between Eastern and Northern Khanty—are considerable. In a familiar variation on Siberian themes, some complained that the way Soviet linguists had homogenized the language when it was transferred from the Latin alphabet to the Cyrillic in the late 1930s had masked important vocal nuances. Kazym teachers had been using a basic elementary-school text by K. F. Khvatai and Alexei M. Obatinov (1958), one of their own former teachers. Little material was available for the upper grades. Galina Obatina, Alexei's daughter and also a teacher, was only just creating a text in the 1990s for the fifth grade, to reach bored Khanty students with the excitement of Khanty literature, poetry, and bear festival songs. The Khanty writers she featured were Eremei Aipin, Tatiana Moldanova, Vladimir Valdin, and Nikul Shilgin, plus Nenets poet Yuri Vella and the Mansi Yuvan Shestalov. Funds for publishing such texts, available in moments of late- and post-Soviet optimism, have become scarce, so that once again a cruel expectation gap has occurred between educational hopes and reality.[37]

On the state of Khanty children's language abilities, Galina explained in 1991 that over 50 percent of the children did not know the Khanty language well when they arrived in school. In Kazym, however, Khanty children outnumbered others and by the 1990s were learning their language and culture more thoroughly in school. Galina was still wary and scared. She had created a cautionary poster to illustrate the devastation of local Kazym life wrought on Khanty young people. Half the children attending her school, she said, would not live to see old age. On a hauntingly dark side of her poster, she depicted alcoholics and suicides and individuals split between their own light and dark sides. She called them "half-dead Khanty," because she said the dark, not the light, side was taking over inside many people. In this context, she idealized "traditional" Khanty ways of education:

> The children in camps had their education naturally. . . . They were not taught. Every morning they woke up and just saw what their parents were doing around them. They repeated this. They learned from experience. They saw their mother preparing fish and their father making traps. They learned to hunt naturally, by example. We in school teach stiffly, and our children in their free time do nothing productive. [The boys even get into trouble playing with campfires in the woods.] . . . If they were living the old way, they would be hunting and fishing, not fooling around.

Part of the education crisis was and is the quality of the teachers themselves. While some of the worst Soviet-style non-indigenous drill sergeants disappeared by the 1990s, the same life conditions that demoralized other Khanty affected Khanty teachers as well. One young woman, a Khanty teacher, had poisoned herself not long before I arrived in 1991. Her husband worked in construction in Beloiar, but they had been living in a shack in Kazym, begging local authorities (in particular, Fillipov, the Zyrian (Komi) head of the village council) for a decent apartment. A colleague explained: "The apartment was the main thing that would have made their lives together work. . . . [The teacher] even went to Fillipov and said that if she were a teacher from outside, he would have found a place for her, and he agreed that it was true. I cannot think of this without breaking down."[38]

The debates about the quality and quantity of education and socialization appropriate for Native children spring from a deeper issue: whether the old Khanty ways enabled Khanty to think differently, more profoundly, more spiritually. This is a question that goes to the heart of "shamanic" ways of knowing and of tapping into one's intuition. Some Khanty friends (and others elsewhere in Siberia) argue that Soviet and even post-Soviet education ruins this intuitive capacity by its emphasis on logic and objectivity:

> In childhood I had a gift of being able to find lost objects. I found papa's watch in the snow. He had come home without it and was upset. I dreamed where it was and we found it. Another time I found a cow and calf. We had lost the mama while she was calving, and I dreamed where they were. Then I lost this talent. I became too involved in getting 5s [As] in school and learned how to think European-style. I lost my sense of depth, of connectedness to Khanty culture. But I never really got deep into Russian. At least my dreams Russian-style are very superficial.

This speaker, a Khanty leader, has begun to cure using dreams. "I also have neutral dreams. But my most important dreams are the Khanty ones. I have begun to get my depth back." As in most shamanic traditions, curing oneself is a first priority:

> I cured myself, to the point where I was supposed to have an operation but then did not have to have it. Doctors thought I had a tumor and then could not find it. A month before, I had gone into the same deep, multileveled worlds, dreaming as I had as a child. And I think that when I was in that state, I cured myself. In modern terms, maybe I used bioenergy on myself. I do not know. In Khanty terms, I turned into a god. Or rather, I used a spirit helper to help me find my way. [*Shyly and hesitantly*] I dreamed that I ran in the image of a bear.[39]

Analysis of shamanic thinking did not stop here, for this educated Khanty leader had read some psychology and was interested in the cognitive workings of symbols. "The relation of a person to symbols is crucial, especially in a dream. You must try to act on the symbol, to effect it, to make the cure work." I asked about relevant training or counseling with Khanty elders specifically versed in dream interpretation and was told: "I myself know the material, I guess because I know a lot from talking to many people about traditional Khanty culture. However, I got much from the beginning of my life, from growing up with my grandmother for the six years before I went to school."

In the multiethnic world of oil boomtowns, delinquent children, and threatened Khanty lands and obshchiny, the need for Khanty lawyers, doctors, and psychiatrists educated to defend their people is critical. Many leaders acknowledge that they need more, not fewer, people with

Western-style higher education. They point out that medical practitioners who acquire this higher education without losing the talents of their shamanic backgrounds can be very valuable to their communities, as has happened elsewhere in Siberia (Balzer 1996).

Compromises between the positions of those who encourage young people to go back to the woods after grade three and those who want them to obtain university and professional degrees are possible. First, requiring education at least through grade six allows the most talented Khanty children to be spotted and encouraged to continue their education, to become leaders and intelligentsia of and for their people. Second, school programs that are more flexible and closer to the people in villages and camps could and should be the bulwark of a new approach to indigenous education (cf. Bloch 1998).

Native American model programs have put computers in some backwoods homes in Alaska and Canada, enabling creative home study programs for children, combined with regular but not daily school attendance.[40] In Alaska, oil money has paid for small villages to have their own high schools, so that children have not been forced out of the communities for schooling, after the Molly Hootch 1976 court case (Case 1984). However, such programs, guaranteeing education for Northern children without forcing them into residential schools, notorious on both sides of the Bering Sea, cost enormous amounts of money. And, as the Sakha sociologist Uliana Vinokurova pointed out at a Moscow Congress of Women Leaders in 1997, funds must be found for indigenous minorities' schools throughout Siberia and the Far East to have indoor plumbing before they can buy computers.[41]

Some Khanty argue that energy profits and compensation money from ecology disruptions should be used to finance innovative educational programs that keep Khanty children with their families as long as possible. New "tent" schools are advocated by leaders like the Sopochins, in an ironic return to some of the experiments of the first decade of Soviet rule. But this time, there are educated Khanty wives in the camps, ready and willing to be schoolteachers for the elementary grades.

CONCLUSION: CREATIVE RESISTANCE AND DEFENSIVE NATIONALISM

The larger question is who will be left to educate. One of the most important aspects of Khanty identity is their sense of themselves as a besieged minority. Evidence for why they feel this way is clear from stories of oil company intimidation, sacred grove desecration, and reindeer poaching. Often, they have turned their anger against themselves, with family tragedies and suicide destroying already impoverished lives. But they have also taken organized political action to recover their sense of cultural dignity, through the Association for the Salvation of the Ugra and through the organization of obshchiny. Such actions need support, monetary and moral, to be sustained.

A sense of being besieged helps people in remote areas maintain ethnic boundaries and forces them into creative resistance and adaptation in camps, villages, and towns. Decisions about resistance or restraint change with interpersonal power contexts and must be analyzed with sensitive attention to local explanations and ambiguities (Ortner 1995:176, 191).[42] Khanty have developed diverse strategies in response to the various crises and encounters of Soviet and post-Soviet regionalization. Khanty leaders are astonished when they are called "nationalist," in part because of the pejorative way this word is used in Russian and in part because they feel fully justified in their strategies, from school language programs to roadblock protests and armed defense of sacred groves.

At a Kazym dinner table in August 1991, a Khanty leader, having been called a "nationalist" by a local Ukrainian, asked, "What is wrong with being proud of your own people?" Another added, "How can Khanty be chauvinist, when we never opposed anyone violently?" This provoked a debate about history, in which someone admitted that in the past Khanty had fought wars with Nentsy as well as Russians, but "not as aggressors." Theories that stress "defensive nationalism" need to take into account the situational nature of defense and aggression and the varied ways that multiple sides in ethnic conflicts perceive themselves as "nonaggressive" through their constructions of history (cf. Shnirelman 1996; Tishkov 1997).

Tensions between Khanty and Nentsy in Salekhard and Khanty and Mansi in Khanty-Mansiisk were acknowledged to me privately in the 1990s, usually with expressions of sorrow. The tensions that are most dominant, however, remain those between the indigenous peoples of West Siberia and the usually Slavic "newcomers," who have inundated [illegible]y with oil derricks. Khanty resentment is expressed in var[illegible]. Especially vivid was a 1991 story about the Kazym grave[illegible]rbed by the laying of a gasline with a caterpillar tractor: [illegible] graves that were disturbed were the Khanty ones, not the Russian ones, as if specially." Khanty were sure energy workers had robbed the graves of gravegoods, a complaint that eerily echoed reports I had read from the nineteenth century.

A contrasting approach to issues of identity and change comes from Russian sociologists Rybkina, Kosals, and Kovalkina (1992:44–48), who interviewed a cross-section of experts on indigenous peoples of the

Photo 6. Khanty artist Nadezhda Taligina, of Salekhard. Photo taken in Moscow, 1993, at the seminar "Traditional Cultures and Their Environments."

North, two-thirds of whom (eighty-two people) were Natives, members of the Association of the Peoples of the North, Siberia, and the Far East. Over two-thirds of the respondents thought that settlement of reindeer breeders had been "more negative" than positive; and about two-thirds said the same of the "placing" of children in boarding schools. These were likely the indigenous respondents. The only Soviet policies that received significant positive scores were the development of literacy and the establishment of the "National Okrugs." Seventy-four percent felt that a "stronger legal territorial structure for peoples of the North" was crucial for further guarantees of self-determination. A smaller, but still significant, 58 percent were ready to advocate the "return to a traditional way of life."

"Neotraditional" nostalgia is often unrealistic in the context of the late twentieth century, although it is easy to see why people are tempted by it. Rather, flexible opportunities for Siberian peoples need to be legally established, along philosophical lines and literal boundaries (on and under the land) that they define themselves, in negotiation with outsider-others. Power and resources are being redistributed in Siberia. Will there be anything left for the Natives? Can a Siberian-style regionalism support multiethnic civic society? A key to Native strength in engaging these questions is their spirituality.

CHAPTER SEVEN

The Tenacity of Ethnicity: Spirituality and Identity

Those who do not love the ancestors, maybe it will be bad for them.

(Tegy fisherman, 1976)

One of the 1991 bear festival musicians is also shamanizing. At least, he dances with a drum, and people are starting to come to him for cures. He is twenty-six.

(Kazym leader, 1991)

SELF-MADE AND REMADE

In 1993, the talented young Northern Khanty artist Nadezhda Taligina astounded attendees at a suburban Moscow conference on "Traditional Cultures and Their Environments" (photo 6) by asserting that most of the Khanty she knew had been given reincarnation soul names, *liaksum*. She assured me privately that the tradition of naming according to soul beliefs was alive and well in the Khanty North—but that it had been kept quite secret in the Soviet period. Was she telling the anthropologist what she wanted to hear? Yes, but our conversation, during a walk in the woods, had begun with my assumption that this ritual was among those that had been curtailed among all but a few Khanty. The lesson was ironic, for even I, who had been arguing that shamanic beliefs persisted far into the Soviet period, was not fully prepared for the implications that Khanty, especially women, had so successfully counteracted Soviet ideology in this crucial, identity-reproducing realm. Khanty beliefs about the soul constitute the core of Khanty confidence in their continuity as a people, and that confidence has been badly shaken in both the Soviet and post-Soviet periods.

Adherence to specific traditions cannot define Khanty, or any other, ethnicity. Yet spiritual concepts directly related to ideas of the self are difficult to kill, especially when they are not replaced by equally deep or satisfying concepts. Ethnicity for individuals is stimulated by the interaction of Russians and Khanty in a social-political process rooted in local histories and local ways of knowing. Awareness of history and of cultural difference can lead to pride in traditions or to rejection of personal roots.

People often test various paths, at different times. A great range of Khanty religious practice has remained valuable and viable, while personal cultural choices have widened. From the 1970s to the 1990s, Khanty consultants carefully explained aspects of rituals and soul beliefs that I had assumed were either obsolete or secret. Religion, broadly defined, has been integral to ethnic identity, because it is a major aspect of what sets many Khanty apart from others in the Ob North.[1]

The fracturing of cultural cohesion in many colonial and postcolonial contexts makes it unrealistic to stress holistic cultures as "relatively fixed and integrated shared systems of values and meanings" (Fox 1995: 1–5; Ortner 1995:181). Yet ethnic groups can use religion in identity-empowering ways, and religion may provide a stimulus for political cohesion. While Khanty ancestral teachings are reinterpreted and changed to accommodate the modern world, the power of moral and spiritual upbringing remains strong. Like the Khanty language, ancestral teachings shape the ways Russian culture has been received. This has helped bind some Khanty to each other and to "traditional" villages like Amnia or camps like those under siege on the Yugan. Religion can be an idiom for everyday behavior and small acts of conscious protest, but it is more often the basis for rituals that reaffirm values, involving life passages of birth, marriage, sickness, and death.[2]

Soviet anthropologists, as activists for a new style of ethnicity that was supposed to evolve into some advanced New Soviet Person, frequently dismissed the significance of religious identity, characterizing traditional Northern rituals as "cultural survivals" of a "primitive" past, destined to die out for lack of contemporary meaning (Sokolova 1971; Anisimov 1969). They trivialized the significance of religion in relation to ethnicity by calling religious beliefs "confessional factors" important to only a few.[3]

Many Khanty indeed reject aspects of Ugrian religion, including the isolation of women in menstrual huts. But many also endow key religious concepts and actions with multiple symbolic significance. Key concepts include (1) reincarnation, evident through birth and naming rituals; (2) soul beliefs, seen in burial and remembrance rituals; (3) lineage identity, manifest through marriage rites and animal sacrifice; (4) reverence for sacred animals, played out in bear festivals; and (5) shamanic power, revealed in séances, dreams, and curses.[4]

REINCARNATION, BIRTH, AND NAMING

Belief in reincarnation (transmigration of souls) is especially salient for the maintenance of ethnic identity. Northern Khanty villagers and urban residents alike explain that at birth they received a special reincarnated soul and, traditionally, the name of an ancestor. Relatives call one another by terms reflecting their own relationships and those of the ancestors whose souls are said to guide their behavior and personality. Thus, a young Khanty woman can be considered to have the soul of her grandmother, and her aunt may call her "mother" (*anka*) (Sokolova 1976:110–12). Or, as Nadezhda Taligina explained in 1993, "I am, for instance, my grandmother. I have her soul, and so some of her children called me "mother" when I was still just a child. One of my children died recently at a fairly old age. The generations are all mixed up in this system. But we know who we are, and feel the continuity."

In this system of thought, a Khanty child is more than a tabula rasa, ready for cultural imprinting and socialization. Rather, newborns represent the accumulated knowledge and customs of the Khanty. Babies are wiser, in this sense, than their own mothers. Eastern Khanty leader Joseph Sopochin emphasized to me in 1995 that "[t]his is not merely an idea, it is an occurrence that will exist as long as there are Khanty."[5]

Divination of ancestral names after birth was and is directed by a shaman (male or female) or an elderly female relative of the newborn. In 1976, concepts underpinning this ritual were alive in Tegy. I was told that "children without teeth can talk with shamans," and can therefore reveal what ancestor they re-embody. A newborn child was considered "clean, like a pure spirit, and strong." Children at birth were said to understand their futures and other aspects of their family's fate that they may forget later. "Parents do not say anything later of this to the child," because it would make life seem too predetermined.

In Kazym in 1976 and 1991, I learned that reincarnated souls were being divined—not only by elderly women, but also by younger Khanty women like Tatiana Moldanova, who were determined to keep the tradition alive. Tatiana told me (and Nadezhda confirmed), "Many know how to do this, to understand whose soul has been reincarnated, not just old women." Nadezhda continued, "To identify a liaksum, and to divine in general, we use a swinging cradle, and an axe or a knife is placed with the baby. Shamans are better at this than others, but are not mandatory." The iron knife or axe is placed under the cradle as a symbol of strength, continuity, and spiritual power. Names of relatives dead within memory are recited as the cradle is lifted. The specifics are still concealed from outsiders, to the point where a Russian woman in Kazym, married to a Khanty man, had not been allowed to see the divination for her child's reincarnation name. She explained that her daughter has the name of an aunt who had drowned, but that "Even though I was the mother, they did not let me see the ritual for figuring out the soul."[6]

A recent incident in the Tromyugan River area involved shamanic divination with a swinging axe during a crisis. A sick newborn was supposed to have the soul of one of two sisters, his aunts. They had each died of tuberculosis, and each was trying to get into the child, to be reborn. The shaman coaxed their spirit-souls into backing off, by insisting that the soul of the elder sister should occupy the boy. She had been born earlier and had died earlier, so the younger sister would have to wait. This agreed, the child recovered and was named.[7]

In previous generations, after the ancestral name (Northern Khanty, *liaksys* or *liaksum*; Eastern Khanty, *nams'ung*) had been divined, the Khanty slipped beads, made by elderly women, onto the child's wrist or ankle. Elders claimed that without beads, a child would not grow. Some Khanty continue to wear these talismanic beads (*yauornukhail*) throughout their lives. In Amnia, they were made by older women specialists. In 1976 and 1991 I observed the beads, especially on women, and had their spiritual significance confirmed. However, far from all Khanty wear such beads.[8]

Rituals of birth and naming link Khanty across time through the sharing of ancestral souls. Khanty narratives reinforce these rituals. According to one recounted to me in 1976 in Tegy, all people once lived forever, because the Sky God, Numi-Torum, made them out of iron. But the spiritual and physical strength of iron was offset by its liabilities. Iron was too heavy for easy walking, and too many people came to inhabit the earth. The Sky God let everyone die and then remade people out of clay and water. "He made men and women, and he put them on the earth in pairs by nationality. Six pairs fell from the Sky God—of Khanty, Mansi, Russians, Zyrians, Permians, and Tatars." Clay and water Khanty became flesh and blood Khanty, who could die and return to the earth, to be reborn as Khanty children when their time came.

As in many indigenous communities, high mortality rates meant that the Khanty long put a premium on fertility and virility. Boys were particularly valued. In the 1970s, some Khanty mothers considered that the spirit who guides birth, Pugos-imi, was punishing them when they had daughters (Kulemzin and Lukina 1977:209–11). However, contrary to early reports, daughters were included in naming traditions (cf. Zuev 1947:66; Balzer 1981:864). By the 1990s, Khanty women friends insisted that girls had become "almost as valued" as boys.

Public "cover names," often Russian, enabled Khanty to keep true personal names secret. A beautiful Khanty name like Kalis was masked by a completely dissimilar Russian name. Babies were sometimes given nicknames like Rubbish or Insect, intended to hide the child's value for the first few precarious years of life. Family names have remained the Russian ones first given during tsarist taxation and Christianization campaigns.

Since World War II, birth rituals have changed more than naming. Yet some prebirth rituals in northern areas include the ancient Ugrian practice of making thumb-sized birch-bark dolls in the fifth month of pregnancy, to help divine the health of mother and child. Older female relatives and midwives guide such rituals. Chances for easy birth are considered improved with the confession of sexual and other transgressions, especially of the mother, but sometimes the father (cf. Rombandeeva 1968). Various local prohibitions guide the behavior of conservative pregnant women. For example, Vakh River Khanty say that a pregnant woman should not step over a dog, and Vasyugan Khanty forbid her to eat rabbit heads—infractions could mar the appearance of the child.[9]

As recently as the 1930s, most Khanty births took place in small birth and menstrual huts (*ai-khot*) in the forest. Khanty women themselves described these huts as uncomfortable, chilly, and unclean (Balzer 1981, 1984). Birth involved elaborate rituals of prayer (to the birth mother spirit Pugos-imi or Kaltash-imi), and purification (with steam and the musk-perfumed smoke of roasted beaver). On the Vasyugan, a specialist played a stringed Khanty instrument during birth, but this musical inducement of easy labor was probably not widespread.[10]

Isolation after birth could last two to three "moons" (*tilis*), during which the child was transferred from a temporary cradle to a longer, more substantial one. Both cradles were baskets with a woven wood grouse (*vursik*) design for protection of a special Khanty soul believed to guide sleep and dreams (Chernetsov 1963:21). A mother's old and contaminated birth clothes, along with the first cradle, were placed as high as possible in trees near the birth hut. This stage was marked with a modest celebratory meal of fish or meat with wine or tea. The hanging cradles served as a warning for men not to come near this special female ritual area, considered dangerous to men but sacred to women.[11]

Return to normalcy was marked by purification of the mother with beaver smoke as she reentered her house, accompanied by an older female relative who carried her child, wrapped in a bright scarf. Among Ob-Ugrians, this woman became the child's "mother-by-carrying,"and the woman who cut the placenta became the "navel mother."[12] These rituals reinforced shared guardianship of children within a community.

Menstrual and birth huts were outlawed in the 1930s. A somewhat exaggerated contemporary song proclaimed, "Where earlier stood the impure birth hut, today stands a tall new building" (Gudkov and Senkevich 1940:97). Many Khanty women have welcomed more comfortable medical alternatives for childbirth. But the very act of leaving home for a maternity ward is perceived by Khanty women and men as reinforcing traditional ideas concerning the contaminating and dangerous nature of birth, thus establishing a cognitive link between old and new ways.[13]

By the 1970s, many Khanty women gave birth in regional medical facilities and later consecrated the experience with private rituals. In Tegy and Kazym I saw cradles bearing the protective image of the vursik, wood grouse. Khanty women explained that children live through their first difficult years if their birch cradles stay well up in the trees for a long time. This ensures the safety of their souls.

DEATH AND SOUL BELIEFS

In the 1990s the safety of his reincarnation soul was very much on the mind of a Khanty friend:

> I have the feeling that I some time or another fought, that I was in battles. I am wondering if I have got the soul of someone who went through terrible fear. I have dreams about this. In my dream I am about to fight, and it gives me awful fear, or I see someone coming up at me. Perhaps my soul was inside some sort of soldier in the past. This is my personal struggle. I wake in horror and with relief understand that it is a dream.[14]

Khanty soul beliefs vary somewhat among different groups. Ob-Ugrians generally identify multiple souls for each individual.[15] Some attribute five souls to men and only four to women (Balzer 1980; Chernetsov 1963:3–45). The four main souls include *lil*, the reincarnation or breath soul; *is-chor*, the material or shadow soul; *ulém*, the soul that comes to a person in sleep and at death clings to clothing of the deceased until it can be coaxed to fly off into the forest as a bird; and *urt* (*ort*), the sickness soul that leaves a person in sickness or death and travels northward to the afterworld. The fifth soul, with which men are uniquely blessed, is, according to a Tegy woman, "strength."

The gender-linked numbers four and five are symbolically repeated in many ways, such as in the boards on top of a grave house, the times a grave is circled during burial, and the number of remembrance feasts due a dead person. Nonetheless, in 1993 Nadezhda Taligina cautioned me that Russian ethnographer Chernetsov may have been too eager to neatly categorize:

> The souls *lil*, *ilés*, *ort*, and *ulém* are the main ones. . . . The reincarnation soul or breath soul, *lil*, is most important. Sometimes, souls live in the

graveyard—*iis [ilés] khor*. And some souls are encouraged to live in an *itarma*, a soul-keeper image, kept in the house, so the soul will not do harm but will help the family. *Ura* is the place for the souls of the dead that do not stay in this world. But they can return from *ura*. It is not clear where *ura* is, above, to the west, below—different people think differently.

By the 1970s, burial rituals were still elaborate, although somewhat simplified due to Soviet pressure. Major goals were to prevent spirits or souls of the dead from becoming restless or vengeful and to accommodate the reincarnation soul-spirit for a future life. A story told to Tegy children illustrates unease about improper treatment of the dead:

> There lived three brothers who went on hunts, as all hunters do. But once, just before a planned hunting trip, their mother died. They decided to bury her next to their house. They went on living there peacefully, but it seemed to them that soon their mother began to haunt them. They decided to go away from that house—it was terrible for them to live there. They traveled through the woods, living there. But it seemed that their mother followed them. When they made fires, she seemed to be looking at them. And when they skied, she seemed to knock on the wood of their skis. Her shadow followed them. One night at their campfire, they heard her spirit on the other side. "Your mother has come," she said. The brothers tried to give her a piece of fish, but it fell into the fire. The mother jumped to get the fish. She ate it, and fell over on the far side of the fire. On the next day, the brothers went further, but their mother still seemed to follow. At their new campfire, the mother came again, dressed in duck feathers and a fur coat. The brothers again tried to toss her a fish. But they were afraid. They decided that she had become evil. The three brothers together held her and threw her into the fire. After burning her, they fled. They built a third campfire but were upset and restless. They went back to the site of the second fire. They found their mother's bones in the ashes, but arranged as if to come back to life in the fire. The brothers rebuilt the fire and reburned the bones. Then they returned to the third campfire, built a hut there, and lived without fear.

In this story, the purifying old-woman fire spirit, Tut-imi, was enlisted to help save the living from the dead, even from their own mother. Brotherly guilt was a main theme: the brothers were in such a hurry to hunt that they had not given their mother a proper burial. Burials usually occurred the third or fourth day after death, following a constant vigil over the body and then a procession to a more removed location.

By the 1970s, coffins could be squared-off canoes but were usually larchwood boxes large enough to accommodate grave goods. The dead were preferably buried a considerable distance from the family dwelling, in areas reserved for specific families or lineages. In Tegy and

Kazym, communal graveyards had separate areas for Khanty and Russians, and further subdivisions for family groups, and for those who died violently or in childhood. All these practices have continued into the 1990s.

In Tegy and Kazym, preparations for burial focus on concern that multiple souls can follow their proper afterlife courses.[16] The "breath soul" needs to be kept under a shroud and then transferred to the itarma image of the deceased. Eventually, it is relinquished to live in the Khanty afterworld, so that it can return as the reincarnation soul. The "shadow," or "material," soul, considered capable of getting drunk, has to be encouraged to live in the graveyard. Other souls, variously defined by different groups of Khanty, are said to fly into the forest as birds or become evil, soul-stealing spirits.

When the last breath escapes from a dying person, a new fire is started in the hearth. In Kazym, the fire is kept burning next to the body. As the household fire spirit, Tut-imi, it symbolizes the need for purification in the presence of death and the familial link between the living and the dead. As a result of Russian influence, bodies are usually washed, along with articles of the deceased's clothing. Respected specialists or elders prepare the body, rather than close relatives of the deceased. Elaborate appliquéd and beaded clothes are sometimes bound around the arms and legs of the deceased with a special "knot of the dead," so that wandering spirits can be recognized. In some northern areas, a death mask is also created by sewing beads on a shroud.

Relatives, their hair cut in mourning, watch over the deceased after death. During my 1976 visit, a Tegy elder explained that the deceased is at this stage "a spirit of the parallel world," who can travel to all the places he or she had visited in life, "even Moscow or America." Kazym Khanty with whom I consulted in 1991 confirmed that they were visited, not only in dreams, by recently deceased kin taking such farewell journeys (cf. Ridington 1988:289). In Kazym, but not in Tegy, corpses are brought outside on the second day, so that "friends and relatives who had lived at some earlier time can come to meet the dead. It is easier and better for the living if they meet outside."[17] The house is purified with smoke, sometimes accompanied by noises to frighten unwanted spirits.

During the procession to a forest or riverside grave site, close relatives stay with the deceased, while others travel ahead, tempting the material soul to follow. They usually bring a table, kettle, food, tea, and liquor. At the site, women prepare food over a campfire, while men dig the grave, ensuring a northwest orientation. In 1976, three campfire areas were spread among approximately forty Tegy graves; twelve were interspersed among two hundred graves in Kazym. By the 1990s, sections had expanded, as had Kazym itself. Several Khanty, showing me the graves, explained: "It is dangerous for too many graves to be in too many different places. There will be more deaths. Spirits are still around the graves."

By the late twentieth century, burial was marked by restrained weeping, reverent silence, and deeply felt parting kisses. This contrasts with earlier reports of dramatic wailing, hair tearing, and face scratching (Novitskii 1884:45; Zuev 1947:67). Laments, sung by close relatives of the same gender as the deceased, serve as powerful memorials. They depict deeds in the deceased's life and link that life to the kin group.

Grave goods are gender correlated, with the quantity and quality diminishing over the years (Balzer 1980:81; Rudenko 1910:36–37). In Tegy and Kazym, a knife, a tobacco pouch and pipe, a flint, a hunting belt, and bear-tooth amulets may be men's coffin offerings. A woman's coffin usually contains her sewing bag, beads, needles, and extra lengths of cloth. Grave goods too bulky to fit in a coffin are placed on the grave. These may be reindeer sleds, oars, boats, or skis, depending on what transport the deceased preferred in life, and what the family can afford. Such items, placed upside down, may be purposely broken, since the goods are then ready for use in a northern land of the dead conceived to have an upside-down and opposites orientation. In recent times miniature sleds or oars have been placed on adult graves, with the rationale that miniatures are appropriate in an inverted land of the dead. This spares relatives from sacrificing valuable and useful goods and reduces fear that they will be stolen.

Various goods piled on grave houses reveal Khanty interest in covering all spiritual options. Russian Orthodox crosses combine with deliberately broken sleds, skis, or boats. Graves of World War II heroes are decorated with plastic garlands strung around Soviet red stars—plus sleds, and grave houses with windows for feeding the deceased. In Soviet times, however, a red star was never combined with the Russian Orthodox cross.

Two rituals were once considered mandatory for the well-being of mourners and the deceased alike: animal sacrifices, to provide the deceased with adequate transport in the afterlife, and divination to discover the cause of death. Extravagant animal sacrifices sharply declined after collectivization. One Tegy matron boasted in 1976 that two horses were killed at her father's brother's burial, with some of the meat eaten at the grave, some given to the deceased, and some apportioned to relatives to take home. I saw evidence of animal sacrifice in the Kazym graveyard in 1991 and have confirmed that in the 1990s both divination and reindeer sacrifices are desirable, if not common.[18]

Shamans or elders led graveside divinations during the Soviet period. In 1976, divination occurred at the burial of a progressive Khanty schoolteacher, who was asked as the coffin was lifted, "Why did you leave so early? Was your [material] soul maybe heavy?" In 1991, divinations were performed to mollify the deceased, especially if death resulted from violence or suicide, and to learn more about individual life spans and community fortunes. An elder who had hoped for a grandson named Vladimir Ilich (after Lenin) was told four times during such divinations that he should sacrifice a reindeer, and he finally complied.[19]

Concern for the fate of Khanty souls has ensured the maintenance of some mourning and remembrance rituals. Depending on the gender of the deceased, outward signs of mourning last at least four or five days. These include cutting the hair and wearing it loose, reversing scarves, and avoiding knots in clothing. Before the demands of Soviet collective organization, mourning also involved moving cabin or tent sites, and avoiding work.[20]

Remembrance feasts combine Russian Orthodox–influenced timing and Khanty rationale. Forty-day wakes (*pominki*) occurred at gravesides into the 1990s, and additional rites were performed after close relatives had dreams about the deceased. Tobacco, tea, wine, and vodka are offered at the grave house window, after awakening the dead with a burning match. During remembrance feasts, relatives and friends "cook, eat, and drink. After the eating, everyone then goes to graves of their own relatives, kisses them, knocks at them, and then puts out tea and food to feed them. . . . All leave together"[21] (photos 7 and 8).

The solidarity (communitas) fostered by such rituals has contributed to their longevity, despite a long history of pragmatic individual adaptation to Russian Orthodox and Soviet life. Young male Communist Party members and elderly women who could not speak Russian all participated in Khanty burials up to the end of the Soviet period. Burials in the 1990s are performed with renewed attention to detail and heightened anxiety, given the stepped-up incidence of tragedies in Khanty communities.

Khanty solidarity is reflected in beliefs about an idealized northern land of the dead, where, according to a Kazym fisherman in 1976, "each nationality goes to its own place." Significant group cohesion was once defined in very specific clan and phratry terms but eventually incorporated more expanded local, as well as ethnic, self-identities.

LINES OF CONNECTION: MARRIAGE AND ANIMAL SACRIFICE

When I asked in 1976 how local Khanty identify themselves to each other, consultants proclaimed, "I am Mos," or "I am Por." One Tegy woman jumped up from her bed, beating her chest, shouting "I am

Photo 7. Amnia woman on her way to a remembrance feast, 1976. In her birch bark container is a modern thermos, filled with tea. She is wearing her scarf backward, in mourning, and carries a tobacco offering for the deceased.

Mos, and my son is Por." She proceeded to identify in patrilineal-phratry terms everyone else in the room, to their amusement and surprise.[22] Por and Mos are the names of the two exogamous patrilineal phratries (moieties) that have existed among the Ob-Ugrians and the nearby Samodeic Sel'kup since precolonial times. By the 1990s, Joseph Sopochin warned: "This is complex. There has been too much written and said improperly about this, even by our own people."[23]

Photo 8. Kazym grave with Russian Orthodox cross and sled, 1976.

Phratry designations in the 1990s retain personal and emotional meaning for some Khanty, although the designations do not necessarily imply the strict exogamy-enforcing marriage-alliance functions of the past. As recently as the 1930s, Ob-Ugrians on first meeting identified themselves as Por or Mos from a given place before exchanging family names. Patrilineal phratries were the major divisions of traditional Ugrian social organization, often more immediately salient than linguistic and ethnic divisions, although these were known.

The designations Por and Mos have religious as well as social connotations, and this helps to explain Joseph's warning. Khanty believers do not separate the social from the sacred; they associate Por and Mos at once with marriage rules, ancestors, and sacred, protected and protecting animals. To be a Por means to be linked by ancestry to the "great sharp-clawed old man of the forest," the bear. To be a Mos means to be the proud descendant of a shamanic goddess who can turn into a hare or a goose.[24]

Por and Mos are sometimes associated with taiga spirits, who protect their members but behave mischievously toward members of other groups. Por are aligned with spirits called *menk*, while Mos are associated with *mis*, from whom they possibly derived their name. A Por elder in Tegy explained that menk are "just like humans, only they are spirits of the parallel forest world." A Mos man similarly noted "mis are like people, they can be hooligans or moody . . . or they can help with hunting and fishing."[25] One Tegy man, refuting the Christian view of these spirits as devils, explained: "The spirits have helpers—their families, sons and daughters. I do not know how they work, whether they have stone houses or wooden, or whether they build airplanes. They have various kinds of intents, good and bad."

Some Ugrian histories, similar to many other origin narratives, differentiate the Por as people who ate their meat half-raw, from the Mos, who ate their meat fully cooked (cf. Lévi-Strauss 1975).[26] While Mos and Por narratives are sometimes partisan to a given group, group intermarriage and intercommunication mitigated against extremes of rivalry and divisiveness.

Khanty definitions of Por and Mos stem from explanations of how *khylim*, "local people," came to be divided in ancient times. In Tegy, I was told about the origins of competitive Por and Mos ancestresses. Other versions describe the incestuous union of a Mos brother and sister.[27]

Marriage formed the basis of an intricate web of social obligations that many Khanty respected well into the Soviet period, and in some cases beyond. These obligations included rituals introducing a timid and veiled worker-bride into her husband's extended family.[28] They were sealed with bride wealth (*netyn*, usually glossed as "bride price") and dowries that probably had once offset each other in a balanced but staggered reciprocal exchange (see chapter 1). By the 1970s, many Khanty had abandoned traditional rituals, while maintaining ideals of reciprocity and feasting among in-laws. Judging from marriage records of Tegy and Kazym collectives, and from Khanty comments, some preferred not to marry into the same phratry. In 1990, to counteract Soviet propaganda about traditional marriages as little better than "slavery," the Association for the Salvation of the Ugra sponsored an elaborate Mansi marriage ceremony and filmed it.

In Northern and Eastern Khanty camps, lineages continued to have economic and sacred meaning. But by 1991, Kazym Khanty lamented not being able to fulfill Por and Mos marriage rules because the demography of their area made it difficult to find appropriate mates. One friend admitted, "People hide their phratries [from each other] and do not usually reveal the animal versions of who their gods are." She named bear, goose, loon, elk, hare, wood grouse, eagle, seagull, burbot, pike, and sturgeon as associated with particular lineages. "The images of these gods are important, and [lineage members] are forbidden to eat their meat, to hunt them. This part of the sacred world is especially important, sacred still"[29] (fig. 3).

Khanty kin group identity has for centuries been solidified through active supplication to ancestors and protected animals, represented in locally worshiped images. Ritual life centers around lineages and phratries that express their unity periodically and during crises by means of offerings and animal sacrifices, led by shamans or knowledgeable elders. Nadezhda Taligina, young and recently married, in 1993 described her introduction to her husband's family's sacred world:

> When I married my husband, we went with his family to their sacred territory—well, their traditional family territory. It was not a grove but an open spot with some bushes, and we camped there, built a fire, and made offerings. Then later we went farther, to a stilt storehouse [*ambar*], where sacred images were kept, among many scarves. My mother-in-law, who is very kind to me, told me to offer a scarf to the ambar, as a kind of introduction to my husband's ancestors. I had a nice new scarf with me, and offered it. I'm a woman from another clan, from far away, and needed to be blessed, to have the spirits help me. We offered prayers that the spirits should protect me, and protect my child, my family, from sickness, from any kind of unhappiness. I'm Por. My husband is from the [Northern] Ob, far from my own family. . . . People say it is best to take a wife from afar.

Through the 1930s, most Khanty men participated in the large religious ceremonies of their kin networks, in phratry rituals occurring once every seven years, and in more modest and frequent extended-family rituals. By the 1950s, animal sacrifice was secret and less common, but cloth and coin offerings to ancestral images persisted in sacred groves. In the 1970s, offerings and correlations of lineages with sacred animals continued. In Tegy, crow, red fox, and pike were among the sacred animals associated with kin groups. In Kazym, the fox, frog, and cat were named as totemlike protectors.[30]

Among the less known yet remarkable phenomena of the 1980s and 1990s was the reemergence of Khanty animal sacrifices, usually of reindeer. In Northern Khanty areas, these occurred in places of historical resonance, such as Num-to and Yuilsk, and also in places less famed. The sacrifices increased in number and broadened in constituency, although they were advertised selectively. For some communities, they represented an appeasement of ancestor spirits thought to be furious at their neglect in stricter Soviet times. In remote Eastern Khanty camps, they remained expressions of normal ritual respect.

Eastern Khanty shaman- and elder-led reindeer sacrifices at the

Little and Big Yugan River Area:

Tromyugan River and Pur River Areas:

Obdorsk and Berezovo areas:

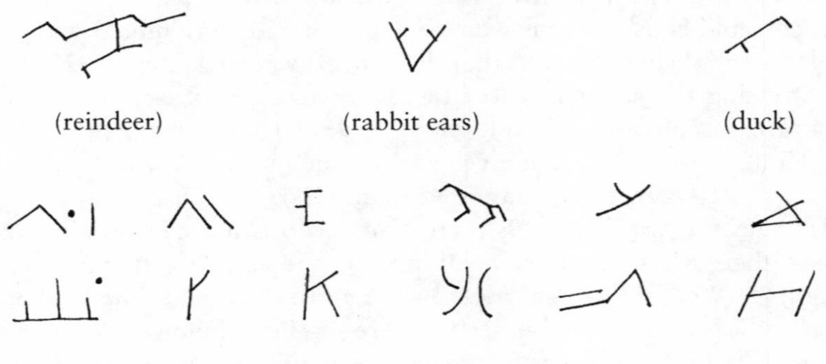

Vakh River Area:

Konda and Upper Pelym River Areas:

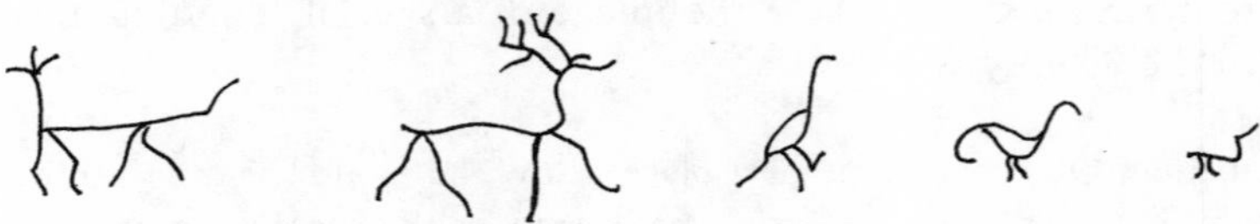

Figure 3. Tamgi: Family and Clan Signs

Sources: Startsev 1928; Gumuev 1990a; author's field notes.

Vakh, Tromyugan, and Vasyugan Rivers have maintained the strict rule barring women from the crux of the action, focused on lineage perpetuation and virility. Recently, a few outsiders have witnessed and even filmed sacrifices, sometimes involving seven or more reindeer, contributed by participating families and consecrated with white, red, and, sometimes, black cloths (see appendix B). Prayers preceding the sacrifice were oriented toward the sun at an altar, laid out in a wooded grove near a river. Participants gave coins and cloths to the ancestral images. Contributions of diverse manufactured goods were also accepted. A prayer leader, called *multé-ku* (spirit gatherer), directed others in the swift stunning of the deer with an axe blow between the antlers. Instantly afterward, the deer were stabbed in the heart with a long knife, so that no visible blood was shed and omens could be read in how the animals fell. Relatively rare white deer were especially valued, white being associated with the sky, black with the underworld and sickness, red with the earthly, fertile middleworld. In addition to local deities, prayers and consecrations were to Sankë and Torum, linked with white, solar symbolism similar to that described by Karjalainen (1927).[31]

Stressing the significance of the Tromyugan as a sacred area for all Khanty, Joseph Sopochin told me in 1995: "The Tromyugan is the river of God. This is the main river and the main God of the Khanty people. . . . At Ugut, there is another main God. He too is important, and his protector just died." "Is there a son who is his successor?" I asked. "Yes, there is a son, and he is taking over the duties." "If there were not a son?" "Well, they might need a shaman to determine [the new protector], or a brother would inherit." "Are sacrifices involved?" "Yes, there should be. When images are transferred, this is certainly done with a reindeer sacrifice."[32]

Although many sacred groves were disbanded with Soviet antireligious pomp, their "idols" carted away to museums, others survived, in secret locations. Worship in the groves was adapted to new conditions: "with the resettling of people [in collectivization and after World War II], the images of ancestors were disrupted. A few acquired new masters and generated new legends" (Sokolova 1971:216). In 1976, I learned of a grove near Kazym, where the image of a special founding ancestress of all the Khanty was revered:

> Yu Khan Ob is the name of a place below the mouth of the river, on the right bank. The name refers to the dryness of the bank there. It is not far from the old village of Mazomova, now nonexistent. People say the real Kazym is there. It is hard to travel there, even by motorboat. When people go by there on the way to the Ob, they stop there, so that more fish will be caught. Yes, people still go there, but some are afraid. Those who do not

love the ancestors, maybe it will be bad for them. Earlier the fishing was better, when everyone made sacrifices. At this dry sacred place, people place food, on the hot sunny side. There we remember the spirits—Numi-Torum and others.

The grove probably featured Earth Daughter, transferred from a sacred storehouse in Yuilsk in the early 1960s, when other images and rich offerings were taken to a museum.[33] The Yuilsk disbandment created havoc, as a friend related: "Mama was there. We were all there, watching. The Yuilsk Goddess-spirit put a curse on us, even on the children." The Earth Daughter is the Goddess many Khanty call "the mother of all fertility," whose image was romanticized and sought even by pre-Soviet Russians as the "zolotaia baba"—the golden woman, although she was made of wood. The Earth Daughter, called Kaltash-angki by Northern Khanty and Pugos (or Angki Pugos) by Eastern Khanty, was honored in a particularly dramatic reversal of fortune in 1991, after Kazym celebrants sacrificed to her in Yuilsk. There, in conjunction with a bear festival, they performed a less public ritual in the forest. One participant explained: "We feel our gods are near to us, not far up in the sky somewhere. They are our ancestors. When we did the bear festival, we also wanted to have forty-nine reindeer sacrificed, seven times seven. . . . People volunteered their own deer. But in the end, the 'black shaman' Karamzin [a local Khanty Communist official] allowed us only seven. They were consecrated to two of our main gods, Torum and Kaltash."

Thus, despite the supposed liquidation of one sacred grove, the most precious images were transferred to another, still ratified by kin group histories and ritual. And eventually, the sacred grove of Yuilsk was restored. A hunter reported that the Goddess had left a mark on a birch indicating her return. School groups today visit the Yuilsk grove with offerings.[34]

DANCES WITH BEARS

During the Yuilsk and other bear festivals, songs and dances were addressed to Kaltash, among many other sacred beings of varied ranks and relationships. Considered the mother, wife, or child of Torum in various versions of Ugrian historical narratives, she is also close kin of the important Khanty deity Mir-susné-khum (World Surveyor Man) and the bear. In the interconnected world of Khanty religion, the bear looms large (Schmidt 1989:187–232). Through festivals, also called "bear games [*pupi tulyglap*]" or "dances for the beast [*voi iak*]," sacred human-spirit relations and sacred geography are reaffirmed and communicated to new generations. The bear may be hunted, but only with special precaution and respect.

Ceremonies celebrating the capture or killing of a bear were common throughout the North, and patterns of circumpolar worship have been extensively analyzed (Hallowell 1926; Zolotarev 1937). Among the Khanty, ceremonies honoring the bear persisted even after Soviet propagandists proclaimed the practice dead. In 1995, Vladimir Kogonchin confirmed: "Even in the Soviet period, people did not stop doing bear festivals. Sure, people hid that they were still held, but they were held in most regions."[35]

The exuberance of bear festivals was so striking that Soviet authorities first attempted to de-claw the tradition by declaring it secularized. However, a universal and mystical reverence for the bear has been revealed in every one of my conversations with Khanty about bear festivals, from 1976 to 1998. As explained in chapter 2, the bear (part animal, part human, part god) is revered not only as an ancestor of the Por people but also as a son, or sometimes younger brother, of the Sky God Numi-Torum.

In 1976, a Tegy fisherman elaborated: "The bear is admired by the Khanty as if he were human. He is like a human but is considered to have come from the sky. The bear has movements like a human and looks at humans as a human. He is like a son of God. He is intelligent. If a hunter sees a bear and the bear presents himself, then that means the bear is ready to die. It is the hunter's fate to kill that bear or evil will befall him. It is a rare man to whom the bear presents himself."

Given their belief in the bear's suprahuman intelligence, Khanty, like many Northern hunters, do not risk offense by saying the name of the bear outright. Khanty refer to the bear by various euphemisms, such as "old man with claws," "lair dweller," "berry picker," or simply "the great animal" or "beast" (*uy*, *voi*). A hunter who stressed the bear's human characteristics also noted: "It is forbidden to kill the bear while he is sleeping. That is like killing God." Bear reverence was evident in such statements as: "We must all be frightened of him. He is older than us all. He is the biggest and most important being in the world" (Tegy). Bear clairvoyance or revenge was implied repeatedly: "It is forbidden to make stupid jokes about the bear, even in the house"; "If in a dream a person kills a bear, this is considered unlucky and a close relative might die within the year" (Kazym).

Hunters wore bear teeth amulets on their belts despite Soviet antireligious propaganda (photo 9). Khanty hunters have long preferred not to hunt the bear but have done so when confronted with a lair, fresh tracks, or the bear itself. Killing the bear has long been forbidden for

Photo 9. Pëtr Moldanov and Franklin Keel at Nulki Lake (Northern Canada), near the Stoney Creek Reserve potlatch house, during a seminar for Native Siberian and Native American leaders, 1996. Pëtr Moldanov is wearing a hunter's belt with a bear tooth amulet.

Por phratry members, except during the ordained Por ritual, occurring every seven years. Once a lair was found, "fathers with their sons would leave the house separately and then rejoin each other in the woods, so that the women would not know" (Tegy hunter, 1976). The hunters used a special language, saying the reverse of what they meant: instead of "shoot," they said "do not shoot" (cf. Startsev 1928:106). Such language does not foil an "all-seeing" bear but is the etiquette of respect for the bear. Bear traps and direct shooting at the heart or eye are acceptable means of killing. But with any method, it is customary to blame someone else, including the Russian from whom the gun was bought.[36]

Once killed, the bear's coat was removed (skinned) and the bear treated as an honored guest. When Khanty hunters returned to their village, their gunshots and jubilant shouting alerted residents that a bear had been killed. Women showered the hunters with snow or water, and sometimes also greeted them with purifying smoke (cf. Karjalainen 1927:199–200).

In 1991, I saw (on video) that the Yuilsk festival room and celebrants were smudged, after which a female bear was brought in, to acclaim and cries of delight.[37] Dogs were shooed out, and a drum was fetched. The bear was placed on a table that became an altar; bells and scarves were draped upon her head. Her fur was stuffed with straw, forming an *immet*, a god receptacle, suitable for offerings and divination. Participants circled the bear, kissing and greeting her and placing money in a nearby bowl. Their host, the main hunter-celebrant, greeted his guests, saying: "We do not need to scold each other. We need to come together. Welcome. All singing people, tell all who know old songs and dances to come. This is a dance house of celebration." Another elder proclaimed: "This is a day we need to worship, to pray. We need to acknowledge the sky. They have brought a bear to us." A small child in furs was brought over to kiss the bear, and, most awkwardly and to poorly hidden amusement of other participants, a local Communist "third Secretary" kissed the bear too. Gifts of oranges and candy were brought, and beads were placed on the bear. Nearby were also sacred dough figures of animals.

The crowd was spritzed (purified) by a merry elder toting a bucket of water. As more people came in, a clowning old man smudged them. People, dressed in elaborate family-heirloom appliquéd dresses, robes, and shirts, of red, white, blue, and sometimes purple, with protective family designs, had come from all over Khanty and Mansi territory.

Dancing began, as two musicians strummed the five-string dulcimer-like *narsus*, joined by the player of a lap harp, *khutang* ("swan") (photos 10–12). Elderly men swayed and waved their arms in graceful bird-like motions, setting the pace, joking, and gaining more dancers. They wore large ritual mittens and tall triangular hats, in the sacred colors white, red, and blue. They sang that the gods were coming down, that humans had dressed for the occasion and were ready. A chorus of men joined the musicians, singing: "To honor the bear, [the god] Torum Shiashi has allowed the bear to come to earth, the beautiful golden earth." They chanted a richly metaphoric song of how the bear first came to earth, as son of the Sky-God. Young men and boys, just learning the words, joined the group.

Some of the songs were sung from the bear's point of view, or in dialogues: "'Here comes a person. A person has come. Why do you touch my deer, my horned animals?' the bear asked. The man answered: 'I have nothing else to eat. Nothing more to collect.'" Another song

Photo 10. Tegy elder playing the *narsus*, 1976. This instrument is often used in Ugrian ceremonies honoring the bear.

told of competition with the bear for beloved berries, and yet another had the refrain "We have come to join [not eat] the bear. Let us join the bear." The songs were not all fixed and "traditional"; some improvisationally touched on glasnost' and the ensuing confusion after so much repression of religion. Masked dancers were introduced, their masks newly made of birch bark for the occasion. A song by a masked man referred to a sacred ancestral place, describing its nearby river as "dark, beautiful, flowing to the sky."

Bawdiness crept into the singing and dancing, especially after masks were in place and men played women's roles. Long epic songs followed mime and satirical theater, during four days of celebrations and feasting. One play depicted the capture and beating of a fish thief. Each masked combatant used pillows to protect himself from sticks, to the riotous laughter of the crowd. As with other festivals, depictions of Por-Mos tensions and founding stories of sacred groves and ancestor-heroes (*urt*, *wort*) were integrated into the cathartic and solidarity-building art form. One masked hero wearing bells had a head covered in fox fur. Another dressed and moved like a crane. Both represented local lineages. The festival culminated in the masked arrival of the Yuilsk swan goddess, announcing, "I am the sacred mother. . . . Everything comes through my hands. . . . I set the fate of people's lifetimes." Kaltash had come home.

Photo 11. Bear festival play. Mansi territory on the Sosva River, ca. 1898–1900. U. T. Sirelius. National Museum of Finland no. 36:358.

Photo 12. Bear festival dance. Khanty territory (Vasyugan?), ca. 1898–1900. U. T. Sirelius. National Museum of Finland no. 36:359.

The soul of each bear festival is reincarnation, or the connectedness, continuity, and circularity of spirit life (cf. E. Turner 1996; Mills and Slobodin 1994). The ethnographer V. N. Chernetsov (1968) witnessed a periodic Por phratry festival at the ritual center near Vezhakary on the Ob in 1965. Khanty and Mansi celebrants came from over one hundred kilometers away to enjoy the rare festival, held once every seven years and conducted intermittently from December to March. Hundreds of songs, dances, and dramas were performed, both classics (cf. Gondatti 1887b) and improvisations.

The opening rites depicted the fate of the first female bear, who, after eating the plant called *pori*, gave birth to two bears and the first Por girl. She addressed her daughter: "Tomorrow people will come. They will kill me, your brother, and sister, and will take you with them. When the people cook my meat, look on, do not eat, and when night comes, go to the back corner of the house" (Chernetsov 1968:109). The captive-daughter complied and found the spirit of her mother, who taught her in three consecutive nights how to smoke the meat and preserve the bones of the bear. The mother receded into the sky, to become the constellation called "Little Bear" (*Kurina Voi*). This was how the bear ceremony was born and why every bear who is killed can return to the sky for eventual rebirth.[38]

The climax of a phratry bear festival featured Khanty dressed as ancestral spirit figures, in sensational costumes and birch-bark masks. A crane representing the Mos people danced with giant, hinged wooden scissors for a beak and pantomimed the theft of food offerings to the bear, symbolic reenactment of Por and Mos antagonism. A spirit called "Double Image Being" had two faces and four hands, possibly symbolizing the duality of Por and Mos and the duality of gender. A humpbacked woman called "Wet-Handed" was probably associated with the water purification conspicuous in bear ceremonialism. Like all female roles in the dramas, "Wet-Handed" was played by a man. Impersonators of a gadfly and mosquito jumped into the audience, stinging them. In the midst of this melee, two sacred bird figures, a wood grouse and a wide-billed duck, pushed onlookers into disarray by rubbing their faces with coal, symbolizing their sinfulness. It is unclear whether specific victims were singled out.

Finally, messengers announced that *menk*, the ancestral forest spirits, were approaching from the river "to chastise people for their wickedness and their breaking of taboos" (Chernetsov 1968:109). Although doors were jammed shut, the menk burst in with huge birch masks covered with hair made of hay. They were hastily given two wooden figures, a man and woman soiled with blood, representing "the concentration of all evil" (Chernetsov 1968:109). The scapegoat figures were carried away by the menk, who beat them and then delivered them to a nearby sacred forest storehouse, after dancing in a swaying circle yelling "O-xo-xo-xo" in resounding voices that echoed through the forest.

The satirical plays featured at both spontaneous and periodic bear ceremonies gave the festivals relevance, freshness, and humor. Such plays reflected changing social, including ethnic, relations, as well as time-honored concepts. Some stressed the bear's revenge on humans who had not been respectful (cf. Karjalainen 1927:210–11). Some mocked male-female relations, while others satirized Nentsy, local Russians, or incompetent hunters.[39]

In one historical play, a Russian tsarist fur-tax collector demanded every fur that an impoverished Khanty hunter had and then had the nerve to ask for *votlep* leaves, used as all-purpose napkins. At this last request, the hunter turned on the Russian and his Khanty assistant, beating them until they ran away. A popular play about Khanty and Nentsy competition for a woman ended with the Khanty wife getting her husband drunk on a concoction of vodka and hallucinatory mushrooms, in order to go off with her Nentsy lover. In a third play, a cowardly hunter let his wife shoot a bear.[40]

Role reversal was in keeping with the language of opposites used in the bear hunt, with the use of female impersonators in all festival plays, and with the raucous behavior permitted women, usually shy, during some festivals (cf.Startsev 1928:108). At the end of Kazym and Yuilsk festivals, Khanty men walked backward during part of their trek to a local sacred storehouse, carrying the remains of the bear skin, bones, and meat.[41]

Following Bakhtin (1975:484–95) on ritual dialogics, Babcock (1978: 13–36) on reversal rituals, and Zemon Davis (1975:130–31) on carnival, I see bear festival improvisations as establishing a tone and language for dealing with, or at least exposing, the tensions and frustrations of value change. Satires on tsarist tax collectors gave way to fresh parodies, with new targets, in the Soviet period. At a 1970s bear festival in Shekure, a few dramas partially reflected the Communist Party line discouraging "idol" worship, traditional marriage, and shamanism. Performers included local brigade leaders. In one play, a father coped with the illness of his two children by making an image of an ancestral spirit, placing it in a sacred corner, and giving it food offerings. When this failed and his wife fell ill, the father beat the image and threw it to the ground. In another satire, a senile old man tried to buy a wife with the traditional netyn, but the bride he had selected ended up marrying his son, for free. A third drama mocked a female shaman, richly decked out in a fur coat and fancy blue head scarf.[42]

Such "people's theater" revealed not only Communist influence but also unresolved ironies. It was propaganda in Ugrian terms, and the act of performing the plays with double entendre shows that "idolatry," "bride price," and shamans were viable and controversial issues. As Khanty opened themselves to Soviet-Russian influences, the plays lost some of their occasionally cruel, insider-joke, anti-Russian quality. But Russian authorities, with reason, have watched them warily.[43]

In the post-Soviet period, some of the leaders of bear ceremony revivals are also the leaders of the Association for the Salvation of the Ugra. The largest and relatively open festivals have been sponsored by the Association, and the theme of Ugrian solidarity in the face of development and Russian land incursion has been prevalent. Tatiana Gogoleva saw the Yuilsk festival in 1991, which lasted ten days for some participants, as creating a chance for representatives of the Khanty and Mansi to discuss political strategy as a group. "We are small and scattered," she sighed. "At Yuilsk, we had reindeer sacrifices as well as the bear dancing. Although conditions were not conducive to advertising, many found out and came. It was popular. We had rituals and meetings to discuss our future."

The festivals have become crucial for morale building, but they are also venues for mass carousing, with alcohol. This has led the folklorist Olga Balalaeva (personal communication, 1993) to distinguish between the deeply religious, quite private, elder-led festivals that occur on the back rivers of Eastern Khanty camps and the larger, more popular festivals led by Association members as well as elders. Even so, in the midst of all the politics, the sacred bear is not forgotten, and people are touched by the rejuvenation of the festivals, with, as I was told in Kazym, "men and women crying at the end of the festival."

SHAMANIC POWER IN THE SPIRIT OF CHANGE

During the 1991 Yuilsk festival, in the middle of a multiverse song, one man sang, half-jokingly, "Gorbachev gave us permission to shamanize. But who wants to do this now? Who is left to do this now?" He had a point, for Soviet persecution of shamans had been serious, sustained, and effective. Plays presenting shamans as charlatans, not healers, were typical of Soviet propaganda from the 1920s onward. Soviet policy created a climate of doubt and confusion regarding at least some shamans, who had been figures of ambiguous, potentially dangerous, power in Khanty conceptions even before the Soviet period. In the 1930s, shamans were hunted into the forest like animals, or turned in by their children.[44]

In the Kazym area, as in many others across Siberia, postwar persecution became more subtle than the brutal repressions of the 1930s, but it was still sinister. Those with shamanic proclivities were deemed, by definition, to be crazy and thus candidates for "psikushki," psychiatric prisons, where debilitating drugs were administered to people broadly defined as "schizophrenics." A brilliant Khanty man with shamanic ancestry on both sides confessed that he was afraid of such "clinics" and had therefore tried not to heed the compelling call of shamanic spirits, although they sometimes tortured him. By the 1990s, he occasionally cured himself by using a drum in the forest. He was considering becoming more open about his shamanic proclivities by trying to help cure others.

In 1976, some Khanty consultants volunteered stories of shamanic failure. "I had a brother who was sick," said one woman, "and we invited a shaman, but my brother died. The shaman came in his everyday clothes and tried to collect the evil spirits causing sickness, in order to shoot them with arrows. The shaman tried to touch the areas where brother was sick and draw out the evil spirits, but on the fourth day, my brother died. I do not know—I was very young. Shamans are no kind of help."

This same woman acknowledged the continuing power, for some Khanty, of shamans and shamanic beliefs, exclaiming, "How can people say there are no shamans? Of course there are." Shamanic power was based on the conviction of shamans and their clients that manipulation of the spirit world was possible in spiritual emergencies. Khanty shamans, like most Siberian shamans, were more than medical practitioners. They were healers of the body politic as well.[45] The best shamanic curers, as defined by Khanty consultants, used their talent to aid both individual patients and their communities. They were leaders by virtue of their personality, spiritual knowledge, and experience in saving interlinked body-souls. As mediators of multiple worlds, they made predictions, provided spiritual shields for the living against danger, acted as intelligence agents during interethnic or intercommunity rivalries, and were veterinarians, psychiatrists, entertainers, and judges (cf. Siikala and Hoppál 1992).

While bear festivals helped Khanty participants communicate with the spirit world in times of joy and renewal, shamanic séances provided settings for communication in times of sorrow, fear, and sickness. Appropriately, the most renowned shamans claimed to harness the power of the bear as a spirit helper (Chichlo 1981:35–112; Schmidt 1989: 190). Given multiple sickness etiologies plus various types of séances and curers, Khanty shamanic practice does not lend itself to systematization (Kulemzin 1976:3–154; 1984; Kulemzin and Lukina 1992). A useful approach is to explain the terms for various shamanic spiritual practitioners in Khanty communities. This also enables differentiation of less powerful shamans (often women), whose practices have survived, albeit crippled, from most "big man" shamans, whose practices were too public to escape notice.

A *ëlta-ku* (Eastern Khanty) is a male séance leader, likely to use a drum for contacting the spirit world; while an *arekhta-ku* is a singer of legends and player of the sacred, spirit-contacting narsus. Powerful spirit intercessors are the *isyl'ta-ku* or *isyl'ta-ni*, crying man or crying woman, reputed to cure by "eating" the illnesses of others, taking and neutralizing bodily harm (in ways similar to the "sucking" of other indigenous curers). The (male) *niukul'ta-ku* is a specialist in hunt forecasting through séances. Less powerful, but crucial to community spiritual life, are the elder prayer leaders, usually men, called *multé-ku*, spirit gatherer. They operate with knowledge known to any elders who managed to learn rituals at any time in their lives, usually in retirement, when Soviet authorities ignored them. Women, in turn, are more often *ulom-verta-ni*, literally "dreams doing woman," adept at dream interpretation and shamanic prediction and diagnosis.

A Northern Khanty generic term for a shamanic fortune-teller is *térden-kho*, while Eastern Khanty say *t'erteng-ku*. Northern Khanty séance practitioners of various levels are sometimes called *chiart-kuat*, derived from the Russian word *chert*, glossed as devil dealers. A Northern Khanty friend confided in the 1990s that if someone did not want a Russian to know that a discussion was about a shaman, the euphemism was "sem pet lichen Khanty-kho," meaning roughly, "Khanty man who sees, hears, and seeks."

Two séances of the early Soviet period illustrate how shamans attempted individual or collective cures by appealing to community spirit. The first was on the Vakh River in 1925, when shamanic power was strong and shamans openly exhorted followers to conform to traditional morality and avoid unnecessary contact with Russian newcomers. Since the séance was for a sick child, soul loss was suspected rather than a breach of "taboo" that required confession. An audience of well-wishers crowded into the yurt of the child's family while the shaman's huge drum was warmed over a fire. After looking once at the child, the shaman began the first of two night sessions of drumming, dancing, and chanting. He built momentum slowly, sometimes tossing drumsticks to the audience, sometimes touching members of the family while singing or calling to his spirit helpers. The first session continued until five in the morning and included seven séances. During breaks, the shaman told his audience which spirits had come to him. With each séance, he became more "ferocious," as he reeled and bowed to incoming spirits. (Shamans were judged by the number of spirit helpers they could control.) He was particularly agitated when he called a spirit woman, Niem-lil, who was his main conduit for diagnosing the illness. After the first night, his eyes were rolling and he was in convulsions, with barely enough strength to promise that the child would be well. On the second night, the shaman used information gained by his spirit helpers to go on an underground journey to recover the lost soul from deceased relatives.[46]

In 1926, a major Vakh River shaman consented to perform an elaborate séance that required a flight through seven layers of the sky. His patient was the Khanty people, who felt their lands and way of life threatened by incoming Russians.[47] During the flight on his eagle-spirit helper, the shaman encountered evil beings, who tortured him into cries and contortions. But he finally rose to the golden yurt of the highest Sky God, where he explained: "There, where our land is, it is bad to live. For some, there are no fish, birds, or animals. Some are ailing, and some have actually died" (Shatilov 1931:128). He asked where the Khanty could live better and begged the "Greatest Elder" to become "aware" of his people. The Sky God reassured him that he could return with a message of hope.

This remarkable séance should be seen as a plea for spirit aid during a period of extraordinary tension, flux, and chaotic interethnic relations. Shamans often tried to be harbingers of hope rather than prophets of doom. But when their credibility diminished, so did the hope-producing power of their messages. The self-abandon that shamans and their audiences exhibited during séances was not always enough to restore a cathartic sense of well-being—a balance of integrated natural, cultural, and spiritual cyclical worlds. Into this gap came old fears about shamanic sorcery, as well as newer awareness of Soviet propaganda and advantages of other kinds of medicine.

In the 1970s, local Russians and Khanty in Tegy feared one "swine shaman," who lived as a recluse in the forest, literally and figuratively on the borders of village life. Some believed that "when he curses people, they may die." I was told this shaman had driven his brother-in-law to suicide with the chilling curse, "May there be blood on your floors" (Balzer 1983:65).

Many shamans in the Soviet period ceased being effective community leaders, because a process of mutual polarization blinded Soviet policy makers to the benefits of shamanic healing and rendered wounded shamans immune to the possibilities of modern European medicine. This has posed a dilemma for those Khanty who believe in shamanic illness etiologies and spiritually based ways of maintaining unified mental-physical health. Although their faith in folk healing was shaken, their confidence in modern medicine was never complete, especially given insufficiencies of Soviet health care. The number and power of shamans diminished, but older, conservative women became increasingly involved in passing on some shamanic traditions.[48]

Khanty consultants mournfully recite the names of the greatest shamans of the past. They are nostalgic for the great singing, séances, and cures of the Eastern Khant Yakov Umsanov, who died in the 1990s, or the Tegy shaman Ta'gyn Kola. They celebrate the feats of the Northern Khant Timofei Moldanov, who was jailed twice, once for the Kazym hostage-taking and once for practicing shamanic séances. "He cured a lot of people. He also had songs in which he foresaw the future of his people." Especially significant, a few younger Khanty have felt spirits calling them and have begun to try to cure by relying on information from both elders and the spirits. Reversing the Soviet line, one said, "People go crazy or die if they cannot shamanize."

CONCLUSION: SOUL-FULL

Khanty still living in their family territories or near their sacred places have a worldview and spiritual intuition that transcends appeal to specific shamans. A hunter from a renowned shamanic family recently recalled: "Sometimes, in the woods, maybe you are hunting and something feels not right. You can just sense it, something out of place or too much in place. But if you are drunk, you do not catch the feeling. Drunks die, because they do not feel the danger signals."

Understanding of Siberian religions is only superficially served by overgeneralizing labels like "animism," "paganism," "ancestor worship," "totemism," and "shamanism" (Humphrey with Onon 1996). Each term, with its historiographic or pejorative loads, conveys only part of the multidimensional and changing social-religious world of the "traditional" Ob-Ugrian Khanty.

Shamans have ceased being the major galvanizers of ethnic awareness, but shamanic spiritual revival is part of a desperate and uneven Khanty ethnic revival, playing out in conditions of trauma. Aspects of shamanic belief live on in Khanty approaches to life crises, and many Khanty of the 1990s selectively perceive positive as well as negative aspects of shamanic practice. Shamanic values include not only patriarchalism but also potential for female power; not only sorcery but compassionate group therapy; not only animal sacrifice but ecological prudence. These values are being resurrected in new ways and in new contexts.

As seen across the North, respect for ancestors, inherent in beliefs about souls and reincarnation, combined with ideologies of environmental and social regeneration are part of complex, interrelated religious beliefs that have proved both tenacious and syncretic (de Laguna 1972; Fienup-Riordan 1990; Mills and Slobodin 1994; E. Turner 1996). Concepts of rebirth are powerful bolsters of Khanty hope and, as such, stimulate ethnic pride. Bear festival revitalization is at once the symbol and mechanism to communicate that pride. As Timofei Moldanov said in 1991: "The bear festival is the core of our culture. You can see most of our values, traditions, and beliefs reflected in the songs and plays and dances." Similarly, Agrafina Sopochina remarked in 1998, "Bear festival songs constitute a whole philosophy for us" (photo 13).

Is there a unique Khanty consciousness, and is it religious? All Khanty do not think alike, any more than all Russians do. However, patterns in Khanty thinking emerge as they confront the Soviet and post-Soviet worlds. This interethnic dynamic may have led Caroline Humphrey (1983:441) to write of Buryat Sovietization: "Rather than an insertion of a Buryat native content into Soviet modes of explanation, we find the reverse: the phenomena of the Soviet world appear, disconnected from their theoretical origins, structured by a Buryat consciousness." The Khanty too were active receivers and shapers of Soviet messages, in their own terms, although hardly on their own terms. That legacy suggests that post-Soviet spiritual revitalization has a base from which to grow in perilous times.

Photo 13. Agrafina Pesikova Sopochina with alligator, at a seminar hosted by the Seminole Tribe, Florida, 1998.

CONCLUSIONS

A Siberian Saga in Global Perspective

EACH CHAPTER in this book analyzes processes of change that have intensified ethnic identity in interethnic contexts. I argue that ethnic identification can be a process of transcending victimhood. The tenacity of ethnicity need not mean maintenance of specific cultural traits, frozen in time. Rather, ethnic interaction creates reciprocal social-political change, redefinitions of "traditional" social groups, and disparate personal approaches to cultural heritage. Historically specific dynamics have caused many analysts to emphasize the situational and variable character of ethnicity (Cohen 1978; Royce 1982; Connor 1994). Anthropologists should acknowledge both cultural context and the necessity of comparisons that enable theoretical generalizations about social trends. Analysis of multiple levels of political identity in an increasingly interconnected, multiethnic world can help resolve seeming contradictions between cultural specificity and the commonality of human, including group, rights (Appadurai 1996; Ortner 1995; Chatterjee 1993).

Analysts need not choose between the extremes of "primordialism," stressing ethnicity rooted in tradition, and "construction," stressing the political nature of identity (Smith 1981, 1986; Anderson 1991). Within one group, multiple ways of seeing and feeling identity may coexist, and various theories may apply. Many Eastern Khanty, still scattered in riverbank and forest camps, are isolated from the excitement of politically charged bear festivals and Association for the Salvation of the Ugra agitation, yet they have a sense of themselves as Khanty.

Attempts to generalize about the nature of "culture contact" led to an early literature on the trials and pain of "acculturation" and "culture loss" for minorities (Redfield, Linton, and Herskovits 1938). Patterns of creativity, adaptation, and resistance, stimulated through interethnic contacts in many parts of the world, were underemphasized. I have attempted to go beyond assumptions of "acculturation" to an "interaction" approach, without claiming ease of adaptation, uniformity of cultural persistence, or consistency of power dynamics. In the case of Ugrian-Slavic interactions, ethnic contacts were too complex and too varied over time for easy characterization. But structured relationships and trends have nonetheless emerged.

The ways such trends are analyzed depend on the theoretical perspectives of the researcher (Marcus and Fischer 1986; Herzfeld 1987, 1997; Clifford 1988). A positivist conceit is to assume that "objective" data dictate analysis. Yet many anthropologists are, to various degrees, "neo-positivists," attempting to report observations in contexts as radically changing and hard to predict as the post-Soviet transition societies.[1] Diverse, multiethnic consultants' voices should be in the foreground as we try to identify processes that generate or confirm useful theories without assuming a priori the validity of one theory or model.

As I have searched the thickets of hermeneutic, symbolic, structural, poststructural, ecological, psychological, materialist, and neo-Marxist thought, I have often found that theories others perceive to be contradictory may be complementary, or operating on different levels of interpretation. Unsystematic fieldwork among fellow ethnographers has taught me that I am not alone in frustration with those who try to polemicize or put theoretical labels on themselves or others. Multiple perspectives have relevance to ethnicity, because analysts of ethnicity and ethnonationalism have recapitulated many debates in anthropology theory. I have tried to select from and adapt those recent and older theories that best apply to Khanty interaction with others, without limiting myself to one theoretical position.

ETHNICITY THEORIES

The importance of ethnicity has been recognized at least since the 1930s by scholars searching for flexible ways to view social process without ignoring cultural constraints. Many scholars have contributed to understanding ethnicity in plural or multiethnic societies by focusing on particular theoretical or topical aspects of its dynamics, from boundary behavior and politics to language maintenance and psychology (fig. 4). Others strive for more integrative or practice-driven approaches. Some, with Western or Soviet backgrounds, have searched for predominant themes or factors fostering ethnic awareness and conflict in multiethnic socialist societies, once proclaimed to discourage or eliminate the need for ethnic divisiveness.[2] Their conclusions derive from avowed theoretical orientations as much as from the nature of the ethnographic examples they have studied.

Analysis of Khanty and Russian interaction should begin with Fredrik Barth (1969). Barth's emphasis on the maintenance of ethnic boundaries leads to exploration of how ethnic interaction may have enhanced rather than eroded Khanty self-identity. Historically, pride building and ethnocentrism were stimulated in both Russian and Khanty commu-

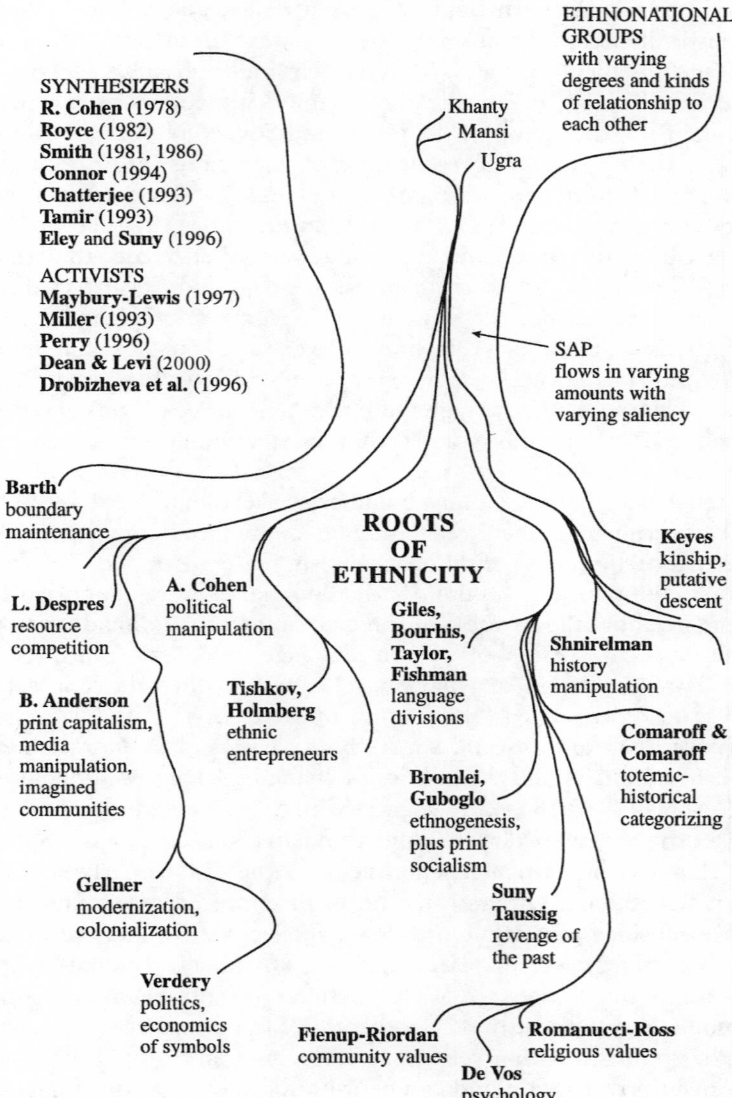

Figure 4. The ethnicity tree: a view of selected theories.

The roots of the tree represent diverse theories of ethnonationalism. The sap from the roots leads to various groups, in complex relations to each other, in the tree branches. Alongside are synthesizers and activists less easily integrated into the tree.

nities. Uneasy trade partnerships, intermarriages, and political alliances synergistically led to the unstable social context for violent Native reactions, such as the 1830s Vavlyo movement and the 1930s Kazym hostage crisis. Terming them "rebellions" implicitly collaborates with the rhetoric, if not the views, of the tsarist and Soviet colonizers.[3]

Many Khanty reacted to early Cossack incursions into their territories by fleeing north and east into forbidding (to Slavic settlers) areas that became ethnic enclaves (cf. Castille and Kushner 1981; Perry 1996). During Christianization campaigns that were in effect de-ethnicization efforts, Khanty fought for their ancestral images and resurrected them when they were burned (cf. Taussig 1987; Hefner 1992; Rambo 1993). The harshness of the clash mellowed over time, but boundaries were never completely erased by either side, even in relatively southern areas. In precisely those areas of greatest contact, ethnicity was intensified through mutual prejudice and ethnic stereotyping by Russian and Khanty individuals.

In the Soviet period, ethnic boundaries were influenced by mixed-signal government policies encouraging multiethnic communities and affirmative action laws. Ethnonationalism festered or was limited to folkloric cooption (cf. Connor 1994). Boundaries were supported literally and symbolically by the political geography of national districts and by cautious sponsorship of written languages and performing arts (cf. Grant 1995). This led to what Suny (1993), writing about larger national groups, has called "the revenge of the past."

It is necessary to transcend Barth's boundaries and Connor's ethnonationalism to understand the politics of changing Khanty self-definitions. Leo Despres (1975:185–207) suggested that, for most multiethnic societies, a primary factor determining ethnic divisions is resource competition. This may be particularly pertinent for the chaotic early Soviet period, when Russian settlers came north in unprecedented numbers. Its salience subsided somewhat after Soviet collectivization and affirmative action programs were in place. In the 1980s, macroregional competition—for example, between West Siberia and Central Asia—was more common than ethnic resource competition.[4] But ethnic resource competition has returned with a vengeance in the internal regional struggles of post-Soviet privatization and competition for energy-producing lands.

A larger lesson is that the complex ecology of the Ob River region, and its historically changing division of resources, must be considered in any discussion of ethnicity and demography in the area (cf. Krupnik 1993). Those Khanty, and Siberian Natives in general, who pursue traditional occupations of hunting, fishing, and reindeer breeding as their predominant means of livelihood have maintained ecological niches that correlate with long-standing cultural values. But a direct correlation between ethnicity and occupation is too simple and plays into the hands of privatizers who wish to cut off urban and village Natives from rights to land. Soviet resource allocation was controlled through a centralized economy with limited local adjustments, ubiquitous greed and corruption, and some consideration for the legal rights of Native peoples. Post-Soviet resource competition has made a mockery of legal protections: the political context is intertwined with the economic.

Abner Cohen's early emphasis on ethnicity as based on interconnected economic and political relationships is helpful. Cohen noted (1974:iv): "One need not be a Marxist in order to recognize the fact that the earning of livelihood, the struggle for a larger share of income from the economic system, including the struggle for housing, for higher education and for other benefits . . . constitute an important variable significantly related to ethnicity." Cohen's analysis applied particularly to urban, postcolonial multiethnic environments in Africa, but fits wherever groups, operating at multiple levels, need to formulate or reinforce informal, symbol-laden social organizations for political purposes at multiple levels using the idiom of ethnicity. In the Soviet paternalistic environment, when dominant Soviet Russians provided a flow of goods and resources into the North and established "culture bases" with hospitals and schools, Cohen's theory was less relevant. In the post-Soviet context of regionalization, Cohen's approach has new applications.

After initial violence, the politics of ethnicity in Soviet Siberia involved changing "autonomous district" structures, and fluctuating degrees of affirmative action in education and employment. Although officials in principle strove toward egalitarian ethnic relations, in practice they implemented policies unevenly. Sometimes they favored Siberians over Russians in access to higher education. But, as is the pattern with attempts at affirmative action, backlash set in. Members of Native elites rarely occupied more than token, local positions. With the demise of local "councils" after 1993, even such formal positions were eliminated. Native leaders have used accommodation and opposition strategies in the post-Soviet period, building on a legacy of diverse and sometimes ambiguous resistance (cf. Comaroff 1985; Watson 1994; Ortner 1995).

From the Stalin to the Gorbachev periods, limited ethnicity-based "interest group" responses to Soviet policies occurred through permitted Communist Party channels, inside district (okrug), autonomous or union republic administrative frameworks. Even the geographic boundaries of republics were adjusted this way. In contrast (if not opposition), informal networks that tapped ethnic feelings came to be the bases for sanctioned and unsanctioned politics, "making use of kinship, friendship, ritual, ceremonial and other symbolic activities" (Cohen 1974: xvii). This kind of ethnicity flourished in the late 1980s, with the founding of such groups as the Association for the Salvation of the Ugra and its counterparts throughout the North.

Charles Keyes stresses that, for smaller ethnic groups, such informal networks are often based primarily on claims of kinship and common history. This return to an early focus in anthropology stems from Keyes's (1976:204) understanding of the Thai term *chat*, which relates ethnicity to birth and karma. Keyes's (1981) linkage of ethnicity with descent is neither rigid nor racial, but it does highlight structural and hierarchical aspects of ethnic group dynamics as seen from within a community. Ethnicity-centered history and putative shared descent can also play important roles in the dynamics of ethnic change. This becomes particularly messy when ethnic "mythologies" (historical narratives) conflict (Shnirelman 1996).

Focus on the constructedness of kinship and history correlates well with the patrilineal and reincarnation-oriented Khanty. Identities based on putative kinship indeed provide multiple and expanding points of social reference, including the new post-Soviet variations on older land-based communities, obshchiny. Individuals, after acknowledging Por or Mos phratry identity from a particular camp, village, and family, may claim to be Berezovo (in contrast to Kazym) Khanty, Northern (not Southern or Eastern) Khanty, or Khanty (not Mansi). These distinctions carry the seeds of mildly politicized ethnicity, but they are especially significant in the context of trends toward broader social-cultural group consciousness. Khanty activists are increasingly defining themselves as Ugra (not Russians). They also stress commonality with other Northern indigenous groups (especially Nentsy) and categorize people as Native as opposed to Newcomer, in increasingly polarized contexts.[5]

Many putative kinship identities happen to be congruent with linguistic distinctions, although they need not be. Language distinctions alone do not "make" ethnicity. But local politics may influence interpretations of ethnolinguistic origins, exemplified by a few budding Khanty linguists, historians, and folklorists who criticize overgeneralizing ethnographers for masking local distinctions. In environments where interpretations of history and language are politicized, outside researchers need tact and caution. Terming all indigenous interpretations of competitive pasts "mythologies" renews old, artificial distinctions between Scientists and Natives.[6]

Any quest to understand the dimensions of Khanty ethnicity should include the political and psychological significance of language. Howard Giles, Richard Bourhis, and Donald Taylor (1977:308–18) developed a complex structural model of ethnolinguistic vitality that places language use and cognition at the center of ethnic identity. Their language-centrism, however, is balanced by acknowledgment of the variable importance of demography, power relations, and institutional support in assessing the vitality of an ethnic group. Intellectual successors of Johann Gottfried Herder and Edward Sapir recognize the potential for language to shape the ways interethnic relations are perceived and cultural values are transmitted (Irvine 1993). This reinforces what Joshua Fishman (1977:25–26) called "the recurring symbolic role of language in the ethnicity experience." While some groups or individuals may have lost their language, or have come to see it as less significant than assertion of their ethnic identity, language is often a prime symbol of ethnicity, with meaning beyond its communication function. International attention to "endangered languages" in turn resonates with indigenous concerns (Vakhtin 1993; Grenoble and Whaley 1997).

Language has been an emotional marker of belonging for many Khanty, but their ethnic consciousness did not interfere with their desire to learn the Russian language in order to understand what goes on in collective meetings and to get ahead in the multiethnic Soviet and post-Soviet worlds. Most in the younger generations incorporated bilingualism, just as many strove for some degree of biculturalism. This meant neither automatic Russification nor Sovietization. Some Khanty are trilingual, knowing Nentsy or Mansi as well. As opportunities to study the Khanty language and use it in school declined in the late Soviet period, a declining Khanty majority upheld the Khanty language as their mother tongue.[7] In the post-Soviet period, emergency language recovery through cultural revitalization activism is beginning to have some effect. Changing 1990s school policies encourage students to use the Khanty language extensively, while learning Russian as well.

The written language that became standard for the Khanty was adapted in the 1930s from the Eastern Khanty dialect (Tereshkin 1981). While a few families find themselves in the awkward position of having a grandmother who speaks only the Khanty language and a young schoolchild who speaks only Russian, this is not the norm. During the Soviet period, the Khanty language, as symbol and marker of Khanty ethnicity, was maintained privately in Khanty homes, semiprivately in Khanty rituals, and officially in Khanty books, newspapers, and radio programs. This was more "print socialism" than "print capitalism" (cf. Chatterjee 1993:4–9; Anderson 1991:67–82), but it did lead to pride in the printed vernacular and hopes that the small Khanty intelligentsia could nourish and be nourished by both the Russian and Khanty languages. Current nostalgia for the rich language of ritual and folklore and regret over its loss are understandably strong (e.g., Vella 1996; Moldanova 1990).

George De Vos and Lola Romanucci-Ross (1995:349–79) stress the psychological factors important to ethnic survival. They recognize multiple sources and uses of ethnicity but focus on cultural separateness as crucial to a sense of self-worth. While acknowledging the situational salience of "passing," they argue that ethnicity answers psychological needs by providing continuity with the past. Following George Herbert Mead, they see this as accomplished partly through life-cycle rituals and religious ideologies that help maintain an individual's "integrity," a consistent sense of self.

For the Khanty, as for other minority indigenous groups under siege, rituals, particularly of birth and burial, have been among the most persistent aspects of cultural vitality. These rituals have provided fulcrums for solidarity or solace (a kind of "communitas") in difficult moments when individuals need community support. Rituals enable Khanty to actualize an ideology of reincarnation in a striking version of widespread Asian and Native American soul cosmologies (cf. Mills and Slobodin 1994). Emotional, "liminal" periods are created in the ritual process, providing opportunities for cultural renewal and change (cf. Turner 1977; Bakhtin 1975; Zemon Davis 1975).

Rituals have been central to the maintenance of Khanty ethnicity, not only helping to forge links with the past but also to negotiate an uncertain future (cf. Fienup-Riordan 1990). Appropriately, the Association for the Salvation of the Ugra has sponsored the revitalization of marriage and bear ceremonies in their bid to reintegrate and activate Khanty and Mansi consciousness. Insiders and outsiders may question the "authenticity" of such intellectual efforts at cultural (re)construction, but they are sincere and motivated by an expressed sense of cultural threat.[8]

Through cultural values exposed, upheld, and sometimes questioned in ritual, community support and a sense of cultural difference have been fostered in West Siberia before and after 1917. Rituals have transmitted messages of ethnic pride, renewal, and, occasionally, chauvinism. While ritualized protests and revitalization did not lead to a new syncretic religion, they illustrate periodic resurgences of shamanic practice. Native Siberians, out of their pain and disharmony, created rituals of identity and temporary multigroup solidarity as dramatic as the Native American Ghost Dance.

In many interethnic contexts, the ethics of "ethnics" have led to an explosive clash of moral commitments, identity, and politics.[9] In most of the Soviet period, Khanty religious identity was only a submerged, quiet, and often private marker of ethnicity, predominantly but not exclusively led in each generation by elderly, conservative women. Despite Soviet educations, they rekindled the flame of prayer as they grew older. After the repressions of the 1930s, religion posed little threat to Soviet political goals. Yet it provided a potential base from which cultural-political activism could arise in the late 1980s, long after many thought all the shamans had died. The renewal of animal sacrifices in the 1990s beautifully illustrates the correlation of ethnic consciousness with religion. But it is no accident that some of the worst extremes of local Russian violence against Khanty occurred following an unusually public mass reindeer sacrifice scheduled just after the 1995 International Finno-Ugric Congress. Assertions of perceived primitive "otherness" met their match.

THEORY AND PRACTICE: AN EXPLANATORY METAPHOR

Imagine a large and shapely tree, grown old, with a profusion of limbs supporting many branches in a chaotic, vital fashion. Underneath such a tree, to enable it to survive, would have to be an enormous network of spreading and exploring roots. If these roots can be taken as a metaphor for the ethnicity theories just reviewed (and others), then the tree may also serve as a model for the interaction of ethnic groups with each other and with their analysts. The branches and limbs represent various ramifying relations of ethnic groups to each other, sometimes with linguistic and dialect correlates, and sometimes without such easily identifiable links. The roots, at different depths in the soil, represent concepts about the primacy of various dominant sources of ethnicity. Thus boundary behavior, resource competition, political maneuvering, history manipulation, putative descent, language identity, psychological needs, community values, and religious experience all have their places in the root system of ethnicity theory (fig. 4).

The task for a researcher confronted with this dense foliage is not to pick one dominant ethnicity theory and run with it up the tree trunk to a likely case study, but rather to analyze the branches to understand where they get their life and how they are intertwined over time. One branch is likely to derive vitality from all possible sources, yet different amounts of sap may course through the trunk at different times from various roots. An analytical challenge is to determine which theories best apply, which sap is most nourishing, and when the sap ebbs as well as flows.[10]

For Khanty during the Soviet period, ethnicity was stimulated and maintained largely through the legal and political structures of the Tiumen Oblast (Region) and the Khanty-Mansi Okrug (District). Official policies designed to both regulate and relax boundary behavior influenced Khanty ethnicity, not always in the directions planned. Some policies—for example, collectivization and influxes of non-Siberian labor—

indirectly strengthened boundaries through disruptive demographic realignments. Other policies directly appealed to ethnic awareness through affirmative action decrees, the sometimes token stimulus of written language programs, and encouragement of multiple identities. This affected some Khanty more than others, young male draftees, for example, more than elderly women.

Private (domestic) and semiprivate (secretive local community) means of maintaining cultural survival reinforced the official stimuli of ethnic awareness. Rituals marking life passages were performed by retired villagers with nothing to lose politically, and also by Communist Party members, who could be reprimanded or worse. Religious values concerning ancestor respect, reincarnation, animal spirit rebirth, female fertility, male virility, and shamanic healing (of linked physical-spiritual ills) retained a power not easily dislodged by Soviet antireligious propaganda or replaced by Soviet "secular rituals." Bear "games" lost some of their sacred meaning in some places, but they were not so thoroughly secularized or eliminated as Soviet officials wished. The satirical plays and rituals of reversal honoring bears represented indigenous philosophy and addressed tensions, not fully resolved, concerning ethnicity and gender. Like most satire, they were played out in different registers or codes, so that the culturally/symbolically initiated caught their meaning, while outsiders did not.

Renewed political-cultural vitality grew from such ambiguous resistance, as soon as group activism and vocal leadership became possible during perestroika. The Association for the Salvation of the Ugra and the more local obshchiny (land-based, council-led communities) sprouted for a few short years in the 1990s. However, their shoots are being stunted by the land grabbing and environmental despoliation associated with energy development, and the more metaphorical pollution of the Siberian social environment by Russian chauvinism and the energy politics of Native cooption.

In sum, in the mid to late Soviet period, ethnic boundaries were not barriers to social and cultural change. The post-Soviet period has seen increasingly mobilized, frightened, and politicized Khanty, reacting to conditions of even greater destabilization in their everyday lives. It is a prescription for cultural polarization.

POTENTIAL FOR CIVIC (CIVIL) SOCIETY

As with all models and metaphors, the ethnicity tree has only limited interpretive power. For the model to bear fruit, additional dimensions and theories are needed. First, the interrelations of limbs, branches, and leaves are not well defined, for in many interethnic situations an individual or group's self-definition changes in response to prejudice and to the mergings or splinterings inherent in social-political interaction. While one group might be grafted onto another—for example, refugees after a war or protest crack-down—another may split and move during periods of competition for scarce resources. Groups may or may not be minorities in a particular microregion. These distinctions, as well as problems of nomad-settler relations, race discrimination, and class, led Ronald Cohen (1978:387) to define ethnicity as "a series of nesting dichotomizations of inclusiveness and exclusiveness." Such a nesting may be correlated to the hierarchical way in which ethnonational categories were defined in the Soviet period. Hierarchies continue in the Russian Federation. The problem for the smallest ethnic groups, like the Khanty, is to avoid being cut out by the process of political and economic redefinition going on in regions and the wider society.[11]

A related problem concerns the failure of organic models to convey the politically contextualized, negotiated making of new ethnicities (Handler 1988). Evolutionary models of Progress, including old-fashioned Soviet studies of ethnogenesis (Dolgikh 1962; Gurvich 1975, 1985), also fail to capture political realities. Ethnonationalism can develop from smaller ethnic subgroup allegiance, as in the Ugrian (Khanty-Mansi) case, and from groups not originally formed solely on the basis of ethnic identity, as with the Siberiak culture that evolved from intermarriage between Cossacks of military communities and various Native Siberian groups (Balzer 1994a). In political contexts of the 1990s, it is significant that Khanty and Siberiaki acknowledge the salience of multiple levels of identity, including their membership in the Russian Federation. Members of both groups call themselves "Rossiiany (multiethnic citizens of Rossiia)," not "Russkie (Russians)."

Beyond ethnicity, theories stressing multiple, situational identities incorporate the possibilities of broad, civic-society citizenship. Hopeful analysts have searched for indicators of civic identities transcending "narrow nationalism" in post-Soviet, postsocialist states (Przeworski 1995; Hann and Dunn 1996); and elsewhere (Eley and Suny 1996:403–508; Periwal 1996; Deak 1990). Ironically, the Soviet propagandist-ethnographer Yulian Bromlei (1983:82; cf. 1984:86), in his discussion of hierarchic ethnic communities, suggested the term "meta-ethnic" for a level of social consolidation that is evolving beyond ethnic affiliation into citizenship. His "meta-ethnic" *Homo sovieticus* did not grow up as expected, though some loyal Soviet mixed-ethnic citizens, including those with minority Siberian backgrounds, mourn the demise of the Soviet Union.[12]

In contrast, in the post-Soviet context, former nationalities minister

Valery Tishkov (1997) analyzes the polarizing trends that have led to ethnic conflict and a tragic hardening of chauvinist ethnonational identities through the "ethnic entrepreneurship" of selfish ethnonational leaders, including Russians and Chechens. The Khanty are such a tiny minority that few of their leaders have the luxury of becoming ethnic entrepreneurs. *Homo xenophobicus* is also an inappropriate image for those Khanty and other indigenous peoples actively searching for international support,[13] or creating groups like RAIPON.

The complex relationship among changing state structures, laws, and ethnicity formation needs to be better understood, particularly in post-Soviet transition societies described as struggling toward "civic (civil) society." My omnibus conception of "civic society" is that it enables a multileveled development of citizen psychology, through social and professional associations separate from state control, as well as the networking of these associations and their interaction with state institutions.[14] During a 1997 seminar in Washington, D.C., two Russian governors from West Siberia, Yuri Neelov (of Yamal-Nenets Okrug) and Aleksander Filipenko (of Khanty-Mansi Okrug), downplayed the need for political parties or Western-style democratic processes, while lauding economic change and international partnerships. They were giving the mixed signals that have become typical for regional leaders in post-Soviet Siberia.

Anya Peterson Royce (1982:10–11) long ago noted that regulation of behavior by the state or by dominant ethnic groups does not always coincide with cognitive shifts in ethnicity (cf. Perry 1996). Royce's synthesizing view of ethnicity centers on three dimensions: power (the political context), purpose (strategies for ethnicity), and perception (the way all parties and groups view themselves and each other). More recent analysts of civic society presume these dimensions, but focus on how diverse, ethnically based interest groups form in the expanding post-Soviet space between the individual and state institutions (Gellner 1994, 1994a; Hann and Dunn 1996). Their analyses are far more complex than the simple formula that nationalism has sprung up in the vacuum-creating absence of communism (cf. Khazanov 1995).

Some theorists stress the ambiguity of everyday behavior and the risks of resistance in widely ramifying state and cross-state contexts (cf. Ortner 1995; Perry 1996; Levi and Dean 2000). Globalizing and local contexts are relevant. Ethnonational politicization centers on community mobilization, even when outside agitators and nonlocal media are involved. In Alaska, for example, Yupik community activism has reinforced consensus values. Elders selectively guide how traditions can be integrated in subtle processes of negotiated change (Fienup-Riordan 1990). In Siberia, communities are experimenting with different kinds of consensus-oriented obshchiny and new styles of leadership that give greater voice to women and spiritual leaders. Predictably, disputes break out over who speaks for whom, and at what level.

Individuals and groups often have difficulty adjusting to the clashes of values implicit in "bizness" and in new legal contracts, especially land deals. Privatization of land is among the most painful unresolved issues of post-Soviet politics. When reindeer breeder and poet Yuri Vella was told that he needed to acquire a deed to his family lands, he first responded, "Do hares have a document?" He adapted quickly to legal realities, however, and learned to lead effective Native protest demonstrations. By 1997, at least some local politics were moving from the street to the negotiating table: when Vella merely threatened a mass demonstration, Khanty-Mansiisk authorities agreed to meet with indigenous leaders to discuss diverse grievances.[15] Meetings were also scheduled over the proposed United Nations model Yugan biosphere project, although the commission in charge of this, appointed and led by the governor, appears to be mere window dressing.

TRIBALIZATION AND GLOBALIZATION – TOGETHER?

Each example of relatively productive local interethnic negotiation builds a climate of better chances for creating a civic society from the rubble of discredited communist ideas. Yet the reverse danger of polarization and failed communication is as real as the nearest sensational(ist) TV newscast, now readily available in Siberian villages. Ideas of ethnic purity (ethnocentrism) have appeal in many multiethnic societies, even as wider political and economic interrelations are becoming possible (Cheah and Robbins 1998). This is less a paradox than a correlation; not a universal social process, but one happening in many places, particularly in postsocialist states. Social theorists such as Michel Maffesoli (1995) proclaim a return to "tribalism" within mass (Western, French) society, but multiethnic politics operating at multiple levels of multiculturalism are far more fraught, fragmented, and exciting. Tribal peoples themselves are "tribal" no longer, unless, like Native Americans, they use the designation along with many other identities. Several major, interrelated trends are affecting contemporary post-tribal political dynamics, with different degrees of force in different places (cf. Friedman 1994).

Imperial implosion. A well-recognized trend is the break-up of neocolonial and quasi-colonial empires, including socialist states (Gellner 1993, 1994a). Diverse definitions of "empire" can be accepted in this context, especially those stressing hegemonic power of one nation over others for political and economic exploitation (regardless of brotherhood-of-the-peoples rhetoric). The expression of ethnonational, politicized consciousness, while reveling over discredited dominant group ideology (communist), has been easily observable at numerous levels within the Newly Independent States. But in the Russian Federation (Rossiia), unlike some parts of the former Soviet Union, this does not necessarily mean the physical retreat of local "ethnic" Russians from once predominantly indigenous regions.

Punished peoples' polarization. The general processes set in motion by imperial implosion are correlated with and sometimes intensified by ethnic group recovery from specific, targeted state repression (cf. Perry 1996). In the post-Soviet context, this entails interpreting and acting on the legacies of such governmental policies as the deportation of whole ethnic groups ("punished peoples"), the widespread imprisonment of cultural and political leaders, and haphazard yet massive terror. Native Siberians experienced relatively little of this kind of repression, which can stimulate bitterly polarized nationalism. But they were not completely immune, as their leaders, analyzing the previous climate of fear and Soviet policies of population displacement, readily admit. Communities moved by fiat "from above," for economic as well as political reasons, are likely to have a high proportion of ethnonational "radicals."

Blow-back. A correlated trend is polarization of the insidious sort known in the intelligence community by the sinister term "blow-back" (Weiner 1994). Used mostly in the context of the terrorist and drug-trading ramifications of the Afghan war, the metaphor can be broadened to include spun-out-of-control unintended consequences of government policies focused on short-term goals. Soviet state nationality policies can be seen as creating the massive "blow-back" of Soviet dis-Union, together with the 1990s turmoil of Trans-Dniestr, the North Caucasus, Karabakh, and Tajikistan. Potential for "blow-back" in other local, indigenous contexts also exists and can be linked to national and transnational gun, drug, and crime policies and practices. Native Siberians discuss the "boomerang" effects of ill-conceived local and central government planning on them and their neighbors. In the 1990s, for example, mafia groups have begun to infiltrate indigenous obshchiny businesses to launder money and take advantage of state policies that give obshchiny some tax privileges. In Siberia, blow-back involving criminalized youth has begun to occur; it should be acknowledged as a first step toward prevention.

Creative federalisms. A more positive trend is fin-de-siècle creativity in attempts to negotiate new federal relations. The end of the century and millennium highlights a need for closure or reflection in the midst of the chaos within Newly Independent States. Ethnonational intelligentsias in many areas, and certainly within Rossiia, are stimulated to rethink their positions, vis-à-vis each other and cross-cutting, newly aligning regional powers. It is a time for new alliances, and skepticism, if not rejection, of old ones. The ethnonationalism that results may be far from chauvinist and can be a healthy force for change in interethnic relations and the construction of some minimal degree of federalism. The best antidote for virulent (potentially secessionist) nationalism is well-managed federalism, in a world where each ethnic group cannot have its own country. But a federalism that reaches down to local, community levels is possible only if indigenous minorities can negotiate meaningful, legally enforced territorial homelands.

Economy-security nexus. Federal relations function within the larger, shifting context of interlocking global economic and security arrangements. Those who are outside the International Monetary Fund, World Bank, North Atlantic Treaty Organization, or European Union (or who are objects of their limited largesse) often resent conditions dictated for participating in "the good life." Wanting membership in international clubs on their own terms, leaders of Newly Independent States and recently politicized ethnonational groups send mixed signals. A foreign policy that zigzags between approach and avoidance generates rhetoric that may sound xenophobic, especially just after behind-the-scenes security supplications have been rejected or major economic negotiations have gone sour. The Russian Federation's international politics of backlash and ambivalence have hindered but not eliminated the ability of its indigenous peoples to seek aid from World Bank and United Nations programs.

Ecological-social fallout. Ecological strife and its accompanying social fallout constitute a particularly unfortunate trend for indigenous peoples. In a climate where the wealthy industrialized "first world" has committed mistakes its members hope developing nations will not repeat, the world's "First Nations" are yet again the primary victims or objects of social experiment. In reaction, indigenous groups are trying to protect their remaining homelands and their own local natural resources. Siberia is prime turf, on the front line of new mineral and energy development. Without rejecting sustainable development, indigenous groups are uneasily aligning themselves with ecological activists and practicing new variations on Fredrik Barth's (1969) theme of "ethnic boundary maintenance". This can put transnational oil companies on the defensive and can make any humanitarian, community outreach deals they reach, beyond strictly monetary agreements, very important and public.

Spiritual connections. Endangered natural, social, and psychological environments have created contexts for renewed spirituality. The intertwined "body-minds" of indigenous peoples are often in as much disarray as their "body politic" (cf. Romanucci-Ross and De Vos 1995: 365–66; Comaroff 1985). Newly reclaimed spiritual authorities use a language of purging and curing of impurities, while mechanisms of society-wide healing are yearned for but not found. This can result in diverse forms of millenarianism and is a deep response on personal and group levels to fear of what is sometimes mistermed "genocide" through alcoholism and crime. Out of expressed concern with "cultural degradation" come personal and public reinterpretations of religious values and rituals. In such conditions, it is no surprise that activist indigenous healers, including controversial urban shamans who know how to manipulate cultural symbols, are popular and to various locally defined degrees, successful. One person's charlatan may be another's savior.

While these seven trends can be expanded upon and supplemented, they constitute the seeds of an interrelated analysis that incorporates post-tribal peoples of the Russian Federation (Rossiia, not Russia) into transnational indigenous politics. Native Siberian leaders are actively looking for models of interethnic communication for their global-economy influenced political negotiations. Anthropologists, too often concerned with a false dichotomy between "applied" and "theoretical" anthropology, can learn from indigenous experience about the interrelationship of theory and practice.

SEARCHING FOR MODELS AMONG FIRST NATIONS

This book is not a memoir, and in the text I have highlighted the Khanty, not myself. Nonetheless, a degree of reflexivity is appropriate. In graduate school, I cut my anthropological teeth on the mantra "No African models in Melanesia." In a more subtle way, I naively absorbed messages about the greater heuristic value of American anthropological theory over British or French models, mired as they were in both colonialism and postcolonial debates.[16]

When I finally arrived in the field in Siberia, after much bureaucratic, emotional, and political strife, I rebelliously was determined to reject Melanesian models for Siberians and to generate my own "models" (photo 14). Acutely aware of how little Westerners knew about Russian anthropology, I was also curious to determine whether there was anything to be salvaged from what I considered pseudo-Marxist Russian/Soviet ethnography. I was hardly a Marxist myself (as some have presumed on both sides of two oceans), but I was fascinated by Soviet propaganda that the history of Russian contact with Siberian peoples had been somehow softer, more humane than the his-

Photo 14. With Tegy friends, 1976. (Photo by Nina Nicharchova, Khanty librarian.)

tory of American Indian decimation through European colonization. And I was seared by the two Indian tragedies at Wounded Knee, nearly a century apart.

I plunged into archives of the tsarist period and gradually decided that American and Siberian colonization histories had been more similar than dissimilar, given parallel horrors of conquest, epidemics, trade exploitation, and land theft. But the "Russian side" of the Bering Sea featured a slower and more haphazard history of settler contacts, and perhaps a more benign experience of Christian "conversion." Russian Orthodox missionaries in the North came to accept greater degrees of syncretic incorporation of shamanic beliefs faster than did most Protestant ones. It was in the Soviet period that Native Siberians experienced the most ambitious degree of revolutionary brainwashing, along with literacy, limited local political representation, and relatively modern health care. In contrast, by the 1960s Native Americans were able to fight harder for their rights to self-determination, ritual vitality, and articulate legal defense in an increasingly judiciary, if not judicious, world.

The issue of Native American–Native Siberian parallels haunted me for over twenty years, as I oscillated between thinking Native American experiences were relevant for Native Siberians and rejecting Native American models as too constrained by the specifics of reservation politics or the Alaska Native Claims Settlement Act (ANCSA) of 1971 (with crucial "1991 amendments" passed by Congress in 1988). I became far too aware of the history of Stalinism and the poverty of Siberian villages to believe Native Siberian experience could be any model for Native Americans, as some poorly informed Westerners seemed to think. Not until the post-Soviet period, during meetings with indigenous leaders of America and Siberia, have I come to understand the degree to which they can offer each other not only dialogue and advice, but also adaptable aspects of their own models, constructed and reconstructed from interactive histories with Russian/Slavic and Euro-American/Anglo others.

Despite all the problems with Native American reservations, Bureau of Indian Affairs legacies, and conflicts over degrees of sovereignty in Canada, Alaska, and the "lower 48" states, Native Americans clearly have a head start in dealing with development, self-determination, and legal self-defense. While I have mixed feelings about wishing on any group the means to become more litigious, one of the most significant changes in Native American ability to defend themselves against further land theft has been the increased proportion of liberally educated Native American leaders, especially but not only lawyers. Many have rejected full assimilation while accommodating themselves to living with dignity in the Anglo world. On both sides of the Bering Sea, multiple identities on multiple levels, activated situationally with flexible style, have become normal for indigenous leaders, if not for all their peoples.

This returns me to the question of ethnic consciousness. Many Native American intellectuals reject a sense of themselves as somehow the same kind of "ethnic" as other ethnic groups in North America. Indigenous nations, First Nations, have a different order of rights and sovereignty than immigrant ethnic interest groups competing in the unmelted, eclectic marketplace of American identity politics (Deloria and Lytle 1984; Nagel 1997). Yet with charm and irony, the Seminole chief James Billie told Siberian guests to address their questions to "those who look ethnic, for example, those wearing Seminole-style shirts."

Wearing the word "tribe" with pride, Native Americans also claim nationhood within the federal United States and Canada. Many proclaim an unbroken cultural vitality, against the odds of Western "civilization," mass-marketed stereotypes, alcoholism, and suicide. A Pueblo potter reinforced to me in 1997 what has become a common refrain: "We are rich in our culture, not our pocketbooks." To boost the confidence of future generations, Native Americans are reluctant to stress that current cultural-political and economic (re)vitalization comes in the context of dire need. They well know the past histories of each tribe's sufferings and are trying to transcend them.

First Nations of the United States and Canada have organized at multiple levels, reflecting identity and solidarity beyond reservations, incorporating regional, pan-Northern, and pan-Indian activism. In Florida, in 1998, the elder Bill Day introduced himself to Siberians, saying, "I am of the Tunica-Biloxi tribe, and also Choctaw, Cherokee, French, and English, but my strong genes are Indian." He and others also made clear the difficulties of activism at regional and pan-Indian levels, when economic and political interests are sometimes diverse or competitive.[17]

Khanty intellectuals, few but growing in number, use neither the words "nation" nor "tribe" with ease. "Nation" would imply a greater sense of separateness from the fledgling Russian Federation (Rossiia) than they feel, and "tribe" seems too tied with a primitive past. Some prefer to focus on being "indigenous" (in Russian, *korenny*) or "aboriginal" (*aborigeny*). For many, a sense of ethnonational identity has been shaped by the Russian words *national'nost*, a nationality that is part of some larger whole, and *narod*, a people. In most Khanty areas, a word for "people" in the broadest sense is *mir*, perhaps originally from Russian. *Syr* denotes "clan" or "lineage," as does the Russian *rod*; while *kaasel* (Eastern Khanty) is "family" and *khanekhe* (Eastern Khanty) or *khantakh* (Northern) is "person." A group at the obshchina (community) level is called *iakh*, and this can also be expanded to broader levels of belonging, as in As-iakh, the Ob people, the term from which Ostiak was derived during early trade contacts (cf. Kulemzin and Lukina 1992:22).

Khanty leaders rarely act at the level of mass political identity by speaking for their whole people. More often, they prefer to defend a particular group, such as the Eastern Khanty of the Yugan River, who are fighting for their rights to land against oil companies. Yet when leaders founded a political movement in the late 1980s, Khanty together with Mansi chose to call themselves "Ugra," stressing their common roots. Their activism is one variation in a broad range of potential nationalisms and attempts at cultural empowerment. More accurately, it is a form of nonchauvinist ethnonationalism, a politicized yet usually liberal ethnic consciousness born of the need to defend their cultural heritage and lands. It fits with membership in the wider community of Native-rights agitation represented by the Association of Peoples of the North, Siberia, and the Far East, led first by Nivkh writer Vladimir

Sangi, followed by the Khanty writer Eremei Aipin and the Nentsy politician Sergei Kharyutchi. Their RAIPON is in turn in communication with other indigenous-rights groups, such as the Inuit Circumpolar Conference and the Saami Nordic Council.

The word "liberal," used in conjunction with nesting levels of ethnonationalism, requires explanation. While eschewing models taken as nondigestible wholes, I have nonetheless searched the anthropological and historical literatures for cases of moderate, nonchauvinist ethnonationalism. It is urgent to understand the dynamics of how mildly politicized ethnonationalism, oriented toward positive goals, can be maintained by the minorities of the Russian Federation, without turning into the polarized, embittered nationalisms of former Yugoslavia or Chechnya. Polarization stems far more often from the "center," in this case Moscow, than from powerless peoples on the periphery, but their radicalized responses can spin out of control, creating a storm of mutually self-defeating hatred (Balzer 1994; Balzer 1995; Drobizheva et al. 1996).

Theories from non-Western, multiethnic scholars, often trained in the West, such as Yael Tamir (1993) and Partha Chatterjee (1993), have the potential to bridge a conceptual gap between large national group activism and small minority group mobilization within state systems. Tamir's "liberal nationalism" reopens Mazzini's creative approach to nationalism in the context of the Middle East. Chatterjee's "the nation and its fragments" helps us understand how a Bengali intelligentsia seared by British colonialism in India can get beyond its "imagination" being forever shaped by others (cf. Anderson 1991). These case-oriented theorists teach the inescapability of interrelations and interpenetrations of multiethnic societies in global contexts, as does Arjun Appadurai (1996: 48–65), describing multiplex "ethnoscapes" of transnational individuals. Globalization need not mean homogenization, and transnational trends in history have taken many forms, operating at various levels.[18] Indigenous groups were never as isolated or apolitical as stereotypes about them depicted. It was to outsiders' advantage to render them alien and to alienate them from each other.

No society or people, not even the remotest Siberian Nentsy reindeer breeders in the Yamal peninsula, falsely rumored to have escaped Sovietization, should be romantically described in the late twentieth century as untouched by the technology and ideas of "outsiders." But people must be given more and better choices concerning how much interpenetration they want, how the dialectic of interaction and creative negotiation evolves. Siberians can flee the "noise" of Russian civilization no farther: they have been pushed to the limits of their territories and their health. To survive, they must learn, with multiethnic awareness and through multileveled political action, better routes to self-defense, self-determination, and self-guided development.

Siberian leaders suggest that their options must include a selected return to "traditional" life-styles and values. This was also the message of the late humanist demographer Aleksander Pika, when he stressed the growing "neotraditionalism" of Native Siberians (Pika and Prokhorov 1994:6). In times of national economic crisis, the greater self-reliance of indigenous communities on natural resources provides a crucial cushion. Yet the few communities experimenting with neotraditional return to reindeer breeding are struggling with defections and are embroiled in contested land claims (cf. Fondahl 1995, 1997). Official policies should be attuned to local conditions for the development of community consensus according to cultural norms. Native consensus-style democracy (not necessarily United States majority-rule democracy) may be a means toward ensuring more liberal varieties of ethnonationalism.

Encouraging respect for land-based tradition, the founder of the Association for the Salvation of the Ugra, Tatiana Gogoleva, explained in 1991: "Land is the most important thing. We still have many people scattered, living in small encampments, traditionally. . . . Degradation comes when people must move, when they are forced to move." Her approach and that of the Association are predicated on the defensive ethnonationalism of a small and scattered minority. They did not initially aspire to a mass political movement but find themselves in the midst of a series of cruelly chaotic transitions that require engagement. All too predictably, when I spoke with Tatiana Gogoleva in 1997, we discussed how to find a good lawyer, well versed in Russian Federation and international indigenous-rights legislation.

THE KHANTY IN SIBERIAN, SOVIET, AND POST-SOVIET CONTEXTS

One of the tragedies of Siberian Native histories viewed over a "longue durée" is that each time indigenous peoples have responded to outsider encroachment with adaptation, escape, or other strategies, new challenges and greater numbers of unsettling settlers have changed yet again the uneasily but creatively evolved demographic and power balances. This is why the chapters in this book describe "-ization" processes that were never quite complete.

When coercive, Soviet policy led to considerable ethnic polarization, further stimulated by establishing administrative territories like the Khanty-Mansi and Yamal-Nenets Okrugs. Eventually, some officials, especially those who were themselves Native Siberians, or part-Native, shifted to a partially successful strategy of waiting for outlying villages to be abandoned, young people to be educated, and shamans to die. An interactive approach meant that the pace of forced change slowed, and the pace of intermarriage picked up. But gradual, organic change was disrupted yet again by the greed of energy companies, stealing "communal" land, displacing local people and ignoring the weak pleas of poorly mobilized indigenous groups. Energy development campaigns, begun in the 1960s and intensified in the 1980s, became unbearable in the divisive, regionalizing, profit-oriented 1990s.

For the few Siberians not (yet) battling the energy industry, and able to continue reindeer breeding, the 1990s have brought some relief. The Northern Khanty reindeer breeder Mikhail Taishin, descendant of the elite Taishin family, owns around four hundred reindeer and helps herd fifteen hundred of those that remain from collective herds. He comes into a small village of ten homes for supplies, bartering meat and furs, but says that more than two days in the village is "hard, and noisy." He recently traded furs for a TV, video machine, and Japanese diesel motor, but no money. For Taishin, reform means choosing to be left alone, so that no one can touch his deer or force his children into boarding schools. However, Taishin expects a government pension (Kakovkin 1998:4).

Native Siberians are quite aware of differences in their experiences of Sovietization, despite propaganda stressing homogenized "nationalities policies" and affirmative action for minorities of the North (see appendix C). Some of these differences stemmed from demography and geography, reinforced by Soviet structures, definitions, and mythology. The ultimate symbolic "aboriginals" were the Chukchi, about whom ethnic jokes were generated, for they lived the farthest to the east and were the most exoticized as the "primitive" other.[19] Russians placed the peoples of the Amur and Sakhalin, such as the Nivkh, described by Bruce Grant (1995), in a similar alienating category. In particularly dire straits were the tiny in number Yukagir of Yakutia and Chukotka, devastated by disease in pre-Soviet times and then by Soviet-style assimilation.[20]

Those larger groups that gained their own so-called "autonomous" republics within the Soviet system, the Sakha (Yakuts), Tyvans (Tuvans), and Buryat, fared relatively better and were considered by the smaller minorities as well as Russian newcomers to be in a different category of privilege and dominance (Balzer 1994; Humphrey 1983). Resentment of historical Yakutization is almost as sharp as resentment of Russification among some of my Yukagir, Even, and Evenk friends in the Sakha Republic. Indeed, Sakha (Yakut) elites are relatively numerous, and their presence in the political hierarchy, along with local and newcomer Russians, enabled a more active voice for Sakha priorities even in the Soviet period. The Sakha have been able to maintain a strong degree of ethnonational identity as well as to sustain ethnic and territorial boundaries. In the Sakha Republic (Yakutia), the Sakha, numbering around four hundred thousand, have used their relative social-political advantages to forge a new and unprecedented relationship with President Yeltsin's Moscow government, through a controversial "bilateral treaty" signed in 1995 (Balzer and Vinokurova 1996). The degree to which Moscow will honor the treaty or Sakha Republic officials will share the mineral and energy wealth of the republic with its indigenous minorities remains to be seen.[21]

Those indigenous groups included among the twenty-six Northern minorities defined as protected by Soviet law came to see themselves as in a different kind of special group. It was they, plus several others not formally acknowledged earlier, who established the Association of the Peoples of the North, Siberia, and the Far East in 1989. Their legal protections, while progressive-looking on paper, were in practice far from uniformly applied or observed at all. By 1993, twenty-nine of these groups were recognized in Russian Federation law, though they were often lumped with other minorities, such as those of the North Caucasus (Kriazhkov 1994). In 1998, the Association encompassed thirty-one different groups, but their legal *l'goty* (privileges, especially in tax and education matters) had dwindled, as a major protest letter indicated (see appendix A.) Their current caught-between-systems plight can be seen as dependency without sustenance.

In retrospect, the Soviet experience teaches that some interethnic milieus were more conducive than others to enabling ethnic group members to adopt multiple social identities more readily and sincerely. In the Khanty-Mansi Okrug, where the Khanty were long a tiny minority in their own lands, bi- or multiculturalism and multilingualism for many Khanty (not most Russians) became an expected and necessary way of life. By the late Soviet period, ethnic identity and loyalty rarely correlated with political dissent, unless Soviet officials themselves made the correlation and provoked polarized opposition. Resistance, not widespread, was more private and subversive. By the post-Soviet period, many in authority had learned from the coercion mistakes of the Stalin era. But power plays by the non-Native energy industrialists and administrators at many levels limited indigenous self-determination in new, ethnically charged ways.

Late twentieth-century analysts of the dizzying zigzags of ethnonational interaction are now in a position to engage in reciprocal thinking and practice. Our theories should help the people from whom they are derived, not just ourselves. Theorizing is an interactive process. With education have come Native elites open to new intellectual stimulation and creative sparring. Contemplative Khanty, knowledgeable about their culture, remind us that when a Khanty clan died out, it was said that the fire had gone out in their hearth. Khanty fear that while hearth fires are burning out for their own people, other fires are burning out of control and all too hotly after oil spills through the North. Khanty ethnicity may not be tenacious forever. We must not dismiss as cliché or stereotype indigenous defense of the environment. As the Khanty leader Joseph Sopochin explained in 1995, when he was my houseguest: "You know there is an aura of soulness that the very earth has. In your yard too, there is this. . . . A mosquito dies without much substance of soul to give back. Even so, it is part of the general soulness of living beings."

APPENDIX A

A 1996 Protest Statement by Social Organizations and Movements of Indigenous Peoples of the North

Discrimination against Indigenous Peoples of the North in the Russian Federation

We, the directors and leaders of various social and public interest groups representing indigenous peoples of the North in the Russian Federation, in connection with:

- the acceptance of the Russian Federation as a member of the European Council and with the adoption of the Charter of the European Council and General Agreement on Privileges and Immunities of the European Council and its protocols,
- the signing of the Convention on Defense of Human Rights and Basic Freedoms, November 4, 1950, and its protocols,
- the signing of the Ramok Convention for Defending National Minorities, February 1, 1995, and the new obligations of the Russian Federation toward the indigenous people of the North resulting from these;

Considering the diminishing number of our peoples and the extreme climatic conditions of life in the Arctic;

Stating the devastating fact that in the last century Rossiia has lost such nationalities as Ain, Vod, Kamasinets, Kerek, Omok, and Yug;

Further stating the fact that such nationalities as the Aleut, Ket, Nganasan, Negidal, Orok, Oroch, Tofalar, Enets, [and] Yukagir are on the verge of extinction;

Noting the abuse of political rights of indigenous peoples: in the 1989–91 period eighteen indigenous representatives were seated in the Supreme Soviet (Parliament) of the USSR and RSFSR, where they developed a code of law defending indigenous rights and interests; in 1995 only two deputies were elected to the State Duma, the Federal Assembly (Parliament) of Rossiia;

Further noting that the majority of the autonomous regions are no longer capable of defending the rights of indigenous peoples of the

North and in the latest elections these regions experienced intense pressure from financial and industrial groups that promote interests not in keeping with the issues facing indigenous peoples of the North;

Stating that article 69 of the new Federation of Rossiia Constitution does not "guarantee the rights of indigenous peoples" because normative acts have not been passed that provide for the representative needs of our peoples [namely]: "Basic Election Right Guarantees for Citizens of the Federation of Rossiia," "Election of Deputies to the State Duma of the Federal Assembly of the Federation of Rossiia," and "Formation of the Council of the Federation of the Federal Assembly of the Federation of Rossiia;"

Noting that the resolution "Critical Economic and Cultural Conditions of Indigenous Peoples of the North, Siberia, and Far East," passed by the State Duma at its first meeting, was not followed up with appropriate action by the president or the government of Rossiia, while at the same time the government remains indifferent to repeated appeals of the Association of Indigenous Peoples of the North on issues of the survival of these ethnic groups;

Pointing out that our Native lands are being annexed and barbarically destroyed by rapacious petroleum and natural gas, coal, gold, and nonferrous mining interests, without any form of just compensation directly to organizations and indigenous enterprises of the North, and this phenomenon deprives us of our lands and rights to part of the resource wealth, [and thus] deprives us of our basic right—a right to life;

Underscoring that the Federal Law "Fundamentals for the Legal Status of Indigenous Peoples of Rossiia" was passed twice in 1995 by the State Duma: the first time on July 21, and then, with the president's edicts, on November 17th, and both times was tabled by the president of Rossiia, the guarantor of the Constitution, [and] that the reform movement of President B. N. El'tsin that was optimistically supported by indigenous peoples of the North has not met these peoples' expectations;

Recognizing that the government of Rossiia lacks any kind of policy for the twenty-nine endangered indigenous groups of the North, numbering two hundred thousand people, for whom the transition to a market economy is characterized by a total breakdown of traditional economic activities and way of life, an uncontrolled growth of unemployment and impoverishment, life-threatening levels of crime and alcoholism that undermine traditional outlooks on life, sharp decline in the health of our peoples, and death rates that are one-and-a-half times the average in the country;

Expressing the will of the most socially unprotected and needy ethnic groups within Rossiia, who have become outcasts in their own land, based upon the mentioned facts concerning their political and economic situation, we are making a statement on

DISCRIMINATION AGAINST INDIGENOUS PEOPLE
OF THE NORTH IN THE RUSSIAN FEDERATION

We address the president and government of Rossiia as well as international organizations and individuals representing the interests of indigenous peoples with our appeal. From the president and the government of Rossiia, based on the fundamental right of indigenous peoples to freedom, housing, food, and education, we demand the start of a negotiation process between the government of the Federation of Rossiia and indigenous peoples of the North, as represented by its social organizations and movements, in order to resolve fundamental issues essential to the survival and development of our peoples:

1. Procedures for direct compensation to organizations and indigenous enterprises for the damage inflicted to their lands and economic activities as a result of annexation and industrial development.
2. Direct licensing procedures that provide for the study of ways to develop coal/mineral deposits, production quotas, and land tenure that guarantee traditional resource use and economic activities.
3. Creation of an economic development corporation for indigenous peoples of the North.
4. Negotiation procedures between the government of Rossiia and representatives of indigenous social organizations.
5. Creation, within the office of the president of the Federation of Rossiia, of a fully empowered agency to advance the rights of indigenous peoples of the North.
6. Creation of a government fund to support indigenous peoples of the North.
7. Organization of a system of local, ethnic, self-management bodies for peoples of the North.
8. Guaranteed minimum representation for peoples of the North in federal and regional representative bodies and executive branches.
9. Creation of a Department of the Arctic and appointment of a government ambassador to coordinate, at the international level, issues concerning the development of regions and peoples.
10. [Ratification of the] Federal Law "Fundamentals for the Legal Sta-

tus of Indigenous Peoples of Rossiia" and "Status for Peoples of the North."

11. Events marking in Rossiia the International Decade of Indigenous Peoples of the World 1995–2005.

While it is still not too late, while hope is still alive among our people, we CALL UPON the president of the Federation of Rossiia, chairman of the government, leaders of the Council of Federation and the State Duma to carefully examine the demands of our peoples and to not let them disappear from the face of the earth. We appeal to political parties and movements, to the Russian public, to all people of good will, to whom the life and rights of every nationality is dear to SUPPORT the aims of minority peoples of the North of Rossiia for self-preservation. In this extremely difficult time for indigenous peoples of the North, we appeal to the international community and CALL UPON the Council of Europe, the UN General Assembly, the UN Commission on Human Rights, the governments and parliaments of the world, government and nongovernment organizations and institutions, all honest citizens that have contact with the higher organs of power TO SUPPORT OUR CALL in the name of survival and development of the indigenous peoples of the Arctic and preservation of their lands.

This declaration is being sent to:

B. N. El'tsin—President of the Russian Federation
V. S. Chernomyrdin—Chairperson of the Russian Government
E. S. Stroev—Chairperson of the Federation Council of the Russian Federation
G. N. Seleznov—Chairperson of the State Duma

March 4, 1996
Moscow

The current statement in the name of the indigenous peoples of the North was signed by:

A. V. Evai', *President*
Association of Indigenous Peoples of the North
Yamalo-Nenets Region

A. V. Krivoshapkin, *President*
Association of Indigenous Peoples of the North
Republic of Sakha (Yakutia)

N. V. Novik, *President*
Association of Ket

P. S. Stepanov, *President*
Association of Indigenous Peoples of the Republic of Buryatia

G. N. Psyagin, *President*
Association of Indigenous Peoples of the North, Sakhalin Island

P. P. Kosygin, *President*
Kamchatka Association of Kamchadal

V. I. Gayul'skii, *President*
Fund for the Survival and Economic and Cultural Development of Indigenous Peoples of the North
Deputy, State Duma

Yu. A. Samar, *President*
Fund for the Indigenous Peoples of the North

T. S. Gogoleva, *President*
Association of Indigenous Peoples of the North
Khanty-Mansi Autonomous District

E. A. Gaer, *General Secretary*
International League of Indigenous Peoples and Ethnic Groups

E. D. Aipin, *President*
Association of Indigenous Peoples of the North, Siberia, and Far East

A. N. Nemtushkin, *Chairperson*
Coordinating Committee
Association of Indigenous Peoples of the North
Krasnoyarskii Krai

Selection of Films about Siberia

Alekseev, Eduard, and Elena Novik; cameraman, Andres Slapinsh
1990 [orig. version, 1982] *Time of Dreams*. Smithsonian Institution film archive. On shamans of the Far East.

Badger, Mark, and Eva Schmidt
1991 Numto family consecration and reindeer sacrifice. University of Alaska, Fairbanks, film archive.

Badger, Mark, and Asen Balikci
1992 *Siberia through Siberians' Eyes*. University of Alaska, Fairbanks, film archive. Sampler from 1991 Kazym film seminar.

Balalaeva, Olga, and Andrew Wiget
1997 *Khanty: People of the Taiga*. New Mexico State University, Heritage Center archive. On Yugan Khanty and ecology.

Balikci, Asen
1990 *Sireniki*. University of Montreal film archive. On the Sovietization of Chukotka.

Gumuev, I. N., and A. M. Sagalaev; cameraman, Andres Slapinsh
1994 *Bogi i bogatiry Mansi* (Mansi gods and bogatyrs). Novosibirsk Institute of Archeology and Ethnography film archive.

Hoppál, Mihály
1994 *Shamans Past and Present*. Budapest Institute of Ethnography film archive.

Kerezsi, Ágnes
1992 *Eastern Khanty Shamanism*. Budapest Institute of Ethnography film archive. See also Kerezsi 1993.

Kirosawa, Akira (with Nikita Mikhalkov)
1974 *Derzu Uzala*. Story of a Siberian hunter–Russian friendship. (Feature).

Konchalovsky, Andrei
1979 *Siberiade*. Epic of Siberian village life. (Feature).

Kostin, V. Iu.
1931 *Khandy-Iokh* (Khanty People). Tobol'sk film archive. Documentary.

Lukina, Nadezhda V.; cameraman, Arkady Mikhailev
1992, 1993 *Rechnye Liudi Iagun-Iakh* (River People of Yugan);

Zima Rechnykh Liudei (Winter of the River People). Tomsk University film archive.

Pentikäinen, Juha
1991 *Reindeer Sacrifice of a Khanty Shaman*. State Audio-Visual Center of Finland.

Soosaar, Mark
1997 *Father, Son and Holy Torum*. American Museum of Natural History, Margaret Mead Film Festival Archive. On changes in Ob-Ugrian values.

Vitebsky, P., G. Johnston, L. Dodd
1991 *Siberia—After the Shaman*. Channel 4, England, "Nomads" series.

Yernazarova, Raisa; cameraman, G. Raspevin
1991 *Kolybel'* (The cradle). Novosibirsk State TV-Radio.

Yernazarova, Raisa; cameraman, Sergei Tchavchavadze
1991 *Poslednyi Shaman* (The last shaman). Novosibirsk State TV-Radio.

APPENDIX C

Indigenous Peoples of the North: Historical and Current Names

Official Soviet Twenty-Six Peoples of the North ("Small," "Protected") (listed in order of size in 1989 census, with alternative names):

Nentsy (Samoyed, Yurak)	34,665
Evenki (Orochon, Tungus)	30,163
Khanty (Ostiak, Ugra)	22,521
Eveny (Lamut, Tungus)	17,199
Chukchi (Luoravetlan, Oravedlan)	15,184
Nanaitsy (Nanei, Goldy)	12,023
Koriaki (Nymylan, Chavchuven)	9,242
Mansi (Vogul, Ugra)	8,474
Dolgany (Sakha)	6,945
Nivkhi (Gilyak)	4,673
Sel'kupy (Ostiak-Samoyed)	3,612
Ul'chi (Nanei, Mangun)	3,233
Itel'meny (Kamchadal)	2,481
Udegeitsy (Udekhe, Ude, Taz)	2,011
Saami (Lapp, Lopari)	1,890
Eskimosy (Yuit, Yupigit)	1,719
Chuvantsy (Chukchi)	1,511
Nganasany (Tavgi, Nia, Samoyed)	1,278
Yukagiry (Odul, Vadul, Omuk)	1,142
Kety (Yenesei Ostiak)	1,113
Orochi (Orochili, Nani)	915
Tofalary (Tofa, Tufa, Karagas, Altai Turk, Oirat)	731
Aleuty (Unangan)	702
Negidalsty (El'kan Beienin)	622
Entsy (Eneche, Mady, Yenisei Samoyed)	209
Oroky (Ul'ta, Ul'cha)	190

Note: Some early Committee of the North lists included Aliutor and Kerek, recorded in later censuses under Koriak. Current minority groups differentiating themselves include Aliutor, Chavchuven (Koriak), Chelkan (Lebedin, Altaitsy), Chulym (Khakas), Kerek, Kumandin (Altaitsy), Nymylan (Koriak), Shor (Altaitsy), Soyot (Karagas), Taz (Udegei), Telingit (Telengut, Altaitsy), Teleut (Altaitsy), and Tubalar (Chelkan, Kumandin, Altaitsy). Larger groups with territorial recognition are Komi (Zyrians), Sakha (Yakuts), Buryat, Tyvan (Tuvans), and Khakas.

Notes

Introduction
From Romanticism to Realism

1. I am grateful to the Nenets poet Yuri Vella, for giving me, summer 1997, information on the organized protests, in which he and his Khanty wife have been active, along with members of the Association for the Salvation of the Ugra. I have also gained insight from the Nivkh ethnographer-politician Evdokiia Gayer, a Supreme Soviet deputy who participated in the Yamal protest; from Khanty attending the 1995 Moscow seminar "Problems of the Peoples of the North"; and from Vladimir Kogonchin and Joseph Sopochin when they were my houseguests (spring 1995).

2. A transcript of the 1990 congress was given to me by Aleksei Tomtosov, to whom I am very grateful. See also Tomtosov 1990. A 1996 protest letter to President Yeltsin's government was signed by leaders of each of the northern Native activist groups that have organized (and split from each other) since 1989 (appendix A).

3. A few other Westerners have been privileged to do fieldwork in Siberia, including what the Russians call the Far East. The French anthropologist Roberte Hamayon (1990) of l'École Pratique des Haute Études en Science Sociale and the British social anthropologist Caroline Humphrey (1983) of Cambridge University have studied the Buryat. Francis Cooley (1983) of the Scott Polar Research Center at Cambridge was able to spend a month in Yakutsk in the early 1980s studying education and returned in 1990. Piers Vitebsky (1996) of the Scott Polar Research Center began work with Even, Evenk, and Yakut (Sakha) in 1987 and has returned frequently. His student David Anderson (1996) has worked with the Evenk, as has Alexia Bloch (1998) and Gail Fondahl (1995, 1997). See also Bruce Grant on the Sakhalin Nivkh (1995), Anna Kerttula (1996), and Debra Schindler (1991) on Chukotka and indigenous politics. Patty Gray of University of Wisconsin has also worked in Chukotka, while Eileen Espiritu (1997) has studied ecology and politics in Canada and Siberia. Columbia University anthropologist David Koester (1997), Petra Rethmann (1997), and University of Virginia graduate student Alexander King have worked in Kamchatka. The Russian-American team Olga Balalaeva and Andrew Wiget (1997) are working in Western Siberia with Eastern Khanty, and the legal rights expert Gail Osherenko (1993, 1995) has published on Western Siberia. Especially respected is the work of Hungarian anthropologist Eva Schmidt (e.g., 1989), who has lived several years in West Siberia and founded a Khanty archive.

4. For Native American comparisons, see especially P. Deloria 1998; Kan 1998; Walker 1997; Nagel 1997; Mancall 1995; Kroeber 1994; Limerick 1987; Swann and Krupat 1987; Martin 1987; V. Deloria and Lytle 1984; Berkhofer 1978; V. Deloria 1969.

5. Compare Arutiunov 1978, 1989, 1997; Tishkov 1992, 1997; Vakhtin 1993; Pika and Prokhorov 1994; Drobizheva 1994, 1996; Golovnev 1993, 1995. The Siberian ethnographies of two émigré anthropologists, Igor Krupnik (1993) and Boris Chichlo (1981, 1987, 1990, 1994), are especially relevant.

6. Most of my visits, from 1991 to 1995 and in 1997, have been to the Sakha Republic, with additional travel for comparative perspectives on Siberian minorities. Sakha Republic ethnic relations are the subject of several articles (e.g., Balzer and Vinokurova 1996) and a planned book. Sakha reactions to my work on the Khanty have also afforded insights.

7. Participants included Tania's sister Olga Kravchenko, one of the librarians with whom I had a mutually wary relationship in 1976. Friendly without worry, she had become a schoolteacher in the vanguard of a program to introduce "cultural anthropology for national schools" into Khanty elementary classes.

8. Zyrians (Komi) live mainly in the Komi Republic of Northern Russia (Rossiia). Zyrians of Kazym prefer "Zyrian" to "Komi," saying "Komi" implies greater Russification. The Komi numbered 345,000 in the 1989 census and are known for their relative demographic dominance, compared to other northern minorities. They have an historical rivalry with the Khanty, who stress "Zyrian" reputation as traders, middlemen, and leaders.

9. Asen Balikci and Mark Badger were the organizers of the Kazym seminar. The site was chosen partially because of Association for the Salvation of the Ugra preferences and partially because Asen had read my doctoral dissertation. See Balikci and Badger 1992 for a discussion of seminar goals.

10. Limits on my knowledge of Khanty spirituality are considerable, including certain sacred ancestral names, some aspects of shamanic seances, and specifics concerning animal sacrifices (off bounds for women). In addition, as elsewhere, Khanty consider that bragging about spiritual prowess is a sure way to lose it.

11. I left Kazym several days earlier, but was told that reactions to the coup were subdued, given fear that it might reverse glasnost, make foreigners unwelcome, and roll back perceived advances in community ability to voice local concerns. The Zyrian president was particularly conflicted, shunning seminar participants during the coup but friendly in its aftermath.

12. Philip Lineton (1978), an advisee of Caroline Humphrey, visited a village in the Khanty-Mansi Okrug in the summers of 1975 and 1978. In Humphrey's description of Lineton's experience (1983:16–17), he found most villagers "almost permanently drunk" and demoralized. This was not my experience in 1976, although I was in the same general area, under the same Leningrad University auspices. The difference may lie in timing or in my friendships with Khanty women and with Khanty men and women who were involved with traditional religious life. My access to Khanty homes was easy, and I was far from the most "exotic" person in our group, for it included an African exchange student who spoke little Russian.

13. I also observed other indications of belief in woman-as-dangerous, for example, the covering of women's faces with scarves before elder male in-laws (cf. Balzer 1983).

14. I spent most of each day and evening with eleven Tegy Khanty consultants of various ages and both genders and with twelve in Kazym.

15. Due to this complex situation, I have mostly avoided using personal names from my 1976 fieldwork, although I am deeply grateful for warmhearted Khanty cooperation. I mostly spoke Russian with the Khanty, although I learned key concepts and everyday phrases in the Khanty language. Since I was not given permission to work with the Khanty far enough in advance, I occasionally had to rely on two Khanty women (who were released from library jobs) to help with translations or on children of elderly consultants when their parents preferred to speak in the Khanty language.

16. Goskomsevera, absorbed in 1998 by the Ministry of Regional Affairs, sponsored several conferences discussed in this book, due to the interest of then associate minister Anatoly Volgin, who has become an advisor to Duma chairman Gennady Seleznov. Berezovo is an old Russian fort and trading town on the Malaia Ob, with dirt roads and low wooden houses gaily painted and carved in Russian folk tradition.

17. See also West Siberian ethnographies by Lukina (1985), Gumuev and Sangalaev (1986), Sokolova (1990), Kulemzin and Lukina (1992), and Golovnev (1993, 1995). Classic ethnographies of Siberia, such as Shirokogoroff 1935, or those from the turn-of-the-century Jesup North Pacific Expedition are used here, where appropriate, for comparison. For an annotated bibliography, see Balzer 1982.

18. Said by Arjun Appadurai at a crowded 1996 American Anthropological Association session honoring the work of Partha Chatterjee (1993). See Appadurai 1996.

19. On complexities of the term "Native" and for samples of "Native anthropology" in Russia, see Balzer 1995. See also Narayan 1993 and Limon 1991. Perspectives of Ob-Ugrian writers are integrated in this study (Aipin 1989, 1990, 1991; Kravchenko 1996; Moldanova 1990, 1993; Shestalov 1973, 1985, 1985a).

20. These standards are similar to those of the Annales school of French historical analysis, which productively differentiates among "events," "trends," and "structural changes" (Braudel 1973). A trend in one time period may become structural change in another, however. Compare Ortner 1984:158; 1995; Geertz 1980:5; Vansina 1978:10; Van Stone 1979; and Paine 1977.

21. Analysis becomes a "multilogue," an effort to see history through multiple points of view. Compare Romanucci-Ross and De Vos 1995; Fox 1991, 1995; Bakhtin 1975; Schutz 1970; Jarvie 1983.

22. Compare Barth 1969; Gellner 1983; Smith 1986; Suny 1992; Eley and Suny 1996.

23. The theories of Despres (1975), concerning ethnicity as stimulated in situations of resource competition, and of Cohen (1974), defining ethnicity through political factionalism, became especially relevant to the Khanty-Russian interethnic situation in the 1990s.

24. See, for example, Bromlei 1973, 1984, 1987; Arutiunov 1978, 1989; Guboglo 1984; Drobizheva 1979, 1981; Arutiunian and Bromlei 1986. See also my editor's introductions to Soviet ethnosociology in *Soviet Anthropology and Archeology* and later, contrasting articles in my successor journal, *Anthropology and Archeology of Eurasia* (e.g., Zhukovskaia 1993; Chvyr' 1995–96). Compare Drobizheva 1994, 1996; Tishkov 1994, 1994–95, 1997.

25. Goodenough (1971) was among the earliest American anthropologists con-

cerned with multicultural individuals. See also Handler (1988:183–96), who stresses internal debates on the "politics of culture" and shifting levels of identity and authenticity. R. Cohen (1978:395–98) mentions the varied "saliency" of ethnicity, and Fishman (1977:32–34) analyzes the "mutability of saliency." Arutiunov (1978:3–14; 1989) discussed similar contextual issues, when this was rare in the Soviet Union. Too often the situational nature of identity is ignored in tirades against the dangers of nationalism (e.g., Hobsbawm 1990; Gellner 1983:43–49).

26. See especially Tambiah 1986, 1989 and Kapferer 1988. Compare Eriksen 1993; Levin 1993; Bailey 1995; and the monograph of former Russian Federation nationalities minister Tishkov (1997).

27. On acculturation, see Hallowell 1967:310–44; Padilla 1980; Castille and Kushner 1981. For historical perspective, see Redfield, Linton and Herskovits 1938. For refinement and reevaluation, see Benson 1981; Merrill 1988; Ridington 1988; Fienup-Riordan 1990, 1994; E. Turner 1996.

28. Until 1997, passports had a line for "nationality." Abolishing the line has led to howls of pain from some non-Russians, who want special recognition. In debate are compromises that may provide a separate page for citizens of the "ethnic-based" republics.

29. Marxism was, however, turned on its head with Gorbachev's stress on the priority of mental restructuring (H. Balzer 1991). See Slezkine 1993 for an excellent historical summary of shifting Russian approaches to indigenous Siberians. Bartels and Bartels 1996 and Kuoljok 1985 are cursory and not based on extended fieldwork in Siberia (Balzer 1997).

30. In Marx's original passage, religion assuaged suffering by providing a superficial high that masked the underlying depravity in the social system. Religious addicts were not to be persecuted but pitied and saved. They were not expected to abandon their "false consciousness" until basic structures of the socioeconomic system were demystified and detoxified (Marx 1963:41; Firth 1981:582–60l; McClellan 1973:88–89). Compare Tokarev 1979–80.

31. Despite their "patri" orientation, the Khanty historically have had pragmatic, flexible approaches to social grouping, and non-unilineal (cognatic) descent can be significant in birth rituals. In most areas, patrilineages are organized loosely into phratries, whose elders regulate important property and ritual transactions. Two major phratries, Por and Mos, earlier constituted the basis for identifying proper marriage partners; in the 1990s, they sometimes define marriageability.

32. Gasprom, Lukoil, and Rosinvestneft control most investment and planning, along with local Russian subsidiaries, such as Surgutneftegaz and Kogalymneftegaz. A few foreign firms have experimented in West Siberia, including Occidental Petroleum, Amoco, Exxon, Mobil, Bechtel, CanBaikal, and a Texas oil venture called "White Nights."

Chapter One
Colonization: Forming Groups in Interaction

1. The context was the workshop he was hosting for Native Siberians and Native Americans. He tactfully added, "Even generalizations about our culture are better than nothing. I'm proud of our culture."

2. Chernetsov and Moszynska (1974) see an Early Khanty culture developing even before the ninth century. See also Shimkin 1965 and Sokolova 1971a. Hungarian scholar Peter Vereš (1975:52) explains that exogamy lessened enmity between aboriginals and newcomer Ugrians, leading to the ethnonym "Khanty" and preservation of older phratry terms.

3. I owe this comparison to anthropologist Sergei Arutiunov (personal communication, July 1996). For oral histories, see Patkanov 1891, 1891a, 1892; Harva 1964. Acknowledging debates, M. F. Kosarev (1984:155) concludes, "Archeological materials, folklore, and written historical sources depict the existence of quite a developed social-political organism—almost at the level of a state formation . . . [certainly] to the level of "war democracy."

4. See Shishonko 1884:713 on sacrificed captives. I first read Khanty history without benefit of relatively recent archeological finds and publications, and I tended to downplay the folklore evidence of human sacrifices and elaborate military-political organization. Rereadings of multiple sources have convinced me that Khanty groups of the tenth to seventeenth centuries had a far more complex political organization, at least in river-system communities if not at the pan-tribal level, than they came to have in the eighteenth to twentieth centuries. See also Pallas 1788:302–5.

5. Agrafina Sopochina (personal communication, June 1998). A full version, transmitted through bear festival songs, has been collected by Tatiana and Timofei Moldanov.

6. For example, *Permskaia Letopis* in Shishonko 1884. By 1998, the archeologist Konstantin Karacharov unearthed, at a middle Ob site near Surgut, a sensational Russian Orthodox cross dated at the beginning of the eleventh century, earlier than previously known Slavic contacts.

7. Compare Prokof'yeva et al. 1964:514; Zenkovsky (translated chronicle text) 1974:82; Hadju 1963:45. Historian Janet Martin (1986) has analyzed archival material on the Novgorodian-Ugrian fur trade of this period.

8. For examples, see Shatilov 1931:23 and Patkanov 1891, 1891a, 1892. Tensions lasted into the period of Russian hegemony. I use the linguistic term Samodeic here, since it has superseded the more derogatory Samoyedic. In Russian "Samoyed" originally meant "self-eater," before it became a general ethnolinguistic term for the group encompassing Nentsy, Entsy, Nganasan, and Sel'kup (cf. Comrie 1981; Golovnev 1995).

9. Compare Hadju 1963:44–46; Boarshinova and Shunkov 1968:25.

10. See Eliasov and Tarnevskii 1969 and Aleksandrov 1897. While sources differ, Ermak was probably a Don Cossack.

11. Tsarist orders authorized the establishment of strongholds along the Irtysh and Ob, to pacify any unruly "Ostiak" (Khanty), "Vogul" (Mansi), or Tatars (Miller 1787:69).

12. Boarshinova and Shunkov 1968:30, 34, from Stroganov family records. Compare Prokof'yeva et al. 1964:514. Cossacks, led by Commander Trahaniutov, pushed deep into Ugrian territory, founding a town at the Khanty fortress Sugut-Vash, or Berezovo.

13. On hostages, see Miller 1787:158–63; 260–63. One of my most significant discoveries, after months of archival work, concerned the child hostages (TsGIA, church records, fond 796, opis 11, delo 504, list 1ob.).

14. Miller (1787:158–63, 260–63) found documents among the Khanty that record these complaints. See also Businsky 1899; Shatilov 1931:18; and Prokof'yeva et al. 1964:515.

15. Compare Miller 1787:127; Prokof'yeva et al. 1964:515; Shatilov 1931: 19–22.

16. This definition of colonialism avoids the cliché that it is an exploitive system of extracting raw materials for processing elsewhere, though that definition too fits much of Siberian history. A. Irving Hallowell (1971:310–33) provided a North American (Ojibwa) perspective, describing a "cultural gradient" of change on the Berens River. Comparing the Ojibwa to other indigenous peoples led Hallowell to suggest numerous Native responses to colonization. Possibilities ranged from rejection of traditional modes of life to limited adaptation to withdrawal into aboriginal and conservative cultural forms. European dominance was not always the norm. Ethel Lindgren (1938:605–21) described Cossack and Tungus (Evenk) "trade friendships" in Manchuria. More penetrating recent studies by Taussig (1987) on South America and Stoler (1996) on Southeast Asia uncover the colonial contexts of sometimes mutually terrifying ethnic interactions that stimulated shifting definitions of "self," "other," and "métis."

17. TsGIA fond 1264, opis 1, delo 166, list 145–48ob. Compare Dmitriev-Mamonov 1884:256.

18. My perspective derives from Dmitriev-Mamonov 1884; Iadrintsev 1891; Dunin-Gorkavich 1904–11; and Minenko 1975; as well as the Siberian administration archive TsGIA fond 1264, opis 1, delo 265, and Kolesnikov's (1982) compilation of the Tobolsk region record book.

19. No Khanty lived permanently or officially within Surgut city limits. Scattered in the Surgut township were about a dozen Khanty yurt settlements and villages, plus several additional Russian villages (Iadrintsev 1891:283–86).

20. Dmitriev-Mamonov 1884:389. In the Tobolsk region in 1880, Khanty constituted only 1.18 percent of the total population, Mansi 2.05 percent, and Tatars 10.23 percent. In the Tomsk region that year, only 2.32 percent were Khanty, 3.96 percent Tatars, and 1.60 percent Nentsy (Iadrintsev 1891:268, table 2).

21. My interpretation of norms and exceptions is from TsGIA fond 1264, opis 1, delo 265.

22. On the economics of fishing, and cedar nuts, see Poliakov 1877:80–83; Iakobii 1893:46–48, 51; Patkanov 1911:177; Shvetsov 1888.

23. Compare Anonymous (Grigorovskii ?) 1859:11; Shvetsov 1888:59–61, 80–82; Iadrinstev 1891:86–87.

24. See also Soviet scholar Minenko 1975:59, 71 and prerevolutionary observers Iadrintsev 1891:76 and Patkanov 1911:177.

25. The work of Michael Taussig (1987) on the colonization of Latin America provides comparative perspective. Status gradations of creolization (or mestization) in countries conquered by the Spanish resemble similar creole patterns in Siberia. See also Sergei Arutiunov (1997) on Spanish/Russian empire correlations.

26. The degree to which this was "tolerance" and not sexual exploitation is open to question. See also Aleksandrov 1964:119–20; and Kolesnikov 1972:6, 14–18. Compare Ann Stoler (1996) on Southeast Asia.

27. This was especially true in the Kalmyk and Kyrgyz areas, according to Iadrintsev (1891:169), but also occurred in Khanty territory, according to Abramov (1857:348).

28. On the laws, see TsGIA fond 1264, opis 1, delo 265, list 77. For perspective, see Iadrinstev 1891:170.

29. The Soviet scholar Minenko (1975:117) uncovered Tobolsk archives (GATOT fond 156, delo 114, list 6) describing an amorous Surgut priest keeping two Khanty girls, one of whom had borne him two children.

30. Grigorovskii 1879:8, 15, 27; Engelhard 1899:124–27. Opportunities for Khanty men to marry Russian women improved after 1826, when it became legal for exiled Russian women to marry Native Siberians, "although without the right to return with their husbands to Russia" (Pamiatnaia Kniga 1881:99). This reform, like many others of its period, legalized an existing practice (cf. Dmitriev-Mamonov 1884:219–24).

31. The Polish exile Felinska (1853(1):193), who lived with a Cossack trading family in Berezovo, wrote of failed and sabotaged agricultural experiments.

32. Iadrinstev 1893:283–85, citing the 1875 census. Khanty were numbered at 9,618 (5,047 men and 4,571 women), Russians at 1349 (680 men and 661 women). In the town of Berezovo itself, an additional 1,888 Russians (982 men and 906 women) lived in 180 houses. Similarly, in 1875 in the Obdorsk region (part of the Berezovo administrative area), Natives, including Khanty and Nentsy, were numbered at 13,458, while Russians totaled only 167 (Bartenev 1896:9). The town of Obdorsk numbered only 378 Russians, 95 Khanty, 100 Nentsy, and 290 Komi by 1891 (Bartenev 1896:9).

33. Winter settlements constituted the longest period of Khanty residence in one place. Felinska (1853(1):170) claimed that the Khanty and Nentsy "baffle all attempts at census registration."

34. See Iadrinstev 1891:283 for administrative distinctions. The *volost'* was the smallest tsarist subdivision, while an *upravlenie* was a larger local category.

35. Patkanov 1911:195, 177. At one center of Russian fishing, on the Northern Ob near the Nadym river, up to eighty Russian and Zyrian fishers, from as far south as Tobolsk, competed for Native riverbank rentals and lucrative commercial fish hauls of salmon, sturgeon, and pike (Iakobii 1893:46).

36. My Khanty consultants remembered prerevolutionary lists, confirmed by Felinska 1853(l):198, (2):166; Bartenev 1896:29; and Murashko and Krenke 1996: 37–66. While most items came from traders with links to Tobolsk, some iron goods were forged in Berezovo. Khanty commissioned Berezovo Russians to fashion their iron or metal-embellished "idols" (*sheitan*) to specification (Skalozubov 1907:7). Before Russian arrival, Khanty smiths made their own sheitan.

37. Khanty and Nentsy techniques were copied by Zyrian and Russian women of Obdorsk (Bartenev 1896:29). Value was measured in rubles, red fox, sable, squirrel, and a northern fish, *muksun* (Voronov 1900:30). See also Abramov 1857:406; Minenko 1975:163.

38. For instance, forty pounds of flour, costing a mere fifty kopecks in Tobolsk in the mid-nineteenth century, could be sold to a Khanty family for one white fox skin worth three silver rubles (Felinska 1853(1): 196–97).

39. This is confirmed in numerous sources (e.g., Minenko 1975:124, 130, from GATOT 1884 fond 156, delo 417, list 2–3; and Bartenev 1896:20).

40. Shvetsov 1888; Grigorovskii 1884. Obdorsk and Berezovo traders on journeys south felt no fear of robbery as they stayed in or passed by Northern Khanty settlements. When they reached the Irtysh area, where Khanty had begun to "lose their marvelous honesty," they were less secure (Voronov 1900:40).

41. Iakobii 1893:48; Poliakov 1877:78. Other trade fairs were held in September or July, crucial transitional times in the seasonal transhumant economy, so that they were less well attended by Natives (Potanin 187?:199).

42. Pamiatnaia Kniga 1881:100. See also Felinska 1853(2):131; Potanin 187?; TsGIA fond 1264, opis 1, delo 266.

43. Bartenev 1896:21, 31–33. Although Kornilov (1828:77), a sympathetic commissioner, had encouraged early Native use of schools and hospitals, many of these programs failed. On the issue of Native alcoholism, the National Institute of Health's "Collaborative Study on the Genetics of Alcoholism (COGA)" has isolated genes said to be associated with susceptibility to alcoholism. A gene for an enzyme that helps to break down alcohol may be lacking in Asians and Native Americans. Scientists associated with this work include Theodore Reich at Washington University and Cindy Ehlers at Scripps Research Institute. However, definitions of alcoholism are disputed (e.g., World Health Organization, American Psychiatric Association), making categorical assertions of genetic susceptibility problematic (Okie 1998; Manson 1982).

44. Bartenev 1896:30. The first documented sale of reindeer occurred in the 1780s, when a Cossack *ataman* of Berezovo bought 180 (Minenko 1975:78, citing Tobolsk archives).

45. TsGIA fond 1264, opis 1, delo 2, list 8. The court records of 1881–1901, titled "Complaints, Disputes, and Crimes of Natives," were edited by Zibarev (1970). Other sources on Siberian customary law include Samokvasov 1876; Dmitriev-Mamonov 1884; and Voronov 1900; but they provide data on ideals without substantial description of practices. Zibarev (1970:21) interprets typically harsh court sentences as examples of Native powerlessness, but Khanty elders had a say in sentencing. Native elders sat in judgment over local Russians as well as local Khanty and Nentsy.

46. Zibarev 1970. In 1893 a complex case came before two Khanty elders, Taishin and Tobolchin. It was brought by a "peasant" of Obdorsk, Mesheriakov, and a Khanty man named Tel, against a Khanty employee of Mesheriakov named Levrin. It was representative in that it involved drunkenness, repeat offenses, and the jurisdiction of Khanty princely elders. The elders sentenced the Khanty thief Levrin to a lashing and awarded full compensation to his victims.

47. While Native American reservation laws are quite diverse, some of the configurations of judicial power are similar to those described here. On Siberian criminal law, see *Polozhenii ob Inorodtsakh*, formulated in the 1820s; TsGIA fond 1264; and Zibarev 1970:156. The lack of formal princely distinctions is noted by Russian observers Kornilov (1828:78), Felinska (1853(2):126–29), Abramov (1857a:217–19), and Popov (1890:457–60). Patkanov's (1891, 1892) focus was on earlier periods, when war leaders may have been princes.

On the debate in the Soviet period, see Bakhrushin 1935; Minenko 1975; and Sokolova 1983:147.

48. Popov (1890:458), a local Russian resident, knew both the Taishins and Artanzeevs. A successful reindeer-breeding Taishin descendant is mentioned in my conclusion.

49. Felinska 1853(2):126. Taishin had demanded punishment of a Russian doctor for lack of respect, but the proceedings resulted in the "prince" himself being horsewhipped. They were conducted in Russian, with a bribed Native interpreter misrepresenting the case. Taishin's lack of Russification was clinched by his approach to Christianity. Taishin, though nominally Russian Orthodox, never gave up "the idol worship of his ancestors" (Popov 1890:457–58).

50. In official church intermarriages, as opposed to sexual liaisons, the children were usually brought up as Russians. Three families were formed by the union of very poor Russian women with wealthy Khanty men. In local eyes, these men "had managed to rise above their usual situation, get rich, learn some craft, and in general become civilized" (Bartenev 1896:24–25).

51. See chapter 7; Gondatti 1887:83; and Karjalainen 1927:218.

52. See Balzer 1994a and Sverkunova 1996. Siberiak is today, and was more so in the past, a self-ascription for those Russian peasants and Cossacks who were permanent residents of Siberia and who syncretized Native lifestyles with traditional North Russian-Ukrainian culture. In Babkin and Levashov's dictionary of Soviet inhabitants (1975:467), "Siberiak" is a current and historical self-ascription for Siberian-Russians. See also Minenko 1975:117–18.

53. Given seminomadism and Russian reliance on Khanty elders for population reports, individuals and even families were able to escape record keepers (Dmitriev-Mamonov 1887:2–3). Evasion was counteracted somewhat by the unfair administrative habit of keeping Khanty males on tax records after their deaths.

54. Compare Felinska 1853(2):197; Grigorovskii 1884:1–2; Dmitriev-Mamonov 1884:202–3, 210, 257. Few administrators were as thorough as Abramov (1857) in reporting local populations. Official census figures for 1875 are less reliable than later, local figures of ethnographers (e.g., Shukhov 1916:29).

55. One source (Anonymous [Grigorovskii?] 1859:6) mentioned that Khanty families were "sometimes more than one hundred versts apart" on the Vasyugan. Grigorovskii (1884:57) claimed it was necessary to go two thousand versts to meet 726 people in the Vasyugan region.

56. By the 1850s they were numbered together as 853 (Abramov 1875). In 1914, Shukhov (1916:29) counted 1132 (588 men and 546 women) in six Khanty villages. Khanty population density peaked during the fall-winter season at about 4.8 persons per square verst, or 3.2 per square mile. In open tundra, density was even lower.

57. Compare Abramov 1857:331; Sokolova 1975:200–201; Murashko and Krenke 1996:37–66. However, a few backwoods settlements were Cossack outposts with government support. Campaigns for colonization from 1846 to 1879 encouraged 43,753 people to settle in the whole Northwest Siberia Tobolsk Gubernaia jurisdiction (Dmitriev-Mamonov and Golodnikov 1884:256–57). Many of these colonists eventually moved further east.

58. The Khanty calendar began with spring, well before ice and snow gave way to warm weather. In the Kazym area, Khanty families moved from their winter settlements to scattered sites in the forest or along the banks of streams. Birds flying south were downed with guns and arrows. Reindeer were rounded up, and boats were prepared for summer travel northward or to the lower Ob. By late May, many moved to fishing sites on or near the Ob, where fish (white salmon, sturgeon, carp, and pike) were netted and trapped as they arrived to spawn. Before autumn snows, Khanty returned to yurts in Kazym villages, to catch grouse, collect berries, and prepare for winter hunting and trapping. Some used their yurts as bases from which to tend small herds of reindeer. Others spent the winter in skin tents (*chums*), nomadizing with large herds that required extensive lichen and moss pasturage. In January, Khanty men, sometimes with families, traveled to the sacred ancient village of Yuilsk for a local interethnic market and winter festivals. While this cycle was typical of the early twentieth century, its roots go back to initial periods of Russian colonization. Details varied with time and ecology.

59. Grigorovskii (1884:57, 61–68). Old Believers were a group of Russian Orthodox conservatives who felt that the reforms of Patriarch Nikon in the seventeenth century had destroyed the church. Many Old Believer families fled to Siberia to practice their faith. See their journals, e.g., *Staroobriadcheskaia mysl'*; and Pascal 1938; Fedotov 1966; Crummey 1970; Billington 1975; Nichols and Stavrou 1978; and Beliajeff 1980.

60. For a sense of changing technologies, compare Felinska 1853(2):192; Iadrinstev 1891: 190, 284; Orlova 1926:70; Potapov 1964:162; Minenko 1975:80-l06.

61. Compare Shvetsov 1888:59; Grigorovskii 1879:1. The late British historian Terence Armstrong (1965:97) termed acculturation of Russians to Native ways "the line of least resistance," but it was the line of best adaptation.

62. The tax records studied by Sokolova (1975:206–7) document extensive Native intermarriage, confirmed by Murashko and Krenke's (1996) study of burials. Wife and daughter sharing had the unfortunate label "prostitution hospitality" in Siberian literature, but there is no evidence that Natives thought of it as prostitution. A Siberian friend explained that this practice had practical value for tiny communities that did not want to become too inbred.

63. For instance, on the Kazym in 1914, the settlement of Khulor had 105 men and 95 women; Ilbe-gort, 185 men and 169 women; and Yuilsk, 89 men and 70 women (Shukhov 1916:29; Abramov 1857).

64. Back-river intermarriage usually meant accelerated Khantization for a Siberiak wife and her children. On the Vasyugan, a rich Khanty hunter married a Russian peasant girl (Grigorovskii 1884:7). They lived in a Khanty settlement, with their language and household organization Khanty in orientation. Their children spoke no Russian, leaving little doubt that locals would consider the next generations to be Khanty.

65. This analysis builds on Fredrik Barth (1969), who accepts a wide range of ethnic boundary maintenance and crossing possibilities and contexts (personal communication, November 1996). The variables are similar to those identified by Ronald Cohen (1978:379–403) in a review of ethnicity theory, though

he especially stresses a typology of ethnic-based power relations. A more fluid approach leaves open an even greater range of interaction patterns.

66. Some Native American activists have criticized the term "nomadism," since they perceive it as implying aimless wandering without a traditional sense of territoriality. But Siberian nomads practiced a controlled pattern of transhumant adaptation on carefully defined kin-based territories.

67. For Native American views of contact, see V. Deloria 1969; Nabokov 1991; and P. Deloria 1998. For an analysis of Yugoslavia that does not descend to generalizations about "tribalism," see Woodward 1995. For post-Soviet cases, see Schoeberlein-Engel 1994 and Drobizheva, Gottemoeller et al. 1996. Useful anthropological anatomies of ethnic conflicts include Salzman 1980; Kapferer 1988; and Tambiah 1989:335–49.

68. The history of Pocahontas is itself an allegorical Rorschach test of differing interpretations. A standard school text version was that she fell in love with Captain John Smith and saved him from the torture decreed for him by her chiefly father, Powhatan. But she married John Rolfe. A revisionist version is that she and her father were purposefully trapping John Smith and John Rolfe for economic exchange benefits. The legends began with John Smith's own account of his salvation in 1607, but Ronald Sanders (1992:262–96) charmingly points out that Smith was saved several times by high-born women in his autobiography and that he had no common language with the Indians he befriended. Powhatan himself, while chief of a loose federation, was not the "emperor" or "king" that Englishmen like John Smith made him out to be for their own glorification. See also Gleach 1997.

Chapter Two
Christianization: Processes of Incomplete Conversion

1. Khanty consultants consider flight from conversion a plausible explanation of why Ugrians left the southern steppes. The "legend" was reported by one of the first missionaries to the Khanty, Grigory Novitskii (1884:24), who worked with Metropolitan Filofei Leshinskii (Fedor) under Peter the Great, in 1712–14. Historian Gerhard Friederich Miller (1787:126–27) supplemented Novitskii's account.

2. Khanty stress continuities over time, although they and I are aware that concepts and practices uninfluenced by Christianization and Sovietization are impossible to document. Khanty explanations are correlated here with early sources such as the missionary Grigory Novitskii (whose 1715 account was not published until 1884) and the historian and traveler G. F. Miller (1787 [1750]: 126–27). See also Finsch and Brem 1882; and Brem 1897. These compare with strikingly similar descriptions by the Finnish ethnographer Karjalainen (1927) and by Soviet ethnographers Chernetsov (1939, 1947, 1963, 1968), Sokolova (1971, 1975a, 1975b, 1976, 1983, 1991), Kulemzin (1976), and Kulemzin and Lukina (1977, 1992).

3. Abramov 1854:16, from Tobolsk church records.

4. Compare Miller 1941 [1763]:13–20; Abramov 1854:17; Lantzeff 1943: 176–77; Kolesnikov 1982; Forsyth 1992:5–6.

5. Businskii 1893:33, from Miller archives. Cf. Zelenin 1936.

6. Miller 1941 [1763]:67–73; Abramov 1854:21–25.

7. The famous schism within Russian Orthodoxy came in 1667. The great schismatic Old Believer priest (*protopop*) Avvakum, who spent considerable time in Siberia, was burned in 1681. See Avvakum 1960; Klibanov 1982.

8. Lantzeff 1943:192. See also TsGIA, church records, fond 797, opis 96, delo 220, list 1–10. Other examples include 1697 instructions to Tobolsk (*Polnoe Sobranie Zakonov*, 3: 355–56) and a 1754 reprimand from the Senate to Governor Miatlev, cited in Abramov 1854:51. Golovnev (1995:105) makes clear that Christianization was far from peaceful in the eighteenth century, when Berezovo documents labeled Natives "zlodei" (evil people), and Native princes were hanged for insurrection. He concludes, "these horrors are not mentioned here to make the reader's hair stand on end, . . . [but to show that] Christianization was received by samodeic and ostiak reindeer herders as normal war."

9. Novitskii 1884:71; Ogrysko 1941:75, from Tobolsk mission records. For an idealized view of Filofei, see Soldatov 1977. The Old Man Ob image was recreated, and in the 1890s it was still the most revered by Ob-Ugrians for providing luck in fishing, according to church historian Businskii (1893:21). It reappeared in the Yugan area in the late twentieth century. See also Novikova 1995:51–63.

10. Sokolova 1991:229, from the Tiumen Oblast archive, fond 156, opis 1, no. 80. Reasoning behind the sacrifice ritual, for regeneration, is similar to that of other Northern peoples (cf. Ridington 1988; Fienup-Riordan 1990; E. Turner 1996).

11. TsGIA, church records, fond 796, opis 11, delo 504, list lob. See also Ogrysko 1941:76–78.

12. Compare TsGIA fond 1264, opis 1, dela 265, 266, on the Speranskii reforms, and Ogryzko 1941:78–98, from Tobolsk mission records.

13. TsGIA, church records, fond 796, opis 11, delo 504.

14. *Pamiatnaia Knizhka Zapadnoi Sibiri* 1881:40.

15. For more on the Siberian conquest see Lantzeff and Pierce 1973; Gibson 1969, 1972; Armstrong 1965; and Martin 1986.

16. Following the advice of Edith Turner's (1996:xxii) Iñupiat friends, I avoid calling Khanty sacred narratives "myths," though "mythic thinking" can be seen as having its own reality (Ridington 1988:71).

17. I recognize, on the basis of arguments with Russian friends, that it is difficult for some Russians to accept that minority peoples of the North were only partially converted to Russian Orthodoxy, since they were described in official church sources and some Soviet historical works as "Orthodox." However, conversations with Khanty and study of local contemporary sources indicate that multidimensional faith and cynicism about Christianity were common. See Felinska 1853(2):19–21; Bartenev 1896:95.

18. See also Dunin-Gorkavich 1911:48–49. Russian adoption of Siberian beliefs was confirmed by disapproving Soviet historians. Bakhrushin (1929:60) claimed that peasants and officials were affected by the whole Native complex of "primitive" shamanic beliefs. Minenko (1975:128) concluded, "Northerners were susceptible to believing in the appearance of spirits before native shamans

and even addressed themselves to local shamans with requests to predict or divine concerning lost reindeer and other articles."

19. The Soviet ethnographer Georgi Startsev (1928:86) observed Slavic and Khanty shamanic parallels in the 1920s, but pre-Soviet sources were more explicit, especially Felinska (1853(1):284, (2):2, 132–83); Shvetsov (1888:76–78); and Bartenev (1896). See Balzer 1996, 1997 for a syncretic analysis of theoretical approaches to shamanism; and Humphrey with Onon 1996 for a critique of overgeneralizing about shamanic worldviews by use of the term "shamanism."

20. For more on Russian religion and the hotly debated concept of Slavic peasant double faith (dvoeverie), see Maikov 1869; Billington 1970:18; and Balzer 1992. For contemporary cognitive ramifications, see Ries 1997.

21. For analysis and description of seances, see Siikala 1978: 217–25; and Balzer 1983, 1987.

22. More than simple generalizations about "double faith" are involved here. My analysis owes much to Bakhtin's dialogics (e.g., 1975) and to Michael Taussig (1987). See also Ames 1964 and Kan 1987, 1989, 1998.

23. See also Geertz 1973; Basso and Selby 1976; Fischer 1977; Hymes 1979; V. Turner 1979:9; Dougherty and Fernandez 1981; Schneider and Lindenbaum 1987:1–8; Fernandez 1991; and Irvine 1993, on the symbolic and linguistic structuring of change. In the Russian context, see Ries 1997.

24. On Northern Christianity, see Fienup-Riordan 1990; Ridington 1988; Kan 1987; and Harkin and Kan 1996. In Siberia and Inner Asia, complex syncretic thinking is found in the Lamaism of Baikal Buryats and in Altai Burkhanism (Krader 1954, 1956, 1978; Humphrey 1994, 1996). Patterns of receptivity and resistance to proselytizing religions, including Islam and Buddhism, are described in Tambiah 1976, Geertz 1968, and Yalman 1964. On anticlericalism, see Riegelhaupt 1984 and Fried 1987.

25. Compare Chernetsov 1963; Diószegi 1978; Novikova 1996.

26. Compare Gondatti 1887:78–79; Kharuzin 1905:145; Dunin-Gorkavich 1911:37; Sokolova 1972:74.

27. For a superb review of widespread Northern concepts and ceremonies regarding the sacred bear, see Hallowell 1926. See also Chichlo 1981 and Novikova 1991 on fraternal kin priorities. Patriliny fit in either tradition.

28. While the main Sky God was usually associated with thunder wielding Numi-Torum, a major Sky Goddess was called Sankë in southern Khanty territories, after a word for "holy light." On the Sky Gods, see Czaplicka 1914:288–90; Chernetsov 1963; Karjalainen 1927; Diószegi 1978; Gemuev 1990; and Kulemzin and Lukina 1992:88–102.

29. Ridington's (1988) context was the Dunne-za (Beaver) Indians. My interpretation adapts those of Lévi-Strauss (1967, 1975), Turner (1968, 1979, 1982), Douglas (1967:49–69), Adams (1977), and Babcock (1978). Structural and symbolic analysis need not mask the messy details of syncretic process and power inequity.

30. See chapter 7 for how these narratives are interpreted in ceremonies honoring the bear. Compare Lévi-Strauss 1967, 1975; Chernetsov 1968; Chichlo 1981; Sagalaev and Oktiabr'skaia 1990; Novikova 1991.

31. I first saw such plates in Tegy in 1976. For a correlation of totemic and

ethnic categorizing, see Comaroff and Comaroff 1992:49–67. The potential of bear ceremony songs for Freudian and Jungian analysis is clear from Geza Roheim (e.g., 1954). Compare Kannisto 1938–39; Munkácsi 1995; Gemuev 1990.

32. See Kulemzin and Lukina 1992:101 on Mikkola Torum. Some accounts attribute to Mikkola Torum the power to punish breaches of social norms. His association with the Milky Way may correlate with its significance for Ob-Ugrians as the "Way of Birds," the path from north to south of migratory birds, symbols of seasonal renewal and fertility (cf. Hoppál 1995:194).

33. Sacred objects made or adorned with metal are in the National Museum of Finland collections of Potanin, Alquist, and Karjalainen. I am particularly indebted to curator Ildigó Lehtinen for interpretation of these collections. See also Chernetsov 1963:14; Moszynska 1968; and Prokof'yeva 1971:10.

34. Gemuev (1990:40–42) elaborates: "not only was it easy to add elements, seemingly alien and not meaningful, but sometimes it was possible to give those elements explanations that fit into the worldview of the people."

35. The symbolic coopting of significance for crosses was different from the wearing of crosses as markers of Russification by some southern Khanty workers and traders. I am following Peirce's use of "symbol," but I use "marker" in a broader sense than his term "index" (1960:18–25, 156).

36. In contrast, Caroline Humphrey with Urgunge Onon (1996:271) explain Mongol shamanic ritual as often "without ideology, without there even being an explanation." On hidden structures of cognition in ritual, see also Rossi 1974:60–106. Latent cognition, mystical experience, and public explanation are all part of shamanic ritual.

37. Tobolsk seminary archives, fond TDK, delo 1746, no. 31, list 49–50, are quoted on this case by Ogrysko (1941:101). For more on animal sacrifices, see chapters 3 and 7.

38. For striking comparison, see Taussig 1987:188–208.

39. Chernetsov (1968) observed this drama as late as the 1930s. For more on bear festivals, see chapter 7.

40. Compare Turner (1968) on ritual liminality with the debate between religious philosopher Theodore Jennings (1982:111–27) and Williams and Boyd (1993:63–68) on the relationship of change in ritual to the generation of new knowledge. Lutz and Lughod (1990) and Fox (1991, 1995) have provided healthy critiques of the coherency of culture. But analysts must still account for patterns of socialization and cognition.

41. The problem of cultural paradigms and change was addressed by Lévi-Strauss (1975:199) and Eva Hunt (1977:247–83), among many other structuralists, in their use of the terms "armature," "code," and "message" to describe increasingly adaptable aspects of cultural symbol-system logic. Compare Elena Novik (1997) and Roberte Hamayon (1990) on patterns, logic, and pragmatism in Siberian shamanism.

42. Unorthodox Orthodoxy is well documented by Zherebina (1983) and Shishigin (1991) for the Sakha (Yakut); and by Sergei Kan (1989, 1998) for the Tlingit.

43. Boris Chichlo (1998:27–28) plausibly argues that the very comparability

of Slavic newcomer and Native Siberian cultures meant that insecure Russians were less likely than other Europeans to place Natives on a "noble savage" pedestal.

Chapter Three
Revitalization: The Battleground of Religion and Politics

1. The premises guiding my interpretation of revitalization stem from anthropological studies of such movements in many parts of the world: Kroeber 1948; Linton 1943; Wallace 1956, 1970, 1974; Kopytoff 1964; LaBarre 1971; Aberle 1972; Schwartz 1976. Critiques of overgeneralizing traditions in social anthropology are also relevant, for example, Herzfeld 1989, 1997; Lutz and Abu-Lughod 1990; Fox 1991, 1995.

2. Compare the Soviet analysis by Butinova (1973) with the more psychological analyses of Wallace (1956, 1956a) and Aberle (1972: 527–31).

3. Wallace's primary model for such a religion is the syncretic Seneca Code of Handsome Lake, notable for its relatively successful (albeit painful) evolution into an established Native religion. The teachings of Handsome Lake helped some Iroquois to change from a disintegrating way of life based on hunting, diplomacy, and warring to agriculture and peaceful accommodation with White society (Wallace 1972).

4. Contrast Worsley 1957:21; LaBarre 1971:20–27. The significance of repetitive religious movements was recognized early by Wallace (1956a) in his study of Delaware Indian religions. Schwartz's (1976) interpretation is thus more a refinement than a contradiction of Wallace.

5. Interpretations of Vavlyo's movement vary, so that the "facts" of the case are buried in ideology. Soviet historians Budarin (1937, 1952, 1964, 1968) and Minenko (1975) claim Vavlyo was a leader in the Decembrist revolutionary tradition, destined to fail but noble in his demands for justice and his fight against rich reindeer breeders, tsarist officials, and some Native elders. They avoid discussion of his identity as a religious leader. Soviet anthropologist Tokarev (1936:110) stresses "the clear class character" of the "rebellion" and also mentions Nentsy and Khanty anger at Orthodox missionizing. The nineteenth-century Russian official Abramov (1857) and the priest Gerasimov (1909) saw Vavlyo as an illegal gang leader with dangerous pagan and anti-Russian pretensions. The Polish exile Felinska's account (1853(2):299–307), though devoid of the rich detail of Budarin or of documents on the case (Vauli 1940), comes closest to a compromise view of begrudging popular admiration for Vavlyo's exploits. Siberiak scholar Golovnev's (1995:155–62) use of archive and informant data makes his version especially rich.

6. The proceedings are recorded in Vauli 1940:20–24.

7. Budarin 1952:97, from the Omsk Gosarkhiv fond 3, delo 1960, list 34–36.

8. I am deeply grateful to Yuri Vella for sharing this song in July 1997. I asked him whether he had ever thought of himself as a modern-day Vauli/Vavlyo. Startled and shy, he lamented that he regrets the time spent in political

activism that had caused him to miss fully recording a Vauli [Vavlyo Neniang] legend from his recently deceased neighbor.

9. Budarin 1952:98, from Omsk Gosarkhiv fond 3, delo 1960, list 39.

10. Felinska (1853(2):306) reported the smith's secret formula: "Smelt the nail from a horseshoe with the iron, and it will then be proof against all charms." This reveals a local association of the horse with Russian spiritual power.

11. Vauli 1940:25–26.

12. Vauli 1940:25.

13. Vauli 1940:27. On Pani, compare Tokarev 1936:110; Budarin 1952:104; Golovnev 1995:162–63.

14. See also Novikova 1995:54; I am grateful to her for this clue. She notes that sacrifices to reincarnated "Old Man Ob" images among Vasyugan Khanty included roosters, clearly obtained from Russians and associated with virility.

15. Compare Schwartz 1976; Gerlach and Hine 1970:78; Kopytoff 1964.

16. TsGIA, Siberian Committee records, fond 1264, opis 1, dela 2, 265, 266; Raeff 1956. The third category, *osedlii*, or "settled," was under still further legal restriction. The legal definitions applied to whole ethnic groups, although some members did not fit the definition. However, Golovnev (1995:158) may be correct in suggesting that Vavlyo never intended to give Murzin power.

17. On interethnic marriages of Khanty and Nentsy, compare Khomich 1976:153; Vasilev 1979; Kriukov 1989. Golovnev notes (1992:164) that about half the Nentsy considered themselves as belonging to a core group they called "nenei nenneche" ("real people"); the others were called "nesei tenz" ("the other part"). Functioning like a phratry (moiety) system for marriage, the first group is associated with the Kharyutchi lineages, famed to this day for producing Nentsy leaders. The second group are associated with the Vanuita lineages, more ethnically intermixed with the Khanty, Entsy, and others. Vavlyo's followers were predominantly but not exclusively from this second group.

18. Mixed tundra clans came to include the Salinder, Nerkygy, Niadangy, Pando, Porongui, Tibichi, and Lar (Golovnev 1992:162). By transferring loyalties to Vavlyo, Khanty families were aligning themselves with a movement considered threatening to many of their clan leaders. According to Felinska (1853(2):305), Taishin made arrangements with Vavlyo in 1840–41 in good faith and was then duped by Russian officials. The Soviet analyst Budarin (1952:100–101) saw Taishin as fully party to the plot.

19. Because Dunin-Gorkavich concluded the movement was not a political threat, he may have decided not to publicize the name of the Vakh Khanty leaders involved in it. Since the initial dream-seer was a woman, Dunin-Gorkavich may also have felt it less important to print her name. Khanty also may have kept it secret.

20. Compare Dunin-Gorkavich 1911:35–36, 44, 45, 1904:43; Karjalainen 1922:40–44; Shatilov 1931:121; Kulemzin 1976:31, 1984:78–86; and Kulemzin and Lukina 1992:88. Differentiating gods and ancestor spirits is difficult. The Finnish ethnographer Karjalainen (1922:40), who knew more names than most, observed that "no single person is able to calculate the exact number and names of all the spirits."

21. Note that "Lar" was on the list of "mixed" groups farther north. Compare Kulemzin and Lukina 1977: 193; Sokolova 1983:111–14).

22. These dual goals make the Vakh events similar to other revitalization movements. The significance of diseases introduced from outside is crucial to the symbolism and psychology of the nearly contemporary 1890s American Ghost Dance. Bishop Hare, an Episcopal minister among the Sioux during Wounded Knee, stressed the despair: "The people said their children were all dying from diseases brought by whites, their race was perishing from the face of the earth, and they might as well be killed at once" (Mooney 1896:841–42).

23. Compare Kulemzin 1976: 46, 52–68); Golovnev 1991:219; and Balzer 1981, 1983 for insights into the cultural context, though not the Vakh movement specifically.

24. On the celestial gods, see Shatilov 1931:99–100, 121); Startsev 1928:77–88. Torém Sankil Ni is the full Vakh Khanty name for the Sky Goddess (Tereshkin 1981:421). See also Cástren 1860:265; Karjalainen 1927:248–50; Eliade 1972:15; Minenko 1975:207.

25. Compare Karjalainen 1927:69–164; and Siikala 1978:217–25.

26. This is still not accepted in some areas, for example, on the Yugan, according to Khanty friends and Kulemzin (1984:95). For more on the reasoning behind female restrictions, see chapter 7 and Balzer 1981. Women had their own sacred groves, linked to rituals of childbirth.

27. Compare Novitskii 1884:47–52; and chapter 1. However, I. N. Gemuev (1990:87) has shown that the Mansi used wooden swords as means of divination through the twentieth century. See also Kulemzin 1984:160–66.

28. Traditional groves along the Vakh River used as sites for the sacrifices of 1896 were carefully observed, photographed, and depicted by Dunin-Gorkavich (1911:36, appendices) and the Soviet ethnographer Shatilov in 1926 (1931:102–9, 115–19). Also relevant are sacred site photographs in the collection of the National Museum of Finland, for example, nos. 324.33–324.41, taken by Karjalainen in the Surgut area. See also appendix B.

29. Compare Shatilov 1931:107, 24–25; and Gumuev and Sagalaev 1986: 136–41 on this kind of sacred grove.

30. Compare Kulemzin and Lukina 1992:98; Bartenev 1896:33–34; Iakobii 1895:6–7; Turskii 1898:34.

31. This idealized vision of traditional life was also expressed in the Khanty view of an afterlife devoid of Russians, described to me in 1976 (Balzer 1980).

32. Compare Turner's (1977:94–130) "communitas." The sacrifice of large numbers of animals was more common at lineage ceremonies that occurred, according to some Khanty consultants, as rarely as once in seven years. Chernetsov (1968) associates such ceremonies with male initiation rites. Nearly a century later, a similar number of animals were sacrificed at Kazym, amidst arguments about the wisdom of killing so many reindeer (see chapter 7).

33. Polygamy was accepted only for those Khanty rich enough to support it, however. It was increasingly rare on the Vakh River by the late 1800s.

34. Compare Thomas and Humphrey 1994:1–12; Ohnukhi-Tierney 1990:1–25. An example of a partially cyclical pattern can be found in Wallace's (1956a) study of the Delaware religions.

35. Compare Slavnin 1911:3–10; Tokarev 1936:10. Later, in the 1930s, a Iamal Nenets protest was called Mandalada, or time of "gathering in earthly war." Its ramifications continued to 1943 (cf. Golovnev 1995:163–64, 183–94; Petrushin 1991:19–21).

36. Burkhanism was named after a Mongol term for one of the manifestations of Buddha. See especially Anokhin 1927; and Sherstova 1997. Krader's (1956) summary of the movement was path-breaking but not meticulous.

37. Trott (1997) stresses missionary-influenced "prophet movements," with resistance and millenarian potential. A recent distinction is Whitehouse's (1995) "doctrinal mode" versus "imagistic mode," formulated after he and his wife became objects of a splinter "cult" in Papua New Guinea. Kopytoff (1964:81) elaborated on Linton's (1943) distinctions of "magical/ rational means" and "revivalistic/ perpetuative ends." Ames's (1957) categories for "nativistic" movements were "resistive/ reformative" in matrix with "aggressive/ non-aggressive."

38. At a comparative level, a few researchers have probed underlying cognitive and emotional processes inherent in movement dynamics (Gerlach and Hines 1970). But focusing on the unifying or even addictive psychology inherent in dance, animal sacrifice, or violence does not mask the need for cultural and social specifics (Firth 1963:12–24; Leach 1976:81–93; Trompf 1990).

39. Khanty intellectuals discussed this in our 1991 Kazym seminar. Sergei Arutiunov affirms that the Khanty were involved in secretive religious activities that could be construed as revitalization efforts, beyond those documented here (personal communication, July 1996).

40. Wallace (1979:192) calls this the code of a "transfer" culture. However, not all movements begin with negative messages, as Wallace (1956:278) has shown. Some emphasize love and cooperation until outside authorities polarize leaders into increasingly nativistic or chauvinistic messages.

41. Outside pressures easily radicalize movements. Ghost Dance prophet Wovoka's original ideology, attuned to the spiritual Pauite and Arapaho, was more "realistic" and conciliatory than later versions. Wovoka preached: "You must not fight. Do no harm to anyone. Do right always" (Mooney 1896:777). Pine Ridge Sioux ideology was more hostile, and lost followers after Wounded Knee. Mooney reported (1896:790): "When one of the women shot in the Wounded Knee massacre was approached as she lay in the church and told that she must let them remove her ghost shirt in order to better get at her wound, she replied, 'Yes, take it off. They told me a bullet would not go through. Now I don't want it any more.'"

42. Wallace 1956:278–79; 1969. Terrorist movements may be successful in their own terms but are beyond the framework of revitalization discussed here. Success and realism are also hard to judge when a movement shifts emphasis from its original social goals (cf. LaBarre 1971:10).

43. Economic aspects, however, may have been exaggerated by Soviet sources, for example, Budarin (1968). Some distinctions used here come from Kopytoff's (1964) literature review, but the Siberian cases, and I suspect many others, crosscut most typologies.

44. Compare Turner 1977:131–65; Falk-Moore and Myerhoff 1975:33–67; Anderson 1991:160.

45. See especially Gerlach and Hines 1970:66, 78, 99–91 on this famous concept of Max Weber's (1947). See also Herzfeld's (1989:193) application of Weber's related idea of "habituation" to the discipline of anthropology itself. For an excellent critique of Weber using data on contemporary Korean shamans, see Kendall 1996.

46. Compare Wallace 1956:275; 1970:196–99); Falk Moore and Myerhoff 1975:231; Peacock 1990:246–67; and Fox (1991:1–16).

47. Compare Lewin 1974:334–35) and Tumarkin 1983:1–23 on Russia, and Fischer 1979:181–84 on Iran, with Anderson 1991:160. As LaBarre (1971:13) noted long ago, "Even the most rigorous and relentless tyrannies and orthodoxies do not make the deeply entrenched prior culture simply disappear."

Chapter Four
Sovietization: Hot and Cold Wars

1. Compare Skachko 1931:108; Sergeev 1955:212; Golovnev 1995:164.

2. *Izvestiia*, December 25, 1921, quoted in Shestalov (1974:15).

3. Tomsk Gubkom [Governing Committee] 1923 records, cited in Onushchuk 1973:59–60.

4. See appendix C; Skachko 1930, 1930a; and Sergeev 1964:4. These "small peoples" were termed *narodnosty*, or *malyi narody*, denoting groups smaller than "nationalities" (*natsional'nosti*). They are the Saami (of North Russia); the Khanty, Mansi, Nentsy, Entsy, and Nganasan (of West Siberia); the Sel'kup, Ket, Dolgan, Evenki, Even, and Yukagir (of Central-East Siberia); the Tofalar (of the Altai area); the Negidal, Nanai, Ul'chi, Udegei, Oroch, Orok, and Nivkh (of the Amur River area); and the Chukchi, Koriak, Itel'men, Chuvan, Eskimo (Yuit), and Aleut (of the Bering Sea area).

5. *Sobranie Ukazov* [Collected Decrees] RSFSR, 1924, number 57:556 and 1925, number 12:79, reprinted in *Sovetskii Sever* (1934(2):11). For more on Committee of the North policies, see Slezkine 1994:167–280.

6. For the debates, see especially Bogaraz (-Tan) 1922, 1923 1932; and the Committee's journal *Sovetskii Sever*. Compare Zibarev 1968:119; Gurvich 1971:18; and Kiselev 1974:104.

7. The decree, *Sobranie Ukazov* 1926, number 73, article 575:861–68, was reprinted in *Sovetskii Sever* (1930(1):5–6), and more recently in Pika and Prokhorov 1994:49–53. Sergeev (1955:231) and Zibarev (1968:124–25) viewed the clan orientation as a mistake. Iakubovskaia (1972:130–31, 90–91) was more sympathetic.

8. In 1924, 154 Khanty, 7 Nentsy, and 8 Mansi participated in executive committee (RIK) and village soviet (*sel'sovet*) leadership. By 1927 the numbers had risen to 243 Khanty, 34 Mansi, and 51 Nentsy, according to Tobolsk party archives cited by Mazurenko (1961:21, 31–32).

9. *Sobranie Uzakonenii i Rasporiazhenii* 1927, number 32, article 330.

10. Statistics are from an anonymous activist reporting to *Sovetskii Sever* (1931(9):144). Party records cited by Mazurenko (1961:29) indicate that by 1930 about 2,840 Khanty, 311 Mansi, and 654 Nentsy were involved in integral cooperatives. For broader perspective on collectivization, see Lewin 1968.

11. Onushchuk 1973:108–9. The ethnographer Sergeev's (1947, 1955) glowing review of these cooperatives and trade points contrasts with a more realistic assessment of bureaucratic problems and strained finances by Skachko (1930), an early organizer for whom the Kazym collective was named at one point, before he was purged.

12. Phrases in quotes are the slogans of the time. See Skachko 1934:37; Onushchuk 1973:134–35; and Gushchin 1980:7–26.

13. *Sovkhozy*, wage-based, government-run collectives, came later, with consolidation of collectivization in the late 1950s and 1960s.

14. The full text is in the "Khronika" of *Sovetskii Sever* 1930 (2):144–46. These conditions provoked the famous Stalin speech "dizzy with success"; even he condemned "left deviationists" for moving too fast.

15. *Sovetskii Sever* 1931(9):146; Onushchuk 1973:137.

16. On party statistics and politics, see Terletskii 1930:6–7; Skachko 1930; Skachko 1930c; Skachko 1931; Taracouzio 1938:278; and Kiselev 1974:133, 145–46).

17. Party records cited by Kiselev (1974:140–41).

18. See Petri 1928:118–27; Chebotarevskii 1930 ; Parkhomenko 1930; and Ustiugov 1930:12–13, for descriptions of culture bases by activists who worked in them; and *Sobranie Uzakonenii i Rasporiazhenii* 1930 for their legal status.

19. Ustiugov 1930. In the Obdorsk area alone, 373 "kulaks, traders, and shamans" lost voting rights in elections to eight Native councils (Ustiugov 1931:201). More than 1,000 kulaks, traders, and religious leaders lost voting rights in the first Okrug elections, according to the historian Kiselev (1974:138), whose father was Khanty and his mother, Russian.

20. Pervukhin (1930:81) notes seventy-six such cases in 1930. The atmosphere of accusations is evident in the Proceedings of the Okrug Party Congress (Vtoroi S"ezd Sovetov 1935). Many of the "plots" were fabricated.

21. Compare Ustiugov 1930:13–18; Skachko 1930a:41–43.

22. *Sovetskii Sever*, correspondence from the field (1931(9):146).

23. *Sovetskii Sever*, correspondence from the field (1931(9):145).

24. Kopylov and Retunskii 1965:167–68. Compare Gudkov and Senkevich 1940:82.

25. Party archives cited by Kopylov and Retunskii (1965:166).

26. Sources for this incident include party archives described or excerpted by Golovnev (1995:165–78); Kopylov (1994:205–305); Kopylov and Retunskii (1965:168–69); and Budarin (1968a:214–27). Background is from the local schoolteacher I. Panov (1937:97–119); and from Tatiana Moldanova's (1990) insider view. I am indebted to Kazym consultants, who first hinted about this in 1976, and whose whispers grew louder by 1991, including members of the Moldanov, Ernykhov, and Kaksin families. Thanks also go to Bulgarian scholar Flora Boldanova for sharing 1991 field data on the "rebellion." I am grateful to the late, meticulous scholar of Northern Native life Alexander Pika for sharing his full typed notes on the most comprehensive relevant document, "Obvinitel'noe zakliuchenie po delu 2/49 'O kontrrevoliutsionnom vooruzhennom vystuplenii protiv Sovetskoi vlasti tuzemtsev Kazymskoi tundry"

(Sostavleno Polnomochnyi predstavitel' OGPU po Obsko-Irtyshskoi oblasti. June 10, 1934.)

27. Alexander Pika transcript of "O kontrrevoliutsionnom vooruzhennom vystuplenii protiv Sovetskoi vlasti tuzemtsev Kazymskoi tundry," *delo* 2/49 of Polnomochnyi Predstavitel' OGPU po Obsko-Irtyshskoi oblasti, June 10, 1934. Cf. Golovnev 1995:168.

28. Although ostensibly drawing on the same OGPU document, Golovnev (1995:172) and the notes of Alexander Pika have small discrepancies in dates, numbers of Natives involved in ritual actions, and the name of the river mentioned here. I have chosen Golovnev's "Liamin" over the name probably in the original document, "Liapino," because the Liamin is closer to the Kazym region, while the Liapino is on the far side of the Ob, in mostly Mansi territory. The mistake may be significant, because it highlights the problem of ascertaining who wrote the final secret service report in 1934. Using court records of Native testimony, it may have been a nonlocal Siberian versed in ways of sacrifice (Nikolai Tereshkin?) or a Russian intent on covering religious and political aspects of the struggle.

29. Timing somewhat differs in Golovnev's (1995:172) account and Alexander Pika's notes from "Obvinitel'noe zakliuchenie." More crucial is the discussion of alliance with "Samoyed," and the variation on the "cargo cult" theme of waiting for "ships" to come bearing salvation, this time in the form of a return of the tsarist Whites. Relatively large supply ships on the Ob (though not the smaller Kazym and Amnia) make this metaphor especially plausible.

30. Golovnev 1995:171; Kopylov 1994:211–12.

31. Prokopii Spiridinov and his family are in some sources depicted as traitors (Budarin 1968a:215; Kiselev 1974:155; "N" 1936(6):108). He died in jail in 1934, but in February 1931, "Comrade Spiridonov" had been featured in the Okrug Native-language newspaper as a sixty-five-year-old nomad taking a Soviet crash course in politics and literacy. He was quoted as saying, "After the courses, I will travel to my nomadic brothers, tell them all, and lead them to Socialism" (Panov 1937:118).

32. Golovnev 1995:175, from "Obvinitel'noe zakliuchenie," correlating with Alexander Pika, from the same document.

33. This version is from Alexander Pika's notes on the "Obvinitel'noe zakliuchenie," although Golovnev's (1995:175) version confirms major points. A short article by the Estonian scholar Art Leete (1998), appearing just as this book was going into print, makes the interesting case, based on field interviews, that the woman Polina Schneider had violated sacred male space at the Num-to island and had thus particularly offended Natives and spirits.

34. Golovnev 1995:175, from "Obvinitel'noe zakliuchenie." Pika's notes from the same source conclude, "the punishment resembles a sacrifice to the spirits of Num-to."

35. The quote on Khanty pulling in sync is from Alexander Pika's notes from "Obvinitel'noe zakliuchenie." Participants in the ritual were likely Nentsy as well as Khanty. The report of scalping may have been mere rumor, since it was not found in other court testimony (Golovnev 1995:176). A relevant discrep-

ancy arises with the issue of whether bodies were later recovered and buried, as Golovnev suggests (1995:176) or were left to drown, as Pika's notes imply. Security forces perhaps rescued the bodies before the ice thawed. Did Astrakhantsev's wife see the bodies? Was she influenced by local tales of ancient Ugra scalping? If scalping occurred, did it mean that the participants, like some Native Americans, saw soul power as residing in hair?

36. This letter is printed in Budarin 1968a:216–17, presumably from party archives. Budarin sensationalizes his account with invented dialogue and use of words like "traitors" and "terrorists" for the "evil" Khanty. But his description of the Khanty secret policeman is fascinating. Zakhar N. Posokhov (1899–1933) was born into a poor Ob River fishing family and inspired by a Russian schoolteacher. He believed the Kazym "rebels" included a vengeful soldier left over from Kolchak's civil war forces, though no evidence supports this. In effect, he died being categorized as "Russian" by other Khanty.

37. I am following Alexander Pika's account of "Obvinitel'noe zakliuchenie" here. Golovnev (1995:177) gives the more astonishing number of twenty-nine shamans, though this may be a misprint.

38. The smallpox scare seems to be missing from court records, but Panov (1937) also mentions it.

39. Moldanova 1990:24–25. I am especially grateful for Tatiana Moldanova's insights, shared in Kazym in 1991, into how the Kazym events resonated in Khanty family histories throughout the Soviet period.

40. I thank Anastasiia Vagatova for sharing these painful recollections (Kazym, 1991), after they had been repressed for so long.

41. See Ortner 1995:173–93 on the multiplicity of resistance dynamics. Compare Comaroff 1985, and Comaroff and Comaroff 1992.

42. Editorial in the successor journal to *Sovetskii Sever*, *Severnaia Arktika*, entitled "Light and Darkness in the Work of Glavsemorput" (1937(1):888). See also Taracouzio 1938:311.

43. Kopylov 1994:305, note 53; Golovnev 1995:178.

44. From Alexander Pika's notes. Compare Golovnev 1995:175.

Chapter Five
Sovietization: Hearts, Minds, and Collective Bodies

1. Western sources are rarely better, whether outdated (Taracouzio 1938; Armstrong 1965; Connolly 1975); too skeptical of Soviet progress (Kolarz 1954); or too accepting of Soviet claims of assimilation and progress (Vuorela 1964; Kuoljok 1985; Bartels and Bartels 1995). Caroline Humphrey's (1983) analysis of Buryat collectives is a notable exception, as is Bruce Grant's (1995) retrospective on Nivkh Sovietization. Slezkine's (1994) focus is more on official Soviet policy in the 1920s and 1930s than on Native responses.

2. For example, Khronika in *Sovetskii Sever* 1930(1):150–52.

3. A furor has arisen in the gender literature over the use of the word "pollution" (Douglas 1966; Buckley and Gottlieb 1988). I use it here because it conforms to concepts Khanty women themselves describe, although I appreciated

the opportunity to debate this when challenged by Child and Child (1985:125–28) in *American Anthropologist*. Compare Balzer 1981:850–67; 1985:128–30); Rombandeeva 1968:77–88; Gudkov and Senkevich 1940:95–97; Senkevich 1934:98–105; and Startsev 1928:74.

4. Compare Petri 1928; *Vtoroi S"ezd Sovetov* 1935:26; Prokof'yeva et al. 1964:534.

5. Leonov 1929:231. In designated areas before 1917, non-Natives needed permission for access to Native domains (see chapter 1). By the 1920s, a legal influx of Russian and Tatar settlers made Native territories everyone's to share (Orlova 1926:71–72; Rubinskii 1928:18; Ostrovskii 1931:114–19).

6. Skachko (1931:102) admitted it was not surprising that some Khanty were ready to retreat further into the taiga and tundra "at the appearance near their camps of Russian settlers."

7. In comparison, the Mansi dropped from 7,473 to 5,754 from 1897 to 1926, and the Russians increased 2.7 percent. Mansi territory was defined more consistently before and after the revolution than Khanty territory. The 1903 figure is from Dunin-Gorkavich 1904:78 for the Khanty of the Tobolsk and Tomsk jurisdictions (cf. Patkanov 1911:25–26). The 1897 census listed Sel'kup (as Ostiak-Samoyed) and possibly others as Ostiak; thus figures in excess of eighteen thousand from the 1897 census quoted by Skachko (1931:91–95) and by Bruk and Kukuzan (1980: 88) are high. Any Khanty population increases were minimal. Mortality among women and children was alarming, and smallpox and typhus epidemics, triggered by contact with Russians, caused serious depletion.

8. Compare Kokosov et al. 1956:12; Iag'ia 1980:15; Diachkov 1979. Problems with the release of unpleasant (purge-, collectivization-, and famine-influenced) 1939 statistics make all 1939 census figures suspect, but these proportions, given the massive Slavic influx, seem appropriate. I am grateful to Professor Murray Feshbach for giving me access to 1939 census data. For subsequent data I have used the official census, *Itogi Vsesoiuznoi perepisi*, unless indicated. Through the 1950s, the population remained under ten persons per square kilometer, with the bulk of new settlement in the southwest, and along the Ob, Irtysh, and Konda Rivers.

9. Khanty ancestors adopted reindeer breeding from neighboring Samodeic peoples. The baseline for my description of local patterns is the 1920s. Sources are Khanty consultants. Compare Pervukhin 1930(1):75–83; Skachko 1931:58–113; Bolshakov 1936:14–24; and Prokof'yeva et al. 1964:521–22. On the historical ecology of nomads, see also Krupnik 1990; Salzman 1980.

10. As reindeer breeders explained to me in 1976, on the Upper Kazym and in the Obdorsk region, the Khanty calendar, reckoned by the sun (*kantl*) and moon (*tilis*), had months named for seasonal changes related to reindeer breeding. June (*lipi tilis*) was the month of leaves on trees and time for travel northward. July (*vonzevoi*) marked the arrival of fish, and August (*shokur*) specifically of pike. In September (*lipi khoti*) leaves turned golden and in October (*lipi pitti*), they fell. November (*pootti*) meant the advent of ice, while December (*van khatlor*) was the dark month of the shortest day. By January (*khantl ros*) "the sun's arms began to spread." February (*munlup*) saw icicles presaging

warmer times. March (*aiker*) was a dangerous month, with storms causing ice upon snow, and April (*vunker*) saw even greater ice coverings on the snow, making foraging especially difficult for reindeer. May (*nopootti*) was the welcome season of river ice breakup, presaging more travel.

11. Khanty reindeer breeders in the Obdorsk (Salekhard) area followed a similar pattern and were like their Nentsy neighbors. Obdorsk herds often were large (over five hundred) and headed north to the sea for summer pastures. Distances for the annual cycle could exceed one thousand kilometers.

12. To succeed in the primarily reindeer-based nomadic cycle, a breeder needed a herd of at least 200. A kulak was defined as having over 400 deer. In the hunting economy of the tundra, 130 reindeer were sufficient and over 300 meant political trouble. In the partially settled hunting-fishing patterns of the forest-tundra and taiga, 54 and 40 deer were enough, respectively, while 200 (in the forest-tundra) and 100 (in the taiga) brought risk of Soviet disapproval. By the late 1920s, 3.2 percent of Northern breeders had over 1,000 deer and 10.3 percent had 250 to 1,000 deer. Thus less than 14 percent of the Native population owned 63 percent of the domesticated reindeer (Skachko 1930a:40; 1930b: 18–24).

13. In the Yamal-Nenets Okrug, settlement of Khanty and Nentsy was less rapid, though some reindeer breeders claimed to be attracted by the "clean new homes" and "cultured life" of the Kharp collective (Brodnev 1936:105–7).

14. I. S. Gurvich (personal communication, June 1985) stressed that most Siberians were not soldiers, but contributed greatly to homefront supply efforts.

15. In the Ob North, Natives constituted 11.5 percent of a total of over twenty-five hundred; 18.5 percent were of Siberian peasant background; and 47.5 percent were women (Kiselev 1974:195; cf. Mazurenko 1961:63–69).

16. In 1976, I heard more statements of pride about relatives in the army than hints that ethnic relations were not smooth. But I also learned about the ethnic jokes and epithets, without soliciting such information. Prevalent were "Chukchi jokes," told about Natives of Chukotka but used to slur all Northern Natives. Many have the theme of the awkward Native bumpkin not knowing how to handle a big city, although occasionally a Chukchi is portrayed as deviously, even politically, clever. (See ahead for further analysis.)

17. Mazurenko 1961:74, from Tiumen archives. In the Khanty-Mansi Okrug, 174 Khanty and Mansi households were recorded as newly settled.

18. I. S. Gurvich (personal communication, April 1984) explained attempts to improve reindeer breeding and decrease nomadism. Given the great variations in the ecology and social organization of reindeer breeding, experiments worked better in some areas than others.

19. This is the notorious shift method, usually used for mining and energy workers in the North. A breeder told Klepikov (1967:141): "Once away from reindeer, they will forget you and you them—[you forget] which are sick, which obstinate, which sovkhoz [collective] owned, which yours. . . . And where would people be found for such shifts?"

20. In the Khanty-Mansi Okrug, only two reindeer collectives survived: Saranpaul (including Khanty, Mansi, and Zyrian) and Kazym (predominantly Khanty). In 1966, the twenty thousand deer of the Kazym sovkhoz enabled the

collective to make a 165,000-ruble profit in reindeer meat sales (Sokolova 1968:29). A decade later breeding at Kazym was productive, although the number of reindeer remained officially twenty thousand. It should have been higher through natural growth. The ratio of deer to herders has increased sharply since the 1920s. Ideally, each brigade included one veterinarian. In 1976, a few privately owned deer were herded along with collective animals, but politics and customary reticence made it difficult for me to gain exact statistics.

21. Compare Kiselev 1974:204–5; Sokolova 1971a:74–75.

22. Large centers resulted from a Central Committee directive (May 30, 1950): "Concerning the consolidation of small kolkhozes and the task of the Party Organization in this matter." By 1958, in the whole okrug, 347 prewar cooperatives had become 125 large collectives. Only 58 of these engaged in successful reindeer breeding, mostly in the Berezovo region (Sokolova 1968:27).

23. Prokof'yeva et al. 1964:54. Outside the okrug, Khanty were affiliated with five predominantly fishing artels in the Aleksandrovsk-Vasyugan region and with several reindeer-breeding collectives in the Yamal-Nenets Okrug. By 1961 in the Khanty-Mansi Okrug, ninety-four fishing, reindeer, hunting, and agricultural kolkhozes were organized into twenty-four sovkhozes (Pika 1982:233).

24. "On measures for aiding the growth of the economies and cultures of the northern regions" (*Postanovleniia* SM RSFSR (1956) number 769; supplement 957, number 300). Laws also strengthened collective control of fishing, limiting private intake and protecting small and spawning fish in the Tiumen Region (e.g., *Postanovleniia* SM RSFSR (1953) number 990). Compare Sokolova 1971a: 75–76; 1968:33.

25. Fish canning enabled the okrug to export a lucrative 15–17 million cans a year by the late sixties (Loshak 1970:40). The notoriously low salaries paid Khanty hunters affiliated with collectives improved somewhat in the 1960s, but hunting cadres markedly decreased (Sokolova 1968:31).

26. Pika 1982:234–36. More numerous fish reception points and processing centers stimulated raises in fishers' salaries. In the 1970s, such salaries ranged from two hundred to four hundred rubles a month, considerably higher than the Soviet average and far above the seventy-ruble minimum.

27. Fish yield declines began as early as the late 1960s and 1970s in some areas, and fishermen had to work harder to catch less and meet government plans. A Tiumen Region report (Kruzhikov 1967:40, 90) reveals a drop from 19.2 thousand tons in 1966 to 14.7 thousand tons in 1967. The general downward trend is confirmed by Pika (1982:237). Drastic and disruptive plans for routing the Irtysh southward toward Central Asia were canceled under Gorbachev, as economically and ecologically unsound.

28. Each type of fish had limited seasonal runs, with some runs stronger than others. Besides brigade salaries, fishermen maintained semilegal nonbrigade net sites and could also receive by-the-job payments from more official channels.

29. Squirrels, sable, muskrats, elk, wild reindeer, arctic fox, wolverine, and lynx were hunted with cartridge hammer guns, and could be reached relatively quickly by snowmobiles. These Soviet-manufactured vehicles, owned in the 1970s by only a few successful Khanty brigade leaders, have become popular

with hunters wishing to be home for dinner from trips once requiring several days (see chapter 6).

30. In the Tiumen Region in the 1970s, fur yields decreased by 50–70 percent, and the number of state hunters declined by two-thirds (Pika 1982:234–36).

31. In the Surgut area, negative effects of government policy on hunting productivity were evident: state-supported hunters declined from 120 to 27 in the 1950s, and the value of the furs they collected went from 40,000 rubles to 8,100 (Pika 1982:236–38). But on the Bolshoi Yugan in the 1950s, a dispersed local population of hunters and fishers were not forcibly moved. By 1979, twenty-two separate settlements had survived as parts of five productive branches of a larger Ugutsk kolkhoz. With this less disruptive model, a relatively stable cadre of 110 hunters turned in furs worth 79,200 rubles from 1971 to 1978.

32. Foxes multiply faster than sable—one of the reasons they were chosen for these farms. For an exposé of a Kazym fur farm, see Yakov Iadne's segment in Mark Badger and Asen Balikci's 1992 film *Siberia through Siberians' Eyes*. On the growth of fur husbandry, see Kokosov et al. 1956:92–94; Mozgalin 1981:130–35. The fur farm economy collapsed in the post-Soviet period; many Native workers have been left unemployed, and many stories circulate of animals smuggled onto the black market in the dark of night.

33. Sometimes these have been the same officials, making a fairly typical transition from Communist Party leader to post-Soviet businessman.

34. Khanty transfers to new homes stemmed from personal decisions, the decline of traditional economies, and official Soviet pressure to meet ambitious economic plans linked with energy industry labor policy. See Salmanov 1970:57–99 for a dramatic inside account of the industry's birth and growth in the region; Shestalov 1970:57–79 for a Native's progress-oriented view; and Gustafson 1983 for a Western view. For further negative ramifications, see chapter 6.

35. The sensitive issue of clashing industrial and traditional values is explored in the novels of the Siberian Russian Valentin Rasputin and in the popular film *Siberiade* (Konchalovsky, 1979). Contrasts between Slavic and Native groups were downplayed in the Soviet period, when brotherhood of the peoples was stressed to the point of blinding Soviet researchers to ethnic tensions. Ethnic tensions, suggested by observations and conversations in 1976, had become obvious by 1991.

36. Attempts to find percentages of Khanty party members in the okrug or oblast revealed that published statistics were rarely broken down by ethnic group, for example, in congress records or the journal *Partiinaia Zhizn'* (Party Life). In 1950, 183 Khanty were in the Tiumen party organization; Khanty, Mansi, and Nentsy constituted 23 percent of the party in 1957 (Mazurenko 1961:65, from party archives). By 1990, that percentage was far lower, given influxes of non-Natives into the region.

37. At the 1981 (twenty-sixth) party congress, only 28 delegates out of about 5,380 were from the Tiumen Oblast. See Rigby 1968:503; KPSS S"ezd 1981:

289–523. The number of Khanty in the Communist Party probably never exceeded 2 percent of their population, lower than percentages for most non-Russian groups.

38. On the day of a meeting, its time and a brief agenda were announced through village broadcast systems in the main square. This was the norm in well-organized Kazym, but not in Tegy.

39. Collective chairmen had three-year terms, extended by local party leadership if they were effective. Humphrey (1983:124) mentions a Buryat chairman so effective in getting people to work through unofficial means that, after he had been dismissed for "alleged malpractices," authorities were forced "reluctantly" to reinstate him.

40. While traveling in Urgench, Uzbekistan in 1976, I was warned not to venture onto the streets at night because of street gangs. Stories also circulated in the Soviet Union in 1976 of occasional violence against interethnic couples.

41. Humphrey (1983:16) notes that her student Philip Lineton reported massive drunkenness, as well as "hooligans," in exile from elsewhere in the Soviet Union; no one wanted the job of local policeman.

42. The psychology of dominance and prejudice is interrelated. See Gioseffi 1993. If weakness breeds contempt, then Russians may have had more respect for Natives early in their contact; later, as Native dependency and alcoholism grew, respect decreased. The more Russians took from Native lands, the more some defensively accused Natives of being "naturally" weak.

43. For statistics and more positive Soviet views on educational advances, see Luks 1930:130; Andreeva 1962:166; Boitsova 1971:141–58; and Timofeev 1974:76–88. Compare Kasten 1998.

44. Sergeev 1947:137–38. But see chapter 6 for further critique of Russian education.

45. Soviet language policy officially promoted bilingualism, not Russification, but the bilingualism that resulted was unbalanced: non-Russians learned Russian, but rarely the other way around. (Compare Guboglo 1984 with Guboglo 1993). A few texts and grammars in the different dialects of the Khanty language were produced, e.g., Tereshkin 1981; S. P. Moldanova et al. 1983; A. M. Sengepov et al. 1988.

46. Compare Drobizheva et al. 1996:39–45, 375; Abrahamian 1993–94:12–23. See also Suny 1993; Balzer 1990.

Chapter Six
Regionalization: Lands and Identities in Crisis

1. The letter was signed by Vladimir S. Kogonchin, Yaun-Yakh President, Yugan Khanty, Surgut region, April 8, 1997. This sale was stopped in the nick of time, not by direct United Nations influence but by realignments of local politics and economics that are still being played out.

2. Ronalda S. Olzhina is a leading Khanty ethnographer; she was part of our 1991 film seminar in Kazym and is one of the founding members of the Associa-

tion for the Salvation of the Ugra. All along the road, and deep into the scarred forest, was strewn a jumble of abandoned car and motorcycle parts, oil rig equipment, and discarded junk.

3. The jokes rarely allowed the stereotyped slow-witted Chukchi to come out ahead. One slyly political exception, probably born in the early 1980s, tells of a Chukchi who comes to Red Square and parks his car. When a policeman tells him he cannot park there because Communist Party Central Committee members pass by all the time, he says "Oh, you are right officer, I did forget to lock up." Chukchi jokes have not died. A 1997 one is at once reflexive and exoticizing, for it is a variation on the "New Russian" jokes about Russian businessmen. A "New Chukchi" goes into a Moscow store and buys a refrigerator, which he loads on his back. "But why have you bought a refrigerator?" he is asked. "Don't you know that you don't have electricity in Chukotka?" "I thought of that," he answers, "so I have also bought a socket for the wall." The joke, a variation on an older one, is also anti-Soviet, given Soviet propaganda that the whole country had been successfully electrified.

4. Claiming the capital was more a tactic than a realistic goal. The newspaper used was Moscow-based and had wide circulation. Newspapers are worth examining as potential catalysts influencing Khanty identity (cf. Anderson 1991), although thus far few Khanty read them. In the 1990s, two newspapers, Mansi writer Yuvan Shestalov's Saint Petersburg based *Belyi Zhuravl* (White Stork) and the Khanty-Mansiisk based *Novosti Ugry* (Ugrian News) are relevant; they are predominantly in Russian, with some columns in Ugrian languages. The Khanty language newspaper *Khanty Iasang* (Khanty Word), based in Khanty-Mansiisk, is the regional political news source of the Communist Party and was founded in 1957.

5. Yaoun Yakh is particularly large (eight hundred members) and has a capable leader, Vladimir Kogonchin. A second Eastern Khanty obshchina is Khanto, organized by Joseph and Agrafina Sopochina. The legal status of the obshchiny is guaranteed in Russian Federation laws, but administrators of the Khanty-Mansi Okrug have been reticent to negotiate with them on local development issues. Some obshchiny are functioning more as economic units than lineage-based political-territorial communities. Some indigenous leaders, for example Yuri Vella, are also skeptical of the effectiveness of obshchiny in areas where people are living scattered and distant from neighbors they sometimes do not trust.

6. My data comes from personal observation as well as discussions with a broad range of Siberians and with anthropologist Bruce Grant. A high-profile example of female leadership is the Nanai (Amur River) ethnographer-politician Evdokiia A. Gayer, who became a deputy to the All-Union Congress in 1989, and who is head of the International Fund for Indigenous Peoples, based in Moscow.

7. Gogoleva also had personal, family reasons to step down.

8. See the Russian Federation Constitution, article 72.

9. My data come from transcripts of the congress, kindly given to me by Sakha leader and former mayor of Yakutsk Aleksei Tomtosov, and from the superb summary by anthropologist Boris Chichlo (1990), who called it the "first

victory" for "Lilliputians" over the Gulliver-like Soviet state. See also Tomtosov 1990; Sangi 1990; Fondahl 1997.

10. By 1997, the elected president was Nenets leader (and former Duma deputy) Sergei Kharyutchi, who succeeded Eremei Aipin. The articulate Kharyutchi is from one of the older Nenets leadership families. In 1994 (when I was privileged to meet him), he participated in a month-long tour of Native American communities, organized by Sakha (Yakut) leader Uliana Vinokurova. Note also the reindeer breeders' union led by Chukotka politician Vladimir Etylin and the indigenous-rights groups of activist-ethnographer Evdokiia Gayer and businessman-ethnographer Yuri Samar, both from the Amur River area.

11. Information is from personal communications from Evdokiia Gayer (November 1991); Eastern Khanty leader Joseph Sopochin (March 1995); Northern Khanty artist Nadezhda Taligina (May 1993); Moscow folklorist and activist Olga Balalaeva (March 1993); West Siberian ethnographer and activist Andrei Golovnev (May 1993, May 1997); and others who may prefer not to be named.

12. I am grateful to Olga Balalaeva for data on the protest (May 1993). Local administrators and oil development executives were at first at odds, until "infrastructure development" was promised as compensation for giving Surgutneftegaz full rights to exploration and development.

13. Data are from an alert put out by the Estonian Society of Ugrians in 1993, titled "Eestilas—Sapmelas Oktavuonta" and from Moscow folklorist Olga Balalaeva (spring 1994). For a more upbeat report on the more public events, see Osherenko 1993:53–55. The festival was supported with energy resource funds from the Surgut region and was in part organized by the Association for the Salvation of the Ugra and the Institute for Ob-Ugrian Revival, based in Khanty-Mansiisk. See also chapter 7 for more on reindeer sacrifice and its meaning for cultural revival.

14. Analysts of the transition in Rossiia might take heed of these examples of how far processes of administrative land claims have gone (cf. Stoner-Weiss 1997; McAuley 1997).

15. I am grateful to Olga Balalaeva (May 1993), for information on this. The referendum also included questions on gas exploration and road building.

16. Later, the Khanty-Mansi Okrug attempted unsuccessfully to pry two Khanty areas from Tomsk, while Krasnoiarsk was targeted in a secession move by the Taimyr Okrug in 1992. I am grateful to West Siberian ethnographer Andrei Golovnev (May 1993) for insights into foiled political boundary maneuvers, also covered in the press.

17. Nikolaev 1995:2. These percentages (covering the Yamal-Nenets and Khanty-Mansi Okrugs together) may be exaggerated, given the energy reserves of the Far Eastern Sakha Republic. Nikolaev reported that the charter of the Khanty-Mansi Okrug was the result of negotiations between Khanty-Mansiisk and Tiumen authorities over the share of the oblast budget that the okrug would pay from taxes, mostly from the energy industry. The share was set at 20 percent, after having been much higher.

18. In the Yamal-Nenets Okrug, according to its governor, Yuri Neelov (Woodrow Wilson Center, Kennan Institute seminar, October 23, 1997), 0.5 percent of Gazprom profits go to indigenous communities. Debates about use of

energy profits to benefit local communities are typical throughout the North, as Native Americans have explained to Native Siberians in 1990s seminars. Contracts for subsurface use of indigenous lands in the U.S. usually designate specific percentages of profits for community infrastructure. But indigenous communities in Siberia have no subsurface rights. Compare Humphrey 1991.

19. I helped arrange this meeting with Bureau of Indian Affairs executive Franklin Keel. Joseph Sopochin's short working career with the oil company was due mainly to his embarrassment over their tactics to gain Khanty land, and also over their treatment of him.

20. This was Vladimir Kogonchin's opening explanation, March 7, 1995, in our meeting with Bureau of Indian Affairs executive Franklin Keel, who is Choctaw and Chickasaw. Vladimir Kogonchin and Joseph Sopochin's visit was in part sponsored by the MacArthur Foundation, through a grant to Olga Balalaeva and Andrew Wiget.

21. This is Olga Balalaeva's story (May 1993), and she is one of the brave activists who tried to expose the deed. See also Sal'nikova 1991:11–15.

22. This horror story and the two that follow come from "Indigenous Reindeer Herders under Siege by Oil Industry: Report from a Fact-Finding Mission to Khanty-Mansi Autonomous Region," an electronic mail report forwarded to me in 1997 by native-l@gnosys.svle.ma.us (original sender, infoe-k@link-gl.comlink.apc.org). While it contains a few mistakes (the translation of Ugra and a few indigenous names), the gist rings true. The authors argue that "consumer countries" (of West Siberian oil), especially in Europe, should protest how their energy is derived.

23. This quote heads the 1997 report, also labeled V. Koeln.

24. Olga Balalaeva, telephone conversation, October 11, 1995. Olga added that there were American energy companies involved. The phrase "village of the town type" is from Soviet programs promoting construction of multistory apartment buildings in villages. They were also supposed to have amenities of town life.

25. The conversation, at a party at the Phillips Collection art museum in Washington D.C., was so stunning that I went home and wrote it down. White Nights was still in West Siberia, Eastern Khanty territory, when I checked in 1997, although other possible investors have pulled out. The nearest "Eskimo" are about three thousand miles away, but his misconception confirms Fienup-Riordan's (1990:1) concerns about popular images of Eskimo.

26. Credit for this concept goes to Andrew Wiget, of New Mexico State University, and Olga Balalaeva, codirectors of the "Khanty Atlas Project,"funded by the MacArthur Foundation. See Wiget and Balalaeva 1997; 1997a, b; and their web site, www.nmsu.edu/~english/hcsiberia.html. In their 1997 film *Khanty: People of the Taiga*, one important meeting with energy representatives ended in a shouting match, and no Khanty signing away exploration rights. This small success resulted from community solidarity and perhaps from pressure put on the company by the film process itself.

27. These are the parcels referred to in the letter of Vladimir Kogonchin to the United Nations. I am grateful to Olga Balalaeva and Andrew Wiget for providing me with a copy of this letter and to Khanty leaders Vladimir Kogonchin and Petr Moldanov for providing earlier background.

28. Governor Filipenko, speaking at the Kennan Institute, October 23, 1997, added that he was concerned about welfare fraud in the Khanty-Mansi Okrug, since a full 20 percent of the population of the region is on welfare. Filipenko (1996) has given lip service to the need to invest in Native communities, but his appointment of a commission on the biosphere project may be a stalling maneuver, since the land involved is so lucrative. His commission, headed by Filipenko, is composed mostly of Russians associated with the energy industry, but it does include Khanty leader Vladimir Kogonchin and one biosphere advocate from the Yugan nature preserve. By late 1998, support of Goskomsevera was in doubt after deputy minister Anatoly Volgin lost his job.

29. In 1997, a Khanty leader purchased a substantial herd of Kazym reindeer and was trying, against some internal community resistance, to get friends and relatives to move back to the forest from their village. This example of "neotraditionalism" in action was threatening to split the community rather than restore it to its former way of life. By 1998, some members had moved back, were building settlement homes with modern amenities, and were supporting a small settlement school.

30. Quite a few indigenous Siberian leaders have interethnic marriages. In part this is because they are among the more traveled and better educated Siberians and have more opportunities to meet diverse people.

31. I am grateful to Nadezhda Taligina, who became a friend in 1993. Zoia Sokolova (1983:126–27) rejected the term "clan" entirely as applied to the Khanty, seeing the Khanty *syn*, glossed as "clan" by Chernetsov, to also mean phratry. Ob-Ugrians had a "dual exogamous phratry system," with marriage, or at least marriage rules, determined by membership in two main groups. Smaller flexible kin formations are the focus of genealogical and territorial groups that in the 1990s form the basis of some obshchiny, and still sometimes have a "totemic" character, that is, are linked with a symbolic system of animal identifications and prohibitions. While "totem" and "clan" are sometimes associated with outdated anthropological "social structure" concepts, precisely "clan" identities, with their animal associations, were discussed with animation among Khanty and Seminoles during a 1998 workshop.

32. If the person doing a divination was already close to the family, as is likely, a pattern could have been noticed and projected onto the spirits. However, Taligina's interpretation hints at fascinating dimensions of Native Siberian concepts of spirit communication and suicide, worth comparing to Native American experiences and expertise (cf. Ridington 1988:287–91).

33. Compare Taussig (1987:111–26), who shows that intermarriage (or cohabitation) is no guarantor of benevolence, and who also discusses the ramifications of oil as well as rubber development in Colombia (176–77).

34. Variations on this story are repeated across Siberia and North America, as Native American friends confirm. On education across the North, see Kasten 1998; Darnell and Holm 1996.

35. On language issues, compare Vakhtin 1993:44–45; Jääsalmi-Krüger 1998:101–12; Pentikäinen 1997:89.

36. See Kravchenko 1996. Olga confirmed the continuity of her "kul'tur-antropologicheskaia" program during a reunion in 1997 in Moscow, but in

1998 I learned that funding was cut off. In the 1990s, Olga too had been able to travel to the American Southwest to study how Native American schools were teaching language and traditional culture. The poet Yuri Vella (1996:5–8; 1996a) has written movingly on the issue of losing linguistic richness.

37. My perspectives on education are formed through conversations at various local levels, as well as with former Russian Federation Minister of Education Edward Dmitrivich Dneprov, a family friend. See also Even activist and writer Andrei Krivoshapkin (1997).

38. In tears, she excused herself. Many of these school and apartment problems also came out more publicly, when our video group called the 1991 town meeting mentioned in the introduction.

39. Because of the personal nature of these quotes, I have not revealed the name or gender of the speaker, to whom I am deeply grateful for insights and friendship. This striking story of a possible shamanic cancer cure is similar to one I learned about in northern Sakha Republic (Balzer 1996:311) and another in the U.S. involving the tumor of a Native American friend, who is a healer and degree-holding psychologist.

40. In 1996, I saw such a cultural program in Northern British Columbia. Native American colleagues in Canada and Alaska explain that, when funds are available, people are experimenting with similar projects where families are widely dispersed. Some Siberian leaders propose more "low-tech" radio programs, followed by a traveling teacher to check student progress every several months.

41. Personal communication, March 1997. Uliana Vinokurova, originally from a mixed-ethnic village in the region of Srednaia Kolyma, is a member of the Sakha parliament (Il Tumen). She is known for strong advocacy of indigenous minority social programs. See also Balzer and Vinokurova 1996.

42. Compare Barth 1969; Comaroff 1985; Comaroff and Comaroff 1992; Marcus 1993. Sherry Ortner (1995:191) reminds: "One can only appreciate the ways in which resistance can be more than opposition, can be truly creative and transformative, if one appreciates the multiplicity of projects in which social beings are always engaged, and the multiplicity of ways in which those projects feed on as well as collide with one another."

Chapter Seven
The Tenacity of Ethnicity: Spirituality and Identity

1. This highlights some Khanty perceptions of difference, rather than denying ethnographic evidence of interpenetrating beliefs and cosmologies among Khanty, Mansi, and Nentsy. See Golovnev 1993, 1995; Kulemzin and Lukina 1992.

2. On life passage (or crisis) rituals in social context, see Turner 1967, 1979. On situational, nonbinding linkage of religious and ethnic identity, see Romanucci-Ross and De Vos 1995. See also Northernists Frederica de Laguna (1972), Ann Fienup-Riordan (1990, 1994), Robin Ridington (1988), E. Turner (1996), and the path-breaking volume on Amerindian reincarnation edited by Antonia Mills and Richard Slobodin (1994).

3. This was evident in 1985 at a Kiev conference on ethnicity, sponsored by the Soviet Academy of Sciences, during which public and private statements of Soviet ethnographers were particularly discrepant. Within two years, with celebrations for the Millennium of Christianity, Russians' and Ukrainians' own senses of ethnonational identities were more openly reintegrated with religion.

4. Although any analysis poses the risk of artificial imposition of order on complex ideologies and practices, my categories reflect explicitly defined areas in which Khanty consultants discussed data or in which I observed religious activity.

5. This conversation took place in my home, in March 1995. Realizing that he might sound too focused on the Khanty, Joseph added, "indeed it [the reincarnation soul] will exist as long as there are Northern people [falling silent] . . . indeed, as long as there are people. This is how human beings have souls." Compare Mills and Slobodin 1994; E. Turner 1996:125 on the interconnections of reincarnation souls and names.

6. Women say that babies will not stop crying unless their souls have been divined, and that even a Khanty girl with a Russian husband will try to have the soul of their newborn divined. Chernetsov, who did fieldwork in the 1930s through 1960s, explains that relatives invoked Khanty ancestors dead within memory, while attempting to lift the cradle. If the cradle stuck to the floor, and the baby stopped crying at the mention of a particular name, participants believed that the child had "taken hold in the direction of that name" (Chernetsov 1963:26).

7. Olga Balalaeva (personal communication, March 28, 1993). The divination was done by a middle-aged Khanty man known for special shamanic powers, Nikita Sopochin.

8. Even less common is tattooing for spiritual strength, although a few elderly women still have tatoos. In the 1940s and 1950s, some of the first young Kazym Khanty schoolchildren to leave their villages were given wood grouse (*vursik*) tatoos on their shoulders, to guard their souls, ensure well-being, and aid safe return (Chernetsov 1963:16, from N.F. Prytkova).

9. Compare Kulemzin and Lukina 1977:209; Kulemzin and Lukina 1992:14–17; and Balzer 1981. More general restrictions for women have been fading with each generation. Yet Nadezhda Taligina explained in 1993 that some prohibitions were indeed tied to menstruation, with its "impure" and "thick" blood, called *shockma*, literally, "heavy." Restrictions include not going into the sacred, male corner of the house (where ancestral images are kept), not stepping over objects related to hunting and fishing, not eating certain animals (bear meat, elk, pike), not participating in animal sacrifice rituals. Purification is with smoke and steam. Tatiana Moldanova in 1991 named similar restrictions, as well as the gesture of covering the face modestly with a scarf before male inlaws. She considered that such prohibitions stem from sexual avoidance tradition. Agrafina Sopochina in 1998 reminded me that men have their own restrictions. She intriguingly added that men doing poorly in hunting sometimes reversed convention by placing weapons where women might step over them.

10. Kulemzin and Lukina 1977:209; 1992:14–15. Compare Kleinman 1995: 214–22 on links between music and healing.

11. If the child was male, a bow and two arrows were tied to the basket, for

future hunting prowess. If the baby was female, household symbols, such as a mortar and pestle, were attached. The groves are the same as those where other lineage-related rituals for women occur, described below.

12. Compare Rombandeeva 1968:81 on Mansi with Kravchenko 1996:44 on Khanty. Kazym Khanty call the navel mother "pukn angki." A "godmother" and "godfather" are "piarna angki" and "piarna ashchi." A further "support mother" is "altym angki."

13. While isolation after birth in clinics or hospitals falls short of earlier Khanty norms, it is long (several weeks) by Western standards. For accounts of standardized Soviet birth and naming, see Kryvelev 1977:44; Feiffer 1973:228; and Lane 1981:68–73.

14. The personal nature of this powerful dream makes revealing the teller's name unwise, although I am very grateful to him. He has lived through enough in this life, including the murder of a brother, to have legitimate fears that he sometimes calms by sleeping with a bear skin.

15. Compare de Laguna 1972:779. Lydia Black (personal communication, 1980) suggests that "multiple souls" may be aspects of one soul. Yet they are separately named. Nonetheless, an Eastern Khanty man influenced by Russian Orthodoxy remarked to me in 1995: "If someone had many souls, then he'd be really sick. But we do say that shamans can see the seat of souls inside people in different places: the heart, the chest, and elsewhere."

16. My description of burial is written in the present tense, since patterns of "traditional" burial that I knew from the 1970s were confirmed in 1990s conversations. The description is schematic: readers should be aware that local variations and individual family decisions can change this generalized picture.

17. One friend said her just deceased father had come to her, and she felt an enormous heavy pulling: "it was as if his soul was reaching out to pull me with him." Relatives sometimes take precautions against the material soul's return by passing the body through a window, smoke hole, or threshold over which an iron knife is placed.

18. Sacrifice of horses or reindeer was sternly discouraged by collective authorities for pragmatic reasons. In the 1990s, people are often too poor to make such sacrifices, although the pace of other community animal sacrifice rituals has increased.

19. He complied after tragedies in his family turned him back to traditional spirituality. Unfortunately, premature deaths have become frequent in the 1990s; fear of these spiritually shattering trends may have turned some to observing rituals that they had been more casual about in the recent Soviet past.

20. Taking time off from work is easier with the demise of the collectives. Remarriage restrictions have remained strict, with one or two years considered liberal. Khanty rules earlier forbade remarriage until four or five years after the death of a spouse.

21. The quote is from a woman of Tegy in 1976. However, friends in Kazym in 1991 made similar statements.

22. Such identities are not usually discussed with outsiders. I later realized that the mirth may have been because she was identifying people by their opposite phratry, as I have learned occurred with at least two other ethnographers in

other villages. I do not here link any specific individuals with phratries or lineages, unless they have given specific permission for it.

23. Joseph Sopochin was referring to the Mansi writer Yuvan Shestalov, as well as others. Eastern Khanty stress lineages over Por and Mos identifications. Given the predominance of two exogamous phratries, it is valid to designate this as a moiety system. Phratry is more often used in the literature, however, especially since a third or fourth major social division has been documented in certain areas. Compare Chernetsov 1939; Chernetsov's letter to McKennan, February 8, 1966, quoted in de Laguna 1975:133–34; and Sokolova 1983.

24. Thus, the loyalties and taboos of Por descendants are linked to the bear, while those of Mos are connected with the sacred hare or goose. Cedar and larch trees are honored by at least some Por, who use their wood to make Por ancestral images. Birch was and is a sacred tree for the Mos. Nonetheless, an origin tale of "Mos'ne," a beautiful girl from an unpeopled village, depicts her as living in a cedar house with a larch door.

25. These quotes are from 1976 field notes. Local variations on these themes should be acknowledged. See also Kulemzin and Lukina 1992: 88–131.

26. In one version of phratry origins, the Sky God Numi-Torum saw that the groups were distinct, and so he gave them names and forbade the Mos to eat raw meat (Chernetsov 1939:21; cf. Gondatti 1887:64).

27. E.g., Chernetsov 1939:40–41. Long ago, the Sky God Numi-Torum told them that they must not live together, and so the Mos man made himself a wife out of a cedar log. His jealous sister eventually destroyed this wife and deceived her brother by wearing the cedar-wife's clothing. When the brother discovered her deception, he killed his newborn son and his sister-wife. From their blood grew the plant called *pori* (*Heracleum sibiricum*). A female bear then ate this plant and gave birth to the first human woman Por, who the Mos man was able legitimately to wed.

28. For detailed description of Khanty marriage ritual, see Balzer 1981; Kulemzin and Lukina 1992. A few symbolic aspects provide insights into patriarchal Khanty gender relations. During marriages up to the 1930s, wedding sheets with blood were displayed and then torn to bits by the bride's mother. This multipurpose signal announced to the community successful consummation, rid the household of virgin blood, and was a metaphor for the breakup of the household caused by the daughter's imminent departure. At a later party in the groom's home, the bride was expected to sit behind a curtain for as long as three days, in a truly liminal and ambiguous position (Balzer 1981:859–61). She emerged to begin work in her husband's household, where she was expected to cover her face with a long scarf before each of her male in-laws.

29. The friend who was speaking was Por. In the Kazym area, Mos predominates, and some say it is because the Por have not observed sacred tradition scrupulously enough. The secrecy of moieties may be a reaction in Soviet times to the demographic distortions: people are embarrassed to reveal that they have married the "wrong" mates.

30. Compare Chichlo 1981. One Kazym consultant said, "The old people say 'do not kill a cat or a frog—allow them to walk.'"

31. Data are from Khanty friends, from Kulemzin and Lukina 1992:93–102,

from Kulemzin 1984, and from conversations with the folklorist Olga Balalaeva. Juha Pentikäinen's *A Khanty Reindeer Sacrifice* (1991), does not show the crucial moment when the two deer are killed. Given the sacred nature of the ritual, led by the Eastern Khanty shaman-elder Ivan Stepanovich Sopochin, reticence is appropriate. The deer were consecrated to the youngest son of the Sky-God (white) and to the God of the Earth (black), on the Tromyugan, described as the most sacred place of the Khanty, the River of Torum.

32. Joseph Sopochin also mentioned that deer are sometimes consecrated to specific gods, designated to be sacrificed, and then killed at special ceremonies every seven years. Vladimir Kogonchin added that "the last major shaman" of the Ugut region, Yakov Nikitovich Umsanov, had died two years previously.

33. Compare Sokolova 1971a:216–17; 1990:58–72; 1991:241. I use "ancestral image," rather than the more loaded "idol." The treasured images sometimes rotated among their families of keepers; the Yu Khan Ob spot was already a sacred grove before the disruption at Yuilsk. For more on Ob-Ugrian sacred places, images, gods, and cosmology, see Kulemzin 1976; 1984; Kulemzin and Lukina 1992; Schmidt 1989; Gumuev 1989:179–87; 1990a, b; Novikova 1990:155–64; 1991:28–36; 1995:51–62; and Kuzakova 1994.

34. In 1997 a Khanty friend clarified that while the Goddess has renewed her good will to those who honor her, her actual image is held by a family in Eastern Khanty territory. Kazym activists are negotiating to get her back.

35. One of the signs of 'glasnost' for Northern Khanty was a small group performance of a bear festival in Hungary in 1991.

36. Kharuzhin (1905:147) reported that hunters said to the bear: "You must forgive me and not judge harshly, since, indeed, it was not I who killed you, but the Russians; from a Russian I received my gun, powder, and bullets. I have always loved and respected you, and to demonstrate this, I will organize a festival in your honor." Compare Sokolova 1976:74. In postwar Soviet years, Khanty in Tegy, Kazym, and Amnia let local Russians kill bears, avoiding Khanty obligation to hold rituals. Yet in winter 1975, joyful snow tossing to greet a bear occurred after a Kazym hunter killed one who had strayed too near the village. Accounts differed as to how much of the rest of the traditional ceremony was celebrated. Similarly, in Tegy in 1976, consultants confirmed that a seven-year periodic Por festival had been held the previous year.

37. The following description comes from watching many hours of uncut film footage shot at the festival by the Estonian Mark Soosaar, at the direction of Association for the Salvation of the Ugra leaders, especially Tatiana and Timofei Moldanov, to whom I am grateful for explanations. The twenty-eight cassettes were labeled "Days of National Culture: The Bear Festival." Another film was made in 1988 by the well-known Estonian filmmaker-ethnographer, later elected president of Estonia, Lennart Meri.

38. Comparative data come from consultants, from tapes of parts of a Tegy bear festival, and from notes and photos in the Finnish National Museum's superb U.T. Sirelius and K. Karjalainen ethnographic collections. Chernetsov (1963:28; 1968:104) was convinced that the once-every-seven-years Por phratry ceremonies were initiatory, and indeed, a play called *Enacting the Death of a Youth* depicted initiations of young boys, who died and were reborn after learning about the ancestral identity of the bear (cf. Gondatti 1887b:84).

39. Consultants' descriptions, combined with an extraordinarily well-documented record from various Khanty areas since the nineteenth century, have allowed me to collect accounts of about seventy dramas. Sources include Gondatti 1887b; Dunin-Gorkavich 1911:55–56; Shukhov 1916, 1916a; Shulz 1924; Karjalainen 1927; Startsev 1928; Kannisto 1938–39; Chernetsov 1968; and Sokolova 1976.

40. These plays continue themes of reversals. The last was seen by Dunin-Gorkavich (1911:54–55) and Karjalainen (1927:215); the second by Gondatti (1887:83) and Karjalainen (1927:218); and the first by Gondatti (1887:83). On the (shamanic) mushroom (*Amanita muscaria*) and vodka concoction, Gondatti noted: "One does not just get drunk. One loses all sense of where one is; one walks into a river or lake, throws oneself into a fire, falls out of trees, and in general does a whole line of illegal things for which it is necessary later to pay."

41. For more on the gender and role reversal dimensions of these fascinating plays, see Balzer 1996. The rites of reversal resemble carnival rituals in symbolism and function (cf. Babcock 1978:13–36). They not only enable a cathartic structure within which to return to the status quo (Norbeck 1974:6) but also can generate an atmosphere through which to create or record change and restlessness (Zemon Davis 1975:130–31; Turner 1977b:69; Bakhtin 1975:484–95).

42. After being summoned by the family of a sick patient, she attempted a cure using a wand and a bucket—to no avail. The angry head of the family then chased her from his house, amidst general laughter. Sokolova (1976: 60–68) witnessed this festival in a predominantly Mansi village. Her presence, or that of other Russians, might have encouraged public adherence to Soviet positions. Audience mirth probably came from political nuances and double entendre that Russian officials missed, as often happened in non-Russian Soviet theaters. Yet these plays should be seen as part of the changing dynamics of bear satires. See also Stites (1989:100), who describes "the muting of the carnival laugh in public ritual" as "gradual and never complete." Other propaganda settings for bear festivals include films made in the 1960s and 1970s and excerpted festival plays performed at secularized winter games.

43. In 1976, I learned of a secret, spontaneous festival held in Kazym in winter 1975. It lasted five nights, since the bear was a full-grown male. (Festivals for female bears lasted four.) Khanty residents were alerted to the festival when celebrants gathered at their doors throwing snow. The bear was brought into the house of the main hunter through the front door, although traditionally it would have been passed through a window or smoke hole to avoid the impure front ("women's") half of the house. After the bear was placed on a cradle of birch bark in the sacred back corner, its skin and head were stuffed with hay, and it was decorated with jewelry, coins, trinkets, and a birch-bark snout cover. At dusk, food offerings of fish, bread, nuts, and baked goods in the shape of foxes and reindeer surrounded the bear, illuminated by candlelight. Each arrival kissed the bear and, bowing, made donations of food, wine, and vodka, which participants later consumed. During the dances, cooked bear meat was eaten, but the bulk of it was smoked after the festival by the men. A male elder presided, seated on the sacred left side of the bear, the side with the heart (cf. Hertz 1960; Needham 1973). Women covered their faces with scarves and danced. "Male hunters took the main roles. . . . It was forbidden to sleep during performances, even though they lasted all night" (Kazym participant).

44. Children were exhorted to turn in their parents for "anti-Soviet" behavior, as had the Russian child-hero Pavel Morozov. Having written on the history of Soviet repression of shamans, I focus here on updating main arguments and data. See also Balzer 1987, 1993, 1996, 1997.

45. Compare Shirokogoroff 1935:393; Balzer 1983:65; 1987; Siikala and Hoppál 1992; Basilov 1992.

46. "Séance" is used as the most appropriate translastion for *kamlanie* and does not have the negative connotations sometimes attributed to it through association with turn-of-the-century European spiritualists. The séance was witnessed by the ethnographer Startsev (1928:94–97), who claimed that the shaman entered a "trance"on the second night. Startsev unfortunately was more concerned about the shaman's negotiation of a reindeer as payment for the séance than he was about the cosmology and ideology behind the séance or whether the child got well. Compare Karjalainen 1927:310–15.

47. This séance was not only witnessed but commissioned by the ethnographer Shatilov (1931:112–29), who seems to have gained the respect of the local Khanty.

48. In the Sakha Republic (Yakutia), shamanic practices have reemerged more forcefully. I have worked with the daughter of a great shaman, Konstantin-*oiun*, who encouraged her to become a Moscow-trained surgeon. In the 1990s, she has integrated shamanic healing into her very successful practice (Balzer 1996:310).

Conclusions
A Siberian Saga in Global Perspective

1. Compare Verdery 1996 and Hann and Dunn 1996. My French colleague Roberte Hamayon defends her confident focus on ethnology as a science by calling it post-postmodernism. I attempt here a balance of reflexivity and multidimensional descriptive text. The phenomenology-based reflexivity that has become integral to sociology and anthropology is crucial for understanding that "of all of the oppositions that artificially divide social science, the most fundamental, and the most ruinous, is the one that is set up between subjectivism and objectivism" (Bourdieu 1990:25).

2. Compare Watson 1994; Verdery 1996; Drobizheva et al. 1996; and former minister of nationalities Tishkov (1997).

3. Compare Bitterli 1989:5, 132. "Rebellion" or "revolt" are terms of a hegemon, while "freedom fight" is from the view of those struggling, and "revolution" is for when they have won.

4. An example is the Ob River diversion project, in which Central Asians finally lost out to the ecological and economic interests of West Siberians (and Soviet citizens in general) in the Gorbachev period.

5. Agrafina Sopochina, at the meeting hosted by the Seminoles of Florida, introduced herself as Khanty from the Eastern Khanty obshchina of Khanto. Her presentation distinguished four main groups in Western Siberia: "traditional aboriginals, aboriginals converted to 'civilized' [ways of life], mixed Tatar-Russians, and newcomers [Russian and Ukrainian] arrived since 1967 oil and gas discoveries."

6. Compare my edited volume featuring indigenous ethnographers of the Russian Federation (Balzer 1994) with Shnirelman 1996. Outsider ethnographers should remember we are writing to be read (sooner or later) by some members of the indigenous groups that hosted us. Methodological and textual sensitivity is also encouraged by Khanty activists such as Agrafina Sopochina, who has written a "Codex of Honesty for the Scientist-Humanist"(1997 MS, my files).

7. Compare Arutiunov 1978:3–14; Guboglo 1993; and Vakhtin 1993:44–49 on bilingualism. The emotion-tinged term "mother tongue" reveals a widespread linkage of language, (cognatic) descent, and ethnicity.

8. In a 1997 electronic mail exchange with me, the German indigenous-rights activist Johannes Rohr expressed concern about a perceived Khanty elite "intraethnic paternalism" regarding "endangered species," "traditionalist" Khanty of the camps suffering from energy industry incursions.

9. Yugoslavia and Sri Lanka are only two of our most recent cases. See De Vos and Romanucci-Ross 1995:356–60. Compare Smith 1981; Kapferer 1988; Tambiah 1989; Petro 1990, 1995; Ramet 1992; Keane 1995:194–95.

10. My cynical spouse, Harley Balzer, suggests that the researcher then becomes like a squirrel, running up, down, and around the trunk and branches, frantically gathering nut-nuggets of data before the whole tree is cut down by development-oriented Soviets or energy executives.

11. Perry (1996) discusses similar processes in the collision of "indigenous peoples and state systems." However, focus on state systems should be supplemented with attention to smaller regional and wider international ramifications. Neo-Marxists Burbach, Nuñez, and Kagarlitsky (1997:156), in their well-titled *Globalization and Its Discontents* put full blame on world capitalism. But indigenous leaders themselves often have more nuanced views of what groups or processes are oppressing them. In West Siberia, home-grown energy industrialists are more exploitive than outsiders, who in a few cases (e.g., Amoco, the World Bank) have taken up indigenous-rights causes.

12. Compare Bruce Grant (1995), who reminds us of Sakhalin Native nostalgia in economically desperate times. My Kazakh student Asel Tulenova calls *Homo sovieticus* "stillborn."

13. See Richard Fox (1995:5), citing Varena Stolcke on *Homo xenophobicus*. Given the huge range of causes in the Russian-Chechen conflict, Tishkov has perhaps exaggerated the significance of arrogant "ethnic entrepreneurs," a term widely applied in the anthropology of recent Yugoslav and African tragedies. Among the first to use "ethnic entrepreneur" was my colleague at Georgetown Gwen Mikell and Carnegie Endowment for Peace president David Hamburg.

14. See especially H. Balzer (1996:300–303). This broadly defined "civic society" differs from more narrow definitions of "civil society," widespread in Eastern European usage, that focus on the development of informal interest-group associations. See also Keane 1988; Cohen and Arato 1992; Hall 1995; Levada 1996. To review relative degrees of democratic changes and "authoritarian reactions" in post-Soviet states, see political scientists Dawisha and Parrott 1997.

15. This story comes from Yuri Vella (personal communication, 1997), who explained he really did not want to organize another demonstration and wor-

ried that authorities would call his bluff. Vella's comment about the land deed comes from the ethnographer Natasha Novikova, to whom I am very grateful for hosting our meeting.

16. I realize the Americas also have their variations on colonial themes and mean no disrespect to my professors at the University of Pennsylvania and Bryn Mawr College, all of whom have left strong imprints.

17. My Sakha colleague Uliana Vinokurova probed about perceived weaknesses of pan-Indian organization, since she sees comparable problems in pan-Siberian group action, which she feels is critical for indigenous survival. Khanty leader Agrafina Sopochina was more philosophical about the difficulties of united action in both Siberia and North America.

18. After writing this, I found it reinforced in Appadurai 1997:11: "globalization is not the story of cultural homogenization." Anthropological histories of transnational relations have come from many sources with many styles (e.g., Wolf 1982; Herzfeld 1987; Bitterli 1989; Friedman 1995; Mintz 1996).

19. Compare Kerttula 1996 and the Jesup North Pacific Expedition classic Bogaras [Bogaraz] (1909). Major differences in history and cultural practices among Siberian peoples must be considered in any analysis. Some Westerners have been overly influenced by English-language stereotypes of Siberians and by Soviet propaganda.

20. Balzer 1995a. Compare Jochelson 1910; and Gogolev et al. 1975. In 1998, the Yukagir won a long-fought battle in the Sakha Republic parliament, which passed a bill legalizing their homeland in the Kolyma region, called Suk Tiul. Data on the Yukagir come from 1990s interviews and friendships, including with the Yukagir linguist and leader Gavril Kurilov. See also the Yukagir writer Semen Kurilov (1983) and the Chukchi writer Yuri Rytheu (1983:215–16).

21. Compared to some regional governments, Sakha Republic authorities are in a potentially better position to legally help their indigenous minorities. Indications include the establishment of the Eveno-Bytantaisk Region in 1989. However, abolishing a special Ministry of Minority Affairs within the republic was a step in the opposite direction. A highly schematized continuum depicting degrees of Sovietization and Russification for various Siberian (including Far East) groups would place the Khanty somewhere near the center and the Sakha and Yukagir at either end of the spectrum.

References

Aberle, David

1972 A Note on Relative Deprivation Theory as Applied to Millenarian and Other Cult Movements. *In* Reader in Comparative Religion, ed. W. Lessa and E. Vogt, 3d ed., 527–31. New York: Harper and Row.

Abrahamian, Levon

1993–94 The Secret Police as a Secret Society. Anthropology and Archeology of Eurasia 32(2):12–23.

Abramov, N. A.

1854 Materialy dlia istorii Khristianskogo prosveshcheniia Sibiri (Material on the history of the Christian enlightenment of Siberia). Zhurnal Ministerstva Narodnogo Prosveshcheniia 81(5):15–56.

1857 Opisanie Berezovskogo Kraia (Notes on the Berezovo Region). Zapiski Russkogo Geograficheskogo Obshchestva 12:329–50.

1857a Ob Ostiakskikh Kniaz'iakh (About Ostiak princes). Tobol'skie gubernskie vedomosti 24:217.

Adelman, Fred

1960 Kalmyk Cultural Renewal. Philadelphia Anthropological Society Bulletin 13(3):36–38.

Aipin, Eremei

1989 Ne neft'iu edinoi (Not by oil alone). Moskovskie novosti (January 8):8–9.

1989a Na perelome: krugli stol (At the breaking point: Round table). Sovetskaia kul'tura (February 11):3.

1989b Tundra: Kak pomoch' narodnostiam Severa sokhranit' etnicheskuiu kul'tury (Tundra: How to help peoples of the North keep their ethnic culture). Izvestiia (June 15):4.

1990 Khanty, ili Zvezda Utrennei Zari (Khanty, or Star of the Morning Dawn). Moscow: Molodaia Gvardia.

1990a Vedenie: O gnezdyshke odinokom (Introduction: On a lonely nest). Literaturnaia Arktika (4):24.

1991 Idet bezzastenchivyi grabezh (Shameless theft is rampant). Severnye prostory (January):3.

Aleksandrov, A.

1897 Pesni, zapisiannykh v Eniseiskom Okruge (Songs, recorded in the Yenisei Region). Zhivaia starina 7:101–5.

Aleksandrov, V. A.

1964 Russkoe naselenie Sibiri XVII-nachala XVIIIv (The Russian population of Siberia, 17th–early 18th centuries). Moscow: Akademiia Nauk.

Ames, Michael M.

1957 Reaction to Stress: A Comparative Study of Nativism. Davidson Journal of Anthropology 3(1):17–30.

1964 Magical-Animism and Buddhism: A Structural Analysis of the Sinhalese Religious System. *In* Religion in South Asia, ed. E. Harper, 21–52. Seattle: Asian Society.

Anderson, Benedict

1991 Imagined Communities: Reflections on the Origin and Spread of Nationalism. London: Verso. [1983].

Anderson, David G.

1996 Bringing civil society to an uncivilised place: citizenship regimes in Russia's Arctic frontier. *In* Civil Society: Challenging Western Models, ed. Chris M. Hann and Elizabeth Dunn, 99–120. London: Routledge.

Andreeva, K. S.

1962 Kul'turnoe stroitel'stvo v Sibiri v 1917–1960 (Cultural construction in Siberia in 1917–60). *In* Sibir' v Periode Stroitel'stva sotsializma i perekhoda k kommunizmu, 154–69. Novosibirsk: Akademiia Nauk.

Anisimov, Arkadii F.

1969 Obshchee i osobennoe v razvitie obshchestva i religii narodov Sibiri (The general and specific in societal development and religion of the peoples of Siberia). Leningrad: Nauka.

Ankudinov, N., and A. Dobriev

1939 Shamany obmanshchiki (Shamans as deceivers). Leningrad: Akademiia Nauk.

Anokhin, A. V.

1927 Burkhanizm v Zapadnom Altai (Burkhanism in West Altai). Sibirskie ogni. (5):162–167.

Anonymous [Grigorovskii, N.?]

1859 Ocherk Vasiuganskogo tundry (A Note on the Vasyugan tundra). Zhurnal Ministerstva Vnutrennikh Del 37 (Combined issue):1–10.

Appadurai, Arjun

1996 Modernity at Large: Cultural Dynamics of Globalization. Minneapolis: University of Minnesota Press.

Appadurai, Arjun, ed.

1988 The social life of things: Commodities in cultural perspective. Cambridge: Cambridge University Press.

Armstrong, Terence E.

1965 Russian Settlement in the North. Cambridge: Cambridge University Press.

Arutiunian, Iu. V., and Iu. V. Bromlei

1986 Sotsial'no kul'turnyi oblik Sovetskikh natsii (The social cultural character of the Soviet nations). Moscow: Nauka.

Arutiunov, Sergei A.

1978 Bilingvism i bikul'turalism (Bilingualism and biculturalism). Sovetskaia etnografiia (1):3–14.

1989 Narody i kul'tury: razvitie i vzaimodeistvie (Peoples and cultures: Growth and interaction). Moscow: Nauka.

1997 The Russian Empire and Its Typological Analogies (Idle Thoughts Looking at the World Map). Acta Slavica Iaponica 15:130–36.

Avvakum

1960 Zhitiie protopopa Avvakuma im samim napisannoe i drugie ego sochineneniia (The life of archpriest Avvakum by himself and other of his writings), ed. N. K. Gudzii. Moscow: Khudozhestvennaia Literatura. [Mid–1600s].

Babcock, Barbara A., ed.
1978 The Reversible World: Symbolic Inversion in Art and Society. Ithaca: Cornell University Press.

Babkin, A. M., and E. A. Levashov
1975 Slovar' nazvanii zhitelii SSSR (Dictionary of the names of the peoples of the USSR). Moscow: Russkii Iazyk.

Bailey, F. G.
1995 The Civility of Indifference: On Domesticating Ethnicity. Ithaca: Cornell University Press.

Bakhrushin, S. V.
1929 Sibirskie tuzemtsy pod Russkoi vlast'iu do revolutsii 1917 (Siberian natives under Russian rule before the 1917 revolution). Sovetski Sever pervyi sbornik statei 1:66–97.
1935 Ostiatskie i Vogulskie kniazhestva v XVI-XVII vekakh (Ostiak and Vogul princedoms in the 16th–17th centuries). Leningrad: Institut Narodov Severa.

Bakhtin, Mikhail Mikhailovich
1975 Voprosy literatury i estetiki: Issledovaniia raznykh let (Questions of literature and aesthetics: Researches of various years). Moscow: Khudozhestvennaia Lit. [1920s, 1930s].

Balikci, Asen, and Mark Badger
1992 Siberian Seminar. Cultural Survival 10(4):68–71.

Balzer, Harley David, ed.
1991 Five Years That Shook the World: Gorbachev's Unfinished Revolution. Boulder: Westview.
1995 Russia's Missing Middle Class: The Professions in Russian History. Armonk, N.Y.: M. E. Sharpe.

Balzer, Marjorie Mandelstam
1980 The Route to Eternity: Cultural Persistence and Change in Khanty Burial Ritual. Arctic Anthropology 17:77–90.
1981 Rituals of Gender Identity: Markers of Siberian Khanty Ethnicity, Status and Belief. American Anthropologist 83(4):850–67.
1982 Peoples of Siberia. *In* Guide to the Study of the Soviet Nationalities, ed. S. Horak, 239–52. Littleton, Col.: Libraries Unlimited.
1983 Doctors or Deceivers? The Siberian Khanty Shaman and Soviet Medicine. *In* The Anthropology of Medicine, ed. Lola Romanucci-Ross, Daniel Moerman, and Lawrence Tancredi, 54–76. South Hadley: Bergin/Praeger.
1983a Ethnicity without Power: Siberian Khanty in Soviet Society. Slavic Review 42(4):633–48.
1985 On the Scent of Gender Theory and Practice: Reply to Child and Child. American Anthropologist 87:128–30.
1987 Behind Shamanism. Social Science and Medicine 24 (12):1085–93.
1990 Nationalism in the Soviet Union: One Anthropological View. Journal of Soviet Nationalities 1(3):4–32.

1992 Dilemmas of the Spirit: Religion and Atheism in the Yakut-Sakha Republic. *In* Religious Policy in the Soviet Union, ed. Sabrina Ramet, 231–51. Cambridge: Cambridge University Press.
1994 From ethnicity to nationalism: Turmoil in the Russian mini-Empire. *In* The Social Legacy of Communism, ed. James Millar and Sharon Wolchik, 56–88. Cambridge: Cambridge University Press.
1994a Siberiaki. *In* Encyclopedia of World Cultures, ed. Paul Friedrich, 6:331–32. Boston: Hall.
1995a Homelands, Leadership and Self-Rule: Interethnic Relations in the Russian Federation North. Polar Geography 19(4):284–305.
1996 Flights of the Sacred: Symbolism and Theory in Siberian Shamanism. American Anthropologist 98(2):305–18.
1997 *Review of* Dennis A. Bartels and Alice L. Bartels, When the North Was Red: Aboriginal Education in Soviet Siberia (Quebec: McGill-Queen's University Press). American Ethnologist 24(1):328–29.

Balzer, Marjorie Mandelstam, ed.
1995 Culture Incarnate: Native Ethnography in Russia. Armonk, N.Y.: M. E. Sharpe.

Balzer, Marjorie Mandelstam, and Uliana A. Vinokurova
1996 Nationalism, Interethnic Relations and Federalism: The Case of the Sakha Republic (Yakutia). Europe-Asia Studies 48(1):101–20.

Bartels, Dennis A., and Alice L. Bartels
1995 When the North Was Red: Aboriginal Education in Soviet Siberia. Quebec: McGill-Queen's University Press.

Bartenev, Victor
1896 Na Krainem Severo-Zapade Sibiri: Ocherki Obdorskogo Kraia (In the Extreme North of Siberia: Essays on Obdorsk Region). Saint Petersburg: M. F. Paikina.

Barth, Frederik, ed.
1969 Ethnic Groups and Boundaries. Boston: Little, Brown.

Basilov, Vladimir
1992 Shamanstvo u narodov Srednei Azii i Kazakhstana (Shamanism among peoples of Central Asia and Kazakhstan). Moscow: Nauka.

Basso, Keith, and Henry A. Selby, eds.
1976 Meaning in Anthropology. Albuquerque: University of New Mexico Press.

Beliajeff, A. S.
1980–81 Articles and Books Relating to the Old Orthodox. Cahiers du Monde russe et soviétique 21(1):109–21; 22(4):489–90.

Bennett, John
1975 The New Ethnicity. Proceedings of the American Ethnological Society. Saint Paul: West.

Benson, Susan
1981 Ambiguous Ethnicity: Interracial Families in London. Cambridge: Cambridge University Press.

Berkhofer, Robert F., Jr.
1978 The White Man's Indian: Images of the American Indian from Columbus to the Present. New York: Knopf.

Billington, James H.
1970 The Icon and the Axe: An Interpretive History of Russian Culture. New York: Random House. [1966].
1975 Neglected figures and features in the rise of the Raskol. *In* Russia and Orthodoxy: Essays in Honor of Georges Florovsky, ed. A. Blaine, 2:189–206. The Hague: Mouton.

Bitterli, Urs
1989 Cultures in Conflict: Encounters between European and Non-European Cultures, 1492–1800. Trans. and intro. Ritchie Robertson. Cambridge: Polity Press.

Bloch, Alexia
1998 Ideal Proletarians and Children of Nature: Evenki Reimagining Schooling in a Post-Soviet Era. *In* Bicultural Education in the North, ed. Eric Kasten, 139–58. Münster: Waxmann Verlag.

Boarshinova, A. Ia., and V. I. Shunkov
1968 Prisoedinenie Sibiri k Russkomu Gosudarstvu (The joining of Siberia to the Russian state). *In* Istoriia Sibiri, ed. A. P. Okladnikov, et al., 2:25–41. Leningrad: Nauka.

Bochner, Stephen, ed.
1982 Cultures in Contact: Studies in Cross-Cultural Interaction. Oxford: Pergamon.

Bogaraz, Vladimir G. [Bogaras, Waldemar; Bogaraz-tan, Vladimir].
1909 The Chukchee. Memoirs of the American Museum of Natural History, 11. New York: Stechert and Co. [Jesup North Pacific Expedition, 7].
1922 O pervobytnykh plemenakh (On primitive tribes). Zhizn' natsional'nostei (1):130.
1923 Ob izuchenii i okhrane okrainnykh narodov; Predlozhenie k voprosu (On the study and protection of border peoples; A proposal concerning the issue). Zhizn' natsional'nostei 3–4:168–80.
1932 Religiia, ka tormoz sootsstroitel'stva sredi malykh narodnostei Severa (Religion as a break on development among the small peoples of the North). Sovetskii Sever 1–2:142–57.

Boitsova, A. F.
1971 Shkola narodov krainego Severa (The school of the peoples of the far North). *In* Osushchestvlenie Leninskoi natsional'noi politiki u narodov krainego Severa, ed. I. S. Gurvich, 141–58. Moscow: Akademiia Nauk.

Bolshakov, M. A.
1936 Problemy osedaniia kochevogo naseleniia (Problems of settling the nomadic population). Sovetskaia Arktika 5:14–24.

Bourdieu, Pierre
1990 The Logic of Practice. Trans. Richard Nice. Stanford: Stanford University Press. [1980].

Braudel, Fernand
1973 Capitalism and Material Life 1400–1800. New York: Harper and Row.

Brem, Alexander
1897 Ostiaki-idolpokloniki (Ostiak idol worshipers). Ezhemesiachnyia literaturnyia prelozheniia k Nive 2:347–83.

Bremmer, Ian
1997 Post-Soviet nationalities theory: past, present, and future. *In* New States, New Politics: Building the Post-Soviet Nations, ed. I. Bremmer and R. Taras, 3–26. Cambridge: Cambridge University Press.

Brodnev, M.
1936 Iz chuma v kul'turnoe zhilishche (From the tent to cultured quarters). Sovetskaia Arktika 3:104–5.

Bromlei, Iulian V.
1973 Etnos i etnografiia (Ethnos and ethnography). Moscow: Akademiia Nauk.
1983 Ocherki teorii etnosa (Notes on the theory of ethnos). Moscow: Akademiia Nauk.
1984 Theoretical Ethnography. Moscow: Nauka Foreign Publ.
1987 Etnosotsial'nye protsessy: teoriia, istoriia, sovremennost' (Ethnosociological processes: theory, history, and modernity). Moscow: Nauka.

Bromlei, Iulian V., ed.
1977 Sovremennye etnicheskie protsessy v SSSR (Modern ethnic processes in the USSR). Moscow: Akademiia Nauk.

Brown, Jennifer S.
1980 Informants in the archives: doing Anthropology through Historical Documents. The Journal of Anthropology 2(2):138–46.

Buckley, Thomas, and Alma Gottlieb, eds.
1988 Blood Magic: The Anthropology of Menstruation. Berkeley: University of California Press.

Budarin, M. E.
1952 Proshloe i nastoiashchee narodov Severo-Zapadnoi Sibiri (The past and present of the peoples of Northwest Siberia). Omsk: Oblastnoe Izdat.
1964 Syn plemin Neniangov (Son of the Neniang tribe). Sverdlovsk: Oblastnoe Izdat.
1968 Put' malykh narodov Krainogo Severa k kommunismu (The path of the small peoples of the Far North to communism. Omsk: Zapadno-Sibirskoe Knizhnoe Izdat.
1968a Byli o Sibirskikh Chekistakh (Tales of the Siberian Cheka). Omsk: Zapadno-Sibirskoe Knizhnoe Izdat.

Burbach, Roger, Orlando Nuñez, and Boris Kagarlitsky
1997 Globalization and Its Discontents: The Rise of Postmodern Socialisms. London: Pluto.

Businskii, P. N.
1893 Kreshchenie Ostiakov i Vogulov pre Petre I (Christianization of Ostiak and Vogul under Peter I). Kharkov: Gub. Pravleniia.
1899 Zaselenie Siberia i byt ee pervykh nasel'nikov (The settlement of Siberia and the life of its first settlers). Kharkov: Gub. Pravleniia.

Butinova, M. S.
1973 Kul't kargo v Melanezii (The cargo cult in Melanesia). Sovetskaia etnografiia 1:81–92.

Case, David
1984 Alaska Natives and American Laws. Anchorage: University of Alaska Press.
Castille, George, and Gilbert Kushner, eds.
1981 Persistent Peoples: Cultural Enclaves in Perspective. Tuscon: University of Arizona Press.
Castrén, M. A.
1858 Etnograficheskie zamechaniia i nabliudeniia o Lopariakh, Karelakh, Samoedakh, i Ostiakakh (Ethnographic remarks and observations about Lapps, Karelians, Samoyeds, and Ostiaks). Etnograficheskii sbornik Russkogo geograficheskogo obshchestva, vyp. 4:219–320.
Chatterjee, Partha
1993 The Nation and Its Fragments: Colonial and Postcolonial Histories. Princeton: Princeton University Press.
Cheah, Pheng, and Bruce Robbins, eds.
1998 Cosmopolitics: Thinking and Feeling beyond the Nation. Minneapolis: University of Minnesota Press.
Chebotarevksii, A.
1930 Kul'turnye bazy komiteta severa (Culture bases of the Committee of the North). Sovetskii Sever 1:117–24.
Chernetsov, Valeri Nikolaevich.
1939 Fratrial'noe ustroistvo Obsko-Ugorskogo obshchestva (Phratry organization in Ob-Ugrian society). Sovetskaia etnografiia (2):20–41.
1947 K istorii rodovogo stroia u Obskikh Ugrov (Toward the history of Ob-Ugrian clan structure). Sovetskaia etnografiia sbornik 6–7.
1963 Ideas of the Soul among Ob-Ugrians. *In* Studies in Siberian Shamanism, ed. Henry Michael; trans. Ethel Dunn and Stephen Dunn. Anthropology of the North 4:3–45. Toronto: University of Toronto Press. [Orig. pub. as Predstavleniia o Dushe u Obskikh Ugrov, in Trudy Instituta Etnografiia 51 (1959):114–59].
1968 Periodicheskie obriady i tseremonnye u Obskikh Ugrov, sviazannye s medvedem (Periodic rituals and ceremonies of the Ob-Ugrians, connected with the bear). Congressus Secundus Internationalis Fenno-Ugristarium. Part 2. Acta Etnologica, 102–11. Helsinki: Societas Fenno-Ugrica.
Chernetsov, Valeri Nicholaevich and Wanda Moszynska
1974 Prehistory of West Siberia. Trans. David Kraus. Anthropology of the North 9, ed. Henry Michael. Toronto: Arctic Institute. [1953].
Chichlo, Boris
1981 L'ours-chamane. Études mongoles 12:35–112.
1987 Histoire de la formation des territoires autonomes chez les peuples turco-mongoles de Sibérie. Cahiers du monde russe et soviétique 28(3–4):361–402.
1990 Pervaia pobeda "malykh narodov" (First victory of the "small peoples"). Strana i mir 5 (September-October):108–12.
1994 Deux visages du séparatisme Sibérien. Revue des Études Slaves 66(1): 165–78.

1998 Korennye narody Sibiri i Rossiia: Osobennosti otnoshenii (Native peoples of Siberia and Rossiia: Specifics of relations). *In* Quest for Models of Coexistence, ed. K. Inoue and T. Uyama, 3–37. Sapporo: Hokkaido University Press.

Chikin, S. Ia., A. V. Sergeev, and K. I. Akulov

1979 Zdravookhranennie v Sibiri i na Dal'nem Vostoke (Healthcare in Siberia and the Far East). Moscow: Meditsina.

Child, Alice B., and Irvin L. Child.

1985 Biology, Ethnocentrism, and Sex Differences. American Anthropologist 87:125–28.

Chvyr', Liudmilla A.

1996 Notes on the Ethnic Self-Awareness of the Uighur. Anthropology and Archeology of Eurasia 34(3):48–68.

Clemhout, Simone

1964 Typology of Nativistic Movements. Man 64:14–15.

Clifford, James

1988 The Predicament of Culture: Twentieth-Century Ethnography, Literature, and Art. Cambridge, Mass.: Harvard University Press.

Cohen, Abner, ed.

1974 Urban Ethnicity. London: Tavistock.

Cohen, Jean L. and Andrew Arato

1992 Civil Society and Political Theory. Cambridge, Mass.: MIT Press.

Cohen, Ronald

1978 Ethnicity: Problem and Focus in Anthropology. Annual Reviews in Anthropology 7:379–403.

Comaroff, Jean

1982 Medicine: symbol and ideology. *In* The Problem of Medical Knowledge: Examining the Social Construction of Medicine, ed. Peter Wright and Andrew Treacher, 49–65. Edinburgh: Edinburgh University Press.

1985 Body of Power, Spirit of Resistance: The Culture and History of a South African People. Chicago: University of Chicago Press.

Comaroff, Jean and John Comaroff

1992 Ethnography and the Historical Imagination. Chicago: University of Chicago Press.

Comrie, Bernard

1981 The Languages of the Soviet Union. Cambridge: Cambridge University Press.

Connelly, Violet

1975 Siberia Today and Tomorrow: A Study of Economic Problems and Achievements. New York: Taplinger.

Connor, Walker

1994 Ethnonationalism: The Quest for Understanding. Princeton: Princeton University Press.

Cooley, Frances

1983 National Schools in the Yakutskaya ASSR: Some Language Issues. *In* Soviet Education in the 1980s, ed. J. J. Tomiak, 278–305. New York: St. Martin's.

Crummy, Robert O.
1970 The Old Believers and the World of Antichrist. Madison: University of Wisconsin Press.
Czaplicka, M. A.
1914 Aboriginal Siberia: A Study in Social Anthropology. Oxford: Clarendon.
Davis, Natalie Zemon
1975 Society and Culture in Early Modern France. Stanford: Stanford University Press.
Dawisha, Karen, and Bruce Parrott, eds.
1997 Democratic Changes and Authoritarian Reactions in Russia, Ukraine, Belarus, and Moldova. Cambridge: Cambridge University Press.
Deak, Istvan
1992 Beyond Nationalism: A Social and Political History of the Habsburg Officer Corps (1848–1918). Oxford: Oxford University Press.
Dean, Bartholomew, and Jerome M. Levi, eds.
2000 At the Risk of Being Heard: Identity, Indigenous Rights and Post-Colonial States. Ann Arbor: University of Michigan Press. (Forthcoming).
Deloria, Philip
1998 Playing Indian. New Haven: Yale University Press.
Deloria, Vine, Jr.
1969 Custer Died for Your Sins: An Indian Manifesto. New York: Macmillan.
Deloria, Vine, Jr., and Clifford Lytle
1984 The Nations Within: The Past and Future of American Indian Sovereignty. New York: Pantheon.
Denisenko, Vasili Semenovich
1957 Na dalekii pivnochi (In the far regions). Kiev: Molod'. (In Ukrainian.)
Despres, Leo
1975 Ethnicity and Resource Competition in Plural Societies. The Hague: Mouton.
D'iachkov, V. I.
1979 Sostoianie i perspektivy razvitiia zdravookhraneniia v Iamalo-Nentskom i Khanty-Mansiiskom Avtonomnykh Okrugakh Tumenskoi Oblasti (Condition and perspectives on the growth of health care in the Iamal-Nenets and Khanty-Mansiiski Autonomous Districts of the Tiumen Region). Zdravookhranenie Rossiiskoi Federatsii 4:20–24.
Diamond, Larry, and Marc F. Plattner, eds.
1994 Nationalism, Ethnic Conflict, and Democracy. Baltimore: Johns Hopkins University Press.
Diószegi, Vilmos
1968 Tracing Shamans through Siberia. Trans. Antia Rajkay Babo. Oosterhout, The Netherlands: Anthropological Publications. [1960].
1978 Pre-Islamic Shamanism of the Baraba Turks and Some Ethnogenetic Conclusions. *In* Studies in Siberian Shamanism, trans. S. Simon, ed. V. Diószegi and M. Hoppál, 83–167. Budapest: Akademiai Kiado.

Dmitriev-Mamonov, A. I.
1884 Iuridicheskie obychai Beriozovskogo okruga (Legal customs of Berezovo district). *In* Pamiatnaia knizhka Tobol'skoi Guberniia na 1884, ed. A. I. Dmitriev-Mamonov and K. M. Golodnikov. Tobol'sk: Tobolsk Gub. Pravleniia Tip.

Dmitriev-Mamonov, A. I., and K. M. Golodnikov, eds.
1884 Pamiatnaia knizhka Tobol'skoi Guberniia na 1884 (Tobolsk record book). Tobolsk: Gub. Pravleniia Tip.

Dolgikh, Boris O.
1962 On the Origins of the Nganasan: Preliminary Remarks. *In* Studies in Siberian Ethnogenesis, trans. Gregory Jacoby, ed. H. N. Michael, 220–99. Anthropology of the North 2. Toronto: Toronto University Press. [Orig. pub. in Russian, 1952].

Dougherty, Janet W. D., and James W. Fernandez, eds.
1981 Symbolism and Cognition. American Ethnologist 8(3).

Douglas, Mary
1966 Purity and Danger: An Analysis of Concepts of Pollution and Taboo. New York: Praeger.
1967 The Meaning of Myth, with Special Reference to "La Geste d'Asdiwal." *In* The Structural Study of Myth and Totemism, ed. E. Leach, 49–67. London: Tavistock.
1975 Implicit Meanings: Essays in Anthropology. London: Routledge and Kegan Paul.

Drobizheva, Leokadiia M.
1981 Dukhovnaia obshchnost' narodov SSSR (Spiritual community among the peoples of the USSR). Moscow: Mysl'.

Drobizheva, Leokadia M., ed.
1994 Natsional'noe samosoznanie i nationalism v Rossiiskoi Federatsii nachala 1990-x godov (National consciousness and nationalism in the Russian Federation, early 1990s). Moscow: Akademiia Nauk.

Drobizheva, L. M., A. P. Aklaev, V. V. Koroteeva, and G. U. Soldatova
1996 Demokratizatsiia i obrazy natsionalizma v Rossiiskoi Federatsii 90-kh godov (Democratization and images of nationalism in the Federation of Rossiia, 1990s). Moscow: Mysl'.

Drobizheva, L., R. Gottemoeller, C. Kelleher, L. Walker, eds.
1996 Ethnic Conflict in the Post-Soviet World: Case Studies and Analysis. Armonk, N.Y.: M. E. Sharpe.

Dunin-Gorkavich, A. A.
1904, 1910–11Tobol'skii Sever (The Tobolsk North). 3 vols. Tobolsk: Gub. Pravleniia Tip.

Edmonson, Munro S.
1960 Nativism, Syncretism and Anthropological Science. Middle American Research Institute 19:181–204. New Orleans: Tulane.

Eklof, Ben
1986 Russian Peasant Schools. Berkeley: University of California Press.

Eley, Geoff, and Ron G. Suny, eds.
1996 Becoming National. Oxford: Oxford University Press.

Eliade, Mircea
1974 Shamanism: Archaic Techniques of Ecstasy. Princeton: Princeton University Press.

Eliasov, L. E., and I. E. Tarnevskii
1969 Fol'klor Kazakov Sibiri (Folklore of the Cossacks of Siberia). Ulan Ude, Rossiia: Akademiia Nauk.

Engelhardt, Alexander Platonovich
1899 A Russian Province in the North. Philadelphia: Lippincott. [1894].

Eriksen, Thomas Hylland
1993 Ethnicity and Nationalism: Anthropological Perspectives. London: Pluto.

Esman, Milton J.
1994 Ethnic Politics. Ithaca: Cornell University Press.

Espiritu, Aileen
1997 "Aboriginal Nations": Natives in Northwest Siberia and Northern Alberta. *In* Contested Arctic: Indigenous Peoples, Industrial States and the Circumpolar Environment, ed. Eric Alden Smith and Joan McCarter, 41–67. Seattle: University of Washington Press.

Fedotov, G. P.
1966 The Russian Religious Mind. Vol. 2. Cambridge, Mass.: Harvard University Press.

Feiffer, George
1973 Our Motherland. New York: Viking Press.

Felinska, Ewa
1853 Revelations of Siberia. 2 vols. London: Colburn.

Fernandez, James W., ed.
1991 Beyond Metaphor: The Theory of Tropes in Anthropology. Stanford: Stanford University Press.

Feshbach, Murray
1995 Ecological Disaster: Cleaning Up the Hidden Legacy of the Soviet Regime. New York: Twentieth Century Fund Press.

Fienup-Riordan, Ann
1990 Eskimo Essays: Yup'ik Lives and How We See Them. New Brunswick: Rutgers University Press.
1994 Boundaries and Passages: Rule and Ritual in Yu'pik Eskimo Oral Tradition. Norman: University of Oklahoma Press.

Filipenko, Aleksandr V.
1996 Mozhno li razmorozit' arkticheskuiu politiku? (Can we freeze arctic politics?) Severnye prostory 3–4:1–3. (Interview by Natalia Novikova).

Finsch, Otto, and A. E. Brem
1882 Puteshestvie v Zapadnuiu Sibir (Travels in West Siberia). Moscow: M. S. Lavrov.

Firth, Raymond
1963 Offering and Sacrifice: Problems of Organization. Journal of the Royal Anthropological Institute 93(1):12–24.
1964 Essays on Social Organization and Value. London: Athalone Press for University of London.

1981 Spiritual Aroma: Religion and Politics. American Anthropologist 83(3):582–601. (Distinguished Lecture for 1980).

Fischer, Michael M. J.

1979 Iran: From Religious Dispute to Revolution. Cambridge, Mass.: Harvard University Press.

Fishman, Joshua

1977 Language and Ethnicity. *In* Language, Ethnicity and Intergroup Relations, ed. H. Giles, 13–57. London: Academic Press.

Fondahl, Gail

1995 The Status of Indigenous Peoples in the Russian North. Post-Soviet Geography 36(4):215–24.

1997 Siberia: assimilation and its discontents. *In* New States, New Politics: Building the Post-Soviet Nations, ed. I. Bremmer and R. Taras, 190–232. Cambridge: Cambridge University Press.

Forsyth, James

1992 A History of the Peoples of Siberia: Russia's North Asian Colony 1581–1990. Cambridge: Cambridge University Press.

Fox, Richard

1995 The Breakdown of Culture. Current Anthropology 36(1):1–13.

Fox, Richard, ed.

1991 Recapturing Anthropology: Working in the Present. Santa Fe: School of American Research Press.

Fried, Morton H.

1987 Reflections on Christianity in China. American Ethnologist 14(1):94–106.

Friedman, Jonathan

1994 Cultural Identity and Global Process. London: Sage.

Gadamer, Hans-Georg

1976 Philosophical Hermeneutics. Trans. and ed. David E. Linge. Berkeley: University of California Press.

Geertz, Clifford

1968 Islam Observed: Religious Development in Morocco and Indonesia. Chicago: University of Chicago Press.

1973 The Interpretation of Cultures: Selected Essays. New York: Basic Books.

1980 Negara: The Theatre State in Nineteenth Century Bali. Princeton: Princeton University Press.

Gellner, Ernest

1983 Nations and Nationalism. Oxford: Basil Blackwell.

1993 What do we need now? Social anthropology and its new global context. Times Literary Supplement (July 16): 3–4.

1994 Encounters with Nationalism. Oxford: Basil Blackwell.

1994a Conditions of Liberty: Civil Society and Its Rivals. London: Penguin.

Gerasimov, V. N.

1909 Obdorsk. Tiumen: Tiumen Izdat.

Gerlach, Luther P., and Virginia H. Hine

1970 People, Power, Change. Indianapolis: Bobbs-Merrill.

Gibson, James. R.

1969 Feeding the Russian Fur Trade. Madison: University of Wisconsin Press.

Giles, H., R. Y. Bourhis, and D. M. Taylor

1977 Towards a Theory of Language in Ethnic Group Relations. *In* Language, Ethnicity and Intergroup Relations, ed. H. Giles, 307–48. London: Academic Press.

Gioseffi, Daniela, ed.

1993 On Prejudice: A Global Perspective. New York: Anchor.

Gleach, Frederic W.

1997 Powhatan's World and Colonial Virginia: A Conflict of Cultures. Lincoln: University of Nebraska Press.

Gogolev, Z., I. Gurvich, I. Zolatareva, and M. Zhornitskaia

1975 Yukagiry (istoriko-etnograficheskii ocherk) (Yukagirs: An historical-ethnographic study). Novosibirsk: Nauka.

Golovnev, Andrei V.

1993 The Khanty Living World. Anthropology and Archeology of Eurasia 32(2):74–92.

1995 Govoriashchie kul'tury: traditsii Samodiitsev i Ugrov (Talking Cultures: Samodeic and Ugrian Traditions). Ekaterinburg: Akademiia Nauk.

Gondatti, N. L.

1887 Kul't medvedia u Zapadnoi-Sibirskoi inorodstev (The bear cult among West-Siberians). Trudy Obshchestva Estestvenii Nauk Antropologii i Etnografii 8:74–87.

1887a Sledy Iazycheskikh Verovanii U Manzov (Traces of pagan belief among the Mansi). Trudy Obshchestva Estestvenii Nauk Antropologii i Etnografii 8:49–73.

Goodenough, Ward

1963 Cooperation in Change. New York: Russell Sage Foundation.

1965 Rethinking "Status" and "Role": Toward a General Model of the Cultural Organization of Social Relationships. *In* The Relevance of Models for Social Anthropology, ed. Michael Banton, 1–20. London: Tavistock.

1971 Culture, Language and Society. Reading, Mass.: Addison-Wesley.

Graham, Loren R.

1974 Science and Philosophy in the Soviet Union. New York: Vintage.

Grant, Bruce

1995 In the Soviet House of Culture: A Century of Perestroikas. Princeton: Princeton University Press.

Grenoble, Lenore A., and Lindsay J. Whaley, eds.

1997 Endangered Languages: Current Issues and Future Prospects. Cambridge: Cambridge University Press.

Grigorovskii, N.

1879 Kresti'ian-Starozhily Narimskogo Kraia (Peasant-Old-Style-Livers of the Narimsk Region). Zapiski Zapadno-Sibirskogo Otdela Imperiatorskogo Russkogo Geograficheskogo Obshchestva, kn.1:1–28.

1884 Opisanie Vasiuganskoi tundri (Notes on the Vasyugan tundra). Zapiski Zapadno-Sibirskogo Otdela Imperiatorskogo Russkogo Geograficheskogo Obshchestva, Kn.6:1–68.

Gryzlov, V. F.

1982 Rastsvet i sblizhenie sotsialisticheskikh natsii (Flourishing and merging of socialist nations). Nauchnyi kommunizm 59(5):9–17.

Guboglo, Mikhail N.

1984 Sovremennye etnoiazykovye prostessy v SSSR (Modern ethnolinguistic processes in the USSR). Moscow: Nauka.

1993 Mobilizovannii lingvisizm (Mobilized linguistic awareness). Moscow: Akademiia Nauk.

Gudkov, I. S., and V. V. Senkevich

1940 Sotsializm v bytu Khantov (Socialism in the life of the Khanty). Sovetskaia etnografiia 4:78–99.

Gufstafson, Thane

1983 The Soviet Gas Campaign. Santa Monica: Rand.

Gumuev, Izmael N.

1990 Mirovozzrenie Mansi: Dom i Kosmos (Mansi worldview: House and cosmos). Novosibirsk: Nauka.

1990a Mirovozzrenie Finno-Ugorskikh narodov (Finno-Ugrian peoples' worldview). Novosibirsk: Nauka.

Gumuev, I. N., and A. M. Sagalaev

1986 Religiia Naroda Mansi (Religion of the Mansi people). Novosibirsk: Nauka.

Gurvich, Ilya S.

1971 Printsipy Leninskoi natsional'noi politiki i primenie ikh na krainem Severa (Principles of Leninist national politics and the application of them in the Far North). *In* Osushchestvlenie Leninskoi natsional'noi politiki u narodov krainego Severa, ed. I. S. Gurvich, 9–41. Moscow: Nauka.

Gurvich, I. S., ed.

1975 Etnogenez i etnicheskaia istoriia narodov Severa (Ethnogenesis and the ethnic history of the peoples of the North). Moscow: Nauka.

1980 Etnogenez narodov Severa (Ethnogenesis of the peoples of the North). Moscow: Nauka.

1985 Etnokul'turnye protsessy u narodov Sibiri i Severa (Ethnocultural processes among the peoples of Siberia and the North). Moscow: Nauka.

Gushchin, Nikolai Iakovlevich, ed.

1980 Kul'turnoe razvitie Sovetskoi Sibirskoi derevni (Cultural growth of the Soviet Siberian village). Novosibirsk: Nauka.

Hajdu, Peter

1963 The Samoyed Peoples and Languages. Uralic and Altaic Series, 63. Bloomington: Indiana University Press.

Hall, John A., ed.

1995 Civil Society: Theory, History and Comparison. Cambridge: Polity Press.

Hallowell, A. Irving

1926 Bear Ceremonialism in the Northern Hemisphere. American Anthropologist 28:1–175.

1967 Culture and Experience. New York: Schocken. [1955].

Hamayon, Roberte

1990 La chasse à l'âme: Esquisse d'une théorie du chamanisme sibérien. Nanterre: Société d'Ethnologie.

Handler, Richard

1988 Nationalism and the Politics of Culture in Quebec. Madison: University of Wisconsin Press.

Hann, Chris M., and Elizabeth Dunn, eds.

1996 Civil Society: Challenging Western Models. London: Routledge.

Harkin, Michael, and Sergei Kan, eds.

1996 Native American Women's Responses to Christianity. Ethnohistory 43(4). (Special issue).

Harva (Holmberg), Uno

1964 Finno-Ugric and Siberian Mythology. Mythology of All Races, 4. New York: Cooper Square. [1927].

Hefner, Robert W., ed.

1992 Conversion to Christianity: Historical and Anthropological Perspectives on a Great Transformation. Berkeley: University of California Press.

Hertz, Robert

1960 Death and the Right Hand. Glencoe: Free Press. [192?].

Herzfeld, Michael

1989 Anthropology through the Looking-Glass: Critical Ethnography in the Margins of Europe. Cambridge: Cambridge University Press. [1987].

1997 Cultural Intimacy: Social Poetics in the Nation-State. London: Routledge.

Hobsbawm, Eric

1990 Nations and Nationalism since 1780: Programme, Myth, Reality. Cambridge: Cambridge University Press.

Hoppál, Mihály

1995 Approaches to Mansi Mythology. *In* Vogul Folklore collected by Bernát Munkácsi, ed. Otto J. von Sadovsky and Mihály Hoppál, 185–206. Budapest: Akademiai Kiado.

Hroch, Miroslav

1985 Social Preconditions of National Revival in Europe: A Comparative Analysis of the Social Composition of Patriotic Groups among the Smaller European Nations. Cambridge: Cambridge University Press.

Hugh-Jones, Stephen

1994 Shamans, Prophets, Priests and Pastors. *In* Shamanism, History, and the State, ed. Nicholas Thomas and Caroline Humphrey, 32–75. Ann Arbor: University of Michigan Press.

Humphrey, Caroline

1983 The Karl Marx Collective: Economy, Society and Religion in a Siberian Collective Farm. Cambridge: Cambridge University Press.

1991 "Icebergs," Barter, and the Mafia in Provincial Russia. Anthropology Today 7:8–13.

Humphrey, Caroline, with Urgunge Onon
1996 Shamans and Elders: Experience, Knowledge, and Power among the Daur Mongols. Oxford: Oxford University Press.

Hunt, Eva
1977 The Transformation of the Hummingbird: Cultural Roots of a Zinacantecan Mythical Poem. Ithaca: Cornell University Press.

Hymes, Dell
1979 The Religious Aspects of Language in Native American Humanities. *In* Essays in Humanistic Anthropology: A Festschrift in Honor of David Bidney, ed. B. T. Grindal and D. M. Watten, 83–114. Washington: University Press of America.

Iadrintsev, Nikolai Mikhailovich
1891 Sibirskie inorodtsy: ikh byt i sovremennye polozhenie (Siberian natives: Their life and modern condition). Saint Petersburg: Sibiriakov.

Iag'ia, N. S.
1980 Zdorov'e naseleniia Severa (Health of the population of the North). Leningrad: Meditsina.

Iakobii, Arkhady Ivanovich, Brother
1893 Ugasanie inorodcheskikh plemen severa (Annihilation of native northern tribes). Doklad Russkogo Obshchestva okhraneniia narodnogo zdraviia. Saint Petersburg: Doma Prizrieniia.
1895 O missionerskom stane v strane Nadym (On the missionary outpost at Nadym). Tobolsk: Tobol'skaia Eparkhial'naia Bratstva.

Iakubovskaia, S. I.
1972 Razvitie SSSR kak soiuznogo gosudarstva 1922–1936 (The growth of the Soviet Union as a unified state). Moscow: Nauka.

Irvine, Judith T., ed.
1993 Edward Sapir's The Psychology of Culture. Berlin: Mouton de Gruyter.

Ivanov, S. V.
1963 Ornament narodov Sibiri (Ornamentation of the peoples of Siberia). Moscow-Leningrad: Akademiia Nauk.

Jääsalmi-Krüger, Paula
1998 Khanty Language in Lower School Education: First Language or Second Language? *In* Bicultural Education in the North, ed. Erich Kasten, 101–12. Münster: Waxmann Verlag.

Jarvie, I. C.
1983 The Problem of the Ethnographic Real. Current Anthropology 24(3): 313–25.

Jenkins, Richard
1997 Rethinking Ethnicity: Arguments and Explorations. London: Sage.

Jennings, Theodore
1982 On Ritual Knowledge. Journal of Religion 62(2):111–27.

Jochelson, Vladimir [Waldemar] I.
1910 The Yukaghir and the Yukaghirized Tungus. Memoirs of the American Museum of Natural History, 12. New York: Stechert and Co. [Jesup North Pacific Expedition, 9].

Kakovkin, Grigorii
1998 Kto na trube (Who is on the pipeline)? Izvestiia (July 14):4.
Kan, Sergei
1989 Symbolic Immortality: The Tlingit Potlatch of the Nineteenth Century. Washington: Smithsonian Institution.
1998 Memory Eternal: Tlingit Culture and Russian Orthodox Christianity through Two Centuries. Seattle: University of Washington Press.
Kan, Sergei, ed.
1987 Native Cultures and Christianity in Northern North America. Arctic Anthropology 24(1):1–68.
Kannisto, Arturri
1938–39 Vogulien karhumenoista: Les fêtes de l'ours chez les Vogouls. Journal de la Société Finno-ougrienne 50:1–39.
Kapferer, Bruce
1988 Legends of People, Myths of State: Violence, Intolerance and Political Culture in Sri Lanka and Australia. Washington: Smithsonian Institution.
Karjalainen, K. F.
1921, 1922, 1927 Die Religion der Jugra-Völker. 3 vols. Folklore Communications, 41, 44, 63. Porvoo: Finnish Academy of Sciences.
Kartsov, V. G.
1937 Ocherk Istorii Narodov Severo-Zapadnoi Sibiri (Essay on the history of the peoples of Northwest Siberia). Moscow-Leningrad: Gos. Sots.-Ekonomicheskoe Izdat.
Kasten, Erich, ed.
1998 Bicultural Education in the North. Münster: Waxmann Verlag.
Kazmina, Olga E., and Pavel I. Puchkov
1994 Osnovy etnodemografii (Foundations of ethnodemography). Moscow: Nauka.
Keane, John
1994 Nations, Nationalism and European Citizens. *In* Notions of Nationalism, ed. S. Periwal, 182–207. Budapest: Central European University Press.
Keane, John, ed.
1988 Civil Society and the State: New European Perspectives. London: Verso.
Kerezsi, Ágnes
1993 The Eastern-Khanty Shamanism (In Light of the Activity of a Genuine Shaman, Leonid Mikhaliovits Sopotsin). *In* Shamanism and Performing Arts, ed. Mihály Hoppál and Pal Paricsy, 97–107. Budapest: Academy of Sciences.
Kerttula, Anna
1996 Antler on the Sea: Chukchi, Yupik and Newcomer in the Soviet North. Doctoral dissertation, Department of Anthropology, University of Michigan.
Keyes, Charles
1976 Toward a New Formulation of the Concept of Ethnic Group. Ethnicity 3:202–13.

Keyes, Charles, ed.
1981 Ethnic Change. Seattle: University of Washington Press.
Kendall, Laurel
1996 Korean Shamans and the Spirit of Capitalism. American Anthropologist 98(3):512–27.
Kharuzin, Nikolai
1905 Etnografiia: Lektsiia chitannyia v Imperatorskom Moskovskom Universitet, IV (Ethnography: Lectures read at the Imperial Moscow University, 4). Saint Petersburg: Gosudarsvennoe Izdat.
Khazanov, Anatoly M.
1995 After the USSR: Ethnicity, Nationalism, and Politics in the Commonwealth of Independent States. Madison: University of Wisconsin Press.
Khomich, L. V.
1976 Problemy etnogeneza i etnicheskoi istorii Nentsev (Problems of ethnogenesis and ethnic history of the Nentsy). Leningrad: Akademiia Nauk.
Khrapal', A. A.
1937 K resheniiu problemy osedaniia kochevykh kolkhozov (Toward a solution to the problem of settling the nomadic kolkhozniks). Sovetskaia Arktika 12:26–32.
Khvatai, K. F., and A. M. Obatin
1958 Bukvar' Khanteiskogo Iazyka (Khanty language primer). Leningrad: Prosveshchenie.
Kiselev, L. E.
1974 Ot Patriarkhal'shchiny k sotsializmu: Opyt KPSS po sotsialisticheskomu preobrazovaniiu v natsial'nykh raionokh Severa (From patriarchalism to socialism: The Communist experiment in socialist upbringing in national regions of the North). Sverdlovsk: Sredne-Uralskoe Knizhnoe Izdat.
Kleinman, Arthur
1995 Writing at the Margin: Discourse between Anthropology and Medicine. Berkeley: University of California Press.
Klepikov, V.
1967 Kochevnikov na Kazyme net (Nomads do not exist on the Kazym). Sibirskie ogni (4):141–45.
Kleshchenok, I. N.
1968 Narody Severa i Leninskaia natsional'naia politika v deistvii (The peoples of the North and Lenin national politics in action). Moscow: Vysshaia Shkola.
Klibanov, Aleksandr I.
1982 History of Religious Sectarianism in Russia (1860s–1917). Trans. Ethel Dunn; ed. Stephen P. Dunn. Oxford: Pergamon.
Koester, David
1997 Childhood in National Consciousness and National Consciousness in Childhood. Childhood 4(1):125–42.

Kokosov, N. M., V. I. Nikulin, and V. I. Kharin
1955 Khanty-Mansiiskii Natsional'nyi Okrug (Khanty-Mansi National District). Sverdlovsk: Akademiia Nauk.

Kolarz, Walter
1954 The Peoples of the Soviet Far East. New York: Praeger.

Kolesnikov, Aleksandr D., ed.
1982 Opisanie Tobol'skogo namestnichestva (Tobolsk administrative records). Novosibirsk: Nauka.

Kopylov, D. I., ed.
1994 Sud'by narodov Ob-Irtyshskogo Severa (The fates of the peoples of the Ob-Irtysh North). Tiumen': Oblastnoe Izdat.

Kopylov, D. I., and V. F. Retunskii
1965 Bor'ba partiinykh organizatsii kraia za kollektivizatsiiu sel'skogo khozaistva i nastuplenie sotsializma po vsemu frontu (The struggle of the regional party organization for collectivization of agriculture and the offensive of socialism on all fronts). *In* Ocherki istorii partiinoi organizatsii Tiumenskoi oblasti, ed. D. A. Smorodinsokov, 141–76. Sverdlovsk: Sredne-Ural'skoe Knizhnoe Izdat.

Kopytoff, Igor
1964 Classification of Religious Movements: Analytic and Synthetic. *In* Symposium on New Approaches to the Study of Religion, Proceedings of the American Ethnological Society, ed. June Helm, 77–90. Seattle: University of Washington Press.

Kornilov, Aleksei Mikhailovich
1828 Zamechaniia o Sibiri (Remarks on Siberia). Saint Petersburg: K. Kraiia.

Kosarev, Mikhail F.
1984 Zapadnaia Sibir' v drevnosti (West Siberia in antiquity). Moscow: Nauka.

Koshelev, Ia.
1930 Integralnaia kooperatsiia v sisteme vsekhokhotsoiuza (Integral cooperatives in the system of voluntary unions). Sovetskii Sever 1:108–16.

Kostrov, Nikolai (Prince)
1873 Narimskii Krai. Tomskie gubernskie vedomosti, vyp. 1, 3, 5.
1875 Sostoiania zhenshchin mezhdu inorodnami Tomskoi Gubernii (The condition of women among Tomsk region natives). Tomskie gubernskie vedomosti., vyp. 24–27, 29–31, 33–34.

KPSS S"ezd
1981 26th Communist Party Congress. Vol. 3. Moscow: Politizdat.

Krader, Lawrence
1954 Buryat Religion and Society. Southwestern Journal of Anthropology 10:322–51.
1956 A Nativistic Movement in Western Siberia. American Anthropologist 58:282–92.
1978 Shamanism: Theory and History in Buryat Society. *In* Shamanism in Siberia, ed. V. Diószegi and M. Hoppál; trans. S. Simon, 181–233. Budapest: Akademiai Kiado.

Kravchenko, Ol'ga
1996 Kem stanet vnuk Velikogo Okhotnika (Who will a great hunter's grandson become)? Severnye prostory (3–4):44–47.
Kriazhkov, V. A., ed.
1994 Status malochislennykh narodov Rossii: Pravovye akty i dokumenty (The status of minority peoples of Rossiia: Legal acts and documents). Moscow: Iuridicheskaia Literatura.
Kriukov, Mikhail V.
1989 Etnichnost', bez'etnichnost', etnicheskaia nepreryvnost' (Ethnicity, lack of ethnicity, ethnic continuity). Rasi i narody 19. Moscow: Nauka.
Krivoshapkin, Andrei V.
1997 The Indigenous Peoples in the North: Is There a Way Out? Trans. I. Vinokurov. Yakutsk, Rossiia: Severoved.
Kroeber, Alfred L.
1948 Culture Patterns and Processes. New York: Harcourt Brace and World.
1966 An Anthropologist Looks at History. Berkeley: University of California Press.
Kroeber, Karl, ed.
1994 American Indian Persistence and Resurgence. Durham: Duke University Press.
Krupnik, Igor
1993 Arctic Adaptations: Native Whalers and Reindeer Herders of Northern Eurasia. Trans. and ed. Marcia Levenson . Hanover: University Press of New England.
Kruzhikov, M. I., ed.
1967 Narodnoe khoziaistvo Tiumenskoi oblasti (Tiumen region economics). Omsk: Statistika.
Kryvelev, I. A.
1977 Sovremennye obriady i rol' etnograficheskoi nauki v ikh izuchenii, formirovanii i vnedrenii (Modern rituals and the role of ethnographic science in their study, formation, and inculcation). Sovetskaia etnografiia (5):36–45.
Kulemzin, Vladislav M.
1976 Shamanstvo Vasiugansko-Vakhovskikh Khantov, konets XIX-nachalo XXvv (Shamanism of the Vasyugan-Vakh Khanty, late 19th to early 20th century). *In* Iz istorii shamanstva, ed. N. V. Lukina, 3–154. Tomsk: Tomsk Universitet.
1984 Chelovek i priroda v verovaniiakh Khantov (Person and nature in Khanty beliefs). Tomsk: Tomsk Universitet.
Kulemzin, Vladislav M., and Nadezhda V. Lukina.
1977 Vasiugansko-vakhovskie Khanty v kontse XIX-nachale XXvv. Etnograficheskie ocherki (Vasyugan-Vakh Khanty at the end of the nineteenth and beginning of the twentieth centuries: Ethnographical essays). Tomsk: Tomsk Universitet.
1992 Znakom'tes': Khanty (Introducing the Khanty). Novosibirsk: Nauka.

Kuoljok, Kerstin Eidlitz

1985 The Revolution in the North: Soviet Ethnography and Nationality Policy. Stockholm: Almqvist and Wiksell.

Kurilov, Semen

1983 Khanido i Khalerkha. Trans. from Yukagir to Russian by P. Palekhova. Moscow: Sovremennik.

Kuzakova, E. A.

1994 Fol'klor Mansi (Mansi folklore). Moscow: Akademiia Nauk.

La Barre, Weston

1971 Materials for a History of Studies of Crisis Cults: A Bibliographic Essay. Current Anthropology 12(1):3–44.

de Laguna, Frederica

1972 Under Mount St. Elias: The History and Culture of the Yakutat Tlingit. 3 vols. Smithsonian Contributions to Anthropology 7. Washington: Smithsonian Institution.

1975 Matrilineal Kin Groups in Northwest North America. *In* Proceedings of the North Athapaskan Conference 1971, ed. F. de Laguna, 1:17–145. Ottawa: National Museum of Canada.

Lane, Christel

1981 The Rites of Rulers: Ritual in Industrial Society—The Soviet Case. Cambridge: Cambridge University Press.

Lantzeff, George V.

1943 Siberia in the Seventeenth Century: A Study of the Colonial Administration. University of California Publications in History, 30. Berkeley: University of California Press.

Lantzeff, George V., and Richard A. Pierce

1973 Eastward to Empire: Exploration and Conquest on the Russian Open Frontier to 1750. Montreal: McGill-Queen's University Press.

Leach, Edmund

1976 Culture and Communication: The Logic by which symbols are connected. Cambridge: Cambridge University Press.

Leete, Art

1998 The Kazym Uprising: The West Siberian Peoples' Struggle for Freedom in the 1930s. Shaman 6(2):171–78.

Leonov, N. I.

1929 Tuzemnye sovety v taige i tundre (Native soviets in the taiga and tundra). *In* Sovetskii Sever pervyi sbornik statei, 200–18. Moscow: Proletarskoe Slovo.

Levada, Yuri A.

1996 Civic Culture. *In* Russian Culture at the Crossroads: Paradoxes of Postcommunist Consciousness, ed. Dmitri N. Shalin, 299–312. Boulder: Westview.

Lévi-Strauss, Claude

1967 Structural Anthropology. Trans. Claire Jacobson and Brooke Grundfest Schöepf. New York: Anchor Books. [1958].

1975 The Raw and the Cooked. New York: Harper and Row.[1964].

Levin, Michael D., ed.
1993 Ethnicity and Aboriginality: Case Studies in Ethnonationalism. Toronto: University of Toronto Press.

Lewin, Moshe
1968 Russian Peasants and Soviet Power: A Study of Collectivization. Trans. Irene Nove. Evanston: Northwestern University Press.
1974 Political Undercurrents in Soviet Economic Debates: From Bukarin to the Modern Reformers. Princeton: Princeton University Press.
1977 The Social Background of Stalinism. *In* Stalinism: Essays in Historical Interpretation, ed. R. C. Tucker, 111–36. New York: Norton.

Limerick, Patricia Nelson
1987 The Legacy of Conquest: The Unbroken Past of the American West. New York: Norton.
1997 Has "Minority" History Transformed the Historical Discourse? Perspectives 35(8):1, 32–36.

Limón, José
1991 Representation, Ethnicity, and the Precursory Ethnography: Notes of a Native Anthropologist. *In* Recapturing Anthropology: Working in the Present, ed. Richard Fox, 115–36. Santa Fe: School of American Research.

Lindgren, Ethel
1938 An Example of Culture Contact without Conflict: The Reindeer Tungus and Russian Cossacks of Northwest Manchuria. American Anthropologist 40:605–21.

Lineton, Philip
1978 Soviet Nationality Policy in North Western Siberia: A Historical Perspective. Development and Change 9:87–102.

Linton, Ralph
1943 Nativistic Movements. American Anthropologist 45:230–40.

Loshak, B., ed.
1970 Obnovlenaia Iugra (Ugrian renewal). Sverdlovsk: Sredne-Ural'skoe Izdat.

Lukina, I. V.
1985 Istoricheskie formy i preemstvennost' v traditsionnoi kul'ture vostochnykh khantov (Historical forms and their continuity in the traditional culture of the Eastern Khanty). Moscow: Universitetskoe Izdat.
1985a Formirovanie material'noi kul'tury Khantov (The formation of the material culture of the Khanty). Tomsk: Universitetskoe Izdat.

Luks, K. Ia.
1930 Institut Narodov Severa, ego mesto i zadachi (The Institute of the Peoples of the North, its place and tasks). Sovetskii Sever 1(1):130–36.

Lutz, Catherine A., and Lila Abu-Lughod, eds.
1990 Language and the Politics of Emotion. Cambridge: Cambridge University Press.

Maikov, L. N.
1869 Velikorusskie zaklinaniia (Great Russian incantations). Zapiski Imper-

atorskogo Russkago Geograficheskogo Obshchestva po otdeleniiu etnografii (2):417–580, 747–48.

Mancall, Peter C.

1995 Deadly Medicine: Indians and Alcohol in Early America. Ithaca: Cornell University Press.

Manson, S. M.

1982 New Directions in Prevention among American Indian and Alaska Native Communities. Portland: Oregon Health Sciences University.

Marcus, George E., ed.

1993 Perilous States: Conversations on Culture, Politics, and Nation. Chicago: University of Chicago Press.

Marcus, George E., and Michael M. J. Fischer

1986 Anthropology as Cultural Critique: An Experimental Moment in the Human Sciences. Chicago: University of Chicago Press.

Martin, Calvin, ed.

1987 The American Indian and the Problem of History. Oxford: Oxford University Press.

Martin, Janet

1986 Treasure in the Land of Darkness: The Fur Trade and Its Significance for Medieval Russia. Cambridge: Cambridge University Press.

Marx, Karl

1963 Karl Marx: Selected Writings in Sociology and Social Philosophy, ed. T. B. Bottomore and M. Rubel; trans. T. B. Bottomore. Harmondsworth: Penguin Books.

Massell, Gregory

1974 The Surrogate Proletariat: Moslem Women and Revolutionary Strategies in Soviet Central Asia, 1919–1929. Princeton: Princeton University Press.

Maybury-Lewis, David

1997 Indigenous Peoples, Ethnic Groups and the State. Boston: Allyn and Bacon.

Mazurenko, G. A.

1961 Torzhestvo natsional'noe politiki Kommunisticheskoi Partii na Obskom Severe (The triumph of the national politics of the Communist Party in the Ob North). Tiumen': Tiumen Izdat.

Mazzini, Giuseppé

1907 The Duties of Man and Other Essays. London: J. M. Dent and Sons.

McAuley, Mary

1997 Russia's Politics of Uncertainty. Cambridge: Cambridge University Press.

McClellan, David

1973 Karl Marx: His Life and Thought. London: Macmillan.

Medvedev, D. F.

1931 O rabote sredi tuzemnoi bednoty i batrachestvo na Tobolskom Severe (On work among the native poor and servants in the Tobolsk North). Sovetskii Sever 2(1):47–49.

Merrill, William

1988 Rarqmuri Souls: Knowledge and Social Process in Northern Mexico. Washington: Smithsonian Institution.

Mikhailov, A. P.

1936 Pervyi itogi raboty s natsional'nym naseleniem (First data on work with the national population). Sovetskaia Arktika (9):31–39.

Miller [Müller], Gerhard Friedrich

1787 Opisanie Sibirskogo Tsarstva (Notes on the Siberian tsardom). Saint Petersburg: Imp. Akademiia Nauk. [1750].

1937, 1941 Istoriia Sibiri (History of Siberia). 2 vols. Moscow-Leningrad: Akademiia Nauk. [1763].

Miller, Marc, ed.

1993 State of the Peoples: A Global Human Rights Report on Societies in Danger. Boston: Beacon, for Cultural Survival.

Mills, Antonia, and Richard Slobodin, eds.

1994 AmerIndian Rebirth: Reincarnation Belief Among North American Indians. Toronto: University of Toronto Press.

Minenko, Nina Adamova

1975 Severo-Zapadnaia Sibir' (Northwest Siberia). Novosibirsk: Nauka.

Mintz, Sidney W.

1996 Tasting Food, Tasting Freedom. Boston: Beacon.

Moldanova, S. P., main compiler

1983 Slovar' khantyisko-russkii i russko-khantyiskii (Khanty-Russian, Russian-Khanty dictionary). Leningrad: Prosveshchenie.

Moldanova, Tatiana

1990 O gnezdyske odinokom (On a lonely nest). Literaturnaia Arktika (4):24–28.

1993 Khantyiskie pesni (Khanty songs). *In* Khantyskie i Mansiiskie pesni, ed. O. V. Mazur and G. E. Soldatova, 11–18. Novosibirsk: Na pravakh rukopisi.

Mooney, James

1896 The Ghost Dance Religion and the Sioux Outbreak of 1896. Washington: Government Printing Office.

Moore, Sally Falk, and Barbara G. Myerhoff, eds.

1975 Symbol and Politics in Communal Ideology: Cases and Questions. Symbol, Myth and Ritual Series. Ithaca: Cornell University Press.

Mosynska, Wanda

1968 On Some Ancient Anthropomorphic Images from West Siberia. *In* Popular Beliefs and Folklore Tradition in Siberia, ed. Vilmos Diószegi, 93–101. Uralic and Altaic Series, 57. Bloomington: Indiana University Press.

Mozgalin, S. E.

1981 Nekotorye problemy formirovaniia naseleniia i trudovykh resursov Obskogo Severa (Some problems in the formation of population and labor resources of the Ob North). Izvestiia Vsesoiuznogo Geograficheskogo Obshchestva 113(2):130–34.

Munkácsi, Bernát
1995 Vogul Folklore. Ed. Otto J. von Sadovsky and Mihály Hoppál. Budapest: Akademiai Kiado. [1892–1921].

Murashko, Olga, and Nikolai Krenke
1996 Burials of Indigenous People in the Lower Ob Region: Dating, Burial Ceremonies, and Ethnic Interpretations. Arctic Anthropology 33(1):37–66.

"N"
1936 Khronika (Chronicle). Sovetskaia Arktika (6):108.

Nabokov, Peter, ed.
1991 Native American Testimony: An Anthology of Indian-White Relations. Foreword by Vine Deloria, Jr. New York: Penguin.

Nagel, Joane
1996 American Indian Ethnic Renewal: Red Power and the Resurgence of Identity and Culture. Oxford: Oxford University Press.

Narayan, Kirin
1993 How Native is a "Native" Anthropologist? American Anthropologist 95(3):671–86.

Needham, Rodney, ed.
1973 Right and Left: Essays on Dual Symbolic Classification. Chicago: University of Chicago Press.

Nemtushkin, Alitet
1988 Stoit li mnozhit' oshibki? (Are errors worth multiplying?) Sotsialisticheskaia industriia (June 28):4.

Nichols, Robert, and Theofanis George Stavrou, eds.
1978 Russian Orthodoxy under the Old Regime. Minneapolis: University of Minnesota Press.

Nikolaev, Ivan
1995 Moskva blizhee Tiumen' (Moscow is closer than Tiumen). Rossiiskie vesti (July 26):2.

Norbeck, Edward
1974 The Anthropological Study of Human Play. Rice University Studies 60(3):1–8.

Nosilov, K. D.
1904 U Vogulov (Among the Voguls). Saint Petersburg: Suvorin.

Novik, Elena
1997 The Archaic Epic and its Relationship to Ritual. *In* Shamanic Worlds: Rituals and Lore of Siberia and Central Asia, ed. Marjorie Mandelstam Balzer, 185–234. Armonk, N.Y.: M. E. Sharpe. [1984].

Novikova, Natalia
1991 Ob Iranskom vlianii v kul'ture Obskikh Ugrov (On Iranian influence in Ob-Ugrian culture). Sovetskaia etnografiia (4):28–35.

1995 Vodianye dukhi obskikh ugrov (Ob-Ugrian water spirits). *In* Traditsionnye ritualy i verovaniia, ed. D. Logashova, 51–63. Moscow: Akademiia Nauk.

1996 Ngém 'Ter—Soderzhimoe zemli (Caretaker of the Land). Severnye prostory (3–4):59–60.

1997 Vzaimodeistvie obshchin korennykh narodov Severa Rossii i neftedobyvaiushchikh korporatsii: vzgliad antropologa (The interrelations of indigenous peoples of the Russian North and oil corporations: views of an anthropologist). *In* Ekologiia, obshchestvo i traditsiia: sotsial'nye i politicheskie krizisy v SNG v kontekste razrusheniia prirodnoi sredy, 42–62. Nauchnye doklady, 15. Moscow: Tsentr Karnegi [Carnegie].

Novitskii, Grigory
1884 Kratkoe opisanie o narode Ostiakom (Short notes on the Ostiak people). Saint Petersburg: Maikov. [1715].

Ogryzko, Joseph Ivanovich
1941 Khristianizatsiia narodov Tobol'skogo Severa (Christianization of the peoples of the Tobolsk North). Leningrad: Ucheb-Pedagogicheskogo Izdat.

Ohnuki-Tierney, Emiko, ed.
1990 Culture through Time: Anthropological Approaches. Stanford: Stanford University Press.

Okie, Susan
1998 Researchers Seek Genes for Alcoholism. Washington Post (May 26): 11 (Health section).

Onushchuk, N. T.
1973 Sovetskoe stroitel'stvo u malykh narodov Severa 1917–1941 (Soviet development among the small peoples of the North). Tomsk: Universitetskoe Izdat.

Orlova, E. I.
1926 Sovremennoe Vasiugan (Modern Vasyugan). Zhizn' Sibiri, vyp. 4:66–81.

Orlovskii, P. N.
1930 Kollektivizatsii na Severe (Collectivization in the North). Sovetskii Sever 1(1):48–58.

Ortner, Sherry B.
1984 Theory in Anthropology since the Sixties. Comparative Studies in Society and History 26(1):126–66.
1995 Resistance and the Problem of Ethnographic Refusal. Comparative Studies in Society and History 37(1):173–93.

Osherenko, Gail
1993 Northwest Siberian Festival Celebrates Revival of Indigenous Culture. Surviving Together 11(4):53–55.
1995 Property Rights and Transformation in Russia: Institutional Change in the Far North. Europe-Asia Studies 47(7):1077–1108.

Ostrovskii, P.
1931 Sovremennoe Vasiugan (Modern Vasyugan). Sovetskii Sever 2(9):114–19.

"P"
1936 Kul'tbazy krainego Severa (Culture bases of the Far North). Sovetskaia Arktika (6):108.

Padilla, Amado, ed.
1980 Acculturation: Theory, Models and Some New Findings. Boulder: Westview.

Paine, Robert, ed.
1977 The White Arctic: Anthropological Essays on Tutelage and Ethnicity. Newfoundland Social and Economic Papers, 7. Toronto: University of Toronto Press.

Paksoy, H. B.
1987 Central Asia's New Dastans. Central Asian Survey 6(1):75–92.

Pallas, Peter Simon
1788 Travels through Siberia and Tatary. Part 1. Trusler's Habitable World Described. London: Trusler. [1773].

Pamiatnaia kniga Zapadnoi Sibiri (Record book of West Siberia)
1881 Omsk: Tipografiia Okruzh. Shtaba.

Panov, Iv.
1937 Gorod v lesu (Town in the forest). *In* Narody Severnogo Urala (Peoples of the Northern Urals), ed. V. A. Popov, 97–119. Sverdlovsk: Sredne-Ural'skoe Izdat.

Parkhomenko, S. G.
1930 Kraevedcheskaia rabota v kul'tbazakh (Regional work in the culture bases). Sovetskii Sever 1(1):125–29.

Pascal, Pierre
1938 Avvakum et les débuts du raskol. Paris: Institut d'Étude Slaves.

Patkanov, Sergei K.
1891 Tip Ostiatskogo bogatyria po Ostiatskim bylinam i geroicheskim skazaniiam (The model Ostiak bogatyr through Ostiak byliny and heroic tales). Saint Petersburg: Khudenkov.
1891a Starodavniaia zhizn' ostiakov i ikh bogatyrei po bylinam i skazaniiam (Ancient life of the Ostiak and their bogatyrs, according to byliny and tales). Zhivaia starina (3, 4).
1892 Ostiatskaia bylina pro bogatyrei goroda Emdera (An Ostiak bylina on the bogatyr of the town of Emdera). Zhivaia starina (2).
1897 Die Irtysch Ostyaken und ihre Volkspoesie. Saint Petersburg: Suvorin.
1911 O Prirost' inorodcheskago naseleniia Sibiri (On the growth of the Siberian native population). Saint Petersburg: Imperatorskaia Akademiia Nauk.

Pavlenko, V. I.
1995 Problemy sotsial'no-ekonomicheskogo razvitiia Arktiki (Problems of arctic social-economic growth). Moscow: Akademiia Nauk.

Peacock, James
1990 Form and Meaning in Recent Indonesian History: Some Reflections in Light of H.-G. Gadamer's Philosophy of History. *In* Culture through Time: Anthropological Approaches, ed. E. Ohnuki-Tierney, 246–67. Stanford: Stanford University Press.

Peirce, Charles
1960 Collected Works: Elements of Logic. Vol. 2. Ed. Charles Hartshorne and Paul Weis. Cambridge: Belknap.

Pentikäinen, Juha
1997 Shamanism and Culture: Essays. Helsinki: Etnika.

Periwal, Sukumar, ed.
1995 Notions of Nationalism. Budapest: Central European University Press.
Perry, Richard J.
1996 . . . From Time Immemorial: Indigenous Peoples and State Systems. Austin: University of Texas Press.
Pervukhin, I.
1930 Na Tobolsk Severe (In the Tobolsk North). Sovetskii Sever 1(1):75–83.
Petri, V. E.
1928 Proekt kul'tbazy dlia malykh narodov Sibiri (The culture base project for the small peoples of Siberia). *In* Pervyi Sibirskii kraevoi nauchno-issledovatel'skii s"ezd, 4:118–27. Tomsk: Krasnoe Znamiia.
Petro, Nicholas N.
1995 The Rebirth of Russian Democracy: An Interpretation of Political Culture. Cambridge, Mass.: Harvard University Press.
Petro, Nicholas N., ed.
1990 Christianity and Russian Culture in Soviet Society. Boulder: Westview.
Petrushin, A.
1991 Mandala. Severnye prostory 44:35–36.
Pika, Alexander I.
1982 Formirovanie zapadnosibirskogo territorial'no-promyshlennogo kompleksa i narody Severa (Formation of the West Siberian industrial complex and the peoples of the North). *In* Sotsial'nye aspekty istorii Sovetskogo naroda kak novoi sotsial'no-international'noi obshchnosti liudei, ed. Iu. S. Kukushkin, 230–38. Moscow: Moskovskogo Universiteta.
Pika, Alexander I., and Boris B. Prokhorov, eds.
1994 Neotraditsionalizm na Rossiiskom Severe. Moscow: Institut Narodnokhoziaistvennogo prognozirovaniia.
Poliakov, I. S.
1877 Pis'ma i otchety o puteshestvii v dolinu r. Obi (Letters and reports on a trip to the Ob River valley). Zapiski Imp. Akademii Nauka 30, prilozhenie 2.
Polnoe Sobranie Zakonov (Complete collection of laws)
1697 Instruktsy Tobol'sku (Instructions to Tobol'sk) 3:355–56.
Ponomarev, G. V.
1973 Changes in Wildlife Populations in the Sos'va Section of the Ob Basin as a Result of Human Activity in the Tayga. Soviet Geography 14(6):356–62.
Popov, T.
1890 Ostiatskie kniaz'ia (Ostiak princes). Russkaia starina. 68:457–60.
Potanin, G. N.
187? Zametki o Zapadnoi Sibiri (Remarks on West Siberia). Russkoe Slovo, 189–214. Saint Petersburg: Russkoe Slovo offprint, no date.
Potapov, L. P., S. V. Ivanov, G. S. Maslova, and V. K. Sokolova
1964 Historical-Ethnographic Survey of the Russian Population of Siberia in the Pre-Revolutionary Period. *In* Peoples of Siberia, trans. Stephen

Dunn, ed. L. P. Potapov and M. G. Levin, 105–99. Chicago: University of Chicago Press. [Orig. pub. in Russian, 1956].

Price, Richard
1983 First Time: The Historical Vision of an Afro-American People. Baltimore: Johns Hopkins University Press.

Prokof'yeva, E. E.
1971 Shamanskie Kostiumy Narodov Sibiri (Shaman costumes of the peoples of Siberia). Sbornik Muzeia Antropologii i Etnografii 27:5–10.

Prokof'yeva, E. E., V. N. Chernetsov, and N. F. Prytkova
1964 The Khants and Mansi. *In* Peoples of Siberia, trans. Stephen Dunn; ed. M. G. Levin and L. P. Potapov, 511–46. Chicago: University of Chicago Press. [Orig. pub. in Russian, 1956].

Proschan, Frank
1997 "We are all Kmhmu, just the same": ethnonyms, ethnic identities and ethnic groups. American Ethnologist 24(1):91–113.

P-rovskii, N.
1866 Berezovo. Tobolskie gubernskie vedomosti 33:237–50.

Przeworski, Adam, et al.
1995 Sustainable Democracy. Cambridge: Cambridge University Press.

Raeff, Marc
1956 Siberia and the Reforms of 1822. Seattle: University of Washington Press.

Rambo, Lewis R.
1993 Understanding Religious Conversion. New Haven: Yale University Press.

Ramet, Sabrina P., ed.
1992 Religious Policy in the Soviet Union. Cambridge: Cambridge University Press.

Raun, Alo
1955 The Ostyak and the Vogul. New Haven: Human Relations Area Files Press.

Redfield, Robert, Robert Linton, and Melville Herskovits
1938 Outline for the Study of Acculturation. *In* Acculturation: The Study of Culture Contact, ed. M. Herskovits. New York: Augustin.

Rethman, Petra
1997 Chto Delat'? Ethnography in the Post-Soviet Cultural Context. American Anthropologist 99(4): 770–74.

Ridington, Robin
1988 Trail to Heaven: Knowledge and Narrative in a Northern Native Community. Iowa City: University of Iowa Press.

Riegelhaupt, Joyce
1984 Popular Anti-Clericalism and Religiosity in Pre-1974 Portugal. *In* Religion, Power and Protest in Local Communities, ed. E. Wolf. Amsterdam: Mouton.

Ries, Nancy
1997 Russian Talk: Culture and Conversation during Perestroika. Ithaca: Cornell University Press.

Rigby, T. H.

1968 Communist Party Membership in the USSR 1917–1967. Princeton: Princeton University Press.

Roheim, Geza

1954 Hungarian and Vogul Mythology. Monographs of the American Ethnological Society, 23. Locust Valley, N.Y.: Augustin.

Romanucci-Ross, L., D. Moerman, and L. Tancredi, eds.

1996 The Anthropology of Medicine: From Culture to Method. New York: Praeger. [1983].

Romanucci-Ross, Lola, and George De Vos, eds.

1995 Ethnic Identity: Creation, Conflict, and Accommodation. 3d ed. Walnut Creek, Calif.: AltaMira/Sage. [1975].

Rombandeeva, E. I.

1968 Some Observances and Customs of the Mansi (Voguls) in Connection with Childbirth. *In* Popular Beliefs and Folklore Tradition in Siberia, ed. V. Diószegi, 77–83. Bloomington: Indiana University Press.

Rossi, Ino, ed.

1974 The Unconscious in Culture. New York: Dutton.

Royce, Annya Peterson

1982 Ethnic Identity: Strategies of Diversity. Bloomington: Indiana University Press.

Rubinskii, V. I.

1928 Pereselenie v Sibiri i na Dal'nem Vostoke (Migration to Siberia and the Far East). Severnaia Aziia 1:13–26.

Rudenko, Sergei I.

1910 Predmety iz Ostiatskogo Mogilnika vozle Obdorska (Objects from Ostiak graves near Obdorsk). Materialy po etnografii Rossii 2:35–56. Saint Petersburg: Imp. Russkii muzei.

Rusakova, L. M. and Minenko, N. A.

1985 Kul'turno-bytovye protsessy u russkikh Sibiri, XVIII–nachalo XXv. (Cultural-customary processes among Russians of Siberia, eighteenth–early twentieth centuries). Novosibirsk: Nauka.

Rybkina, R., L. Kosals, and K. Kovalkina

1992 Malochislennye narody severa: Problemy i puti ikh resheniia (Nonnumerous peoples of the North: Problems and routes of resolution). Vestnik statistiki (4):44–48.

Rytkheu, Yuri

1983 People of the Long Spring. National Geographic 163(2):206–23.

Sadovnikov, D.

1911 S reki Vakha Surgutskogo uezda (From Vakh River, Surgut). Ezhegodnik Tobol'skago gubernskago muzeiia 19:1–21.

Sagalaev, A. M., and I. V. Oktiabr'skaia

1990 Traditsionnoe mirovozrenie Tiurkov Iuzhnoi Sibiri: znak i ritual (Traditional worldview of the Southern Siberian Turks: Sign and ritual). Novosibirsk: Nauka.

Sahlins, Marshall

1981 Historical Metaphors and Mythical Realities: Structure in the Early

History of the Sandwich Islands Kingdom. Ann Arbor: University of Michigan Press.

Salmanov, F. K.
1970 Put' k bol'shoi nefti (Road to big oil). *In* Obnovlenaia Iugra (Ugrian renewal), ed. B. Loshak, 57–79. Sverdlovsk: Sredne-Ural'skoe Izdat.

Sal'nikova, Liudmila
1991 Parallel'naia zhizn' (Parallel life). Ogonek (August):11–15.

Salzman, Philip Carl
1978 The Proto-State in Baluchistan. *In* State Origins: A Controlled Comparison, ed. R. Cohen and E. R. Service, 125–40. Philadelphia: ISHI.
1980 When Nomads Settle: Processes of Sedentarization as Adaptation and Response. New York: Praeger/Bergin.

Samokvasov, D. Ia.
1876 Sbornik obychnogo prava sibirskikh inorodtsev (Collection of Siberian native customary law). Warsaw.

Sanders, Ronald
1992 Lost Tribes and Promised Lands. Foreword by Michael Dorris. New York: Harper Perennial. [1978].

Sangi, Vladimir
1990 Konventsiia-26: Assotsiatsii malochislennykh narodov severa Sovetskogo Soiuza. (Convention of 26 [Peoples]. Association of Minorities of the Soviet North). Manifesto MS.

Schindler, Debra
1991 Theory, Policy and the "Narody Severa." Anthropological Quarterly 64(2):68–80.

Schmidt, Éva
1989 Bear Cult and Mythology of the Northern Ob-Ugrians. *In* Uralic Mythology and Folklore, ed. M. Hoppál and J. Pentikäinen, 187–232. Budapest: Academy of Sciences; Helsinki: Finnish Literary Society.

Schneider, Jane, and Shirley Lindenbaum, eds.
1987 Frontiers of Christian Evangelism: Essays in Honor of Joyce Riegelhaupt. American Ethnologist 14(1).

Schoberlein-Engel, John
1994 Conflict in Tajikistan and Central Asia: The Myth of Ethnic Animosity. Harvard Middle Eastern and Islamic Review 1(2):1–55.

Schwartz, Theodore
1976 The Cargo Cult: A Melanesian Type-Response to Change. *In* Responses to Change, ed. George. A. DeVos, 157–206. New York: Van Nostrand.

Sengepov, A. M., E. A. Nemysova, S. P. Moldanova, et al.
1988 Khantyiskii iazyk: Uchebnik (Khanty language: textbook). Leningrad: Prosveshchenie.

Senkevich, V.
1934 V Voitkhovskikh iurtakh (In the Voitkhovsk yurts). Sovetskii Sever 4(6):98–105.
1935 Skazka i pesni Khantov (Khanty tales and songs). Sovetskii Sever 6(3–4):151–59.

Sergeev, Mikhail A.
1947 Malye narody Severa v epokhu sotsializma (Small peoples of the North in the epoch of socialism). Sovetskaia etnografiia (4):126–58.
1953 Narody Obskogo Severa (Peoples of the Ob North). Novosibirsk: Akademiia Nauk.
1955 Nekapitalisticheskii put razvitiia malykh narodov severa (The noncapitalist road of the small peoples of the North). Moscow-Leningrad: Akademiia Nauk.
1964 The Building of Socialism among the Peoples of Northern Siberia and the Soviet Far East. *In* Peoples of Siberia, trans. Stephen Dunn; ed. M. G. Levin and L. P. Potapov, 487–510. Chicago: University of Chicago Press. [Orig. pub. in Russian, 1956].

Serkin, I. O.
1937 Ob oshibkakh obdorskogo politotdela (On mistakes of the Obdorsk political section). Sovetskaia Arktika (10):9–15.

Shalin, Dmitri N., ed.
1996 Russian Culture at the Crossroads: Paradoxes of Postcommunist Consciousness. Boulder: Westview.

Shashkov, S.
1864 Shamanstvo v Sibiri (Shamanism in Siberia). Saint Petersburg: Morichegovskogo.

Shatilov, M. B.
1931 Vakhovskie Ostiaki (Vakh Ostiak). Trudy Tomskii kraevogo muzeia, 4. Tomsk: Tomsk Kraevogo Muzeia.
1977 Dramaticheskoe iskusstvo Vakhovskikh Ostiakov (Dramatic art of the Vakh Ostiak). *In* Iz istorii shamanstva (From the history of shamanism), ed. N. V. Lukina. Tomsk: Tomsk Universitet.

Shavrov, V. N.
1871 Kratkie Zapiski O Zhiteliakh Berezovskogo Uezda (Short notes on the inhabitants of Berezovo). Moscow: Universitetskaia Tip.

Sherstova, L. I.
1997 Burkhanizm v gornom Altae: Istoki nastional'noi ideologii i tendentsii ee razvitiia (Burkhanism in the Altai Mountains: Sources of national ideology and its development). *In* Narody Sibiri, ed. Z. P. Sokolova, 171–215. Moscow: Akademiia Nauk.

Shestalov, Yuvan
1973 Iazycheskaia poema (Pagan poem). Moscow: Sovremenik.
1974 Shag cherez tysiacheletiia (Step across a thousand years). Moscow: Politicheskoi Izdat.
1985 Samaia chistaia radost' (The most pure joy). Leningrad: Lenizdat.
1985a Zeml'ia Iugoriia (Land of the Ugrians). Moscow: Sovetskaia Rossiia.

Shilnikov, Sergei
1995 Soglasie obychno gde khochetsia (Consensus usually comes with receptivity). Tiumen'skaia pravda (December 23):1–2.

Shimkin, Demitri
1965 Western Siberian Archeology: An Interpretive Summary. *In* Selected

Papers of the Fifth International Congress of Anthropological and Ethnological Sciences, ed. A.F.C. Wallace, 648–61. Philadelphia: University of Pennsylvania Press.

Shirokogoroff, Sergei
1935 The Psychomental Complex of the Tungus. London: Kegan Paul, Trench, Trubner.

Shishigin, Egor S.
1991 Rasprostranenie Khristianstva v Iakutii (The spread of Christianity in Yakutia). Yakutsk: Yakutskii Nauchnyi Tsentr.

Shishonko, B., ed.
1884 Permskaia letopis' c 1253–1881 gg., c 1645–1676 gg. (Perm Chronicle). Perm': Gub. Pravleniia Tip.

Shnirelman, Victor A.
1996 Who Gets the Past? Competition for Ancestors among Non-Russian Intellectuals in Russia. Washington: Woodrow Wilson Center, with Johns Hopkins University Press.

Shukhov, I. N.
1916 Reka Kazym i ee obitateli (The River Kazym and its inhabitants). Ezhegodnik Tobol'skogo Gubernskogo Muzeia 27:1–57.
1916a Iz otcheta o poezdke vesnoiu 1914 goda k Kazymskim Ostiakam (From a report on a trip in spring 1914 to the Kazym Ostiak). Sbornik Muzeia Antropologii i Etnografii 3:103–12.

Shulz, L. R.
1924 Ostiaki. Tiumen: Tiumen'skogo Obshchestva Nauchnego Izucheniia Mestnogo Kraia.

Shutz, Alfred
1970 On Phenomenology and Social Relations. Chicago: University of Chicago Press.

Shvetsov, S. P.
1888 Ocherk Surgutskogo Okruga (Essay on the Surgut Region). Zapiski Zapadno-Sibirskogo otdela Russkogo geograficheskogo obshchestva 10:1–87.

Sibirski Vestnik
1885 Rasprostraneni Khristianstva (The spread of Christianity), vyp. 3: 9–10. (Editorial).

Siikala, Anna-Leena
1978 The Rite Technique of the Siberian Shaman. Folklore Communications, 220. Helsinki: Finnish Academy of Sciences.

Siikala, Anna-Leena, and Mihály Hoppál
1992 Studies on Shamanism. Helsinki: Finnish Anthropological Society; Budapest: Akademiai Kiado.

Simchenko, Iurii B., ed.
1992 Narody Severa Rossii (Peoples of the North of Rossiia). 3 vols. Narody i Kul'tury series. Moscow: Akademiia Nauk.

Skachko, Anatolii E.
1930 Problemy Severa (Problems of the North). Sovetskii Sever 1(1):15–37.

1930a Klassovoe rassloenie, mery borb'y s kulachestvom i kollektivizatsiia (Class distribution, measures in the struggle with kulachestvo and collectivization). Sovetskii Sever 1(2):38–49.

1930b Imushchestvennyie pokazateli sotsial'nykh grupp u malykh narodov Severa (Property indicators of social groups among the small peoples of the North). Sovetskii Sever 1(3):5–28.

1930c Sed'moi plenum komitet Severa (Seventh Plenum of the Committee of the North). Sovetskii Sever 1(4):7–23.

1931 Zemliia Iugorskaia i Obdorskaia v leto 1930 (The land of Ugorsk and Obdorsk in the summer of 1930). Sovetskii Sever 2(2):58–113.

1934 Narody Krainego Severa i rekonstruktsiia severnoi khoziaistve (The peoples of the Far North and reconstruction of the northern economy). Leningrad: Gos. Izdat.

Skalozubov, N. L.

1907 Ot Tobol'ska do Obdorska (From Tobolsk to Obdorsk). Ezhegodnik Tobol'skogo Gubernskogo Muzeia 16:1–18.

Slavnin, P.

1911 Samoedy-grabiteli v Obdorskom krae (Samoyed-robbers in the Obdorsk region). Tobolsk: Tobol'skii Gubernskii Muzei.

Slezkine, Yuri

1994 Arctic Mirrors: Russia and the Small Peoples of the North. Ithaca: Cornell University Press.

Smidovich, P. G., S. A. Buterlin, and N. I. Leonov, eds.

1929 Sovetskii Sever: Pervyi Sborniki Statei (The Soviet North: First collection of articles). Moscow: Komitet Sodeistviia Narodnostiam Severnykh Okrain pri Presizdiume VTsIK.

Smith, Anthony D.

1981 The Ethnic Revival in the Modern World. Cambridge: Cambridge University Press.

1986 The Ethnic Origins of Nations. Oxford: Basil Blackwell.

Smith, Eric Alden, and Joan McCarter, eds.

1997 Contested Arctic: Indigenous Peoples, Industrial States and the Circumpolar Environment. Seattle: University of Washington Press.

Smith, Marian

1959 Towards a classification of cult movements. Man 59:8–12.

Sokolova, Zoia Petrovna

1968 Preobrazovaniia v khoziaistve, kul'ture i byte Obskikh ugrov (Transformation in Ob-Ugrian economics, culture, and life). Sovetskaia etnografiia (5):25–39.

1970 Sovremennye etnicheskie protsessy u obskikh ugrov (Modern ethnic processes among the Ob-Ugrians). *In* Preobrazovaniia o khoziaistve i kul'ture i etnicheskii protsessy u narodov Severa, ed. I. S. Gurvich and B. O. Dolgikh, 87–92. Moscow: Akademiia Nauk.

1971 Perezhitki religioznykh verovanii u Obskikh Ugrov (Survivals of religious belief among the Ob-Ugrians). Sbornik Muzeia Antropologii i Etnografii 27:211–39.

1971a Postanovleniia partii i pravitel'stva o razvitii khoziaistva i kul'tury narodov Krainego Severa, iuridicheskie akty (Resolutions of the party and government on the growth of economics and culture of the peoples of the Far North: Legal acts). *In* Osushchestvlenie Leninskoi natsional'noi politiki u narodov Krainego Severa, ed. I. S. Gurvich, 66–116. Moscow: Akademiia Nauk.

1975 K voprosu o formirovanii etnograficheskikh i territorial'nykh grupp u Obskikh Ugrov (Toward the question of the formation of ethnic and territorial groups among the Ob-Ugrians). *In* Etnogenez i etnicheskaia istoriia narodov Severa, ed. I. S. Gurvich, 186–210. Moscow: Akademiia Nauk.

1975a Nasledstvennye, ili predkovye, imena u Obskikh Ugrov i sviazannye s nimi obychai (Hereditary or ancestral names and related customs among Ob-Ugrians). Sovetskaia etnografiia (5):42–52.

1975b Novye dannye o pogrebal'nom obriade Severnykh Khantov (New data on burial rituals of the Northern Khanty). Polevye issledovaniia Instituta Etnografii 1974, 165–74. Moscow: Akademiia Nauk.

1976 Strana Ugrov (The country of the Ugrians). Moscow: Mysl'.

1978 The Representation of a Female Spirit from the Kazym River. *In* Shamanism in Siberia, ed. V. Diószegi and M. Hoppál; trans. S. Simon, 49–501. Budapest: Akademiai Kiado.

1979 Pokhorony u Kazymskikh Khantov (Burial among Kazym Khanty). Polevye issledovaniia Instituta Etnografii 1977, 249–53. Moscow: Akademiia Nauk.

1983 Sotsial'naia organizatsiia Khantov i Mansi v XVIII-XIXvv: Problemy fratrii i roda (Social organization of the Khanty and Mansi in the eighteenth and nineteenth centuries: Problems of phratry and clan). Moscow: Akademiia Nauk.

1990 Endogamnyi areal i etnicheskaia gruppa (na materialakh Khantov i Mansi) (Endogamous area and ethnic group, [based] on Khanty and Mansi materials). Moscow: Akademiia Nauk.

1991 Problemy izucheniia obsko-ugorskogo shamanstva (Problems of studying Ob-Ugrian shamanship). *In* Obskie Ugry (Khanty i Mansi), ed. Iu. Simchenko, 225–41. Moscow: Akademiia Nauk.

Sokolova, Z. P., N. I. Novikova, and N. V. Ssorin-Chaikov

1995 Etnografy pishut zakon: Kontekst i problem (Ethnographers write the law: Context and problem). Etnicheskoe obozrenie (1):74–88.

Soldatov, G. M.

1972 Mitropolit Filofei, v skhime Fedor, Prosvetitel' Sibiri, 1650–1727 (Metropolitan Filofei, following Fedor, Enlightener of Siberia, 1650–1727). Minneapolis: Soldatow.

Solov'ev, Aleksandr I.

1987 Voennoe delo korennogo naseleniia Zapadnoi Sibiri: Epokha srednevekov'ia (Warfare of the West Siberian native population: Middle Ages). Novosibirsk: Nauka.

Startsev, Georgii Afanasevich

1928 Ostiaki: Sotsial'no-etnograficheskii ocherk (Ostiak: A social-ethnographic study). Leningrad: Priboi.

Stites, Richard

1989 Revolutionary Dreams: Utopian Vision and Experimental Life in the Russian Revolution. New York, Oxford: Oxford University Press.

Stoler, Ann

1996 Sexual Affronts and Racial Frontiers: European Identities and the Cultural Politics of Exclusion in Colonial Southeast Asia. *In* Becoming National, ed. Geoff Eley and Ronald Grigor Suny, 286–322. Oxford: Oxford University Press.

Stoner-Weiss, Kathryn

1996 Local Heroes: The Political Economy of Russian Regional Governance. Princeton: Princeton University Press.

Suny, Ronald Grigor

1993 The Revenge of the Past: Nationalism, Revolution, and the Collapse of the Soviet Union. Stanford: Stanford University Press.

1994 The Making of the Georgian Nation. Bloomington: Indiana University Press. [1988].

Suslov, I. M.

1930 Raschety minimal'nogo kolichestva olenei, potreblenogo dlia tuzemnogo seredniatskogo khoziaistva (Accounting of the minimal number of reindeer used in middle-income native households). Sovetskii Sever 1(3):29–35.

1934 Piatnadstat' severnyikh kul'tbazy (Fifteen northern culture bases). Sovetskii Sever 4(1):28–37.

Sverkunova, N. V.

1996 Fenomen Siberiaka (The Siberiak phenomenon). Sotsiologicheskie issledovanie (8):90–94.

Swann, Brian, and Arnold Krupat, eds.

1987 I Tell You Now: Autobiographical Essays by Native American Writers. Lincoln: University of Nebraska Press.

Tambiah, Stanley J.

1976 World Conqueror and World Renouncer. New York: Cambridge University Press.

1989 Ethnic Conflict in the World Today. American Ethnologist 16(2):335–49.

Tamir, Yael

1993 Liberal Nationalism. Princeton: Princeton University Press.

Taracouzio, Timothy A.

1938 Soviets in the Arctic. New York: Macmillan.

Tarasenkov, G.

1938 Ostiatsko-Vogulskii Natsional'nyi Okrug (the Ostiak-Vogul National Okrug). Sovetskaia Arktika (9):43–61.

1939 Skhola na krainem Severa (School in the Far North). Sovetskaia Arktika (9):97–100.

Taussig, Michael

1987 Shamanism, Colonialism, and the Wild Man: A Study in Terror and Healing. Chicago: University of Chicago Press.

1993 Mimesis and Alterity: A Particular History of the Senses. New York: Routledge.

1997 The Magic of the State. New York: Routledge.

Teleshev, I.

1932 God raboty v Ostiatskoi shkole (A year of work in an Ostiak school). Sovetskii Sever 2(5):125–30.

Tereshkin, Nikolai I.

1981 Slovar' Vostochno-Khantyiskikh dialektov (Dictionary of East Khanty dialects). Leningrad: Akademiia Nauk.

Terletskii, P.

1930 Natsional'noe raionirovanie Krainego Severa (National divisions of the Far North). Sovetskii Sever 1(7–8): 5–28.

1936 Sostav naseleniia krainego severa. Sovetskaia Arktika (11):36–41.

Thomas, Nicholas, and Caroline Humphrey, eds.

1994 Shamanism, History and the State. Ann Arbor: University of Michigan Press.

Tishkov, Valery Aleksandrovich

1994–95 Soviet Ethnography: Overcoming the Crisis; Post-Soviet Ethnography: Not a Crisis but Something More Serious. Anthropology and Archeology of Eurasia 33(3):14–39, 87–92.

1997 Ethnicity, Nationalism and Conflict in and after the Soviet Union: The Mind Aflame. London: Sage, for PRIO, UNRISD.

Tishkov, V. A., ed.

1994 Etnichnost' i vlast v polietnichnykh gosudarstvakh (Ethnicity and power in polyethnic states). Moscow: Nauka.

Tokarev, Sergei A.

1936 Vosstaniia narodov severa protiv tsarskogo rezhima (A rebellion of the peoples of the North against the tsarist regime). Sovetskaia Arktika (4):103–10.

1979–80 Religion as a Social Phenomenon. Soviet Anthropology and Archeology 20. (Critic's responses, SAAE 21, 22).

Tomtosov, Aleksei

1990 Net malykh narodov (There are no small peoples). Soiuz 13(March):2.

Trexler, Richard C.

1995 Sex and Conquest: Gendered Violence, Political Order, and the European Conquest of the Americas. Ithaca: Cornell University Press.

Trompf, G. W., ed.

1990 Cargo Cults and Millenarian Movements: Transoceanic Comparisons of New Religious Movements. Berlin: Mouton de Gruyter.

Trott, Christopher G.

1997 The rapture and the rupture: Religious change amongst the Inuit of North Baffin Island. Études Inuit 21(1–2):209–28.

Tumarkin, Nina

1983 Lenin Lives! Cambridge, Mass.: Harvard University Press.

Turner, Edith

1996 The Hands Feel It: Healing and Spirit Presence among a North Alaskan People. DeKalb: Northern Illinois University Press.

Turner, Victor

1977 The Ritual Process: Structure and Anti-Structure. Ithaca: Cornell University Press. [1969].

1979 Dramatic Ritual/Ritual Drama: Performance and Reflexive Anthropology. Kenyon Review 1(3):80–93.

Turner, Victor, ed.
1982 Celebration: Studies in Festivity and Ritual. Washington: Smithsonian Institution.

Turskii, D.
1898 Ostiaki. Moscow: Obshchestvo Rasprostraneniia Poleznykh Knig.

Ustiugov, P.
1930 Tuzemnye Sovety i zadachi ikh ukrepleniia (Native soviets and the tasks of their strengthening). Sovetskii Sever 1(9–12):5–41.
1931 Perevybory sovetov na Krainem severe (Reelections of Far North soviets). Sovetskii Sever 2(3–4):193–227.
1971 Put' narodov Severa k sotsializmu: Opyt sotsialisticheskogo stroitel'stvo na Eniseiskom Severe. (The road to socialism of the peoples of the North: An experiment in socialist development on the Enisei). Moscow: Mysl'.

Vakhtin, Nikolai B.
1993 Korennoe naselenie krainego severa Rossiiskoi Federatsii. Saint Petersburg: Evropeiskogo Doma. (Pub. in 1994 as Native Peoples of the Russian Far North [London: Minority Rights Group International]).

Van Gennep, Arnold
1960 The Rites of Passage. Trans. Monika Vizedom and Gabrielle Caffee. Chicago: University of Chicago Press. [1903].

Vansina, Jan
1978 The Children of Woot: A History of the Kuba Peoples. Madison: University of Wisconsin Press.

VanStone, James W.
1979 Ingalik Contact Ecology: An Ethnohistory of the Lower-Middle Yukon, 1790–1935. Fieldiana, Anthropology 71. Chicago: Field Museum of Natural History.

Vatin, V.
1914 K voprosu o tabstve v Sibiri (Toward the question of slavery in Siberia). Sibirskii arkhiv (10):455–57.

Vauli Piettomin [documents].
1940 Iz istorii sotsial'nykh dvizhenii Khantev i Nentsev v XIX veka (From the history of a social movement of the Khanty and Nentsy in the nineteenth century). Omsk: Oblastnoi Izdat.

Vella, Yuri
1996 Belye kriki: kniga o vechnom (White cries: A book about posterity). Surgut: Severnyi dom.
1996a My ne ischeznem s litsa zemli (We are not disappearing from the face of the earth). Severnye prostory (3–4):16–18, 21, 25–28.

Veniamin (Archimandrite)
1855 Samoedy mezenskie (Local Samoyed). Vestnik Russkogo Geograficheskogo Obshchestva 14.

Ventsel, Aimar, and Stephan Dudeck
1998 Do Khanty Need a Khanty Curriculum? Indigenous Concepts of

School Education. *In* Bicultural Education in the North, ed. Erich Kasten, 89–100. Münster: Waxmann Verlag.

Verdery, Katherine

1996 What Was Socialism and What Comes Next? Princeton: Princeton University Press.

Veresh [Vérеš], Petr

1975 Obshchestvennye i etnograficheskie gruppy mansi v xvii-xix vv (Community and ethnographic Mansi groups, seventeenth–nineteenth centuries). *In* IV Mezhdunarodnom congress finnougrovedov, 50–58. Budapest: Akademiai Kiado.

Vitebsky, Piers

1996 The Northern Minorities. *In* The Nationalities Question in the Post-Soviet States, ed. G. Smith, 94–112. London: Longmans.

Voget, F. W.

1959 Towards a Classification of Cult Movements: Some Further Considerations. Man 59:26–28.

Voronov, A. G.

1900 Iurodicheskie obychai Ostiakov Zapadnoi Sibiri i Samoiedov Tomskoi Gubernii (Legal customs of West Siberian Ostiak and the Samoyed of Tomsk Province). Zapiski Russkogo Geograficheskogo Obshchestva po otdeleniiu etnografii 18(2):1–50.

Vtoroi S"ezd Sovetov Ostiako-Vogulsk Natsional'nogo Okruga (The Second Congress of Soviets of the Ostiak-Vogulsk National Okrug).

1935 Ostiako-Vogulsk: Okrug Tip.

Vuorela, Toivo

1964 The Finno-Ugric Peoples. Trans. John Atkinson. Uralic and Altaic Series, 39. Bloomington: Indiana University Press.

Walker, Cheryl

1997 Indian Nation: Native American Literature and Nineteenth-Century Nationalisms. Durham: Duke University Press.

Wallace, Anthony F. C.

1956 Acculturation: Revitalization Movements. American Anthropologist 58:264–81.

1956a New Religions among the Delaware Indians. Southwestern Journal of Anthropology 12:1–21.

1969 The Death and Rebirth of the Seneca. New York: Random House.

1972 Paradigmatic Processes in Culture Change. American Anthropologist 74:467–78.

Watson, Rubie S., ed.

1994 Memory, History, and Opposition under State Socialism. Santa Fe: School of American Research Press.

Weber, Max

1947 Theory of Social and Economic Organization. Trans. A. M. Henderson and Talcott Parsons. Oxford: Oxford University Press.

Whitehouse, Harvey

1995 Inside the Cult: Religious Innovation and Transmission in Papua New Guinea. Oxford: Oxford University Press.

Wiget, Andrew, and Olga Balalaeva

1997 Saving Siberia's Khanty from Oil Development. Surviving Together 15(1):22–25.

1997a National Communities, Native Land Tenure and Self-Determination. Polar Geography 21(1):10–33.

1997b Black Snow: Oil and the Khanty of Western Siberia. Cultural Survival Quarterly 20(4):17–19.

Williams, Ron G., and James W. Boyd

1993 Ritual Art and Knowledge: Aesthetic Theory and Zoroastrian Ritual. Columbia: University of South Carolina Press.

Wolf, Eric R.

1982 Europe and the People without History. Berkeley: University of California Press.

Woodward, Susan

1995 Balkan Tragedy: Chaos and Dissolution after the Cold War. Washington: Brookings Institution.

Worsley, Peter

1957 The Trumpet Shall Sound: A Study of "Cargo Cults" in Melanesia. London: Macgibbon and Kee.

Yalman, Nur

1964 The Structure of Sinhalese Healing Rituals. *In* Religion in South Asia, ed. E. B. Harper, 115–50. Seattle: Asian Society.

Zavalishin, I.

1862 Opisanie Zapadnoi Sibiri (A sketch of West Siberia). Moscow: Popov.

Zelenin, D. K.

1936 Kul't ongonov v Sibiri (Cult of idols in Siberia). Moscow-Leningrad: Akademiia Nauk.

Zenkovsky, Sergei

1974 Medieval Russia's Epics, Chronicles and Tales. New York: Dutton.

Zguta, Russell

1977 Witchcraft Trials in Seventeenth Century Russia. American Historical Review 82(5):1187–1207.

Zherebina, Tatiana V.

1983 Traditsionnye verovaniia iakutov i khristianstvo (Traditional beliefs of the Yakut and Christianity). Avtoreferat dissertatsii, kandidata istoricheskikh nauk. Leningrad: Gos. Muzei Istorii, Religii i Ateizma.

Zhukovskaia, Natalia L.

1993 The Republic of Kalmykia: A Painful Path of National Renewal. Anthropology and Archeology of Eurasia 31(4):85–101.

Zibarev, V. A.

1968 Sovetskoe stroitel'stvo u malykh narodnostei Severa (Soviet construction among the small peoples of the North). Tomsk: Universitetskoe Izdat.

1970 Obdorskoi upravy kniga dlia zapisi prigovorov po tiazhbam, sporam i prostupkam inorodtsev (1881–1901) (Obdorsk governing book for records of disturbances, arguments, and crimes of natives). Tomsk: Universitetskoe Izdat.

Zolotarev, Aleksander M.
1937 The Bear Festival of the Olcha. American Anthropologist 39:113–30.

Zuev, V. F.
1947 Opisanie zhivushchikh Sibirskoi Gubernii V Berezovskom Uezde, inoversheskikh narodov Ostiakov i Samoyedov (Notes on the inhabitants of Siberia in Berezovo, the nonbeliever Ostiak and Samoyed natives). Materialy po etnografii Sibiri vosemnadsatogo Veka. Trudy Instituta Etnografii 5(1):1–95. [1771].

Index